The Handbook of
LGBTQIA-Inclusive Hospice
and Palliative Care

The Handbook of LGBTQIA-Inclusive Hospice and Palliative Care

Kimberly D. Acquaviva

Columbia University Press
New York

Columbia University Press
Publishers Since 1893
New York   Chichester, West Sussex
cup.columbia.edu

Copyright © 2023 Columbia University Press
First edition published 2017 (as *LGBTQ-Inclusive Hospice and Palliative Care:
A Practical Guide to Transforming Professional Practice*) by Harrington Park Press, LLC
All rights reserved

Library of Congress Cataloging-in-Publication Data
Names: Acquaviva, Kimberly D., 1972– author.
Title: The handbook of LGBTQIA-inclusive hospice and palliative care /
   Kimberly D. Acquaviva.
Other titles: LGBTQ-inclusive hospice and palliative care |
   LGBTQIA-inclusive hospice and palliative care
Description: Second edition. | New York : Columbia University Press, 2023. |
   Preceded by LGBTQ-inclusive hospice and palliative care / Kimberly D.
   Acquaviva. New York : Harrington Park Press, [2017], | Includes bibliographical
   references and index.
Identifiers: LCCN 2023008135 | ISBN 9780231206426 (hardback) |
   ISBN 9780231206433 (trade paperback) | ISBN 9780231556477 (ebook)
Subjects: MESH: Palliative Care | Hospice Care | Sexual and Gender Minorities
Classification: LCC R726.8 | NLM WB 310 | DDC 616.02/90866—dc23/eng/20230601
LC record available at https://lccn.loc.gov/2023008135

Cover design: Elliott S. Cairns
Cover illustration: Mohammad Sohan

To Dylan

I'm pretty sure the fact you married a lesbian

and I married a man

will never stop confusing people.

I'm not confused in the least, though.

I love you, goofball.

Contents

About Language in This Book   ix
Acknowledgments   xi
Preface   xv

Introduction: From "Special Population" to Inclusion—
A Paradigm Shift   1

1 Self-Awareness and Communication   25
2 Sex, Gender, Sexual Orientation, Behavior, and Health   50
3 Understanding Attitudes and Access to Care   75
4 The History and Physical Examination   95
5 Shared Decision Making and Family Dynamics   133
6 Care Planning and Coordination   159
7 Ethical and Legal Issues   183
8 Patient and Family Education and Advocacy   210
9 Psychosocial and Spiritual Issues   237
10 Ensuring Institutional Inclusiveness   262
11 Advocating for Change Beyond the Institution   278

Glossary   285
Supplemental Reading List   303
About the Content Expert Reviewers   307
References   313
Index   331

About Language in This Book

In writing *The Handbook of LGBTQIA-Inclusive Hospice and Palliative Care*, I have deliberately avoided opaque prose and used plain language instead. This is a scholarly work written to be accessible, practical, and understandable. I use the term *LGBTQIA+* to be inclusive of all who self-identify as lesbian, gay, bisexual, transgender, nonbinary, gender nonconforming, queer, questioning, intersex, and/or asexual. Terminology continues to evolve, and not every LGBTQIA+ person uses the term *LGBTQIA+* to describe the community as a whole. Other terms used include *LGBTQ+*, *LGBTIQ+*, *LGBTIQA+*, and *LGBTQ2S+*, among others. Terms are explained in chapter 2 as well as in the glossary.

Throughout the text I alternate the order in which I use the terms *hospice care* and *palliative care* in recognition of the fact that the two aspects of the care continuum are equally important. I also randomly arrange the list of professional disciplines so that no one discipline is presumed to be the most important. Whenever possible I have used the phrase "person receiving hospice care or palliative care" or "individual receiving care" rather than "patient." It wasn't possible to remove every instance of the word *patient*, however. For example, the title of the "Patient Perspective" text boxes would have been confusing if I had changed it to "Individual Perspective."

The word *provider* has been replaced by the word *professional* whenever possible. I owe a debt of gratitude to the content expert reviewer Connie Dahlin for making me aware of the painful history behind the term *provider*. Scarff (2021) writes:

> The origin of the term provider is deplorable. During its ascent to power in the 1930s, the Nazi Party promoted the devaluation and exclusion of Jews in German society, including the medical community. Due to its eugenics campaign, the Nazi Party first targeted pediatrics, a specialty in which nearly half of its practitioners were Jewish (Saenger, 2006). Beginning with female pediatricians, all Jewish physicians were redesignated as *Behandler* (provider) instead of *Arzt* (doctor) (Saenger, 2006). This is the first documented demeaning of physicians as providers in modern history. Jewish doctors were soon restricted to treating only Jewish patients and were further persecuted during the Holocaust. Knowing this background, what health care organization would use a term once associated with Nazi ideology? (Nasrallah, 2020)

Definitions for words and phrases that appear in bold type in the text can be found in the glossary at the back of the book. Facebook and GoFundMe posts are reproduced verbatim (including emojis, typos, etc.).

Acknowledgments

This book—a substantially expanded and updated version of my 2017 book *LGBTQ-Inclusive Hospice & Palliative Care: A Practical Guide to Transforming Professional Practice*—would not have been possible without the support and encouragement of a large cast of characters. First, I want to thank Stephen Wesley, my editor at Columbia University Press, for believing in this book—and in me. A multidisciplinary book written in plain language is very different from the rest of the projects in his portfolio. I could not have asked for a more supportive, visionary editor. I had the pleasure of working with a stellar team of professionals on this edition: Marielle T. Poss, Director of Editing, Design, and Production, and Leslie Kriesel, Production Editing Manager, both at Columbia University Press; freelance copyeditor Peggy Tropp; editorial services manager Ben Kolstad at KnowledgeWorks Global Ltd; Elliot Cairns, Designer at Columbia University Press; and Mohammad Sohan, freelance illustrator.

Designing the cover of this book was a ridiculously enjoyable process that would not have been possible were it not for editor Stephen Wesley's willingness to try something new. Instead of relying on the press's in-house designer to come up with an idea for the cover design, I wanted to come up with the cover design. There was one small problem: despite being a huge graphic design nerd, I have zero talent in actually *doing* graphic design. My first attempt at a cover design was atrocious and involved generic soup can labels. (I will forever be grateful to designer Elliot Cairns for pretending he never saw that design). I then spent the better part of a day trying to get Midjourney AI to turn the image in my head into a workable design. After I had the design I wanted, I turned to Fiverr and found freelance illustrator Mohammad Sohan. In less than 24 hours, Mohammad used the AI-generated image as the springboard to create an original illustration. Elliot Cairns then revised *that* illustration and designed the cover. The end result is everything I had hoped for: Wes Anderson-esque, welcoming, and rainbow free.

The feedback I received from members of the content expert review team was a priceless gift for which I will always be grateful. These content expert reviewers read the draft manuscript and validated the content to ensure its accuracy: Charlie Blotner, Danielle Buhuro, Constance Dahlin, Deborah Dunn, Gary Gardia, Judi Haberkorn, Noelle Marie Javier, Alex Kemery, Shail Maingi, Sam Mullen, and Martha Rutland. I am also deeply appreciative of the hospice and palliative care professionals, patients, and families who submitted their stories for inclusion in the "Professional Perspective," "Patient Perspective," and "Family Perspective" text boxes that appear throughout the book: Kathryn Almack, Patrick Coyne, Constance Dahlin, Kunga Nyima Drotos, Deborah Dunn, Gary Gardia, Richard Gollance, Jennifer Hawkins, Kris Helm, Anne G. Huey, Lynne Hunter, Noelle Marie C. Javier, Jay Kallio, Nick Krayger, Jenn Ledbetter, Holly Lux-Sullivan, Vaiana Morgan, Vicki Quintana, Timothy Sandusky, Steve Shick, and Kathleen Taylor.

I would be remiss if I did not also acknowledge the family and friends who supported and encouraged me through the process of writing this book. Their love, support, and encouragement carried me through the process of writing both the first and second editions. My late wife, Kathy Brandt, and our son, Greyson, showed me time and again the value of a chosen family one can count on. Kathy's ceaseless enthusiasm for my book project was an act of love for which I will always be grateful. Both editions of the book are as much hers as mine; without her, I could never have written either of them. My dad, Phil, shared insights from his experience caring for my mom as she was dying, reminding me that there are so many ways we can make palliative and hospice care better for all the patients and families we serve. Last but definitely not least, my spouse, Dylan Ruediger, showed me the value of living and loving beyond labels. His love and encouragement kept me afloat when I felt as though I might drown under the weight of the writing and editing process.

Words cannot begin to express my gratitude to the team at the now-defunct Harrington Park Press for their efforts to produce the first edition of the book. The late Bill Cohen, along with Steven Rigolosi, invested considerable time and effort in making the first edition as strong as it could be, and I will always be grateful to them for their support, guidance, and friendship. Many thanks to Patrick Ciano of Ciano Design for designing such a dynamic cover and for overseeing the innovative design and layout of the interior for the first edition. Julie Hagen had the onerous task of copyediting the first edition's manuscript—a job that required enormous patience on her part to deal with my insistence that "they" be used as a gender-neutral singular pronoun instead of the binary-reinforcing "him or her."

Finally, I want to acknowledge the LGBTQIA+ patients, families, and professionals who helped me realize the need for this book. Their journeys have not been easy ones. My hope is that the lessons we learn from their experiences with hospice and palliative care will help us ensure a smoother journey for those who come after them.

Preface

A year and eight months after the first edition of this book was published, my wife, Kathy, was diagnosed with ovarian cancer. She died six months later.

From the day Kathy was diagnosed, we both knew that she was dying. That's the blessing and the curse of being hospice and palliative care experts: we knew too much to be able to pretend we didn't know. After talking it over as a family, we decided to share everything she was going through—and *we* were going through—on social media. Kathy knew she was dying, and she wanted to share what that process was like with other people. For the six months from diagnosis to death, we used social media to share every aspect of the dying process. We began by sharing posts with family and friends on Facebook, then started posting on Twitter and a GoFundMe page that two friends set up for us. (If you'd like to read my tweets from when my wife was dying, you can find them online under my Twitter name—@kimacquaviva.)

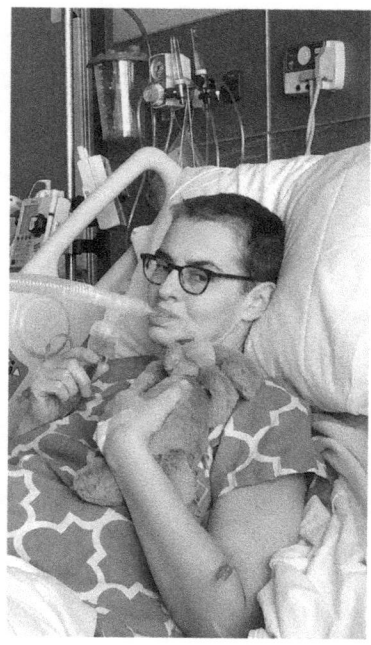

FIGURE 0.1 Kathy Brandt

February 6, 2019

Facebook post from Kim Acquaviva:

Dear family and friends,

One of the wonderful things about Facebook is the ability to stay in touch with so many people from various facets of our lives. While the following may seem like an impersonal way to communicate, when you read it we hope you understand that Kathy and I have limited energy to reach out to our many dear friends to communicate this directly.

Next Tuesday Kathy will undergo surgery for ovarian cancer. She's had a cluster of seemingly unrelated symptoms for the past six months and while she's seen several doctors, the diagnosis wasn't made until last week (on my birthday -that's why I've been so quiet on FB).

As you know our family has had a difficult six months with the death of Kathy's mother and my grandmother. Kathy, Greyson, and I are eternally grateful for the support we've received during this time. We know that many of you will want to continue to be helpful during this time and we so appreciate it.

At this point we are all okay. Greyson is receiving amazing support from friends at Emerson, and Kathy and I have had many wonderful offers of help already.

I'll post an update after the surgery sometime next Tuesday. Until then thank you for the prayers, best wishes, etc. that we know you will send our way.

I put together these FAQ's based on actual questions I've already been asked. 😊

FAQ's

Q: OMG—why didn't the doctor catch this sooner? She had all the classic symptoms of ovarian cancer. How did they miss this? Didn't she go to the doctor?

A: Kathy was first seen by several clinicians for her symptoms in late August of last year. At that time, they thought she had a kidney infection. Since then, she's been seen by a number of fantastic physicians, nurse practitioners, and physician assistants. No one put the pieces of her history together until Kathy self-referred to a gastroenterologist who did bloodwork and then sent Kathy to the emergency room for a CT scan and ultrasound. There's no one to blame—every healthcare professional who saw Kathy over the 6 months she's been symptomatic did the best they could given the limitations of our disjointed healthcare system. Imagine a machine lobbing baseballs at someone rapid-fire. No matter how good a player they are, they're only going to hit a handful of those balls. Blaming the player isn't fair: it's the machine that's broken.

(continued on next page)

(continued from previous page)

Q: Is there a history of ovarian cancer in Kathy's family?

A: No, Kathy's relatives live to be a gazillion years old and then get Alzheimer's. My mom died of ovarian cancer at age 52. Out of every 100 women diagnosed with ovarian cancer, only 20–25 of them have a genetic mutation associated with ovarian cancer.

Q: Didn't you realize Kathy was showing all the classic symptoms of ovarian cancer? It's a textbook case. How did you miss this?

A: Everything seems obvious in hindsight. For example, I just realized you have the emotional intelligence of a gym sock. 😊

Q: Kathy's going to beat this—she's a fighter.

A: The most loving thing you can do for us right now is avoid using war imagery. There is no fight or battle and there is no winning or losing. Kathy, Greyson, and I are Quakers but we're also pretty fiesty. If any of y'all use war imagery in reference to her cancer—e.g. fight, battle, win, lose, etc—I'll punch you in the throat. Lovingly and in a super-Quaker way, obviously, but it'll still hurt. Consider yourselves warned. 😊

Q: How much time does Kathy have? What's her prognosis?

A: Kathy's going to be alive until she isn't anymore. Same with me. Same with you, actually. Each day from now until then, her treatment will be focused on maximizing symptom-free time and our lives as a family will be focused on maximizing normalcy.

Q: What can we do to help?

A: Thank you so much for offering to help. Your support means a lot to us. Here are a few ways you could be helpful:

- Kathy will be in Sibley Hospital starting Tuesday the 12th. I know she'd love visitors starting on the 13th, so if you have time to stop by, text me a few hours beforehand at 202-423-0984.
- Our dogs are kennelled at WOOFS! for the next few week, so we don't need anyone to walk our dogs. (Shout out to Laura Sharkey for taking such loving care of our pups).

> - Put your affairs in order. Seriously, y'all. We worked with Sanju Misra of Misra Law—she's amazing!
> - Keep us in your thoughts. We love you all!
>
> Love,
>
> Kim, Kathy, and Greyson

JoNel Aleccia, a journalist with Kaiser Health News, did a story about Kathy's illness and our family's decision to share our journey publicly. The article she published—"'Living Their Values': Palliative Care Power Couple Faces Cancer at Home"—also ran on NBC News (Aleccia, 2019b). Around the same time, Kathy and I filmed a series of short videos with the Coalition to Transform Advanced Care (C-TAC) about the individual and caregiver experience near the end of life (C-TAC, 2019, 2022). We also participated in a live-streamed Kaiser Health News (2019) panel called "Inclusive Care at the End of Life: The LGBTQ+ Experience" that was later posted on YouTube. Throughout this time, Kathy and I were tweeting and posting about what it was like to experience dying and caregiving as a lesbian couple with a college-age son.

Kathy died on August 4, 2019—three years ago this week. Several stories about our family appeared in the days that followed: Kaiser Health News ran a piece about Kathy's death (Aleccia, 2019a), and the *Chronicle of Higher Education* ran a piece titled "Death Is This Professor's Life's Work. When It Hit Close to Home, She Invited Everyone to Watch" (Stripling, 2019). Six months later, the *Pennsylvania Gazette* ran a long-form piece by Dave Zeitlin (2020) about which *Pennsylvania Gazette*'s editor wrote:

> The couple's Tweets, Facebook posts, and videos were more than simple sharing. . . . Acquaviva told Dave that their hope was to make people "see that death is not scary" and to show solidarity with others in similar situations. After she shared the news of Brandt's death last summer, one

Twitter user replied: "What a wonderful testimony to her life you and your son have offered. In sharing you normalized death for so many others." (Prendergast, 2020)

Throughout the six months that Kathy was dying and afterward when each of these stories ran, I received a flurry of emails and direct messages from people—some LGBTQIA+, some not—about how the things Kathy and I had written, tweeted, or talked about had affected them. After more than half a million people had watched a short documentary about our family that the *New Yorker* released on YouTube in June 2021, I wasn't surprised to see a handful of negative comments underneath the video (as well as under the C-TAC and KHN videos on YouTube). The negative comments, albeit very few in number, still serve as a powerful reminder of why LGBTQIA+ people may be afraid of how hospice and palliative care professionals will treat them. Here's an exchange between a self-identified hospice nurse and another commenter under the *New Yorker* video:

> AK: As a nurse, this is so heartbreaking yet absolutely needed. I've worked hospice and I've always said that when you are witnessing someone actively passing, it's as close to God without yourself passing. I'm so sorry for your loss. I pray for peace and a beautiful life for you and your son.
> CD: Since you've seen alot of deaths. What do you think happens after death?? I'm so curious.
> AK: @CD as a Christian, if they accepted salvation then they'll go to heaven. If they're old enough and mentally able to understand the gift.

This is one of the comments under the Kaiser Health News video, "Inclusive Care at the End of Life: The LGBTQ+ Experience":

> From a Church perspective, the following verses best encapsulate "End of Life Care" for the "LGBTQ+" community: "On that night there shall be two Men in one bed: the one shall be taken and the other shall be Left Behind. Two Women shall be grinding together: the one shall be taken and the other shall be Left Behind." (Luke 17:34–35)

And here's a comment under the C-TAC video of Kathy and me:

We must Repent and put our trust in Jesus Christ death comes so fast.

Throughout this book you'll find social media posts from Kathy and me, along with text boxes containing first-person accounts written by LGBTQIA+ individuals and family members. As you read this book, think about the LGBTQIA+ individuals and families in your own community—the ones whose stories *aren't* told in these pages. What stories could they tell about your palliative care or hospice program? What stories would you *hope* they would tell? You have the power to change the story of how LGBTQIA+ individuals and families in your community experience hospice and palliative care. Thank you for being willing to go on this journey with me.

The Handbook of
LGBTQIA-Inclusive Hospice
and Palliative Care

Introduction

*From "Special Population" to Inclusion—
A Paradigm Shift*

When I began work on the first edition of this book, I set out to write a resource for **hospice** and **palliative care** professionals that would be equally relevant and engaging to palliative care and hospice professionals from multiple disciplines; would change the way readers approach their work with *all* individuals receiving care, not just with those who are lesbian, gay, bisexual, transgender, nonbinary, gender nonconforming, queer, questioning, intersex, and/or asexual (LGBTQIA+); and would show readers that having conservative religious or moral beliefs and providing high-quality, inclusive care to LGBTQIA+ people and their families are not mutually exclusive. While the majority of the book is dedicated to achieving the first two goals, the third goal is equally important.

In the eighteen years that I have been speaking to audiences about caring for LGBTQIA+ individuals with chronic or life-limiting illnesses, one thing has remained fairly constant: health care professionals with more conservative religious beliefs come to my presentations with significant discomfort at the outset—if they come at all. Changing the way LGBTQIA+ individuals with chronic or life-limiting illnesses are cared for requires a paradigm shift in the way we (collectively, as health care professionals) approach the conversation about what it means to be inclusive in our compassion. You don't need to change your religious or moral beliefs to provide good care to LGBTQIA+ individuals. Regardless of your religious or moral beliefs, providing LGBTQIA-inclusive care is part of achieving health equity for all individuals. So if you are unsure about buying or reading a book about LGBTQIA+ people, don't be. At its core, this is simply a book about people.

LGBTQIA-inclusive practice begins with an active choice—a choice to change our practice so that all are welcome and treated with dignity and compassion. I have never met a hospice or palliative care professional who consciously excludes LGBTQIA+ individuals and their families. I do not believe that care professionals make a conscious choice to give poor care to LGBTQIA+ individuals and their families. However, unless palliative care and hospice professionals make a conscious choice to engage in LGBTQIA-inclusive practice, they are, by default, unintentionally choosing to exclude LGBTQIA+ people from receiving the high-quality care that all people deserve. The result of that unintentional choice is, not unsurprisingly, discriminatory and disrespectful hospice and palliative care. We know this to be true because hospice and palliative care professionals have observed it firsthand: in a survey of 865 hospice and palliative care professionals, "53.6 percent thought that lesbian, gay, or bisexual (LGB) patients were more likely than non-LGB patients to experience discrimination at their institution; 23.7 percent observed discriminatory care; 64.3 percent reported that transgender patients were more likely than nontransgender patients to experience discrimination; 21.3 percent observed discrimination to transgender patients; 15 percent observed the spouse/partner of LGBT patients having their treatment decisions disregarded or minimized; and 14.3 percent observed the spouse/partner or surrogate being treated disrespectfully" (Stein et al., 2020).

February 13, 2019

Facebook post from Kim Acquaviva:

Dear family and friends,

I apologize in advance for the Facebook post but I'm trying to be efficient so that I can focus my time and energy on Kathy and Greyson. I waited to post this so that I could talk to Greyson first. Thanks for your patience—I know many of you had a sleepless night worrying and I'm so sorry.

    Kathy went into surgery last night (Tuesday) at 9:15pm. The surgery was over around 1:00am. The surgeon spent almost 45 minutes with me discussing the results of Kathy's surgery. From 1 am until 4:30 am, Kathy was in the ICU for post-surgical recovery. A little before 5 am, they brought her to her room (room 512).

    Here's what the surgeon found: Kathy's cancer is a high-grade serous carcinoma involving both ovaries and fallopian tubes, with metastases to the peritoneum and a spot in the abdomen. There was around 100 cc of ascites. It is either Stage IIIa or Stage IIIb, depending on what the pathologist finds in the omentum. The surgeon was able to remove all visible evidence of the cancer but at this stage, the disease is not curable.

    This news was not unexpected—in fact, last week Kathy and I met with a palliative care nurse practitioner at Sibley Memorial Hospital because we knew the cancer was likely to be at least Stage III and we knew aggressive symptom management would be needed. (Kathy even helped me draft this email to you before she went into surgery because we were fairly certain about what the surgery would reveal). Given that (1) the cancer is not curable, (2) chemotherapy would require that Kathy spend a lot of time in doctors offices and hospitals, (3) any day spent in a medical setting is a bad day in Kathy's book, and (4) her cancer is both aggressive and advanced, Kathy was adamant in the weeks before surgery that she doesn't want to have any treatment other than that which would be palliative to reduce symptom burden.

(continued on next page)

(continued from previous page)

None of this means Kathy has "given up" or "lost hope." It simply means that she's someone who, after considering all the options, has decided to live her life in the least medicalized way possible until she's run out of life to live. Everyone dies—we don't get a choice about that. What we do get to choose is how we want to live.

When Kathy is awake and not under the influence of the anesthesia or pain meds, we'll meet with the oncologist and the palliative care team to discuss what the palliative treatment plan will be. Kathy's oncologist was clear that, without chemotherapy, Kathy would probably have a year or less to live. With chemo, she would likely have more time but the cancer will ultimately come back. This is a choose-your-own-adventure story where the ending always sucks. I respect Kathy's decision to prioritize quality of life over length of life, as does Greyson. If Kathy's choices change at some point down the line, we'll support that, too. She's in charge of deciding how to live the life she has left.

At this time, our family gently asks that you not offer advice about treatment options you think Kathy should consider. Similarly, please don't share stories about the people you know who had/have ovarian cancer but had a positive outcome. We know you're trying to be helpful but it's important to remember that not every person defines their goals of care the same way. What was right for your friend or family member isn't the same as what's right for Kathy and our family.

Kathy will be in Sibley Memorial Hospital for the next 7–10 days. If you'd like to stop by in the coming days, I know she'd love it and I'd enjoy the visits as well. Please bring your love and your smiles—no hanging crepe, y'all. Every day is a gift. 🙂

I can't begin to convey how much Kathy, Greyson, and I appreciate your love and support. I'm So sorry we're not able to respond to all your texts and emails individually. Please know that our lack of response isn't lack of appreciation.

Love and hugs,

Kim

WHY THIS BOOK?

When I wrote the first edition, there were no books written for palliative care and hospice physicians, advanced practice registered nurses, registered nurses, social workers, counselors, and chaplains collectively in a single text. (The first edition of this book did not include physician associates in its target audience. The inclusion of physician associates in the second edition is explained later in this chapter.) Instead, books focused on a narrower target audience, one that was usually bound by a single discipline. There was no shortage of well-researched publications for palliative care and hospice professionals, though. The following seminal works were mentioned in the first edition:

- *Advanced Practice Palliative Nursing* (Dahlin, Coyne, & Ferrell, 2016)
- *Dying in America: Improving Quality and Honoring Individual Preferences Near the End of Life* (Institute of Medicine, 2015)
- *Geriatric Palliative Care* (Chai et al., 2014)
- *Oxford American Handbook of Hospice and Palliative Medicine and Supportive Care* (Yennurajalingam & Bruera, 2016)
- *Oxford Textbook of Palliative Medicine* (Cherny et al., 2015)
- *Oxford Textbook of Palliative Nursing* (Ferrell, Coyle, & Paice, 2015a)
- *Oxford Textbook of Palliative Social Work* (Altilio & Otis-Green, 2011)
- *Pediatric Palliative Care* (Ferrell, 2015)
- *Textbook of Palliative Care Communication* (Wittenberg et al., 2015)

In most of the texts listed, LGBTQIA+ populations are either relegated to a stand-alone chapter, as is the case in the *Textbook of Palliative Care Communication* and the *Oxford Textbook of Palliative Social Work*, or they are mentioned briefly within the context of chapters on sexuality, "special populations," "cultural considerations," or HIV/AIDS, as in the *Oxford Textbook of Palliative Nursing*, the *Oxford Textbook of Palliative Medicine*, and *Geriatric Palliative Care*.

There is a critical need to move beyond ignoring the existence of LGBTQIA+ people, thinking of LGBTQIA+ people as a special population, or conceptualizing LGBTQIA+ people as a group that merits mention only within the context of discussions about disease and dysfunction. When

LGBTQIA+ people are relegated to a single chapter in a book, the clinicians most in need of the information may skip reading it entirely. Even more concerning, this approach to the presentation of content reinforces the idea that LGBTQIA+ people are "other." (In *Advanced Practice Palliative Nursing*, the single mention of LGBTQIA+ people is in a list of other "special populations," sandwiched between "prison inmates" and "individuals with substance use disorders" [Gibson, 2016].)

There is no discussion at all of LGBTQIA+ populations in *Pediatric Palliative Care*, with the exception of a brief mention in a chapter about grief and bereavement where the authors note that "single parents or same-sex parents may not have as many options for support as married parents in a heterosexual relationship" (Limbo & Davies, 2015). *Advanced Practice Palliative Nursing* contains a brief acknowledgment that "the APRN will encounter a wide diversity of patients, such as military veterans; individuals with developmental disabilities; individuals with mental illness and personality disorders; prison inmates; the lesbian, gay, bisexual, transgender, and intersex community; individuals with substance use disorders; individuals who are homeless; and individuals of a low socioeconomic status" (Gibson, 2016), but no content regarding how to provide LGBTQIA-inclusive care. The most glaring absence of LGBTQIA+ persons with serious or life-limiting illnesses, however, is in the 639-page *Dying in America: Improving Quality and Honoring Individual Preferences Near the End of Life*, in which the words and phrases *gay, lesbian, bisexual, transgender, sexual orientation, sexuality, LGBTQ,* and *LGBTQIA+* are never used, not even once.

Since 2017, three of these seminal texts have released new editions. The influence of *LGBTQ-Inclusive Hospice & Palliative Care* can be seen in all three. In the fifth edition of the *Oxford Textbook of Palliative Nursing* (Ferrell & Paice, 2019), LGBTQIA+ people are now mentioned in multiple chapters: "Supporting Families and Family Caregivers in Palliative Care," "Poor, Homeless, and Underserved Populations," "Sexuality and Intimacy in Serious Illness and at the End of Life," and "Cultural Considerations in Palliative Care." This more recent edition notes:

> One of the most profound gender disparities in the delivery of quality palliative care involves providing quality palliative care to those who

are lesbian, gay, bisexual, transgender, or queer/questioning (LGBTQ). It is recommended that the best way to address these disparities is by providing LGBTQ-inclusive palliative care rather than conceptualizing LGBTQ people as a "special population" that is separate from all others. Acquaviva suggests that making subtle changes in the way palliative care is delivered will allow for inclusive, nonjudgmental hospice and palliative care for all persons. (p. 475)

The editors of the second edition of the *Oxford Textbook of Palliative Social Work* (Altilio, Otis-Green, & Cagle, 2022) opted to continue to address the care of LGBTQIA+ people in a stand-alone chapter ("LGBTQ Patient Palliative Care: A Queery Into Quality of Life" by Charlie Blotner and Danae Dotolo). When they approached me to ask whether I would be interested in writing the chapter, I declined and explained why I no longer agree to write stand-alone chapters. Although the editors ultimately decided that a stand-alone chapter was the best way to ensure that LGBTQIA+ content was addressed in the second edition, they did so only after considerable discussion and with full awareness that the other chapters needed to incorporate information about LGBTQIA+ individuals as well.

The third seminal text to release a new edition since 2017 is *Advanced Practice Palliative Nursing*, second edition (Dahlin & Coyne, 2023). Although it had not been released at the time I wrote this chapter in August 2022, the coeditors provided me with the following information about the content of the new edition and the thinking behind their approach:

> Overall, it is a complex situation right now. APRNs state they need the content because they cannot practice what they do not know. Many APRNs receive little to no education or content on LGBTQI+ inclusive care in their academic programs and there is often little to no content in nursing textbooks. Moreover, there are few continuing education offerings on LGBTQI+ inclusive care. However, the current social context is one "should know" which leaves APRNs needing to learn on their own. Adding to the complexity is that APRNs may live or practice in areas where it is not safe to ask or it is unclear to whom to ask about where to learn about care of LGBTQI+ individuals or other marginalized

individuals. The result is that APRNs may learn from a less than ideal vehicle—social media. The second edition of *Advanced Practice Palliative Nursing* has an intentional focus on inclusivity, including language and pronouns, and case studies throughout the book that represent LGBTQI+ individuals with serious illness and their families. To promote further knowledge, there is a section about marginalized populations in which there is a stand-alone chapter about caring for LGBTQI+ individuals with serious illness and their family caregivers, since this community has been marginalized overall within palliative care. (personal communication, August 28, 2022)

In weaving LGBTQIA+ content and case studies throughout the second edition of their book, Dahlin and Coyne appear to be leading the way when it comes to making meaningful strides toward LGBTQIA-inclusive palliative care and hospice texts.

Since the first edition of this book was released in 2017, another seminal text has been published. The fourth edition of the National Consensus Project's *Clinical Practice Guidelines for Quality Palliative Care*, published in 2018, is notable for the way it tries to weave LGBQIA+ inclusion through the guidelines. The introduction to domain 6 ("Cultural Aspects of Care") notes:

Assessing and respecting values, beliefs and traditions related to health, illness, family caregiver roles and decision-making are the first step in providing culturally sensitive palliative care. Palliative care interdisciplinary team (IDT) members continually expand awareness of their own biases and perceptions about race, ethnicity, gender identity and gender expression, sexual orientation, immigration and refugee status, social class, religion, spirituality, physical appearance, and abilities. Information gathered through a comprehensive assessment is used to develop a care plan that incorporates culturally sensitive resources and strategies to meet the needs of individuals and family members. Respectful acknowledgment of and culturally sensitive support for patient and family grieving practices is provided. (p. 38)

Domain 6 of the NCP Guidelines calls upon members of the interdisciplinary team to elicit and document each "patient's preferred name, pronouns, and gender identity" at the time of initial assessment, and to understand "that each person's self-identified culture includes the intersections of race, ethnicity, gender identity and expression, sexual orientation, immigration and refugee status, social class, religion, spirituality, physical appearance, and abilities." **Intersectionality** is an analytic framework for understanding the ways in which the combination of an individual's identities, experiences, and characteristics—each of which may be either oppressing or empowering when looked at in isolation—results in oppression or privilege. An intersectional approach to understanding a person's culture and lived experiences is central to the provision of high-quality hospice and palliative care.

While the *Clinical Practice Guidelines for Quality Palliative Care* and the fifth edition of the *Oxford Textbook of Palliative Nursing* both represent laudable progress in the hospice and palliative care publications arena, there remains a critical need to move beyond thinking of LGBTQIA+ people as a "special population." Since the first edition of my book was published in 2017, I have continued to receive requests to write stand-alone chapters in hospice and palliative care textbooks. Each time I have politely declined, explained why I no longer write stand-alone chapters, and offered to help integrate LGBTQIA+ content throughout the textbook *without compensation*. Each time, the editors have decided to move forward anyway with their plan to have a stand-alone chapter about LGBTQIA+ people.

When LGBTQIA+ people are relegated to a single chapter in a book, the clinicians most in need of the information may skip reading it entirely. Even more concerning, this approach to the presentation of content reinforces the idea that LGBTQIA+ people are "other." As much as it pains me to turn down opportunities to write chapters in prestigious textbooks, the best way each of us—myself included—can push for LGBTQIA+ inclusion in textbooks is to refuse to participate in book projects that are structured in ways that marginalize LGBTQIA+ people. Until LGBTQIA+ scholars (and cisgender, heterosexual "allies") take a unified approach to responding to requests for stand-alone chapters, we are unlikely to see

February 14, 2019

Facebook post from Kim Acquaviva:

I'm pretty sure I have the cutest Valentine ever.

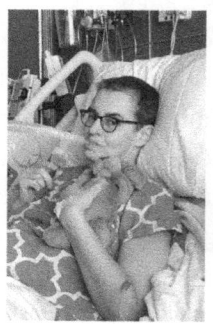

FIGURE 0.1 Kathy Brandt

LGBTQIA+ content woven throughout the chapters of the seminal texts in the field. (See chapter 11 for practical strategies you can use to help make this change happen.)

THE ADDITION OF PHYSICIAN ASSOCIATES

When I wrote the first edition of this book, I sought to create a practical guide to transforming professional practice for palliative care and hospice physicians, advanced practice registered nurses, registered nurses, social workers, counselors, and chaplains. In writing the book back in 2016, I did not include physician assistants, now known as "physician associates" per the American Academy of Physician Associates' (2022) announcement of the title change, in the book's target audience. From 2016 to 2020, the number of certified PAs working in hospice and palliative care grew by 216.2 percent (National Commission on Certification of Physician Assistants [NCCPA], 2021). However, the number of certified PAs listing "Hospice and Palliative Medicine" (NCCPA's term) as their primary clinical position has remained small: 37 in 2016, 96 in 2018, and 117 in 2020 (National Commission on Certification of Physician Assistants, 2019, 2021).

Effective January 1, 2019, section 51006 of the Bipartisan Budget Act of 2018 (Pub. L. 115–123) required that "physician assistants (PAs) be recognized as designated hospice attending physicians, in addition to physicians and nurse practitioners" (Centers for Medicare and Medicaid Services, 2018). With this change it became possible for physician assistants/physician associates to remain involved in the care of individuals when they transition into hospice. Physician associates who are serving as an individual's attending physician in hospice are allowed to order medications for that individual as long as doing so is consistent with the scope of practice laws in their state and the policies of the hospice program (Centers for Medicare and Medicaid Services, 2019; Physician Assistants in Hospice and Palliative Medicine, n.d.). However, there are still limits to the care that physician associates can provide when it comes to hospice. As of August 2022, physician associates are not permitted to certify or recertify that an individual has a terminal illness, a restriction that the American Academy of Physician Associates (2019) hopes to see eliminated.

Although physician associates are a more recent addition to hospice and palliative care, their seminal texts approach the inclusion of LGBTQIA+ content in ways that closely parallel the approaches taken by the disciplines I focused on in the first edition. The seminal physician associate text in palliative and hospice care is currently *Palliative and Serious Illness Patient Management for Physician Assistants* (Dimitrov & Kemle, 2022), the latest addition to Oxford's suite of discipline-specific palliative care texts: *Oxford Textbook of Palliative Medicine*, *Oxford Textbook of Palliative Nursing*, and *Oxford Textbook of Palliative Social Work*. Consistent with the approach taken by editors of other Oxford texts on palliative care, Dimitrov and Kemle have placed content about LGBTQIA+ individuals in a stand-alone chapter titled "LGBTQ Community" in a section called "Special Populations and Communities"—a section that also contains chapters focused on "Patients with Substance Use Disorder" and "Prisoners' and Ex-Offenders' Community," among others.

> February 18, 2019
>
> Facebook post from Kim Acquaviva:
>
> KATHY: Can you order me some sherbet?
> ME: Honey, I love you but you don't have hand cancer. Pick up the phone and order it.
> NURSE we just met 1 minute ago: [*silence*]
> ME: We've been married for 18 years.
> NURSE: Ahhhhhhh. . . .

MAKING THE SHIFT TO LGBTQIA-INCLUSIVE CARE

This book turns the traditional approach to addressing LGBTQIA+ persons in palliative care and hospice upside down in order to help clinicians make the shift from providing special care to LGBTQIA+ people to instead providing inclusive care to *all* people, including those who are LGBTQIA+. When a person receives palliative care or hospice care, they carry with them a complex set of identities, experiences, and characteristics that interact with one another. These identities, experiences, and characteristics are not always visible—for example, you can't tell if a person is LGBTQIA+ just by looking at them. An LGBQTIA+ person shouldn't need to tell you they are LGBTQIA+ in order to get inclusive care, though. This book teaches you how to provide LGBTQIA-inclusive care to everyone, regardless of how they identify or which identities they feel safe sharing with you.

In writing this book, I made a conscious decision to use a conversational tone rather than an academic one. Unlike discipline-specific books that cover dense, foundational content like the pathophysiology of pain, pharmacology, or pain and symptom management, this book seeks to provide both new and experienced hospice and palliative care professionals with the knowledge they need to shift from providing high-quality care to high-quality LGBTQIA-inclusive care. You may be reading this and thinking that you already provide LGBTQIA-inclusive care. You treat every person the same—why would your treatment of LGBTQIA+ people and their families be any different? These are great questions, and ones I hear a lot. Providing LGBTQIA-inclusive care requires a shift in the way you think about hospice and palliative care. Being inclusive is not the same as treating everyone the same. In fact, treating everyone the same is an approach that rarely benefits people receiving hospice or palliative care, regardless of whether they are LGBTQIA+, because people are not all the same. This book will give you clear, actionable strategies to use in transforming the care you provide so that it is truly LGBTQIA-inclusive. The ultimate goal is for LGBTQIA-inclusive care to be what you provide to everyone—not a "specialized" form of care provided to LGBTQIA+ individuals.

February 18, 2019

Facebook post from Kim Acquaviva:

Kathy slept well after the Ativan last night—we only got up for two trips to the bathroom and a quiet vitals check. Just finished walk 1 of 8. Now she's watching a Grace & Frankie episode about vibrators. Life is good.

––––––––––––––

Update: I'm editing this post to add more details for our medical friends who like to see more specifics. The following is hella-boring for non-medical people so please feel free to skip:

Nausea/Vomiting: The round-the-clock Zofran, Reglan, and Protinix combined with Ativan PRN through the IV when severe nausea/vomiting hits seems to be the magic combo. She still can't

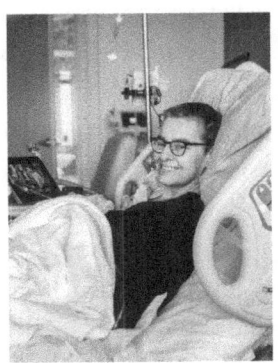

FIGURE 0.2 Kathy Brandt

(continued on next page)

(continued from previous page)

hold down anything other than clear liquids even with all those meds, though, so she's feeling really wiped out. She's slowwwwllly eating a little jello right now.

Pain: Yesterday the seven long walks increased gas production (go farts go!), reducing the abdominal pain and the need for the oxycodone, so we're planning to do eight walks today. (The oncologist wants 6–8 walks/day from her now). Kathy's taking minimal narcotics (just PRN and usually just once a day) and she's taking both ibuprofen and acetaminophen round the clock. A large lidocaine patch cut in half and placed on either side of her lower back before bedtime is giving her significant relief.

Bowels: Gas but no BM since Monday's bowel prep. This isn't all that worrisome to the oncologist because Kathy hasn't been eating anything.

Fluids: Kathy's still receiving IV fluids and she's up 32 pounds from where she was in admission. It's uncomfortable for Kathy and will take a few weeks to resolve but it isn't worrisome to her care team. Her oncologist has been diligent about only using Lasix when her bloodwork and overall condition indicate there's a window of opportunity to do so safely. Lasix two days ago, none yesterday or today. Albumin levels are right where the oncologist wants to see them.

Physical Therapy: PT will be coming by today to begin prepping Kathy to do stairs at home. Fortunately I already knew how to do the patient care stuff (transferring, using the belt for safety during walks, showering, toileting, etc), so Kathy and I have been doing those things without assistance since the day she was admitted. (I'm so grateful to have spent 20+ years working with nurses, physical therapists, and physicians—turns out it pays off to pay close attention to you guys!)

Path Report: We should hear back in a few days whether there were additional mets found in the omentum and/or lymph nodes. It won't change the plan of care either way but I know folks are curious so we'll post the results when we get them.

USING THIS BOOK TO MAKE THE SHIFT

Providing LGBTQIA-inclusive hospice and palliative care involves making subtle changes in the way you approach almost every aspect of care. At first glance, the titles of chapters in this book may appear to reflect topics with which you are already quite familiar. While experienced hospice and palliative care professionals are likely to have a solid background in many of these broad topic areas, the chapters are designed to build on that knowledge rather than duplicate it. To get the maximum benefit out of this book, it is important to read all the chapters. That being said, I have written this for readers in four distinct disciplines: medicine, nursing, chaplaincy, and social work/counseling. Your own discipline's **scope of practice** will determine whether and how you integrate the content into your professional practice. For example, although everyone should read the chapter on conducting a physical exam, if you are a chaplain, social worker, or counselor, you will not conduct physical exams yourself because they are outside your discipline's scope of practice.

Of course, you don't have to be a social worker, registered nurse, chaplain, physician, advanced practice registered nurse, physician associate, or counselor to benefit from reading this book. Clinical psychologists, pharmacists, home health aides, licensed practical nurses, licensed massage therapists, registered dieticians, music therapists, speech-language pathologists, physical rehabilitation therapists, volunteer coordinators, administrators, and educators will find that this book can help change the way they work with individuals, families, staff, students, and volunteers. And if you are a student, it will help you get off on the right foot in terms of LGBTQIA-inclusive practice as you begin your work with individuals and their families.

COMPETENCY-BASED SCAFFOLDING

LGBTQIA-Inclusive Hospice and Palliative Care is built on a scaffolding of learning objectives designed to address the needs of physicians, advanced practice registered nurses (APRNs), physician associates (PAs), registered nurses (RNs), social workers, counselors, and chaplains working in the field of hospice and palliative care. When I wrote the first edition of this book, I developed the learning objectives using discipline-specific competencies, curricular guidelines, and professional standards for medicine, nursing, social work, and chaplaincy. Since there were no existing competencies focused on LGBTQIA-inclusive hospice and palliative care, I set out to find and compile hospice and palliative care competencies first and then LGBTQIA-specific health care competencies. After gathering competencies in these two broad areas for the target disciplines, I planned to create a crosswalk between the areas and develop working competencies for LGBTQIA-inclusive hospice and palliative care for each discipline. At least, that was the original plan. I had mistakenly assumed it would be relatively easy to find hospice and palliative care competencies and LGBTQIA-specific competencies for each of the disciplines and that the challenge would be in converting them into LGBTQIA-inclusive hospice and palliative care competencies.

Unfortunately, of the health care disciplines this book addresses, only medicine has established detailed competencies for both the care of LGBTQIA+ persons and the care of persons with chronic or life-limiting illnesses (see Association of American Medical Colleges, 2014; American Academy of Hospice and Palliative Medicine [AAHPM], 2009; American Academy of Family Physicians, n.d.; Joint Commission, 2011). The social work discipline has indicators for cultural competence and general standards for social work practice in palliative and hospice care but no set of competencies specific to working with LGBTQIA+ individuals (National Association of Social Workers, 2004, 2015; Hay & Johnson, 2001). Similarly, the chaplaincy discipline has general competencies for hospice and palliative care chaplains but no competencies specific to working with LGBTQIA+ people and their families (Board of Chaplaincy Certification, n.d.).

In gathering palliative care and hospice competencies, I looked to the certification requirements outlined by the credentialing bodies in each of the disciplines. The American Board of Medical Specialties administers the Hospice and Palliative Medicine (HPM) subspecialty for physicians, and the American Osteopathic Association's Bureau of Osteopathic Specialists administers the Certificate of Added Qualification (CAQ) in hospice and palliative medicine for osteopathic physicians. Certification requires completion of a fellowship as well as passage of a daylong examination (AAHPM, n.d.a).

The National Commission on Certification of Physician Assistants began administering the CAQ in palliative medicine and hospice care in 2022, with the first group of CAQs anticipated to be awarded in 2023 to physician associates who pass the exam (NCCPA, 2022).

The Hospice and Palliative Credentialing Center (HPCC) administers the Certified Hospice and Palliative Nurse credential as well as the Advanced Certified Hospice and Palliative Nurse credential. Certification requires completion of 500 hours of practice in the previous year (or 1,000 hours in the previous two years) as well as passage of a lengthy examination (HPCC, n.d.a, n.d.b).

The Hospice Medical Director Certification Board (HMDCB) administers the Hospice Medical Director Certification, which requires "400 hours of broad hospice-related activities" and either "two years of work experience in a hospice setting during the previous 5 years" or "current, valid board certification in hospice and palliative medicine through the American Board of Hospice and Palliative Medicine (ABHPM), the American Board of Medical Specialties (ABMS), or the American Osteopathic Association (AOA)" or "successful completion of a 12-month clinical hospice and palliative medicine training program accredited by the Accreditation Council for Graduate Medical Education (ACGME) or AOA" (HMDCB, 2013).

The National Association of Social Workers Specialty Certification Program administers the Certified Hospice and Palliative Social Worker (CHP-SW) credential and the Advanced Certified Hospice and Palliative Social Worker (ACHP-SW) credential. Certification requires several years of supervised practice as a hospice and palliative care social worker, but there is no examination. The Advanced Palliative Hospice Social Work Certification (APHSW-C) is administered by the APHSW Certification Board and requires social workers to pass an examination "based on a national job analysis which defined the areas of specialty and designed a psychometrically sound text of that advanced knowledge" (Advanced Palliative Hospice Social Worker Certification Board, 2022). This exam is in addition to several years of post-degree experience in hospice and/or palliative care.

The Board of Chaplaincy Certification administers the Certified Hospice and Palliative Care Chaplain credential. Requirements for certification are substantial (including a ten-page essay, three years of experience in hospice and palliative care, and three recommendation letters), but no examination is required.

Because the medicine and nursing competencies were so detailed, I was able to compile a spreadsheet of the competencies from each of the disciplines and then develop working competencies appropriate to each discipline to fill in the gaps. This is not the best way to develop competencies, but it gave me a draft set around which to develop the content of the book. I had hoped that the first edition of this book would stimulate leaders from the disciplines to come together to develop competencies in LGBTQIA-inclusive hospice and palliative care, but as of 2022, no such effort is underway. There remains a pressing need for the inclusion of more LGBTQIA+ content in specialty certification exams in the hospice and palliative care disciplines.

FIGURE 0.3 Kathy Brandt

February 20, 2019

Facebook post from Kim Acquaviva:

Kathy came downstairs and cooked her own breakfast (because she doesn't have hand cancer, y'all) while I stood nearby. Rice, poached eggs, and Boursin cheese.

February 22, 2019

Facebook post from Kim Acquaviva:

Things I never thought I'd be doing at age 47:

1. Installing grab bars on our toilet.
2. Decarboxylating medical marijuana.
3. Contemplating a future without my wife in it.

Live your life today like it really counts. Because it does.

HOW THE BOOK IS ORGANIZED

Providing LGBTQIA-inclusive hospice and palliative care requires changes at three levels: the individual, the institutional, and the systemic. At the individual level, hospice and palliative care professionals can shift toward providing more LGBTQIA-inclusive care by adopting a structure of self-awareness and changing the way they assess, interact with, and support the individuals and families they work with. At the institutional level, leaders of institutions should prioritize addressing health disparities experienced by LGBTQIA+ people and dismantle structural barriers including policies that marginalize and/or discriminate against LGBTQIA+ people. Institutions can be either agents of oppression or agents of change when it comes to LGBTQIA+ inclusion.

At the institutional level, organizations can strengthen their inclusion of LGBTQIA+ individuals and their families by (1) updating language on the forms they use, (2) developing LGBTQIA-inclusive messages and outreach strategies, (3) hiring more LGBTQIA+ staff, (4) offering equitable benefits to employees in same-gender relationships and transgender employees, and (5) providing training to employees and volunteers.

At the systemic level, hospice and palliative care professionals and institutions can push for change in the way laws and policies treat LGBTQIA+ people and in the way their discipline writes about, teaches about, and engages with LGBTQIA+ people. Policy makers and insurers can dismantle structures that privilege heterosexual, cisgender people by implementing universal **SOGI data** collection and requiring the collection and use of social determinants of health data.

The chapters in this book build on one another, starting from the individual level in chapter 1 and working up to the systemic level in chapter 11. The following is a brief overview.

Chapter 1 describes a process that hospice and palliative care professionals can use to improve their ability to provide inclusive, nonjudgmental care when planning, engaging in, and reflecting on an interaction with an individual receiving hospice care or palliative care. In addition, the chapter describes communication techniques as well as verbal and nonverbal approaches to facilitating LGBTQIA-inclusive care.

Chapter 2 explains the relationships among sex, gender, gender identity, gender expression or gender presentation, gender incongruence, gender nonconformity, gender dysphoria, gender euphoria, sexual orientation, sexual behavior, sexuality, and sexual health and discusses their relevance in the palliative care and hospice setting. In addition, the chapter describes a two-step process for asking individuals about their sex assigned at birth and gender and explains the use of gender-neutral pronouns.

Chapter 3 explains why, given the historical and contemporary contexts within which LGBTQIA+ people live, it's not surprising that some LGBTQIA+ individuals and families may be reluctant to seek care. The chapter describes three kinds of barriers to palliative care and hospice care—perceptual, financial, and institutional—and offers a two-pronged approach to addressing such barriers.

Chapter 4 describes an LGBTQIA-inclusive approach to taking a comprehensive history that places the primary emphasis on the individual as person. The chapter includes an explanation of how to conduct an organ inventory.

Chapter 5 explains how to coordinate and facilitate a family meeting focused on shared decision making, how to use shared decision making for issues surrounding palliative sedation, and how family dynamics may play a role in the shared decision-making process.

Chapter 6 explains how to help individuals and families identify their own unique goals for care, how to use a set of key questions to refocus interdisciplinary/interprofessional team meetings on person- and family-centered outcomes of care, and how to conduct an environmental and safety risk assessment.

Chapter 7 provides an overview of the ethical principles that guide practice, the elements of advance care planning, and the legal issues that may have an impact on LGBTQIA+ individuals, in particular, as they navigate serious and life-threatening illness and seek to remain the authors of their own lives.

Chapter 8 provides specific, actionable strategies for teaching individuals and families about care skills, end-stage disease progression, pain and symptom management, medication management, disposal of supplies, and signs and symptoms of imminent death.

Chapter 9 explains the developmental tasks of life completion and life closure as well as the roles that despair, hope, and meaning play in the context of advanced illness. The chapter describes LGBTQIA-inclusive assessment skills and supportive techniques for addressing psychosocial and spiritual issues and explains how a spiritual/existential history and a spiritual/existential assessment differ. Finally, this chapter examines the ways in which the members of the interdisciplinary/interprofessional team work in collaboration with one another to support the individual and family in achieving their goals for care in the psychosocial and spiritual/existential domains.

Chapter 10 explains how to assess the structural integrity of an institution's or program's bridge to LGBTQIA+ individuals and their families and how to construct that bridge in order to reach, welcome, and serve LGBTQIA+ individuals and families. After you have finished reading chapter 10, consider ways you can encourage your organization to implement the types of changes described.

Chapter 11 provides specific strategies you can use to advocate for change beyond the organization or program where you provide hospice and/or palliative care. You will learn how to advocate for changes to textbooks, journals, curricula, and conferences to ensure that future and current hospice and palliative care professionals have access to the content they need in order to provide exceptional LGBTQIA-inclusive care to individuals and families. You will also learn how to advocate for changes to laws and policies that affect LGBTQIA+ individuals and families.

Each chapter contains the following elements:

- Chapter Outcomes: What you will be able to do with the information after reading the chapter.
- Key Terms: Words or phrases covered within the chapter and also defined in the glossary at the back of the book.
- Chapter Summary: A brief overview of the chapter.
- Perspectives: Text boxes containing personal stories submitted by palliative care and hospice professionals, individuals, and families.
- Key Points to Remember: A list of the chapter's main ideas or takeaway points.

- Discussion Questions: Questions you can use for self-assessment or to guide team-based or classroom-based discussions about the chapter.
- Chapter Activity: An activity that provides an opportunity for applying or reflecting on the chapter's content.

At the back of the book, you will find a glossary of important terms, a list of the references cited, and brief biographies of the experts who reviewed and validated the content. Additional resources, such as downloadable pocket guides, can be found on the website for *The Handbook of LGBTQIA-Inclusive Hospice and Palliative Care*, http://www.lgbtqia-inclusive.com.

PROFESSIONAL PERSPECTIVE

Though I consider myself a conservative Christian, my eyes have been opened regarding the differences in moral and civil beliefs. Several years ago, I cared for a patient who was a lesbian. As I made my visits and came to know her and the partner she had shared over twenty years of her life with, I realized that this couple was like any loving, committed couple that I had witnessed hundreds of times before. There were family photos throughout the home, children and grandchildren on both sides were involved, along with any number of relationship quirks that go along with a couple that has been together long-term. What grieved me the most about this experience was the fact that her partner . . . was unable to take Family and Medical Leave Act [FMLA] time because they weren't considered to be married. So as the patient continued to decline, her partner, with whom she had shared almost half of her life, continued to have to work six days a week, almost twelve hours a day, because she was unable to take time off.

Now, my own Christian beliefs still dictate to me that a marriage is solely between a man and a woman. However, I have come to the conclusion that any committed couple, who have been together a number of years, should have the same civil rights of those couples who are of opposite sex. The fact that my patient was a lesbian wasn't the eye-opener for me—it was the fact that as she lay dying, the love of her life was literally two blocks away, working, because she wasn't able to take FMLA time. This seemed very wrong to me. I hope you can use my experience. I have come to believe that though my Christian beliefs can be black-and-white, the bottom line for my faith is still "love," and those [who] love should be able to be by the side of those they love, no matter the gender of their partner.

—Jennifer Hawkins, RN, CHPN

February 21, 2019

Facebook post from Kim Acquaviva:

Kathy's oncologist called today with the results of the pathology report. The cancer is a Stage IIIb, which we expected, but we were surprised to learn (as was the oncologist) that Kathy's cancer was ovarian clear cell carcinoma, not a high-grade serous carcinoma as originally thought. Ovarian clear cell carcinomas are rare—comprising only around 5 percent of ovarian cancer cases—and have a much worse prognosis than high-grade serous carcinomas because they are aggressive and generally resistant to chemotherapy. The pathology report confirmed that there was cancer in both ovaries, both fallopian tubes, the omentum, the peritoneum, the surface of the rectum, and the abdomen. In addition, the pathology report indicated that Kathy has malignant ascites, generally considered to be a poor prognostic sign. Kathy's oncologist said it's difficult to know what the disease course will look like but we're definitely looking at a time frame of less than 9 months. The oncologist said we should expect to see the tumors grow back and potentially begin causing bowel obstructions in 3–4 months.

    None of this changes the treatment plan: Kathy will be receiving aggressive palliative care for symptom management through the use

(continued on next page)

(continued from previous page)

of a combination of prescribed medications (e.g. Lovenox, Reglan, Protonix, etc) and medical marijuana. The only thing that has changed is our urgency to make the most of every second of our time together as a family. Greyson will be coming home for spring break in 2 weeks and then he'll be coming home for the summer the first week of May.

Shortly before Kathy was diagnosed, I accepted an endowed professorship at the University of Virginia School of Nursing. In many ways, the timing couldn't be better: UVA has an exceptional palliative care team and Kathy's likely to begin needing more intensive symptom management as we enter the summertime. We hope to move to Charlottesville in late May and I'll continue to work at GW and teach online over the summer until my August 1 start date in my new position. Kathy's oncologist will continue to follow her when we move to Charlottesville and we'll be looking to the amazing palliative care team at UVA for symptom management.

If and when Kathy's symptom management needs exceed what we're able to handle with palliative care alone, we'll look to hospice for support. We're lucky in that we have a large network of hospice and palliative care experts we can lean on for advice and guidance, so Kathy's transition from palliative care to hospice at home will likely be late in her disease trajectory. Because we both work in the hospice and palliative care field, Kathy and I wanted to be upfront early on about this because we don't want people to say in a few months, "OMG—why didn't they call hospice sooner?" As two introverts who value the bubble of quiet that our home provides, we want to maintain that for as long as possible for Greyson, Kathy, and I and our three dogs.

We understand that this news may be hard to process and we're so sorry. Please know that we greatly appreciate your support and the quality time you're making possible for our family.

Love and hugs,

Kim

1 Self-Awareness and Communication

CHAPTER OUTCOMES

1. Reflect on your attitudes, beliefs, and feelings about sexual orientation, gender, and gender expression/gender presentation.
2. Reflect on your attitudes, beliefs, and feelings about the dying process and death.
3. Use a three-step mitigation plan before each interaction to acknowledge the power imbalance between the individual receiving care and the professional and prevent your attitudes and beliefs from having a negative impact on the care you provide.
4. Use empathic and facilitating verbal and nonverbal behaviors in delivering LGBTQIA-inclusive care.
5. Recognize how touch, humor, and self-disclosure can be either helpful or harmful to your relationship with a person receiving care.

Key Terms: assumption, attitude, belief, CAMPERS, compassion, denial, emotions, empathic behaviors, empathy, facilitating behaviors, humor, mitigation plan, nonverbal communication, power imbalance, presence, reactions, reflection, right to self-determination, self-awareness, self-disclosure, touch, unconscious bias

CHAPTER SUMMARY

Providing inclusive care to individuals with chronic or life-limiting illnesses requires **self-awareness**—an awareness of one's **attitudes**, **beliefs**, and **emotions** and the ways in which they shape interactions and care. For hospice and palliative care professionals, self-awareness should be an ongoing process rather than a static state of existence to strive toward. This chapter describes a process that hospice and palliative care professionals can follow to improve their ability to provide inclusive, nonjudgmental care when planning, engaging in, and reflecting on interactions with persons receiving care. In addition, the chapter describes verbal and **nonverbal communication** techniques to facilitate LGBTQIA-inclusive care.

SELF-AWARENESS

Self-awareness is key to delivering LGBTQIA-inclusive care. The mnemonic device for remembering the steps in this process is **CAMPERS**: clear purpose, attitudes and beliefs, mitigation plan, patient, emotions, reactions, and strategy.

STEP 1: KNOW YOUR CLEAR PURPOSE

Before an interaction with an individual receiving hospice care or palliative care, take a minute to think about the reason for that interaction. Every interaction has a purpose. Give conscious thought to identifying your clear purpose before the interaction, but keep in mind that your purpose may (and should) change during the interaction, based on the needs of the individual. Whether you're a physician, an advanced practice registered nurse (APRN), a physician associate (PA), a registered nurse (RN), a social worker, a counselor, or a chaplain, your purpose for an interaction with an individual will generally fall into one or more of the following categories:

- Provide supportive **presence**
- Gather information
- Transmit information
- Clarify understanding of information
- Collaborate to create and oversee a treatment/care plan
- Administer a medication or treatment

STEP 2: KNOW YOUR ATTITUDES AND BELIEFS

As you approach any interaction with an individual receiving hospice care or palliative care, think about your attitudes and beliefs in relation to that person. If you are going to be meeting a new patient for the first time, pay attention to any **assumptions** you might be making based on information on the intake form or referral sheet. Does the first or last name of the patient lead you to make assumptions about their race, ethnicity, religion, or cultural traditions? If so, how do these assumptions lead you to draw other conclusions about the patient—what their home may look like, what their socioeconomic status is, what amount of family support they have, and so on? Take a look at the patient's address. What assumptions do you make based on the patient's zip code or whether the address includes an apartment number? What assumptions do you make based on the type of insurance the patient has? When you look at the referring diagnosis, what thoughts pop into your head? For example, if the diagnosis is lung cancer, do you instantly wonder whether the patient was a smoker? What about a diagnosis of cirrhosis—do you find yourself wondering whether the patient has a history of alcohol abuse? Does a diagnosis of anal cancer make you wonder whether the patient is gay? There is nothing wrong with having any of these thoughts. Human beings sort information based on patterns, prior experiences, and learned social norms. These prejudgments (prejudices) are instinctual, even though they are often inaccurate.

When you find yourself wondering whether an individual receiving hospice care or palliative care "did something" to cause their illness, you may be subconsciously trying to make sense of the patient's illness by sorting the patient into the category of "other"—a category of taboo breakers toward whom you feel comfortably distant or perhaps uncomfortably close. You may feel safe from experiencing a similar fate or fearful that a similar fate might befall you. In reality, of course, no one is "safe" from experiencing a life-limiting illness: nonsmokers get lung cancer, heterosexual people get anal cancer, and nondrinkers get cirrhosis. More important, however, is recognizing that *none* of the individuals you work with should be blamed or shamed for their life-limiting illness. It doesn't matter whether they smoked tobacco, drank alcohol, or had anal sex: illness is not punishment. The challenge for all of us as health care professionals and human beings is to become aware of our instinctual prejudgments and then counteract their ability to influence our decisions and behaviors.

If you are going to be seeing someone you have visited before, pay attention to your attitudes and beliefs. Do you find yourself dreading the visit because the patient has a hoarding disorder or the house seems uncomfortably dirty to you? If the patient is wealthy and lives in a beautiful home, do you find yourself looking forward to that visit a little more than you look forward to others? Do you have more positive feelings about visits to someone who is gay than visits to someone who is straight (or vice versa)? Ask yourself the following questions, and be honest with yourself:

- Which persons do you feel more **compassion** for: someone with lung cancer who smoked or someone with lung cancer who never smoked?
- Which person would you rather spend time visiting: someone who lives in a tent under a bridge or someone who lives in a luxury high-rise apartment?
- Have you ever rushed through a visit after seeing roaches in a patient's home?
- Which person would be harder for you to relate to: an evangelical Christian or a devout Muslim?

- Which person would you rather have assigned to you: a gay man with rectal cancer or a heterosexual ("straight") woman with rectal cancer?
- Do you believe that living life as an LGBTQIA+ person is a sin?
- If you believe in heaven and hell, do you believe that LGBTQIA+ people go to hell after they die?
- Do you feel as though it's "normal" for older people to die but not younger people?

An important part of this step is becoming more aware of your attitudes and beliefs about dying and death. Ask yourself these questions:

- How do you define a "good" death?
- When individuals choose to go to the hospital to die because they don't want to die at home, do you think that this is a bad decision?
- What are your thoughts about the use of medically administered nutrition and hydration at the end of life?
- When family members of someone who is likely days from death insist that the patient be given medically administered nutrition and hydration after you have clearly explained the risks, do you think that they are making the wrong decision and that they're "in denial"?
- When a palliative care patient decides not to pursue potentially life-extending or curative treatment, do you think that the patient has "given up"?
- When an individual receiving hospice care or palliative care has adult children who live nearby, work full-time, and say they cannot help with the patient's care, do you find yourself viewing those adult children negatively?

Thinking about these questions—and answering them honestly, even if the answers make you cringe a bit—is a first step toward becoming more aware of your attitudes and beliefs. Without this self-awareness, you run the risk that an **unconscious bias** will play a detrimental role in your care of individuals—leading you to develop "stories" to fit your bias. For example, your bias could lead you to assume that a person who is unable to stay home to care for their dying spouse doesn't care when, in fact, the person has to work 60+ hours a week in order to provide for the family's basic needs.

PROFESSIONAL PERSPECTIVE

I worked as a social worker in hospice in South Dakota in the '90s and have such fond memories of the men [with HIV/AIDS] we worked with at the end of life, and their partners/families. While it was tragic and very sad to lose such a young, vibrant group of men, they taught me so much in my time with them. Those men taught me that quality of life is defined only by the person going through the illness. I saw a young man that we all felt had no quality of life due to his blindness, chronic diarrhea, pain, nausea, and [other] intractable symptoms but he, at his young age, saw being alive to be with his mother one more day as an acceptable quality of life for him. These men taught me that the strength and bond of a relationship has nothing to do with the gender of the partners, and they helped me see that men can be excellent caregivers to one another. At that time, there was no legal or binding arrangement for their relationships, but I witnessed unbelievable commitment to each other and a resiliency that I didn't often see in the other populations we served. I learned the value of humor in coping with very difficult times. I think the most valuable lesson that I learned was about other people's ability to adapt and overcome their apprehensions in working with LGBTQ people. Parents who were not always comfortable with their sons' sexual orientation were almost always able to allow love to overcome any barrier they had, and they provided wonderful, supportive care at the end of their sons' lives. I [have] worked with nurses who refused to take care of a gay person with HIV/AIDS. One nurse overcame her apprehension and became the nurse to care for all the men on our caseload with HIV/AIDS. She grew to love serving her "boys" and became a strong advocate for these men, their partners, and their families at the end of their lives. As treatment of HIV/AIDS changed, we began decreasing our hospice caseload of patients with AIDS and sometimes even discharged them—a happy end to a very tragic time.

—Lynn Hunter, MSW, CSW-PIP, QMHP

STEP 3: KNOW YOUR MITIGATION PLAN

The term **mitigation plan** is used in the business world to describe an aspect of risk management in which a plan is devised ahead of time to reduce risk (Leonard, 2018). In the context of the CAMPERS self-awareness process, the term refers to the actions you plan to take to prevent the attitudes and beliefs identified in step 2 from having an impact on your interactions with an individual receiving hospice care or palliative care. Your mitigation plan should also include actions you will take to minimize the **power imbalance** between you and the patient. A power imbalance exists when one person in a relationship has more authority, expertise, or access to resources than the other person. Individuals receiving palliative care or hospice care are in a vulnerable position because they may be dependent on the health care professional for meeting some of their most basic human needs, such as relieving their pain, helping them perform the activities of daily living, and easing their emotional and spiritual distress.

Some of the phrases used by health care professionals exemplify the existence of this power imbalance. The terms *noncompliant, nonadherent, difficult, challenging,* and *in denial* are probably the best examples. These terms connote that someone has failed to comply with, adhere to, or accept the care plan developed by a health care professional—and they imply that the patient's role in the relationship between professional and patient is to follow orders. But what does terminology like this say about our respect for an individual's **right to self-determination?** "Noncompliance" and "nonadherence" do not describe individuals' failures; instead, they reflect our inability as health care professionals to help individuals set goals they are motivated and able to achieve. The phrase "in denial" similarly reflects our inability as health care professionals to meet individuals where they are and understand their perspective on their situation. Sometimes **denial** is the coping mechanism a person needs to rely on in a given moment. It is not our right as professionals to take that away from them.

While many hospice and palliative care professionals have abandoned the use of terms like *noncompliant* in favor of more patient-centered terminology, there is still much work to be done at the individual level to mitigate the effects of attitudes and beliefs on the care provided. Your mitigation plan does not need to be complex. In fact, the best mitigation plans are so simple that they can be easily remembered and quickly implemented in less than a minute before each interaction.

The following mitigation plan consists of three concrete steps—three questions and answers that, if you repeat them to yourself each time you meet with someone, will help you mitigate the power imbalance between patient and professional and prevent your attitudes and beliefs from having a negative impact on the care you provide. I have used "I" statements so you can imagine how the plan could be used in your own practice.

- **Who is the narrative about?** The narrative is about the person receiving care. What I believe and my own attitudes have nothing to do with the person's story.
- **Who should be writing the narrative?** I am not writing this narrative. The person receiving care should be the one writing the narrative. They are the author of the narrative throughout this illness and for the remainder of their life.
- **What is my role?** My job is simply to give the person who is receiving care the behind-the-scenes support needed to write the narrative. I won't try to tell them what to write or cast myself as a central character.

STEP 4: KNOW THE PATIENT

At this point, you have identified the purpose for your interaction with the patient, examined your own attitudes, beliefs, and assumptions, and implemented a plan for mitigating both the patient-professional power differential and the impact of your attitudes and beliefs on the care you are going to provide. The fourth step in the self-awareness process is to know the patient. Knowing the patient goes beyond simply knowing their diagnosis and prognosis—you need to get to know who the patient is as a person and what is most important to them. The following list of questions can be asked, after a brief period of rapport-building conversation, when you first meet an individual receiving hospice care or palliative care:

- What name would you like me to call you?
- What sex were you assigned at birth, on your original birth certificate?
- What gender do you identify as now?
- What pronouns would you like me to use to refer to you? (e.g., he/him, she/her, they/them, ze/zir)
- What prompted your decision to seek palliative care or hospice care?
- Who do you consider to be your "family"?
- Who are the important people in your life?
- Who are the people who have been most supportive to you in the past?
- To whom do you turn for support now?
- What do you know about your diagnosis? Prognosis?
- What are your short-term and longer-term goals for your life? For your care?

While several of these questions are standard components of a palliative care or hospice admission visit, the three questions about sex, gender, and gender pronouns may be unfamiliar to you. These questions should be asked of all individuals receiving care—not just those you think may be transgender. The questions are discussed in greater depth in chapter 2.

March 4, 2019

GoFundMe update from Kathy Brandt:

Well, that was no fun. After eating some blue corn chips, I had a repeat of the stomach pain, nausea, and vomiting that plagued me in the hospital. (Luckily no green beans showed up this time—that would have freaked me out). We think my ileus returned (or hadn't totally resolved), which was why my food wasn't being digested, leading to the pain and vomiting. I've been walking more (as that helps resolve an ileus) and eating a very plain diet. There's a kind

(continued on next page)

(continued from previous page)

of [medical marijuana] that is much better than Zofran or Ativan at managing my nausea. It helped a ton Friday and Saturday and by Sunday, I was able to eat rice and keep it down.

I'm feeling much better today but my badass caregiver, Kim, hurt her back lifting a heavy box (She's not supposed to lift anything heavy because she has Ankylosing Spondylitis). She's in a lot of pain but she still did her 7-mile hike early this morning (which cements her badass status in my book). She's already hiked more than 150 miles since I was diagnosed at the end of January. The daily hikes help her back stay strong and they're a huge stress reliever, so I want her to keep going on her hikes every day.

It is so great having Greyson home. He and I fell asleep together in the recliner/loveseat on Saturday, which was awesome. He is a champ and is managing not to be too bored with his low-key spring break. I'm sure many of his friends are doing way more exciting things than we are. For example, today we are going to the grocery store. So . . . much . . . fun!

We continue to enjoy visits every few days from dear friends and plan to have dinner out with two friends on Wednesday—Hard Times Café chili, here I come (again)!!

This week we have a follow-up appointment with the gynecologic oncologist to check my wound, etc. My gynecologic oncologist Dr. Mildred Chernofsky is incredible—I'll be forever grateful to Alyssa McCrea for recommending her. Since I'm not going to be having chemo, I'm interested in hearing Dr. C's thoughts about what we can do to keep me comfortable as long as possible. We also have the outpatient palliative care clinic and all our friends and colleagues providing helpful insights into my plan of care.

Once again, the theme running through our veins whenever we think about all of you who donated is gratitude. You've helped us in ways you can't imagine, especially since I can't work full time as yet. Hopefully in a week or so, but we just don't know for how long. That's the scary part for our family. You've all helped to ease our worries, allowing us to focus on being present with each other in every moment we have together. Thank you so much, for everything!

With love,

KB [Kathy]

GoFundMe update from Kim Acquaviva:

Today we ventured out as a family for the first time since Greyson arrived home Friday night. Our mission: grocery shopping at Harris Teeter. Kathy was exhausted by the time we got to the check-out line so she waited in the car while I paid and the groceries were bagged up. Greyson hasn't complained once about what has to be The World's Most Boring Spring Break—more proof that he's a much better human being than either Kathy or I. When I picked him up at the airport Friday night, he told me he'd been pretty anxious about what being home would be like. There's no playbook for "spring break at home with a dying parent" and he didn't know what to expect. It didn't take long for him to adjust to our family's new "normal" once he got home, though.

I had been hoping Kathy would have more energy by the time Greyson arrived home for spring break but she only has about 10 percent of the energy and "pep" that she had a year ago. It's hard to know whether she'll get stronger in the next week or so or whether this is the best she'll feel and it's all downhill from here. These are the kinds of conversations Kathy and I are having these days: should she power through a dinner out with family & friends because soon she won't feel like going out much at all, or should we wait and see if she feels better in a few days? Sometimes it feels like we're trying to guess the number of jelly beans in a jar that's been painted black. Are there lots of jelly beans in there or only a handful? No one can tell for sure so we're making decisions based on blind guesses.

Meanwhile, we're doing a lot of laughing as a family and we're trying to enjoy every single second of our time together. Life is short . . . every second counts.

Love,

Kim

STEP 5: KNOW YOUR EMOTIONS

The fifth step in the self-awareness process is to learn to recognize your emotions. I still remember one of the first deaths I witnessed as a new social worker. Shortly after the patient took his last breath, I felt my eyes well up with tears and a lump form in my throat. When I glanced over at the patient's wife, though, her eyes were dry and I thought she looked almost bored. I felt a flicker of disapproval. I had just met the man and I was tearful. The word *cold* popped into my mind, followed by a cheek-burning sense of shame that in a split second I had unconsciously imposed my idea of what grief looks like onto her. Recognizing my emotions made it possible for me to put my feelings aside so that I could focus on the feelings that really mattered—those of the patient's wife. I sat with her and reminded myself that I needed to meet her where she was. (Several decades later, *I* was the dry-eyed wife whose spouse had just died. I wasn't bored—I was exhausted and numb.)

As hospice and palliative care professionals, it can be difficult for us to acknowledge experiencing socially undesirable emotions. How often have you heard someone say that you're an "angel" or a "saint" for the work that you do? It can be tough to reconcile the way that others see you (and the way you want to be seen) with the gritty emotions you experience working with individuals and families. The fastest way to shed this sense of cognitive dissonance is to accept the fact you are not and cannot be a saint or an angel. You are a mortal human being doing incredibly challenging work to make the lives of individuals and families better during illness, death, and bereavement. Feeling frustration or disgust or annoyance with someone receiving care doesn't mean you're a "bad" health care professional—it means you are human. Your task is to do whatever you can to recognize those feelings when you experience them and then make a conscious choice not to let them get in the way of your ability to provide the best care possible to people.

STEP 6: KNOW YOUR REACTIONS

The sixth step in the self-awareness process, know your reactions, is closely intertwined with step 5. When you feel annoyance, do you convey that

PROFESSIONAL PERSPECTIVE

I think a really good place to start in caring for the LGBT community is to get on the same page with patients and clients about language (i.e., personal pronouns, words for "partner," etc.). If you don't know, ask! It's OK to show that you don't know, because asking shows you care to get it right. Once you are informed, either directly or indirectly, it's so important to apply what you've learned about the language that people prefer. I once was involved with a situation where a hospice professional, Mr. A., gave a report referring to the male partner of a male patient as his "wife." That seemed unusual to the rest of us on the team because the male partner had clearly identified himself as the patient's husband in his interactions with us. When I asked Mr. A. about it, he said he was told by the male partner to refer to him as the patient's wife. When we sought clarification from the patient's husband about his preferred language, he reiterated that he is the patient's husband. The patient's husband reported that when he told Mr. A. that he was the patient's husband, Mr. A. continued to question it and didn't seem to "get it." The patient's husband finally [gave up and] told Mr. A., "Just think of me as [the patient's] wife." As a community, let's not be dense—let's ask for patient and family preferences and let's honor them!

—Vicki Quintana, MSPH, RN

reaction to others in your facial expressions, body language, and tone of voice? Do you furrow your brow or maybe wrinkle your nose? What about when you feel frustrated with someone? Your goal in step 6 is to gain a better understanding of how your reactions become visible to others so you can make a conscious effort to avoid communicating those personal feelings to individuals receiving hospice or palliative care. One of the medical students I taught years ago would twirl her hair with her finger and bounce her foot up and down, dangling her shoe from her toes, when she was feeling a lack of confidence during an interaction with a person seeking care. Once she was aware of both what she was feeling and her reaction to it, she was able to stop bouncing her foot and playing with her hair and begin projecting more confidence. Another medical student would register shock or surprise by widening her eyes and raising her eyebrows. She worked hard to control her facial expressions and is now a skilled practitioner with a rock-solid yet compassionate poker face.

If you are not sure how you show your emotions, ask your partner or spouse, family members, or friends. Ask them how they can tell when you are annoyed, frustrated, angry, disapproving, or impatient. The insights you glean will help you put this step into practice so that when you are interacting with someone and you recognize that you're experiencing an emotion you would rather not make visible to them, you can make a conscious effort to control your "tells"—the physical reactions like pursed lips, furrowed brows, or crossed arms that reveal your feelings.

STEP 7: KNOW YOUR STRATEGY

The last step in the self-awareness process is to know your strategy. This step involves taking time for a brief period of **reflection** (and, if possible, debriefing with other members of the care team) after an interaction in order to develop a strategy for communicating more effectively in the future. Think about what went well and what did not. Were you surprised by any of the thoughts or emotions you experienced during the interaction? How did those emotions make themselves visible to the person you were interacting with? Were you able to support the individual's role as the author of their own story, or did you find yourself trying to take control of that story at times? Whose goals and needs were met during the interaction—the individual's, yours, both? Based on how the interaction went, consider what you would do differently or better in your next interaction, and devise a strategy for carrying this out in the future.

COMMUNICATION

The CAMPERS process—clear purpose, attitudes and beliefs, mitigation plan, patient, emotions, reactions, and strategy—when paired with good

March 6, 2019

GoFundMe update from Kathy Brandt:

Our adventures have gotten a bit more exciting since the grocery store outing (what's not to love?) We managed to go to Ted's Bulletin yesterday, despite the fact that I was feeling low energy. Spending time out with Grey and Kim was worth the effort, though. Today we head to Hard Times for dinner with Emil and Russ, which will be lots of fun.

My nausea is gone and I am able to eat more but Kim is worried I'm losing weight too fast. I've lost 20 pounds in the past two weeks but I want to lose the remaining 10 pounds of water weight as it is still bothering me. It's mostly in my stomach now, so I look like I'm 8 months pregnant. It's impossible to know whether the weight I'm losing is all water or not. My appetite hasn't been great, but some of it is I'm gun shy about eating too much because of my ileus (which is hopefully gone, but we can't know if it's gone for good). However, I plan on eating ALL the chili that's put in front of me tonight (with sour cream and cheese), so that should slow down the weight loss some.

I love all the Facebook comments and messages, tweets, cards, and texts that I'm receiving from everyone. I wish I could respond to each of you and write individual thank you notes for the donations. Kim keeps reminding me that I have limited energy or "money cookies" (that's what she used to call the gold coins we'd earn playing Lego Star Wars video games) and I need to use the money cookies doing things I have to do (like work and a few chores) and want to do (spending time with family and friends). So, while I have guilt for not writing thank you notes, the money cookies I have are already allocated right now.

If you have a spare supply of money cookies please let me know. Until then please consider each update my thank you to all of you wonderful friends, colleagues, and family members.

Much love,

kb

communication skills, will help you provide inclusive, nonjudgmental care. Communicating with individuals receiving hospice or palliative care and their families is central to your work as a hospice or palliative care professional. APRNs, RNs, physicians, physician associates, chaplains, social workers, and counselors learn communication skills in school, with each discipline putting a unique spin on the communication techniques that are taught. Because the focus of this book is on the skills hospice and palliative professionals need to deliver LGBTQIA-inclusive care, I will not be covering basic communication skills. Instead, this book will highlight communication techniques and other verbal and nonverbal approaches that facilitate LGBTQIA-inclusive care.

Empathic behaviors are the things you say (verbal) or do (nonverbal) to convey to individuals receiving hospice or palliative care that you care about them and are committed to understanding their perspective or experience; **facilitating behaviors** are the things you say or do to foster open communication (AAHPM, 2009). Table 1.1 summarizes the behaviors. The behaviors listed in table 1.1 can convey **empathy** and facilitate open communication, but if carried out clumsily or insincerely, some of these behaviors can be detrimental to forming a relationship with an individual receiving hospice care or palliative care, especially when it comes to being LGBTQIA-inclusive. Three behaviors in particular are open to misuse by well-meaning professionals: **self-disclosure**, **touch**, and **humor**.

TABLE 1.1 Empathic and facilitating behaviors

	Verbal	Nonverbal
Empathic	Silent listening	Touch
	Affirmation	Open posture
	Self-disclosure	Facial expression
Facilitating	Naming normalization	Eye contact
	Reflection humor	Head nodding/shaking
		Eye-level approach

Source: AAHPM, 2009. Reprinted with permission from the American Academy of Hospice and Palliative Medicine, © 2009 American Academy of Hospice and Palliative Medicine.

Self-Disclosure

Disclosing information about yourself can convey empathy and openness, but the disclosure should be made to meet the needs of the patient, not those of the health care professional (you). If you self-identify as lesbian, gay, bisexual, transgender, nonbinary, gender nonconforming, queer, questioning, intersex, and/or asexual, you may find yourself wanting to share this fact with the LGBTQIA+ individuals receiving hospice or palliative care you work with. Before you do, think about your rationale for disclosing this information. Would you be doing it because you want the patient to like you? Trust you? Feel understood by you? Are there other ways you could accomplish those goals more effectively? The same questions hold true for heterosexual hospice and palliative care professionals. If you self-identify as heterosexual and you find yourself wanting to mention your other-gender significant other or spouse during a conversation with an individual receiving hospice care or palliative care, think carefully about your rationale for doing so. Why do you want to disclose your heterosexuality? Whose needs are you meeting—yours or the patient's? Self-disclosure is neither good nor

AUTHOR'S NOTE

Over the years I've been asked many times why lesbian, gay, and bisexual people feel the need to "tell people about their sex lives" by coming out to others. Rather than answer the question directly, I like to respond by asking the questioner to try the following exercise. If you are heterosexual and currently in a relationship with a person of another gender, keep track of how many times you refer to this person (either by name or by such terms as boyfriend, girlfriend, husband, wife) in your conversations with colleagues, friends, neighbors, and family members this week. At the end of the week, reflect on why you felt the need to share your heterosexuality with so many people. This exercise never fails to leave people surprised by how often heterosexuality is casually disclosed in everyday conversations. Mentioning your sexual orientation to others isn't telling people about your sex life; it is sharing a part of who you are as a person.

bad. Use it with intentionality to maximize its potential benefits. There are ways other than verbal self-disclosure to show that you are committed to providing nonjudgmental care to LGBTQIA+ individuals and their families. For example, some professionals wear a rainbow "ally" lapel pin as a way to signal to individuals receiving hospice or palliative care and families that they are committed to LGBTQIA-inclusive care.

Touch

When touch is a part of care delivery—for example, when a nurse puts lotion on an individual's dry skin or a chaplain holds hands with someone in prayer—it can be a powerful tool for conveying a sense of caring and compassion. When touch is used during a conversation between a professional and a person receiving care, however, it can be awkward. Does putting a hand on a someone's knee make potentially difficult news easier to hear, or does it just make us as professionals think we are doing something to lessen that person's pain? As both a social worker and a person who receives care from health care professionals, I view touch as something that needs to be invited. I do not want my health care professionals to pat me on the knee or rub my back, and I don't do those things to individuals I work with who are receiving hospice or palliative care. Touch may be more than unhelpful—in fact, it may be harmful:

> For many trauma survivors, inappropriate or unpleasant touch was part of a traumatic experience. Touch, even when appropriate and necessary for providing care, can easily activate a fight, flight, or freeze response. Nurses are often required to touch patients, sometimes in sensitive areas. This may include helping patients sit up in bed, applying their hospital identification band, listening to their lungs, or examining a wound. Any touch can be interpreted as unwanted or threatening and it is important to ask permission to touch someone and obtain verbal consent before doing so. Touch may be activating for a patient and may bring up difficult feelings or memories. This may lead to increased anxiety and activation of the stress response which can result in disruptive behaviors and even lead to the patient dissociating. Asking permission before you touch

patients gives them a choice and empowers them to have control over their body and physical space. (Fleishman, Kamsky, & Sundborg, 2019)

An understanding of trauma-informed care is essential for hospice and palliative care professionals hoping to provide LGBTQIA-inclusive care:

> Because many intersex patients have experienced medical trauma, they may have a high level of anxiety and distrust when visiting a health care provider. A trauma-informed approach to care can help put the patient at ease and reduce traumatic responses to health care. Trauma-informed care means that providers: are aware that many patients have a history of trauma; understand the impact of trauma on a [person's] health and behaviors; recognize the signs of trauma; help with recovery from trauma; access care for themselves to prevent secondary trauma; and resist re-traumatization of the patient. An example of trauma-informed care would be to recognize that an intersex patient may experience a Pap test as traumatizing, ask the patient for permission before performing the exam, and to suggest an alternative, such as a self-swab, to resist re-traumatization. (National LGBTQIA+ Health Education Center, 2020)

When you work with individuals receiving hospice or palliative care and their families, you should refrain from touching without a person's consent. Hugging is particularly tricky territory. Someone who has a history of sexual abuse, for example, may feel triggered by a forced or unexpected embrace. The power differential between the hospice and palliative care professional and the patient may make it difficult for the patient to refuse a hug initiated by a care professional. Asking someone "Can I give you a hug?" puts the patient in a position that may leave them feeling powerless to say no. Instead, talk with individuals proactively about touch and ask them about their desire for and level of comfort with hugs from you. Instead of asking "Can I give you a hug?" consider asking "What can I do right now to support you?" If the patient wants a hug, they will ask you for one. This may seem like a small thing, but the importance of respecting persons' physical and emotional boundaries cannot be overstated. Each patient you work with will have different preferences in terms of touch; it is important to be cognizant of that.

March 13, 2019

GoFundMe update from Kathy Brandt:

What a week it's been already and it's only Wednesday. There are so many things to tell you about!

    Our kitchen was demolished yesterday and right now there is a very loud saw being used to customize the new IKEA cabinets to fit where the original 1940s cabinets used to reside. The noise isn't pleasant, but I love the smell of the cut wood. Reminds me of my Grandfather Brandt's basement. It's bittersweet that we're finally getting a new kitchen but we'll be listing the house for sale the second it's finished.

    Health-related news is a mixed bag this week. The good news is I'm feeling more energetic—I don't get as tired as quickly (although by 5 I'm usually done for the day if I've been out and about at all). The bad news is that the ultrasound I had on Sunday shows a 2.3 cm nodule on my liver and it wasn't there a month ago. While this doesn't change my prognosis, it does change the staging of the disease to Stage 4 ovarian cancer. Normally I'd like "moving up" to the next level of something, but not so much this time. This doesn't change anything day-to-day, it just confirms for us how aggressive this cancer.

    I'm having trouble keeping my weight up—generally not a problem for me. I've lost too much too fast, so now I'm eating ice cream (thanks Sarah Friebert), cookies and chocolate (thanks Aunt Keiko) and other food to try and stop the weight loss. The problem is I'm not very hungry, although when I saw a bag of potato chips my mouth started watering (so I ate a whole bunch and Kim did too until I took them away from her).

    We've received great news from Emerson College. They are providing a renewable merit scholarship to cover a little more than a quarter of Greyson's tuition. This helps ease Grey's mind as he was worried about how we would be able to afford tuition given my limited ability to work. While he still will need loans, this contribution from Emerson is tremendous. However, it doesn't come close

> to matching all that you have done, as part of this community of donors, to help our family. We are so grateful for each of you, and especially Heather Wilson and Joy Barry for starting this Go Fund Me. Your gifts are helping so much, especially as the medical bills have started rolling in. Yikes—co-pays are expensive for hospital stays involving surgery!!!
>
> Thank you all for your support!
>
> kb
>
> PS—To everyone at the Annual Assembly—have fun and enjoy being in community with our best and brightest palliative care practitioners. And to those who stayed home to care for patients, check out the #HPM19 tweets as they are always illuminating.

Humor

Like touch, humor is a behavior that should be used carefully and with an awareness of the needs and preferences of each patient. A joking comment that seems lighthearted to you may seem callous to an individual receiving hospice care or palliative care or their family member. An individual with a chronic or life-limiting illness—especially someone in physical pain—may not appreciate your attempts at humor. This is not to say that there is no place for laughter in hospice or palliative care; on the contrary, laughter has many physiological and psychological benefits (Mayo Foundation for Medical Education and Research, n.d.a).

There are different ways to use humor, including laughing at oneself, laughing at the other person, laughing at a situation, and laughing at someone other than the two people interacting. Within the context of your relationship with an individual receiving hospice care or palliative care, it is wise to avoid laughing at the patient or laughing at someone else. This kind of humor runs the risk of being interpreted as mean-spirited and hurtful. Laughing at the absurdity of a situation is safer territory, especially if the patient initiates the laughter.

AUTHOR'S NOTE

When I was twenty-six, I was finishing up my dissertation proposal at my childhood home in Texas while caring for my mom, who was dying of ovarian cancer. The morning of the day she died, friends and family members were gathered around her on her bed, telling funny stories and sharing memories. She was minimally responsive—it was clear to all of us that she would die within hours. Suddenly she smiled slightly and said, "You know, I'm not dead yet." Our laughter at her parting joke ended up sweetening all our tears. Had a hospice professional cracked the joke, saying, "You know, she's not dead yet," it wouldn't have been funny at all—it would have come across as cruel. Remember that humor relies on context as much as content.

KEY POINTS TO REMEMBER

- CAMPERS is a process you can use to improve your ability to provide inclusive, nonjudgmental care when you are planning, engaging in, and reflecting on an interaction. The letters in the mnemonic device stand for: clear purpose, attitudes and beliefs, mitigation plan, patient, emotions, reactions, and strategy.
- Every interaction with an individual receiving hospice care or palliative care should have a clear purpose. Give conscious thought to your purpose before an interaction, but keep in mind that your purpose may (and should) change based on the needs of the patient during the interaction.
- Prior to an encounter with an individual receiving hospice care or palliative care, take a minute to think about your attitudes and beliefs in relation to that patient. Become aware of any prejudgments so that you can counteract the ability of those judgments to influence your decisions and behaviors.
- Review your mitigation plan before each patient interaction as a reminder to mitigate the power imbalance between patient and professional and prevent your attitudes and beliefs from having a negative impact on the care you provide.

- Get to know who the patient is as a person and what is most important to the patient.
- Recognize your own emotions during your interactions with individuals receiving hospice or palliative care and make a conscious choice not to let them get in the way of your ability to provide the best care possible. Showing emotion may be an appropriate way to show empathy in some situations, as long as your emotions don't become the focus of the interaction.
- Pay attention to your emotional reactions visible when interacting with an individual receiving hospice care or palliative care. When you recognize that you are experiencing an emotion you would rather not communicate, make a conscious effort to control your "tells" (e.g., pursed lips, furrowed brows, crossed arms).
- Engage in a brief period of reflection (and, if possible, debriefing with other members of the care team) after each interaction with an individual receiving hospice care or palliative care so that you can develop a strategy for communicating more effectively in the future.

DISCUSSION QUESTIONS

1. Think back to when you were eighteen years old. What messages had you heard up to that point from the adults in your life regarding sexual orientation? What about the messages you heard regarding gender and its expression? How did these messages shape the attitudes, beliefs, and feelings you have today?
2. Can you provide LGBTQIA-inclusive care without recognizing and reflecting upon your attitudes, beliefs, and feelings about sexual orientation and gender? Why or why not?
3. Describe how you might use verbal and nonverbal techniques to convey empathy and facilitate communication with an individual receiving hospice care or palliative care who seems reluctant to talk openly with you.
4. Imagine you have been asked to care for an LGBTQIA+ patient. Describe how you would use the CAMPERS self-awareness process before, during, and after your first interaction with the patient.

5. Imagine that you are meeting with a new patient recently diagnosed with the same rare, life-threatening illness that your sibling had. Your sibling was treated ten years ago and has been disease-free ever since. The patient is sobbing and you want to offer some comfort. Give examples of how touch, humor, and self-disclosure might be used inappropriately in this scenario.

CHAPTER ACTIVITY

Use the CAMPERS self-awareness process before, during, and after an interaction with an individual receiving hospice care or palliative care (either a real interaction or one simulated via role playing). Immediately afterward, write down what you were thinking and feeling during each step in the process. Did any of your thoughts or feelings surprise you? If you used the CAMPERS process for your work with all individuals receiving hospice or palliative care, do you think it would decrease the impact of unconscious bias on the care you deliver? Why or why not?

March 18, 2019

GoFundMe update from Kim Acquaviva:

For the first time in 6 weeks, Kathy drove this morning. The siren song of a McDonald's bacon egg and cheese biscuit was too enticing to resist. She said the food "hit the greasy spot." She bought two but could only eat one.

Kathy lost another pound since yesterday so we're trying whatever we can to stop the weight loss. It's shocking to see how skinny her legs are now. She's down to 173 pounds at 5' 10." Foods just don't taste good and foods she *thinks* will taste good end up tasting "meh." Once the stove is installed later this week things will be a little easier because we'll (translation: she'll) be able to cook again.

Kathy's drain is being placed on Friday so yesterday I ordered some pockets to attach to the inside of her clothes to hold the little bulb thingy. I also went to the dispensary yesterday to pick up some more supplies. We seem to have found the right balance so that Kathy's nausea-free and pain-free all day.

With the reality of Kathy's illness continuing to sink in, we're both trying to get used to our new roles. She's grieving the loss of her identity as a super-productive consultant and small business owner. She's not able to work much and the GoFundMe money has ended up being a lifesaver because of this. She had hoped to have a few more months of productivity in her but her rapid decline has been surprising to both of us.

Selfishly, I'm grieving the loss of being treated like a princess by the most badass woman in the world. There is no better wife in the world than Kathy . . . full stop. I've been spoiled rotten for 18 years by the way she's always put my needs and happiness (and that of our son) at the center of her universe. Kathy still does sweet things for me all the time but I know she misses her Starbucks runs as much as I do. Now it's my turn to return the favor and spoil Kathy . . . she definitely deserves it!

Kim

2 Sex, Gender, Sexual Orientation, Behavior, and Health

CHAPTER OUTCOMES

1. Define sex assigned at birth and gender and describe the differences between them.
2. Define gender identity and gender expression or gender presentation and describe the differences between them.
3. Define gender incongruence, gender nonconforming, and gender dysphoria and describe how they differ.
4. Define sexual orientation and sexual behavior and describe the differences between them.
5. Define sexuality and sexual health.

Key Terms: asexual, bisexual, cisgender, gay, gender, gender dysphoria, gender euphoria, gender expression, gender identity, gender incongruence, gender nonconforming, gender presentation, genderqueer, heterosexual, intersex, lesbian, pansexual, sex, sexual behavior, sexual expression, sexual health, sexuality, sexual orientation, transgender

CHAPTER SUMMARY

Providing LGBTQIA-inclusive care requires an understanding of several key concepts: sex, gender, gender identity, gender expression or presentation, gender incongruence, gender nonconformity, gender dysphoria, sexual orientation, sexual behavior, sexuality, and sexual health. This chapter explains how these concepts relate to one another and their relevance in the palliative care and hospice setting. In addition, the chapter describes a two-step process for asking individuals about their assigned birth sex and true gender and explains the use of gender-neutral pronouns.

KNOWLEDGE DEFICITS

When I teach, I never cease to be amazed by the number of student health professionals who lack basic knowledge about human sexuality. Without exception, these are bright students who graduated from good undergraduate programs. People can't know what they haven't been taught: clearly people are not being taught basic information about human sexuality in school. When I was working with a group of graduate students at my previous institution, I gave out a questionnaire so that I could build the weekly course content around their knowledge gaps. I asked them to submit the questions they've always wanted to ask about human sexuality. Questions that the students submitted included the following (reproduced here verbatim):

- "Has being gay become a fad more than an actual identity that one is born with? Do you think some people just give up on the opposite sex or somewhere along the way, they become influenced by friends?"
- "Can someone really be born gay/lesbian?"
- "I have always wondered whether being a gay is a 'social disease'/trend or is it really genetic?"
- "Is it truly possible to be bisexual?"

- "I don't understand transgendered people and I don't know how to gracefully have a conversation with someone who is transgendered without being inquisitive or trying to satisfy my own curiosity about their lifestyle."

To address the knowledge deficits related to human sexuality that seem to be fairly common among health care professionals, this chapter provides a quick overview of the key concepts you need to understand in order to provide good care to all individuals, including those who are LGBTQIA. For a more in-depth exploration of some of these concepts, see Laura Erickson-Schroth's *Trans Bodies, Trans Selves: A Resource by and for Transgender Communities* (2022). Published by Oxford University Press and featuring the voices of more than 150 transgender and gender-expansive individuals, it is the definitive guide to trans health and a must-have for every health care professional's personal library.

March 20, 2019

GoFundMe update from Kathy Brandt:

Have you ever been hungry and not hungry? Every afternoon that happens to me. Because our kitchen is being remodeled, I literally have a table full of food that I love that I both want to eat and really don't want to eat. I order a pizza and the first few pieces are great and then I can't eat more. Not because I don't want to, or I'm worried about the calories—I just suddenly can't eat more. It's like a door closes and I'm suddenly so full I feel like if I eat more I'll be sick.

Every morning I wake up and get on scale hoping I have not lost weight. As someone who has been overweight since elementary school, that's a huge shift. I'm about the weight I was five years ago, a year after giving up sugar (I've since renegotiated my relationship with sugar and am eating it once again). And while the weight I'm at is still higher than it "should" be for my height, I was losing it way too fast.

> The ascites is making it hard for me to eat because it's pressing against my stomach and digestive tract, so I feel full even when I'm not. That's where the medical MJ comes in handy because it helps me to feel hungry even with the ascites. It helps me enjoy the potato chips, pound cake, cookies, bagels, salmon, cheese, eggs, etc that would normally be off the menu.
>
> Those of you who know I have Celiac Disease may wonder— "Kathy, how can you eat bagels and cookies and pizza? You [can't eat] gluten." Well, it turns out when you're dying, the major risk factor from celiac (stomach cancer) isn't as big an issue. So, I reintroduced gluten and I'm loving all the foods I hadn't eaten in years. I'm not having digestive issues and so I'll keep eating gluten to keep the weight on (and because I love it). Cancer isn't fun to say the least but after six years of no sugar and no gluten, at least I can eat cake!
>
> kb

SEX AND GENDER

Two words that you may have heard used interchangeably are **sex** and **gender**. Sex is often described as having to do with the body while gender is described as having to do with sociocultural expectations, roles, and behaviors (Gendered Innovations, n.d.). The distinction between sex and gender is not that simple, though, as writer and activist Julia Serano notes:

> With regards to bodies, [sex] refers to a suite of sexually dimorphic traits that may include chromosomes, gonads, external genitals, other reproductive organs, ratio of sex hormones, and secondary sex characteristics. In our society, these traits are classified in a dichotomous manner as either female or male, and people are assigned a legal sex on that basis. However, variability exists in all these traits, plus these traits may not all "align" (i.e., all male, or all female) within the same person—when this occurs, such traits (and the people who possess them) are often described

as intersex. Some people believe in a strict sex/gender distinction—where sex refers to the realm of biology, and gender refers to the purely social—but I reject that position.... The truth is that, in our culture, "sex" is both a social and legal category in addition to describing anatomy. (Serano, 2022)

A baby isn't born a boy or a girl—they're *assigned* a sex. Most of the time, a midwife, nurse practitioner, physician, or other health care professional simply looks at the baby's genitals and decides whether they look like the genitals of a boy or a girl. When the health care professional delivering a baby says to the new parent, "Congratulations—it's a girl!," they aren't sharing information that required specialized clinical expertise. In fact, I would posit that the vast majority of new parents could look at their new baby and reach the same conclusion. That's because most of the time, a baby's sex is assigned at birth based on congruence between the baby's genitals and sociocultural norms regarding what male and female genitals should look like. While one could argue that genitals and chromosomes are objectively observable phenomena, such an argument cannot be made for sex. A person is born with a "cluster of anatomical and physiological traits that include external genitalia, secondary sex characteristics, gonads, chromosomes, and hormones" (National Academies of Sciences, Engineering, and Medicine, 2022). Whether that cluster of traits is assigned the label "male" or "female" depends on the sociocultural context into which that baby has been born.

Historically, sex has been described as a continuum that has male and female as its two endpoints. Between those two points, the science is imprecise:

Nature presents us with sex anatomy spectrums.... Sex categories get simplified into male, female, and sometimes intersex, in order to simplify social interactions, express what we know and feel, and maintain order. So nature doesn't decide where the category of "male" ends and the category of "intersex" begins, or where the category of "intersex" ends and the category of "female" begins. Humans decide. Humans (today, typically doctors) decide how small a penis has to be, or how unusual a combination of parts has to be, before it counts as intersex. Humans decide whether a person with XXY chromosomes or XY chromosomes and androgen insensitivity will count as intersex. (Intersex Society of North America, 2008)

Within a given sociocultural context in which sex is assigned at birth, the X and Y chromosomes are typically used to determine sex, with most human females having a 46XX chromosomal makeup and most males having a 46XY chromosomal makeup. The role of chromosomes in determining sex is not always clear-cut, however. Babies may be born with sex monosomies (46X or 46Y, missing an X chromosome) or sex polysomies (46XXX, 46XXY, and so on) or with translocations of portions of their chromosomes (resulting in a male with 46XX or a female with 46XY) (World Health Organization, 2020). Babies may also be born with what is known as an **intersex** condition:

> A majority of intersex people identify as heterosexual and cisgender. . . . However, research suggests that people born with variations in sex characteristics have an increased likelihood of identifying as a sexual minority (e.g., gay, lesbian, bisexual, pansexual, queer) or a gender minority (e.g., transgender, non-binary, gender fluid). Some intersex people who are heterosexual and cisgender still identify as part of the LGBTQIA+ community based on common marginalized and/or stigmatized experiences. Like transgender people, intersex people may have a gender identity that does not correspond with their sex assigned at birth or gender of raising. In addition, because intersex people have sex characteristics that transcend typical notions of female and male bodies, they may experience barriers similar to transgender people in accessing affirming health care that respects their bodies, gender identities, and physical needs. (National LGBTQIA+ Health Education Center, 2020)

Regardless of the chromosomes an individual has, the sex assigned to that person says more about the sociocultural context in which that assignment was made than it does about any sort of innate maleness or femaleness of the individual in question. Sex is complex:

Gravity seems pretty straightforward: If you drop your keys, they fall to the floor. But to truly understand gravity, you need Einstein's theory of relativity, with all of its counterintuitive ramifications—like the bending of light and slowing down of time near black holes. Similarly, sex also seems straightforward. Every person superficially appears either female or male. But once we look beneath the surface, things are far more complicated. While there are tangible biological sex characteristics—chromosomes, reproductive organs, hormones and secondary sex characteristics—they do not always fit neatly into male or female classifications, or align with one another within the same individual, as is the case for intersex people. Gender expression, gender identity and sexual orientation also vary within individuals across cultures and throughout history. (Serano, 2019)

As is the case with sex, gender is a social construct that varies across geography, culture, and time. While sex assigned at birth has to do with how the biology and anatomy of a newborn baby are interpreted by health care professionals in a given sociocultural context, gender is about the way the person inhabiting that physical body feels, behaves, and is "read" by the society around them. If gender expression were described as a continuum, its endpoints would be masculine and feminine.

GENDER IDENTITY AND EXPRESSION OR PRESENTATION

An individual's **gender identity** refers to that person's internal sense of being a man or a woman. **Gender expression**, or **gender presentation**, is the way a person outwardly expresses that internal sense. When I speak to groups of health professionals, I often use myself as an example to illustrate the concept of gender identity and gender expression. I was assigned the sex "female" at birth. My internal sense of myself is that I am a woman, and I self-identify as feminine. My gender identity is that of a woman.

When their gender identity aligns with the sex they were assigned at birth, individuals may refer to themselves as **cisgender**, or "cis." For example, let's say Bob was assigned the sex "male" at birth. Bob is a man and

> **AUTHOR'S NOTE**
>
> *I express my gender identity (my internal sense of my gender and, more broadly, my core sense of being) through the way I present my physical self to the world. When I step outside my home, I feel as though I'm walking out into the world presenting myself as a woman. Sometimes I wear lipstick and earrings and high heels, sometimes I wear jeans, flannel shirts, and Doc Marters. But always, no matter what clothing I wear, I am presenting myself to the world as a woman. As a woman with a buzzcut who has had an unreconstructed prophylactic bilateral mastectomy, however, I may be "read" by other people as masculine looking. My gender identity as a woman is unwavering, but how others see my gender may not match how I see myself. Does my flat chest make me a man? Of course not. The absence or presence of breasts has nothing to do with whether a person is female. So whose opinion counts when it comes to determining how to interpret my gender expression or gender presentation—mine or that of the person viewing me? Mine. That's why you should never attempt to make a visual determination of a person's sex, gender identity, or gender expression. Instead, ask. The patient will tell you what you need to know in order to provide the best care.*

presents himself to the world as a man. Bob might use the term *cisgender* to describe himself. This term has both enthusiastic proponents and critics. Some argue that it perpetuates a binary way of seeing the world as either "us" or "them" (White, 2013). Indeed, the Latin prefix *cis-* means "on this side of" while the prefix *trans-* means "on the other side of" (Steinmetz, 2014). Others argue the term is simply a descriptor.

GENDER INCONGRUENCE, GENDER NONCONFORMITY, AND GENDER DYSPHORIA

The word *conformity* is generally used in reference to an external set of rules or expectations. **Gender nonconforming** is "an umbrella term to describe people whose gender expression or gender identity differs from gender norms associated with their assigned birth sex" (American Psychological Association, 2015). When a child is assigned the male sex at birth, for example, and from a very young age insists on wearing only dresses, that child may be described as exhibiting gender nonconforming behavior. Similarly, my flat chest and short hair may be viewed by some people as examples of gender nonconformity. Although you may perceive someone to be gender nonconforming, you should only use the term to describe them if it's a term they use to describe themselves. Some gender nonconforming individuals use the acronym **GNC**.

Gender incongruence and gender dysphoria both rely on an individual's internal perceptions of their own gender. When a person's sex assigned at birth does not align with their gender identity, this may be referred to as **gender incongruence**. Gender incongruence is "a diagnostic term used in the ICD-11 that describes a person's marked and persistent experience of an incompatibility between that person's gender identity and the gender expected of them based on their birth-assigned sex" (Coleman et al., 2022). When the person is distressed over this incongruence, it may be referred to as **gender dysphoria** (American Psychological Association, 2015). Equally if not more important to a discussion about gender incongruence is the concept of **gender euphoria**, "a distinct enjoyment or satisfaction caused by the correspondence between the person's gender identity and gendered features associated with a gender other than the one assigned at birth" (Ashley & Ells, 2018). While gender dysphoria is often mentioned in the literature on gender incongruence, gender euphoria is not. As Beischel, Gauvin, and van Anders (2021) note, "the absence of knowledge about gender euphoria could reify the clinical focus on negative experiences of dysphoria, and could do so at the expense of fostering positive gender/sex experiences."

Some individuals whose sex assigned at birth does not align with their gender identity choose to take steps to bring their gender expression or gender presentation into alignment with their gender identity. These individuals may describe themselves as **transgender**, or they may reject such labels and simply describe themselves using the term that best aligns with their gender identity. Some individuals choose to dress and groom themselves (e.g., facial hair, clothing, hairstyle, makeup) in a way that outwardly reflects their internal gender identity while leaving their physical body as it is. Other individuals choose to make modifications to their physical body, using hormones, hormone blockers, surgery, or a combination of gender-affirming care. When you are working with someone whose sex assigned at birth does not align with their gender, don't assume that the patient has had (or wants to have) surgery to align their body with their identity. There is no right or wrong way for people to bring their gender expression or gender presentation into alignment with their gender identity, and not everyone chooses to do so at all. Gender identity is completely distinct from sexual orientation: a person may be transgender and heterosexual. For example, a person assigned the male sex at birth who is female might describe herself as heterosexual if she were attracted primarily or solely to men.

Some individuals whose sex assigned at birth does not align with their gender identity prefer to use the term **transsexual** rather than transgender to describe themselves. Transsexual is "an older term that originated in the medical and psychological communities [and is] still preferred by some people who have permanently changed—or seek to change—their bodies through medical interventions, including but not limited to hormones and/or surgeries" (Refinery29, 2018). This is an outdated term, so if an individual receiving hospice or palliative care uses the term *transsexual* to describe themselves, you should not use the word in your clinical documentation without also stating that this term is preferred by the patient. Example: "Bill was assigned female at birth and is a man. He prefers the word 'transsexual' over the word 'transgender' to describe his lived experience." Like the term *transgender*, the word *transsexual* is an adjective and should never be used as a noun.

Not everyone identifies as either male or female. Some people refer to themselves as **genderqueer:**

> Genderqueer is a term to describe a person whose gender identity does not align with a binary understanding of gender (i.e., a person who does not identify fully as either a man or a woman). People who identify as genderqueer may redefine gender or decline to define themselves as gendered altogether. For example, people who identify as genderqueer may think of themselves as both man and woman (bigender, pangender, androgyne); neither man nor woman (genderless, gender neutral, neutrois, agender); moving between genders (genderfluid); or embodying a third gender. (American Psychological Association, 2015)

A person who identifies "as being both a man and a woman, somewhere in between, or as falling completely outside these categories" may refer to themselves as **nonbinary** and may (but may not) also identify as transgender (Human Rights Campaign, n.d.a). **Agender** individuals do not identify as any gender (Refinery29, 2018). **Aliagender** individuals identify as a gender other than male or female, using a term that "was coined as a way to talk about a third gender without appropriating the term Third Gender from other cultures" (Refinery29, 2018). Some individuals experience their gender as something that is not static and refer to themselves as **genderfluid** (Human Rights Campaign, n.d.a). That fluidity may extend to both gender identity and gender presentation, with fluctuation between identifying and/or presenting as masculine, feminine, both, or neither (Refinery29, 2018). *Two-spirit* is another term you should become familiar with:

> Though Two-Spirit may now be included in the umbrella of LGBTQ, the term "Two-Spirit" does not simply mean someone who is a Native American/Alaska Native and gay. Traditionally, Native American two-spirit people were male, female, and sometimes intersexed individuals who combined activities of both men and women with traits unique to their status as two-spirit people. In most tribes, they were considered neither men nor women; they occupied a distinct, alternative gender status. In tribes where two-spirit males and females were referred to with the same term, this status amounted to a third gender. In other cases, two-spirit females were referred to with a distinct term and, therefore, constituted a fourth gender. . . . Most Indigenous communities have specific terms in their own languages for the gender-variant members of their communities and the social and spiritual roles these individuals fulfill; with over 500 surviving Native American cultures, attitudes about sex and gender can be very diverse. Even with the modern adoption of pan-Indian terms like Two-Spirit, not all cultures will perceive two-spirit people the same way, or welcome a pan-Indian term to replace the terms already in use by their cultures. (Indian Health Service, n.d.)

With all these terms used to describe gender, definitions vary between and within communities, and the terminology continues to change.

March 20, 2019

GoFundMe update from Kathy Brandt:

"Dead Woman Walking"

Tuesday I was walking down the street in Georgetown when all of a sudden I thought to myself "I'm a dead woman walking." It's surreal trying to go about a "normal" life when you know you aren't going to be around in a few months. I feel less connected to things that a year ago were so important to me, including:

- My work—it is so hard to focus and care about what I'm working on when I know in a matter of months my business will be closed
- Politics and world events—I'm still paying attention, but it's more a passing curiosity since the events that are happening won't impact me
- Most of the TV shows I enjoyed aren't interesting to me—although Kim and I still love our [Law & Order] SVU marathons
- Chit chat with strangers or to fill quiet spaces between conversations
- The Patriots—Gronk's retirement isn't concerning me the way it once would have

When I'm left to my own devices at home I often stream old TV shows. Right now, I'm on season two of the West Wing. Watching the show is an escape to a time when I didn't have cancer, when I didn't have a tube permanently inserted in my abdomen, when I wasn't a dead woman walking.

There's no roadmap for people like me who have a defined time when they will cease to exist. When I'm not watching West Wing, I spend a lot of time thinking about the fact that I won't be here soon, that Kim and Grey will keep living without me. And then, when I spend too much time thinking about this and I end up crying, there's always West Wing.

kb

MAKING SENSE OF COMPLEXITY

So if sex is something that's assigned to a person at birth based on what their body looks like and gender depends on how an individual self-identifies, what can you infer about a person's sex assigned at birth and gender based on the fact that the person checked "male" rather than "female" on an intake form? Unfortunately, the information collected from this patient is useless. Did the person check "male" because they were assigned male at birth or because their gender is male? There is no way you can know what the person meant by their answer. This is a common problem with traditional intake and admission forms—a problem that can be compounded when health care professionals check the boxes on the form themselves without even asking the individual.

The National Institutes of Health tasked the National Academies of Sciences, Engineering, and Medicine (the "National Academies") to develop a consensus report about the best ways to collect data on sex, gender, and sexual orientation. These kinds of data are often referred to collectively as **SOGI data**. The resulting report recommends using a pair of questions:

Q1: What sex were you assigned at birth, on your original birth certificate?

- Female
- Male
- (Don't know)
- (Prefer not to answer)

Q2: What is your current gender? [Mark only one]

- Female
- Male
- Transgender
- [If respondent is AIAN:] Two-Spirit
- I use a different term: [free text]
- (Don't know)
- (Prefer not to answer)

The National Academies report recommended against including "intersex" as a response choice on binary measures of sex assigned at birth. Instead, they recommended the use of "a stand-alone measure that asks respondents to report their intersex status." The report recommends that, when there is a need to know whether a person is intersex, the following question should be used:

Have you ever been diagnosed by a medical doctor or other health professional with an intersex condition or a difference of sex development (DSD) or were you born with (or developed naturally in puberty) genitals, reproductive organs, or chromosomal patterns that do not fit standard definitions of male or female?

- Yes
- No
- (Don't know)
- (Prefer not to answer)

It is difficult to imagine a scenario in which this question would be clinically relevant to the care of an individual receiving palliative care or hospice care, however. As such, this question should not be part of your standard assessment.

In summary, to gather relevant clinical information about sex and gender from hospice and palliative care individuals, you need to ask them two questions at the time of their intake: (1) What sex were you assigned at birth, on your original birth certificate? (2) What is your current gender? These questions should be asked of all persons receiving care, not just those you think might be transgender (Cahill et al., 2014; Institute of Medicine, 2011; Joint Commission, 2011). If these two questions are asked at intake, they should not have to be repeated multiple times by different members of the team.

This two-step method has been found to yield more complete data, and the Centers for Disease Control asserts that "using the two-step data collection method of asking for sex assigned at birth and current gender identity can help to increase the likelihood that transgender people will be accurately identified" (Tate, Ledbetter, & Youssef, 2013). In a study involving four health centers with diverse patient populations, the overwhelming majority of participants understood the questions in the two-step method, and "85 percent strongly agreed that they would answer the birth sex question, and 78 percent strongly agreed that they would answer the current gender identity question" (National LGBT Health Education Center, 2015).

If a person's sex assigned at birth does not align with their gender identity, you can follow up by asking, "What pharmacological and/or surgical steps, if any, have you taken in the past to bring your gender expression or presentation into alignment with your gender identity?" It may be helpful to explain that this information is important for you to know as a health care professional so that you and the patient can work in partnership to plan the most appropriate care moving forward. (See chapter 4 to learn how to conduct an organ inventory.)

PRONOUNS: WHAT YOU NEED TO KNOW

Some people use pronouns other than he *or* she *to describe themselves. A person may feel constrained by gendered (sometimes called "binary") pronouns for any number of reasons. It doesn't mean the person self-identifies as LGBTQIA. For this reason, at your first meeting you should ask about the pronouns an individual uses. This practice helps to facilitate patient-centered care and communication (National LGBT Health Education Center, 2015). If you're not sure how to ask about the pronouns a person uses, here's an example of a good way to start: "I'm Mark and I use he, him, and his pronouns. What pronouns do you use?"*

In table 2.1, the pronouns she *and* he *are followed by just a few of the gender-neutral pronouns you might hear once you begin asking people about the pronouns they use. These are not the only possibilities. There are an infinite number of pronouns as new ones emerge in our language. Always ask someone for their pronouns.*

TABLE 2.1 Pronoun application

Subjective	Objective	Possessive	Reflexive	Examples
She	Her	Hers	Herself	She is speaking. I listened to her. The backpack is hers.
He	Him	His	Himself	He is speaking. I listened to him. The backpack is his.
They	Them	Theirs	Themselves	They are speaking. I listened to them. The backpack is theirs.
Ze	Hir/zir	Hirs/zirs	Hirself/zirself	Ze is speaking. I listened to hir. The backpack is zirs.

Source: Chart © Landyn Pan (Trans Student Educational Resources 2016). Reprinted with permission.

SEXUAL ORIENTATION AND SEXUAL BEHAVIOR

The National Academies of Science, Engineering, and Medicine (2022) define **sexual orientation** as "a multidimensional construct encompassing emotional, romantic, and sexual attraction, identity, and behavior."

A **heterosexual** woman is primarily attracted to men, and a heterosexual man is primarily attracted to women; both are commonly referred to as "straight." A woman whose sexual orientation is **lesbian** or **gay** is primarily attracted to women. A man whose sexual orientation is gay is primarily attracted to men. A man or woman whose sexual orientation is **bisexual** is attracted to both men and women and is commonly referred to as "bi." Individuals who are attracted to people regardless of gender may self-identify as **pansexual**. Some individuals do not feel sexual attraction toward anyone. These individuals may refer to themselves as **asexual** or "ace." The only way to determine a person's sexual orientation is to ask—sexual orientation cannot be inferred from observed or even self-reported sexual behavior.

Since the first edition of this book came out in 2017, I've realized that many hospice and palliative care professionals are less familiar with asexuality than with the other sexual orientations. If you're among those who are unfamiliar with asexuality, that's OK—unfamiliarity is simply a starting point along a learning journey. The first thing you need to know is that asexuality is a sexual orientation, *not* a medical condition like hypoactive sexual desire disorder. An asexual person is not someone who suddenly became less interested in sex or stopped experiencing sexual attraction—an asexual person typically doesn't experience feelings of sexual attraction at all. This does not mean that asexual people move through life disconnected from others:

> Asexuality does not limit a person's emotional needs. As is the case for sexual people, we vary widely in how we fulfill those needs. Some asexual people may still desire romantic relationships. Other asexual people may be most satisfied with close friendships, or happier on their own. Sexual or nonsexual, all relationships are made up of the fabric of interpersonal connection. Communication, closeness, fun, humor, excitement, and trust are all just as important in nonsexual relationships as in sexual ones. (Asexual Visibility and Education Network, n.d.)

Some asexual people experience romantic attraction without sexual attraction and describe their orientation using terms like heteroromantic ("romantically attracted to/desires romantic relationships with the opposite gender"), homoromantic ("romantically attracted to/desires romantic relationships with the same gender"), biromantic ("romantically attracted to/desires romantic relationships with multiple genders"), panromantic ("romantically attracted to/desires romantic relationships without gender being a factor"), and aromantic ("not romantically attracted to or desiring of romantic relationships at all") (Asexual Visibility and Education Network, n.d.). If an individual tells you they're asexual, thank them for trusting you enough to share that. Asexuality is not a medical condition to be solved or a disorder to be cured—it is a core component of an individual's identity and should be respected as such. The "A" in the acronym LGBTQIA+ is intended to be inclusive of asexual individuals.

Sexual behavior or **sexual practices** refers to acts engaged in by an individual with the goal of sexual pleasure, reproduction, or both. Sexual behavior can involve a wide range of activities: oral-genital, oral-oral, genital-genital, oral-anal, genital-anal, digital/manual-anal, and digital/manual-genital contact are just a few of the ways an individual may engage in sexual behavior with another person. Sexual behavior also need not involve another person—masturbation, or self-stimulation, is considered sexual behavior as well.

Sexual expression is a term used to describe the way individuals express their sexual desires, either alone or with partners. It is more than "sex": "Sexual expression is a form of communication through which we give and receive pleasure and emotion. It has a wide range of possibilities—from sharing fun activities, feelings and thoughts, warm touch or hugs, to physical intimacy. It is expressed both individually and in relationships throughout life" (McKinley Health Center, 2009).

AUTHOR'S NOTE

For the past twenty-five years I have identified as a lesbian. When my wife died in 2019, the furthest thing from my mind was dating. A few years passed. In September 2021 I scheduled a risk-reducing hysterectomy for the end of December. On the off chance the surgery might have a negative impact on sexual function, I decided I wanted to make the most of things during the three months before my surgery. I decided to make a Tinder profile, my first-ever foray into the world of online dating and "the apps." I wasn't looking for a serious relationship—the grief from losing my wife was still too fresh. Although I had identified as a lesbian since I was in my twenties, I had dated men in high school and college, so I decided to make a Tinder profile indicating I was open to dating persons of any gender. In my profile I listed that I was a lesbian and that my wife of close to twenty years had just died. Within twenty-four hours I matched with several people: a trans woman, a trans man, and three cisgender men. To my surprise, it quickly became apparent that I felt the strongest emotional connection with one of the cisgender men. He was

(continued on next page)

(continued from previous page)

> *brilliant, funny, and unbothered by the fact I was a boobless lesbian who hadn't dated a man since the year the first color photograph appeared on the front page of the* New York Times. *As I write this a little more than a year later, we are still together—and we just got married. His sense of his own sexuality is an expansive one—so much so that my relationship with him is the queerest relationship I've ever had. When we walk into a health care professional's office together, though, my queerness would be invisible if I didn't take the initiative to disclose it.*
>
> *The next time you encounter a person receiving palliative care or hospice care, remember: you can't know a person's story just by looking at them.*

PATIENT PERSPECTIVE

As a bisexual it's incredibly difficult to be out. Because unless you tell them, there is no way they're going to guess. You know, if you're seen with a same sex partner you're judged to be a lesbian; if you're seen with the opposite sex partner you're judged to be straight. Or you might be by yourself and is it relevant to say anything? You're constantly passing for what you're not, and it's really frustrating.

—Kathryn Almack, PhD
From "The Last Outing: Exploring End of Life Experiences and Care Needs in the Lives of Older LGBT People" (Almack et al., 2014).

SEXUALITY AND SEXUAL HEALTH

To understand the concept of sexual health requires an understanding of a more foundational concept—**sexuality**. The World Health Organization (2006, 2010) defines sexuality as

> A central aspect of being human throughout life [that] encompasses sex, gender identities and roles, sexual orientation, eroticism, pleasure,

intimacy and reproduction. Sexuality is experienced and expressed in thoughts, fantasies, desires, beliefs, attitudes, values, behaviors, practices, roles and relationships. While sexuality can include all of these dimensions, not all of them are always experienced or expressed. Sexuality is influenced by the interaction of biological, psychological, social, economic, political, cultural, legal, historical, religious and spiritual factors.

What's notable about this definition is its assertion that sexuality is "a central aspect of being human throughout life." Whether the patient is thirty years old or ninety, sexuality is a central aspect of that patient's humanity. The same is true for the patient who is weeks or days from death: sexuality remains central to their being.

> Even patients facing terminal illness may desire to remain sexually active if possible. This needs to be placed within the overall context of goals and desires for care. Persons receiving care and their loved ones may feel uncomfortable initiating discussion about sexuality and sexual health needs in the context of palliative care. In most cultures, sexuality, significant illness, and dying are all considered taboo topics, at least to some degree, so it becomes part of the healthcare professional's duty to raise these issues. (Griebling, 2016)

If sexuality is a central part of being human throughout the life span, what does it mean for an individual receiving palliative care or hospice care to experience sexual health? The World Health Organization (2006, 2010) declares that **sexual health** is

> a state of physical, emotional, mental and social well-being in relation to sexuality[;] it is not merely the absence of disease, dysfunction or infirmity. Sexual health requires a positive and respectful approach to sexuality and sexual relationships, as well as the possibility of having pleasurable and safe sexual experiences, free of coercion, discrimination and violence. For sexual health to be attained and maintained, the sexual rights of all persons must be respected, protected and fulfilled.

Individuals receiving palliative care and hospice care can experience sexual health. While sexual health "is not merely the absence of disease, dysfunction or infirmity," the presence of disease, dysfunction, or infirmity does not negate the possibility of a person's experiencing sexual health. In its *Clinical Practice Guidelines for Quality Palliative Care*, the National Consensus Project for Quality Palliative Care (2018) highlights the importance of sexual health by including it in the criteria that need to be addressed. According to guideline 4.2, the interdisciplinary team should conduct a social assessment of the patient and family that includes "the effect of illness or injury on intimacy and sexual expression, prior experiences with illness, disability and loss, risk of abuse, neglect or exploitation, incarceration, or risk of social isolation."

Sexual health is as achievable and reasonable a goal as pain relief for persons receiving palliative care and hospice care, but few hospice and palliative care professionals include sexual health within their assessment and plan of care. Given that sexuality is a central aspect of being human, sexual health should be part of the assessment and plan for every patient receiving palliative care and hospice care. Chapter 4 explains how to incorporate sexual health into the assessment process, and chapter 6 provides specific suggestions for how to incorporate sexual health into an individual's palliative or hospice care plan.

KEY POINTS TO REMEMBER

- Sex is something assigned at birth based on how the biology and anatomy of a person is interpreted by health care professionals in a given sociocultural context.
- Gender has to do with the sociocultural expectations, roles, and behaviors of men, women, nonbinary people, and gender-fluid people. It concerns the way a person inhabiting a physical body feels, behaves, and is "read" by society.
- Individuals may communicate their internal sense of their gender (their gender identity) to those around them through the way they

present their physical self (their gender expression) in the form of clothing, grooming or styling, and so on.
- When you are working with a patient whose gender differs from their sex assigned at birth, do not assume that the patient has had (or wants to have) surgical or other gender-affirming medical interventions.
- Gender identity is distinct from sexual orientation. Many transgender people are straight (heterosexual), and many straight people are attracted to, love, and partner with transgender people. Transgender people may also be asexual, bisexual, gay, or any other sexual orientation.
- The only way to determine a person's sexual orientation is to ask. Sexual orientation cannot be inferred from observed or even self-reported sexual behavior.
- To gather relevant clinical information about sex and gender, you need to ask individuals two questions (ideally at the time of admission or intake): (1) What sex were you assigned at birth, on your original birth certificate? (2) What is your current gender?
- Sexual health is as achievable and reasonable a goal as pain relief for individuals receiving palliative care and hospice care. Sexual health should be part of the assessment and plan for every patient receiving palliative and hospice care.

DISCUSSION QUESTIONS

1. If an individual receiving hospice care or palliative care is assigned female at birth, is a woman, and has been married to a cisgender woman for twenty-five years, what is this patient's sexual orientation? How did you come to this conclusion?
2. Imagine that you are working with an individual receiving hospice care named Maria. Maria was assigned male at birth, is a woman, and expresses her gender identity through her clothes, makeup,

and hairstyle. Maria is about to be transferred from home to an inpatient facility. As you arrange for Maria's admission what information, if any, should you provide to the facility regarding her sex assigned at birth, gender identity, and gender expression? Should you request that Maria be assigned a female roommate or male roommate? Why?
3. Imagine you just walked into the room of an individual receiving hospice care or palliative care and found the patient masturbating. What do you do? Do you say anything? If so, what? What thoughts and feelings do you think you would experience in this situation?
4. Now imagine that you're the patient in that scenario. A health care professional just walked into your room while you are masturbating. What do you do? Do you say anything? If so, what? What thoughts and feelings do you think you would experience in this situation?
5. How many times in an average day do you think you "come out"—as straight, gay, lesbian, bisexual, pansexual, or asexual—to people around you? Is this something you do deliberately, or is it largely an unconscious act? Do you think it would be difficult to hide your sexual orientation for a day? For a week? For a month?

CHAPTER ACTIVITY

For the next week, hide your sexual orientation from everyone you come in contact with. To prepare for the possibility that a visitor may stop by your home or apartment, make sure to hide any photos, books, posters, or other items that might help visitors deduce your sexual orientation. During this week, you may not refer to a spouse or significant other using pronouns that would indicate what their gender is, and you may not hold hands, flirt, or otherwise demonstrate affection in public. Keep a journal throughout the week about your thoughts and feelings during this experience. How much energy did it take to hide who you are from other people? How has this experience changed your thoughts and feelings about the importance of LGBTQIA-inclusive care?

April 3, 2019

GoFundMe post from Kathy Brandt

"A Day in the Life of Kathy Brandt"

    A dear friend asked me the other day "how do you decide what you do each day—how do you filter all the choices into the most important ones?" The problem with that brilliant question is it assumes that this is what I actually do. Now that I know my time is very limited, it makes sense that I would prioritize what I do each moment to make the most of time. But the fact is, I still have things I have to do. Each day I have to:

- Get dressed
- Eat
- Take my medications, including 1 shot
- Check email and respond to work emails
- Work on writing and/or editing projects for clients

    I also want to spend time with Kim and talk to Greyson each day. Then there are the other things I do each week or so—paying bills, getting groceries, going to the marijuana dispensary, spending time with friends (either in person, on the phone or online), getting my hair cut, and going to therapy. Plus, the other things that come up like doctor's visits, etc.

    You may be wondering how I fit West Wing watching into my day, well the reality is all of the things listed above are exhausting to me. If I do a lot of work in the morning, I usually can't do more in the afternoon. If I go somewhere in the afternoon, I typically can't do anything that night. I have limited money cookies (see previous post for an explanation) and I have to spend them wisely. So when I'm tired, I watch West Wing (or Battlestar Galactica) and I try not to feel guilty about it.

(continued on next page)

(*continued from previous page*)

    Your donations have made it easier for me to choose friends and family over work, to feel less guilty when I simply can't do more work on a given day, even if it's only 10:30am. It's frustrating to me, as I've always been a very productive person, and at the same time, my productivity is way less important than it used to be. I feel like I live in a series of dichotomies—

I am passionate about my work --------- I don't care about working
I love to eat --------- I'm not hungry
I love my friends and family --------- I'm feeling slightly disconnected from people
I'm still alive --------- My ghost is always in the room

    Knowing that I have as little as three months to live has certainly shifted my priorities. I want to spend as much time with Kim and Grey and dear friends as possible. I want to only eat food that makes me happy. I won't wear uncomfortable clothes. I'll share my story in the hopes it helps others

kb

3 | Understanding Attitudes and Access to Care

CHAPTER OUTCOMES

1. Recognize the ways historical, political, institutional, and sociocultural factors may influence attitudes about palliative care and hospice among LGBTQIA+ people.
2. Recognize the barriers faced by LGBTQIA+ individuals and their families in accessing hospice and palliative care services.

Key Terms: access to care, barriers to care, employment discrimination, financial barriers to care, institutional barriers to care, perceptual barriers to care

CHAPTER SUMMARY

An important aspect of providing LGBTQIA-inclusive care is understanding why some LGBTQIA+ people may be reluctant either to seek care or to share with you that they are lesbian, gay, bisexual, transgender, nonbinary, gender nonconforming, queer, questioning, intersex, and/or asexual. Historically, disclosing one's status as an LGBTQIA+ person has often come with a high price—and may still do so today. This chapter explains why, given the historical and contemporary contexts within which LGBTQIA+ people live, it's not surprising that some LGBTQIA+ individuals and families are reluctant to seek care. The chapter describes three kinds of barriers to palliative care and hospice care—perceptual, financial, and institutional—and offers a two-pronged approach to addressing barriers to care.

THE PAST AS PROLOGUE

William Shakespeare's words "what's past is prologue" ring especially true when it comes to understanding why some LGBTQIA+ individuals may be fearful about accessing palliative or hospice care. When a person is diagnosed with a chronic or life-limiting illness, their past experiences with health care professionals may shape their openness to receiving palliative care or hospice care. Because of the intersectionality of prejudice and social identity, LGBTQIA+ persons may legitimately **fear** they will receive poor care or unfair treatment based on a combination of factors, including their race, ethnicity, sexual orientation, gender identity, gender expression, religion, and socioeconomic status. These fears may be based on firsthand experience, secondhand stories from family and friends, or thirdhand historical accounts.

Access to care, defined as "the timely use of personal health services to achieve the best health outcomes" (Institute of Medicine, 1993), is an issue of concern regarding the LGBTQIA+ population. In a study of almost five thousand LGBTQIA+ individuals, 56 percent of lesbian, gay, or bisexual respondents and 70 percent of gender-nonconforming and transgender respondents reported having had at least one of the following experiences: "being refused needed care; health care professionals refusing to touch them or using excessive precautions; health care professionals using harsh or abusive language; being blamed for their health status; or health care professionals being physically rough or abusive." Among transgender and gender-nonconforming respondents, close to 21 percent reported that they

> **PATIENT PERSPECTIVE**
>
> *As a fifty-nine-year-old LGBT person, I grew up in an environment that was extremely homophobic. I was traumatized both within my family structure and within the community. LGBT seniors of my age were often exposed to various forms of psychological trauma, emotional trauma, and the mental trauma of isolation as well as not being able to be open about themselves. In addition, there are people such as myself who experienced quite severe physical trauma, assault, being stalked—actual life endangerment. As a cancer patient, [I found] the discrimination continued during the initial medical and surgical treatments. At the moment, though, I am also receiving palliative care, which to me is a godsend. When I am talking about palliative care, I am talking about the whole gamut of psychiatry, social work, the total picture for all the psychosocial support that needs to be present for a cancer patient to successfully negotiate treatment. It is absolutely essential, and many people would fare so much better [in] cancer care and their symptoms would be managed much better if they were connected to palliative care.*
>
> —Jay Kallio, transgender advocate and cancer survivor (August 15, 1955–September 30, 2016)
>
> Author's Note: Jay died before the first edition of this book went to press. Jay wanted to be listed as a "transgender advocate and cancer survivor," so I've honored his choice by listing him as such in both editions of the book.

had been "subjected to harsh or abusive language from a health care professional" (Lambda Legal, 2010).

When issues of race, cultural tradition, and socioeconomic status intersect with or are layered on top of sexual orientation, gender identity, and gender expression, the effects of discrimination and poor-quality care are magnified: nearly 33 percent of low-income gender-nonconforming and transgender respondents in the Lambda Legal study said they had been refused care because of their gender identity. More than 50 percent of lesbian, gay, and bisexual respondents and almost 86 percent of transgender respondents stated that "overall community fear or dislike of people like them is a barrier to care" (Lambda Legal, 2010).

All individuals you meet bring with them their own complex set of experiences, beliefs, and fears, any or all of which may influence how they perceive and receive the care you extend to them. Knowing how to provide LGBTQIA-inclusive care requires an understanding of the intersectionality of oppression and an awareness of how LGBTQIA+ individuals have been treated in the United States over the past, say, seventy-five years. While I could discuss a more extensive history of discrimination against LGBTQIA+ persons in the United States, focusing on the past eighty years (1940–2022) will cover the lived experience of LGBTQIA+ individuals aged eighty and up, as well as provide a relatively recent history for younger LGBTQIA+ individuals.

April 4, 2019

GoFundMe post from Kathy Brandt:

"A Day in Pain"

Until today I've been lucky. My symptoms have been very mild, with very little pain. Today was different—in fact, Kim said it started last night when I was moaning in my sleep. I've had pain in my lower left abdomen all day, fluctuating between a 2–4 on the pain scale. Kim was great, reminding me to eat a brownie, take an anti-inflammatory, and vape as needed to keep the pain to a minimum. Within an hour I was starting to doze on the sofa thanks to the edible. After the nap I took a shower and then Kim changed the bandage. We discovered that the Tegaderm bandage is causing contact dermatitis in several places. Yay! (sarcasm) Kim ordered some skin prep wipes that should arrive tomorrow.

Until today I've been in denial that I will have pain. Those days are over. While the rash is a minor annoyance and the pain is manageable, I'm glad we have a palliative care appointment tomorrow. Originally the appointment was just so that I could get Do Not

> Resuscitate Orders signed for DC, Virginia, and Maine, but now I have a question for the NP: What's our plan if there comes a time when I can't control the pain with medical marijuana alone?
>
> kb

> Author's Note: Kathy chose not to use opioids because she wanted to avoid the possibility she might get a bowel obstruction. She also chose to prioritize alertness over pain management. She was in pain not because palliative care was unable to control her pain but rather, because she chose to manage her pain with only medical marijuana and dexamethasone.

BEING LGBTQIA+ COULD (AND STILL CAN) COST YOU YOUR JOB

At the beginning of the Cold War and the anticommunist McCarthy era in the United States, the federal government secretly investigated the lives of government employees in an attempt to ferret out those who were homosexual. The U.S. Senate issued a report to Congress in 1950 titled *Employment of Homosexuals and Other Sex Perverts in Government*, asserting that homosexuals constituted a security risk because "those who engage in overt acts of perversion lack the emotional stability of normal persons." In what became known as the Lavender Scare, more than 4,300 gay men and lesbians were discharged from the military and more than 500 civilians were fired from their jobs in the federal government (WGBH Educational Foundation, 2011).

In 1953, the president of the United States, Dwight Eisenhower, issued Executive Order 10450, banning homosexuals, alcoholics, and "neurotics" from working for the government or its contractors, based on the perception that they posed a risk to national security (WGBH Educational Foundation, 2011). On June 3, 1953, President Eisenhower said in his televised report to the American people regarding Executive Order 10450, "Employees could be a security risk and still not be disloyal or have any traitorous thoughts, but it may be that their personal habits are such that they might be subject to black-mail by people who seek to destroy the safety of our country" (Eisenhower, 1953).

From 1950 to 1981, it was legal in every state in the United States to fire someone from their job because of their sexual orientation. During this period, in an attempt to provide some protections to LGBTQIA+ people, some cities enacted antidiscrimination ordinances. In 1972, the mayor of New York, for example, put in place antibias protections for city employees fighting against **employment discrimination** based on sexual orientation (Torres, n.d.). The first state to make it illegal to discriminate against someone on the basis of sexual orientation was Wisconsin, in 1982 (WGBH Educational Foundation, 2011).

When I wrote the first edition of this book in January 2016, it was legal in twenty-eight states—Alabama, Alaska, Arizona, Arkansas, Florida, Georgia, Idaho, Indiana, Kansas, Kentucky, Louisiana, Michigan, Mississippi, Missouri, Montana, Nebraska, North Carolina, North Dakota, Ohio, Oklahoma, Pennsylvania, South Carolina, South Dakota, Tennessee, Texas, Virginia, West Virginia, and Wyoming—to deny a person employment or to fire them from their current job based solely on their sexual orientation or gender identity (Movement Advancement Project, 2016). There were no federal protections against employment discrimination for LGBTQIA+ people.

In June 2020, the United States Supreme Court ruled that Title VII of the federal Civil Rights Act applied to sexual orientation and gender identity and, as a result, discriminating against someone based on sexual orientation or gender identity was illegal. Although this provided federal protections for LGBTQIA+ people, as of June 2022 sixteen states and three U.S. territories still had no laws prohibiting employment discrimination on the basis of sexual orientation or gender identity (Movement Advancement Project, 2022).

April 6, 2019

GoFundMe update from Kathy Brandt:

I am so lucky. I really believe that, hard as it may be for a terminally-ill woman to make that statement, it is true.

Most people aren't lucky enough to have a caregiver who is a palliative care expert. Kim recognized that we needed a pain plan beyond the MMJ, found the BEST medication for my symptoms, and knew the correct dosage to ask for when we met with Nicole, the palliative care nurse from Sibley.

Most people aren't lucky enough to have a wife who, within minutes of seeing my contact dermatitis caused by the bandage surrounding my drain, had researched the stuff we needed to put on my skin to protect it from the bandage and ordered it to arrive the next day.

Most people aren't lucky enough to have an amazing son who is somehow managing to have a good freshman year at college, despite losing his two grandmothers and learning that his mother has a terminal illness. He is keeping his grades up, staying engaged in college life, and talking about his feelings.

Most people aren't lucky enough to have friends who take time out of their busy lives to come to a Boy Scout pancake breakfast just to be with them.

Most people aren't lucky enough to have a tremendous support network of people who call and text them pictures and videos of grandkids, goats, or just stupid stuff to make them laugh. Or who send M&Ms and an old Buck Rogers DVD, or cards by the dozens, or random emails to brighten their day.

Most people don't know a college freshman who went to high school with their son who came home from spring break with a blanket from their alma mater (Mount Holyoke) for them.

Most people aren't fortunate enough to have a friend who owns a dog training center/boarding/day care facility who babied their dogs for more than a month and refuses to send them a bill.

Most people don't have friends, colleagues, friends of friends, and Twitter acquaintances who donated and keep donating to a fund to prop them up as they pay medical bills and life expenses with a greatly reduced income.

Cancer didn't make me lucky, it made me realize how lucky I am.

kb

BEING LGBTQIA+ COULD CAUSE YOU TO BE LABELED "MENTALLY ILL"

When the American Psychiatric Association (APA) published its first *Diagnostic and Statistical Manual of Mental Disorders* (DSM) in 1952, it listed homosexuality as a form of sociopathy illness, a designation that lasted for the next twenty years. The APA finally removed homosexuality from its official list of mental illnesses in 1973 (WGBH Educational Foundation, 2011).

The APA has made similar shifts in the way it classifies individuals whose assigned sex at birth does not align with their gender. In 1980, the association added "gender identity disorder" to the DSM, thereby attaching the stigmatizing label *disorder* to transgender individuals. In 2013, more than thirty years later, the APA issued this statement prior to the release of the fifth edition (DSM-5):

> DSM-5 aims to avoid stigma and ensure clinical care for individuals who see and feel themselves to be a different gender than their assigned gender. It replaces the diagnostic name "gender identity disorder" with "gender dysphoria," as well as makes other important clarifications in the criteria. It is important to note that gender nonconformity is not in itself a mental disorder. The critical element of gender dysphoria is the presence of clinically significant distress associated with the condition.

The APA went on to explain why it had not removed the "condition" as a diagnosis: "To get insurance coverage for the medical treatments, individuals need a diagnosis. The Sexual and Gender Identity Disorders Work Group was concerned that removing the condition as a psychiatric diagnosis—as some had suggested—would jeopardize access to care" (APA, 2013a).

BEING LGBTQIA+ COULD (AND STILL CAN) GET YOU EVICTED

In a national survey of 6,450 individuals who identified as transgender or gender nonconforming, 19 percent said they had been homeless because of their gender identity, and 19 percent said they had been refused housing for the same reason (Grant et al., 2011). The U.S. Department of Housing and

Urban Development (HUD) requires recipients of HUD funding to comply with laws at the state and local level that prohibit housing discrimination on the basis of sexual orientation and gender identity. Despite this requirement, as of June 2022 it was still legal in the eighteen states—Alabama, Arizona, Arkansas, Georgia, Idaho, Indiana, Louisiana, Mississippi, Missouri, Montana, North Carolina, Oklahoma, South Carolina, South Dakota, Tennessee, Texas, West Virginia, and Wyoming—to deny a person housing or to evict them from their existing housing based solely on their sexual orientation or gender identity (Movement Advancement Project, 2022).

BEING LGBTQIA+ COULD (AND STILL CAN) GET YOU ARRESTED

Until 1962, sodomy was a crime in every state in the United States. That year, Illinois became the first state to decriminalize sodomy (WGBH Educational Foundation, 2011), and in the 1970s sodomy laws were repealed in nineteen other states: California, Colorado, Connecticut, Delaware, Hawaii, Indiana, Iowa, Maine, Nebraska, New Jersey, New Mexico, North Dakota, Ohio, Oregon, South Dakota, Vermont, Washington, West Virginia, and Wyoming (American Civil Liberties Union, n.d.).

In 2003, the U.S. Supreme Court ruled in *Lawrence v. Kansas* that barring consensual sex between adults is unconstitutional. In 2022—almost twenty years later—consenting adults can still be arrested on charges of sodomy in some states, but because states may not enforce unconstitutional laws, such cases have generally ended up being dropped (Coble, 2015). However, the Supreme Court decision in *Dobbs v. Jackson Women's Health Organization* raises serious questions about whether privacy rights such as those protected under *Lawrence v. Kansas* will endure for much longer (League of Women Voters, 2022).

BEING LGBTQIA+ COULD (AND STILL CAN) GET YOU ASSAULTED OR KILLED

In 1998 in Laramie, Wyoming, a twenty-one-year-old man named Matthew Shepard was tied to a split-rail fence, beaten, and left to die because he was gay (Human Rights Campaign, n.d.b). Twelve years after Matthew Shepard's murder, groundbreaking federal hate crimes legislation was enacted:

> The Matthew Shepard and James Byrd, Jr., Hate Crimes Prevention Act of 2009, 18 U.S.C. § 249, was enacted as Division E of the National Defense Authorization Act for Fiscal Year 2010. Section 249 of Title 18 provides funding and technical assistance to state, local, and tribal jurisdictions to help them to more effectively investigate and prosecute hate crimes. It also creates a new federal criminal law which criminalizes willfully causing bodily injury (or attempting to do so with fire, firearm, or other dangerous weapon) when: (1) the crime was committed because of the actual or perceived race, color, religion, national origin of any person or (2) the crime was committed because of the actual or perceived religion, national origin, gender, sexual orientation, gender identity, or disability of any person and the crime affected interstate or foreign commerce or occurred within federal special maritime and territorial jurisdiction. (U.S. Department of Justice, 2009)

As of June 2022, four states—Arkansas, Indiana, South Carolina, and Wyoming—still had no law against hate crimes. Of those with hate crime laws, thirteen states—Alabama, Alaska, Idaho, Michigan, Mississippi, Montana, North Carolina, North Dakota, Ohio, Oklahoma, Pennsylvania, South Dakota, and West Virginia—did not outlaw hate crimes based on sexual orientation or gender identity (Movement Advancement Project, 2022).

Sadly, LGBTQIA+ people face threats to their physical safety even in states that have hate crime laws on their books. On June 12, 2016, the LGBTQIA+ community in Orlando, Florida, was the target of the second deadliest mass shooting by a sole gunman in U.S. history. The attack, which took place in Pulse, an LGBTQIA+ nightclub, left forty-nine victims dead and more than fifty injured; many of the victims were both LGBTQIA+ and Latino or Latina. As you read the list of the names and ages of those who were murdered in Orlando (City of Orlando, 2016), reflect on how this attack and other hate crimes would be likely to affect LGBTQIA+ individuals in your community, especially regarding how comfortable they

Understanding Attitudes and Access to Care | 85

feel about sharing who they are with people they have never met before. I have listed the victims' names because the phrase "forty-nine people died" doesn't come close to capturing the scope of the tragedy:

Stanley Almodovar III, 23
Amanda Alvear, 25
Oscar A. Aracena-Montero, 26
Rodolfo Ayala-Ayala, 33
Antonio Davon Brown, 29
Darryl Roman Burt II, 29
Angel L. Candelario-Padro, 28
Juan Chevez-Martinez, 25
Luis Daniel Conde, 39
Cory James Connell, 21
Tevin Eugene Crosby, 25
Deonka Deidra Drayton, 32
Leroy Valentin Fernandez, 25
Simon Adrian Carrillo Fernandez, 31
Mercedez Marisol Flores, 26
Peter O. Gonzalez-Cruz, 22
Juan Ramon Guerrero, 22
Paul Terrell Henry, 41
Frank Hernandez, 27
Miguel Angel Honorato, 30
Javier Jorge-Reyes, 40
Jason Benjamin Josaphat, 19
Eddie Jamoldroy Justice, 30
Anthony Luis Laureanodisla, 25
Christopher Andrew Leinonen, 32
Alejandro Barrios Martinez, 21
Brenda Lee Marquez McCool, 49
Gilberto Ramon Silva Menendez, 25
Kimberly Morris, 37
Akyra Monet Murray, 18

Luis Omar Ocasio-Capo, 20
Geraldo A. Ortiz-Jimenez, 25
Eric Ivan Ortiz-Rivera, 36
Joel Rayon Paniagua, 32
Jean Carlos Mendez Perez, 35
Enrique L. Rios Jr., 25
Jean C. Nives Rodriguez, 27
Xavier Emmanuel Serrano Rosado, 35
Christopher Joseph Sanfeliz, 24
Yilmary Rodriguez Solivan, 24
Edward Sotomayor Jr., 34
Shane Evan Tomlinson, 33
Martin Benitez Torres, 33
Jonathan Antonio Camuy Vega, 24
Franky Jimmy Dejesus Velazquez, 50
Juan P. Rivera Velazquez, 37
Luis S. Vielma, 22
Luis Daniel Wilson-Leon, 37
Jerald Arthur Wright, 31

Each life lost was a person—an individual whose death left an indelible mark on the LGBTQIA+ community and whose name should not be forgotten. As you work with individuals and families in the months and years to come, remember these victims and the effect their murders have had on the LGBTQIA+ community. Not everyone will feel safe sharing who they are with you; individuals and families should not have to "come out" to you in order to receive LGBTQIA-inclusive care.

UNDERSTANDING BARRIERS TO PALLIATIVE AND HOSPICE CARE

Given the long and ongoing history of discrimination against LGBTQIA+ people in the United States, it is not surprising that LGBTQIA+ individuals may be hesitant to seek health care of any sort, including palliative care or hospice care. For LGBTQIA+ individuals, **barriers to care** fall into three

PATIENT PERSPECTIVE

Sarah lives with two partners, an MtF woman (Iris) who she was previously married to before Iris transitioned, and Damian, a cis man. Sarah described a period of time recently when she was [feeling] very poorly and [was] in [the] hospital. When she came home she convalesced in a room set up especially for her. She went on to explain: "It was difficult to explain to anybody coming in why this was a change. They would come in, they would see me in that single bed in that single room, and they would see Damian and Iris, and even if they accepted that we are three, they would see they had the main bedroom, and they wouldn't realize or understand that actually normally I would have been in there too, and I would be missing it."

—Kathryn Almack, PhD

Author's Note: In this passage, Almack uses MtF as shorthand for "male-to-female," indicating that the individual was assigned the male sex at birth but is female. This is outdated language and should not be used unless someone uses this term to describe themself. Passage is from The Last Outing: Exploring End of Life Experiences and Care Needs in the Lives of Older LGBT People (Almack et al., 2014).

general categories: (1) **perceptual barriers**, (2) **financial barriers**, and (3) **institutional barriers**. Understanding these barriers will be helpful as you work toward understanding the perspective of LGBTQIA+ individuals and families. Chapter 10 provides detailed information about ways that you and your employer or institution can ameliorate or eliminate these barriers in order to ensure greater inclusion of LGBTQIA+ individuals.

Perceptual Barriers

For LGBTQIA+ individuals with chronic or life-limiting illnesses, perceptual barriers to care may be twofold. First, LGBTQIA+ individuals may have some of the same negative beliefs or fears about palliative care and hospice care as their cisgender and heterosexual counterparts. Common myths and misperceptions about palliative care include:

- Palliative care is for people who are dying.
- Palliative care is just another term for hospice care.
- Palliative care is only for people who need pain medicine.
- If I get palliative care, I won't be able to keep seeing my primary care professional. (National Institutes of Health Clinical Center, 2022)

Some common myths and misperceptions about hospice care are:

- Hospice is for people with cancer, not people with other illnesses or conditions.
- Hospice is a place—a physical facility sort of like a nursing home.
- If I'm admitted to hospice, it means I have given up hope.
- Hospice care costs a lot of money. (Naierman & Turner, 2012; Morii-chi, Dapper, & Vorpahl, 2020)

In addition to the common misperceptions about hospice and palliative care that many people share, LGBTQIA+ individuals may have fears or concerns specific to their gender identity, gender expression, or sexual orientation. Special concerns for LGBTQIA+ individuals may include:

- I will be refused care because of my gender identity, gender expression, or sexual orientation.
- I will have to spend my limited time and energy educating my health care professionals.
- I will be treated like a pariah or a freak.
- I will have to hide evidence of my gender identity or sexual orientation (e.g., photos, books) in my home so that my health care professionals won't figure out I'm LGBTQIA+.
- I will run the risk of being "outed" to my family members.
- I will be treated politely enough, but the care I receive will somehow be less than what others receive.

PROFESSIONAL PERSPECTIVE

"He is a tranny," they said in report. I felt an overwhelming amount of anger followed by a blanket of sorrow wash over me as I narrowed my eyes and told my co-worker that using the word "tranny" ensured everybody knows they are an ignorant boomer. They didn't bat an eye and said I shouldn't be such a snowflake. Well, this snowflake put on their best winter business casual outfit and provided the suffering human fabulous palliative care. Ignorant Boomer was never allowed back in that beautiful, glittery, and loving home for the three months they were on our service. Years later, I watched Ignorant Boomer in a mandatory seminar for appropriate care of the LGBTQIA+ storm out when they "felt uncomfortable" and declare its time to retire because the snowflakes are ruining the world. Yes, Ignorant Boomer . . . it's time you and your hatefully ignorant values retire and never come back in this world with a blizzard of snowflakes piling on love and acceptance.

—Jen Led, RN
Jen Led describes themself as "a registered nurse by weekdays and parent/spouse/volunteer nights/weekends." They identify as queer/demifem.

Financial Barriers

For individuals who have private insurance, Medicare, or Medicaid, palliative care and hospice care are covered either in part or in full. However, because of the complexity of health care costs, copays, and insurance coverage, LGBTQIA+ individuals (like their cisgender and heterosexual counterparts) may be unsure how much their out-of-pocket cost would be for palliative care or hospice care. Transgender individuals receiving hormone therapy may worry that a hospice admission would cause them to lose pharmacy coverage for their hormones. They may also fear that the hospice would not understand that they need to remain on hormones for the rest of their lives. For LGBTQIA+ individuals who do not have health insurance, financial concerns will be even more pressing.

Institutional Barriers

Hospice and palliative care programs may unintentionally erect barriers that prevent LGBTQIA+ individuals from accessing their services. Such institutional barriers can include discriminatory admission and employment policies; noninclusive marketing and outreach materials; and inadequate orientation and training for health care professionals, staff, and volunteers. If your institution's nondiscrimination statement does not include gender identity, gender expression, sexual orientation, intersex status, intersex traits, differences of sex development, and diversity in sex characteristics, you will have a difficult time convincing LGBTQIA+ individuals to enter your program for palliative or hospice care. Addressing institutional barriers to care requires a two-pronged approach: outward facing and inward looking. The outward-facing approach to addressing these barriers involves creating outreach and educational materials (e.g., a website, brochures) that specifically address LGBTQIA+ individuals' myths, misperceptions, and concerns about hospice and palliative care. The inward-looking aspect of addressing institutional barriers to care is even more important. It requires teaching all caregivers, staff, and volunteers how to provide inclusive care to LGBTQIA+ individuals and their families, "to promote comfort and acceptance, identify and diminish bias . . . minimize heterosexual assumptions within assessment and care, and

---

PROFESSIONAL PERSPECTIVE

Back [in the 1990s], we identified the "primary caregiver" on a written fact sheet, by name and relationship to the patient. Most of the time, same-sex partners were listed as "friend" under "relationship to patient." When you think about issues like anticipatory grief and role/relationship changes due to illness, "friend" is not a word that adequately conveys what partners were likely going through. I had several patients tell me the nature of their relationship and ask me not to share [it] with other team members, I assume for fear it would somehow affect their care. I always believed they knew best, and I never shared what I was asked to keep in confidence.

—Kathleen Taylor, MA, LMHC

thus strengthen open communication" (Harding, Epiphaniou, & Chidgey-Clark, 2012). To illustrate this, imagine that the care your institution provides is a box of pasta. Changing how people with celiac disease perceive and experience your company's pasta goes beyond simply slapping a "gluten-free" label on the box. Unless you change how you make the pasta, your company's product will continue to be harmful to people who consume it.

KEY POINTS TO REMEMBER

- All individuals bring their own complex sets of experiences, beliefs, and fears to their interactions with you, any or all of which may influence the way they perceive and receive the care you extend to them.
- Understanding how to provide LGBTQIA-inclusive care requires an understanding of the intersectionality of oppression and an awareness of the ways LGBTQIA+ individuals have been treated in the United States over the past seventy-five years.
- For LGBTQIA+ individuals, barriers to palliative care and hospice care fall into three general categories: (1) perceptual barriers, (2) financial barriers, and (3) institutional barriers.
- Addressing barriers to care requires a two-pronged approach on the part of your hospice or palliative care program: outward facing and inward looking.
- Outward facing: Create outreach and educational materials that address LGBTQIA+ individuals' myths, misperceptions, and concerns about hospice and palliative care.
- Inward looking: Teach all care professionals, staff, and volunteers how to provide inclusive care to LGBTQIA+ individuals and families.

DISCUSSION QUESTIONS

1. Imagine that you are working with Shawn, an eighty-five-year-old man who has lived with Jangus, his "best friend," for almost sixty years. For the past twenty years, the two of them have shared a one-bedroom apartment. Jangus has been very reluctant to access home health care services

to help Shawn with showering, a task he took great pride in managing himself until it became too difficult. What are some of the historical, political, institutional, and sociocultural factors that may have influenced Jangus's attitude toward seeking and receiving care? Would Jangus and Shawn need to "come out" as a couple to the interdisciplinary/interprofessional team in order to receive optimal care? Why or why not?

2. What are some of the barriers faced by LGBTQIA+ individuals and their families in accessing hospice and palliative care services? What are some reasons LGBTQIA+ individuals might be hesitant to seek services from a palliative care or hospice program in your community?

3. If given a choice, would you prefer to be assigned a cisgender heterosexual ("straight") patient or a transgender heterosexual patient? What if the choice were between being assigned a cisgender gay patient or a cisgender straight patient? Why? Do you think your preferences are similar to those of your colleagues in the field or different?

4. Perceptual barriers for LGBTQIA+ individuals include general misperceptions and concerns about palliative care and hospice care as well as concerns specific to their status as LGBTQIA+ individuals. Given the subjectivity of "perception," how can palliative care and hospice programs address these perceptual barriers?

5. Imagine that you are working in a palliative care or hospice program that has decided to address barriers to care for LGBTQIA+ people. Describe how you might address institutional barriers to care, using both outward-facing and inward-looking strategies. Which set of strategies would you recommend tackling first: outward facing or inward looking? Why?

CHAPTER ACTIVITY

In the state where you live, what laws, if any, protect LGBTQIA+ individuals from discrimination? How do you think these laws (or their absence) affect the degree to which LGBTQIA+ individuals in your community feel safe and comfortable seeking hospice or palliative care? Visit http://www.lambdalegal.org/ to find information about your state.

April 12, 2019

GoFundMe update from Kathy Brandt:

"The Long Goodbye"

Years ago, Bill Colby wrote an important book called <u>The Long Goodbye: The Deaths of Nancy Cruzan</u>. While my death won't take as long as Nancy Cruzan's did, it feels as though everything I do is a prelude to goodbye. Everything leads toward the inevitable "leaving" I will take.

I have dinner with a friend and the "leaving" is right there. Next to me. We'll both leave dinner. I will leave the earth. Not today, but soon. We both know it and there's nothing we can do about it. We briefly acknowledge it, talking about death in a fleeting way. Even though we do this work, talking about it is hard. Yet death is insistent. It's right there waiting for me. It knows that it's only a matter of time before I will have to say goodbye to all of it. Everyone.

As I'm looking towards attending the NHPCO [National Hospice and Palliative Care Organization] leadership conference on Monday and Tuesday, the notion of goodbye is front and center. I've been attending NHPCO conferences for 30 years. I grew up in the organization, working there for 16 years. I found my vocation, met my wife, raised my family, and found out I'm dying within the context of my relationship with NHPCO.

And now, as I've done every spring, I'm thinking about my time at the conference, who I'll see, what I'll attend. And yet the educational sessions hold no interest to me. I'm not attending the Town Hall or any policy sessions. I'll go to my Palliative Care Advisory Council meeting and present my section of our panel presentation on Tuesday because I believe in the work and enjoy the people. But I won't be marketing the kb group or doing any solo presentations. I don't need to mingle with the exhibitors, schmooze new people I meet, or make small talk with strangers.

(continued on next page)

(continued from previous page)

My role has changed. By virtue of my diagnosis and prognosis, I am a short-timer—not a business owner. Not a palliative care and hospice professional. I'm a dead woman walking. And that's what I'll be at the conference.

NHPCO has been a catalyst, an organizing hub for my career. But it's the people I've met in the field who have always mattered the most. So, on Monday and Tuesday, those of you attending the conference will see Kim and me there as I say goodbye to friends and colleagues.

I don't want people at the conference to feel like they have to focus their attention on me. At the same time, I don't want to miss the opportunity to say "goodbye" and "thanks," and "remember when we . . ." I've been given an opportunity to say goodbye and while it isn't always easy, it's so important and it's not an opportunity afforded to everyone.

So, if you're reading this update and plan to be at the conference, bring some Kleenex as well as your memories, and laughter. Let's remember all the fun we had, the good we did, and all that we've done together to make care better for people like Kim and me.

kb

4 | The History and Physical Examination

CHAPTER OUTCOMES

1. Conduct a five-dimension comprehensive history with individuals receiving palliative care and hospice care.
2. Distinguish between questions that are relevant and necessary to your care of the patient and questions that stem primarily from your personal curiosity about an individual's life or body.
3. Conduct an organ inventory.
4. Carry out the necessary and appropriate elements of the physical examination.
5. Assess and support "diverse cultural values and customs with regard to information sharing, decision making, expression and treatment of physical and emotional distress, and preferences for sites of care and death" (AAHPM, 2009).

Key Terms: chosen family, comprehensive history, family of choice, family of origin, FICA Spiritual History Tool, Five-Dimension Assessment Model, gender affirmation surgery, organ inventory, Patient and Family Outcomes-Focused Inquiry for Developing

Goals for Care, Patient and Family Outcomes-Focused Inquiry for Interdisciplinary Teams, prognosis, psychosocial history, quality of life, rapport, spiritual/existential/cultural history

CHAPTER SUMMARY

To elicit a complete and accurate history, palliative care and hospice professionals need to establish rapport and communicate a genuine openness to hearing the patient's answers to their questions. This chapter describes a new LGBTQIA-inclusive approach to taking a comprehensive history that places the primary emphasis on the patient as person. Pathophysiology, pharmacology, and differential diagnoses are beyond the scope of *The Handbook of LGBTQIA-Inclusive Hospice and Palliative Care*; this chapter provides information to supplement readers' existing clinical expertise and knowledge.

AN EVIDENCE-BASED APPROACH TO TAKING A COMPREHENSIVE HISTORY

If you have not already done so, take a close look at the National Quality Forum's voluntary standards: "Palliative and End-of-Life Care—A Consensus Report" (2012). Hospice and palliative care professionals are encouraged to use these evidence-based measures, summarized in table 4.1, to collect and report publicly data on the care delivered.

In the fourth edition of *Clinical Practice Guidelines for Quality Palliative Care*, the National Consensus Project for Quality Palliative Care (2018) provides direction regarding elements of the history-taking process according to criteria delineated under eight domains:

- Domain 1: Structure and Processes of Care
- Domain 2: Physical Aspects of Care
- Domain 3: Psychological and Psychiatric Aspects of Care
- Domain 4: Social Aspects of Care

TABLE 4.1 National voluntary consensus standards for palliative and end-of-life care

Domain	National Quality Forum–endorsed measures
Pain management	Hospice and palliative care—pain screening
	Hospice and palliative care—pain assessment
	Patients treated with an opioid who are given a bowel regimen
	Patients with advanced cancer assessed for pain at outpatient visits
Dyspnea management	Hospice and palliative care—dyspnea screening
	Hospice and palliative care—dyspnea treatment
Care preference	Patients admitted to ICU who have care preferences documented
	Hospice and palliative care—treatment preferences
	Percentage of hospice patients with documentation in the clinical record of a discussion of spiritual/religious concerns, or documentation that the patient/caregiver did not want to discuss
Quality of care at the end of life	Comfortable dying
	Hospitalized patients who die an expected death with an implantable cardioverter defibrillator (ICD) that has been deactivated
	Family evaluation of hospice care
	CARE—Consumer Assessments and Reports of End of Life
	Bereaved-family survey

Source: National Quality Forum 2012. Table text © 2012 The National Quality Forum. Reprinted with permission.

- Domain 5: Spiritual, Religious, and Existential Aspects of Care
- Domain 6: Cultural Aspects of Care
- Domain 7: Care of the Patient Nearing the End of Life
- Domain 8: Ethical and Legal Aspects of Care

To elicit a complete and accurate history, professionals need to establish **rapport** with each individual and communicate a genuine openness to hearing the person's answers to their questions. A **comprehensive history** should never be viewed as a checklist or form you have to fill out. With the advent of electronic health records and computer-based charting, the process of taking and documenting an individual's history runs the risk of becoming less intimate and more robotic. However, a skilled hospice or palliative care professional can ask questions while clicking and scrolling through a checklist and drop-down menus and still manage to forge a genuine connection with the individual they are talking with. When an individual begins to provide detailed information that the hospice or palliative care professional wants to capture in the chart, the professional can say something like "This information is important—I want to make sure I get it down accurately to share with the other members of the team." When an individual begins to cry, the hospice or palliative care professional can say something like "Let me put this laptop away and let's just sit together" (Gardia, personal communication, August 14, 2022).

In palliative care and hospice care, registered nurses, physicians, advanced practice registered nurses, and physician associates can elicit the most complete and accurate history by using eye contact and genuine listening. By sitting across from someone, looking them in the eye, and giving them your full attention, you will facilitate their willingness to open up to you and provide an accurate history. Eliciting a complete and accurate history—and building the rapport needed to do so—will save you time in the long run. An assessment should be more of a conversation than an interrogation, so make sure your questions flow naturally and organically.

April 21, 2019

GoFundMe post from Kim Acquaviva:

It's a beautiful morning for a hike. After a day spent painting the driveway with epoxy protectant and then painting the new wainscoting in the basement, it's nice to breathe fresh air.

The past few days have been tearful ones. Kathy's acutely experiencing the pain of knowing she won't be with Greyson and I in the years to come, and so am I. Every time the gaping wound of that sorrow begins to form a scab, we wake to another day and life rips the wound open anew. I don't want to make it sound as though there's some kind of medical crisis going on, because there's not. Kathy's still up and around doing things and laughing a lot and playing with our dogs and FaceTiming with Greyson and enjoying life.

We're both making the most of our time together while getting the house ready to be listed. Our days are joyful yet reassuringly dull in the way that life in a normal household generally is: chit-chat, laundry, trash, bills, inside jokes, gentle teasing. But the sorrow slips in like smoke through a window we thought we'd closed.

Of **course** it's not closed but we forget . . . we forget the whole window is gone and the lawn is on fire and there's no way to 911 our way back to normal. The only way forward: keep living life and appreciating every smoke-free breath.

Kim

PROFESSIONAL PERSPECTIVE

What not to do: assum[e] you know who the patient/client is because he/she is LGBT. It's not meant to be cruel—I know when [professionals] are doing this they're trying to create a trusting bond. The problem is that they're doing it without waiting to find out who the patient/client is. Experiences I've had/observed: [professionals] assuming a gay man identifies with female pronouns/references, [professionals] trying to figure out who in a gay relationship is the "man" and who is the "woman," and "fag hag" [professionals] who love gay men and assume they must be like her gay best friend.

—Richard Gollance, LCSW, MSG (March 11, 1950–November 3, 2019)

COORDINATING AND FACILITATING THE FIRST FAMILY MEETING

As a member of the interdisciplinary/interprofessional team, you are likely to play a role in coordinating and facilitating family meetings. What that role looks like will vary, depending on your discipline, the size of the program where you work, and the particular needs of each patient and family. What the interdisciplinary/interprofessional team looks like will vary as well. If you work in a hospital-based palliative care program, for example, you may be part of a palliative care consultation team. Because Medicare and Medicaid require that the initial assessment of a hospice patient be completed by a registered nurse, a registered nurse on the interdisciplinary/interprofessional team is likely to be the person coordinating the first family meeting for a hospice patient. Within palliative care, a physician or advanced practice registered nurse will likely convene the first family meeting.

You may not think of the first time you meet with an individual receiving hospice care or palliative care as a "family meeting." After all, your focus during the first meeting is typically on taking a comprehensive history, conducting a physical examination, and identifying the patient's goals for care. But when you treat your first meeting with an individual as a family meeting, you will clearly establish from the outset your respect for and recognition of the patient and family as the unit of care. If the individual and family truly are the unit of care, every interaction should take this into account. Thus, the way you coordinate and facilitate the first meeting sets the tone for all your future interactions with the patient and family.

So, what is a "family"? Many people have two kinds of families: the family they were born or adopted into (sometimes called their **family of origin**) and the group of close friends they have chosen to surround themselves with, sometimes called their **chosen family**, their **family of choice**, or, among some LGBTQIA+ people, their lavender family (Breder & Bockting, 2022; Kim & Feyissa, 2021; Lawton, White, & Fromme, 2014; Neville & Henrickson, 2009; Rawlings, 2012; Rosa, Banerjee, & Maingi, 2022). When arranging the first meeting, always ask individuals receiving care whom they consider to be their family and whom they would like to have present at the meeting. The way you ask this question will communicate the degree to which you are open to a variety of familial configurations, so be intentional in your choice of language. For example, instead of asking a female patient, "Would you like to bring your husband or boyfriend?" ask, "Whom do you consider to be your family? Who are the people in your life who are sources of emotional support for you?" Follow up by mentioning that many people find it helpful to invite one or more people to participate in their meeting with the professional, then ask if that's something they might be open to. By suggesting that many people find this helpful before you ask the patient if they want to bring someone to the meeting, you normalize the idea of bringing a support person.

After a patient suggests one or more people they'd like to invite to the meeting, ask, "Is there anyone else you'd like to have there with you?" Some individuals will have multiple family members and friends they would like to bring with them. This can present logistical challenges to you as a professional in terms of scheduling the meeting, but the effort you expend to ensure that the family meeting includes all the key players is worthwhile. Mention that some individuals prefer to have the professional take their history and perform the physical exam with their family member(s) in the room, and some individuals prefer that their family member(s) be invited into the room after the professional finishes taking their history and performing the physical exam. Then ask them if they would like the people they named to be in the room for the physical exam and history, or only for the care planning discussion afterward.

FAMILY PERSPECTIVE

It was incredibly validating when the nurse who was visiting my dad pointed to my partner and me and the dogs and said, "This is your family. You are surrounded by a beautiful family. What better way to be than that?"

—Nick Krayger, MSW

Once an individual receiving care has identified the people they would like to have present at the family meeting, ask whether any of them have mobility, hearing, or visual impairments that you should be aware of, in order to ensure their access and full participation. In addition, ask whether any of the individuals will need an interpreter present. When you ask these questions, you communicate that you see the involvement of their identified "family" as being vitally important to the care you provide. Enlist the help of the social worker or counselor on your interdisciplinary/interprofessional team to make the necessary arrangements for accommodating the needs of the family.

At your first meeting with the patient and family, check in with the patient again to see who, if anyone, they would like to have in the room during the physical exam and/or history. If the patient has one or more family members who will be waiting outside the room, offer them a quiet place to sit. If one or more family members will be in the room with the patient, seat the patient and family member(s) in chairs at the same level as your chair or stool. Direct your questions to the patient but warmly acknowledge the presence of the family member(s), taking your cues from the patient as to how involved the family member(s) should be in the back-and-forth regarding the patient's history. If you notice that the patient appears agitated or impatient each time a family member answers a question, you might subtly turn your body more toward the patient (and away from the family member) and start your next question with the patient's name. For example, "Mary, you mentioned that you had surgery last year. Tell me a bit more about that."

FAMILY PERSPECTIVE

My dad moved in with me over the Christmas holiday in 2012. I noticed his coloring was bad, his health ailing, and over the next two years he went from fully independent to mostly dependent for ADLs [activities of daily living], three-day-a-week dialysis treatment, and transport to all medical procedures and appointments. My father really fell ill in the fall of 2014, and I had to take leave from work. Over those two years, my dad was in and out of the hospital twenty-some times. We discussed his ailing health and he said he wanted to die at home, with me, surrounded by our wiener dogs. He explained what he wanted from his hospice experience, when the time came, and that he wanted to be at home with the dogs.

My dad decided on a Monday that he was stopping dialysis. He had already missed his regular Friday treatment. The doctor called me very matter-of-factly and said, "You realize it will be no more than seven to ten days." That hit like a ton of bricks. I knew that, but to have a doctor state it set it in stone: He [would] die within a week. There was no turning back.

My estranged lover had been gone about six months, and when I told him my dad was receiving hospice care and I was alone, he showed up with his dog and a suitcase and said he was there for the duration. He helped me every day through and past the end. My dad died a beautiful peaceful death. He had Chinese food for dinner. Took a sip of Angry Orchard beer, got last rites from our family priest, and then said to my lover and me, "Well, fellows, it looks like it's my time to go." He [lay] down in his bed. All five of our dogs climbed to their respective spots around him. I rubbed his head. My niece held his hand. We listened to The Snowman soundtrack play and turned the fire up high, with the windows wide open. My lover burned sage, and my dad peacefully left his body and this life within an hour—in his bed, with the ones he loved, surrounded by the dogs. That was his final wish. And it was perfect.

—Nick Krayger, MSW

DEVELOPMENT OF A NEW MODEL FOR ASSESSMENT

A comprehensive history generally contains the following:

- Assessment of the patient's **quality of life**
- Information about the patient's advance care plans (living will; durable power of attorney for health care; health care proxy or surrogate; discussions with family, friends, and health care team; etc.)
- The patient's goals, values, and preferences

- History of the patient's illness and physical symptoms
- The patient's understanding of the illness and **prognosis**
- **Psychosocial history** (including mental health diagnoses and previous treatment) and **spiritual/existential/cultural history**
- The patient's sex assigned at birth and current gender identity
- Sexual orientation and sexual behavior
- Organ inventory
- Surgical history
- Assessment of patient's activities of daily living (ADLs)
- Depression screening
- List of pharmacologic, nonpharmacologic, and complementary/alternative therapies
- List of allergies and drug interactions
- Information regarding substance abuse or dependency

Because of the large amount of information you need to gather when taking a comprehensive history, it is helpful to have an organized framework to follow. Unfortunately, the only place I have found even the roughest beginnings of a clear map of questions clinicians should ask individuals and families is Knight and von Gunten's Module 3: Whole-Patient Assessment: Nine Dimensions (2004), which is no longer available online but is a core component of the Education in Palliative and End-of-Life Care (EPEC) Curriculum (Emanuel et al., 1999–2011).

Each discipline has core texts that are foundational to that particular field and that delineate key questions to ask in certain areas, but I have never seen anything in print that covers the waterfront in a unified way that all the disciplines can work with. The fourth edition of the National Consensus Project for Quality Palliative Care's *Clinical Practice Guidelines for Quality Palliative Care* (2018) comes closest to a multidisciplinary approach in its identification of eight domains for quality palliative care (listed at the beginning of this chapter). The National Consensus Project (NCP, 2013) succeeds in providing "guidelines that delineate optimal practice . . . [and that] rest on the principles of assessment, information sharing, decision-making, care planning, and care delivery." Without a doubt, the NCP guidelines are a triumph in the arena of evidence-based practice.

Where they fall short, however, is in explaining how to ask questions to meet the guidelines for quality palliative care—and how to ask them in an inclusive way.

It's hard for me to imagine someone reading the NCP guidelines and thinking, "No, I don't want to deliver quality palliative care." Where a clinician's good intentions fail to translate to behavior change is in the execution of those intentions. Thus, one of my goals in writing this book and developing a new assessment model was to give clinicians a crystal-clear road map to asking questions and delivering care in an LGBTQIA-inclusive manner. By design, this book is not a dense read, nor is it a replacement for seminal works like the NCP guidelines or the Oxford textbooks (see Altilio, Otis-Green, & Cagle, 2022; Cherny et al., 2015; Ferrell, Coyle, & Paice, 2015a; Ferrell & Paice, 2019). Instead, I am trying to teach clinicians about the language of inclusion in a practical way. As a starting point in developing an assessment model to accomplish this goal, I looked at Knight and von Gunten's Whole-Patient Assessment: Nine Dimensions (2004) and the framework it provides for palliative care and hospice care professionals. The nine dimensions in their assessment are:

1. Illness/Treatment Summary
2. Physical
3. Psychological
4. Decision-Making
5. Communication and Information Sharing
6. Social
7. Spiritual/Existential
8. Practical
9. Anticipatory Planning for Death

A potential limitation of Knight and von Gunten's nine-dimension framework is the way it starts with the primary illness rather than with the patient as a human being. Although their framework is a nominal rather than an ordinal listing of dimensions, the order in which the dimensions are listed could be interpreted as having some significance, even if none was intended. This approach runs the risk of medicalizing rather than humanizing the professional-patient interaction, sending the message to the patient that the professional's focus is on the illness, not on the person.

Given the limitations and gaps in the existing assessment models, I realized that a new, inclusive, patient-centered model was needed—a new assessment tool that I call the **Five-Dimension Assessment Model**. Based on a synthesis of the literature on patient and family assessment for palliative and hospice care, the Five-Dimension Assessment Model is designed to serve as a practical framework for a comprehensive patient history.

Knight and von Gunten's framework is focused more on the illness than on the patient. To address this problem, I added a dimension called Patient as Person at the beginning and end of the new framework and collapsed Knight and von Gunten's psychological, social, spiritual/existential, and communication and information sharing dimensions into this new dimension. Because the members of the interdisciplinary/interprofessional team share responsibility for supporting the patient's and family's plan of care in all domains, including the psychosocial and spiritual, I made a purposeful shift away from creating psychosocial and spiritual "silos"—stand-alone domains for psychosocial and spiritual care. Finally, I incorporated elements of Knight and von Gunten's practical dimension into the other dimensions and changed the name of their physical dimension to Functional Activities and Symptoms, to remind professionals of the focus of this aspect of the history-taking process.

In formulating the spiritual aspects of the Five-Dimension Assessment Model, I made use of Christina Puchalski's **FICA Spiritual History Tool** ©, a widely used model for assessing and addressing spiritual issues with individuals receiving care (Puchalski, 1996, 2014, 2021). While a variety of tools can be used for taking a spiritual history, I like the FICA Spiritual History Tool because it can be used by palliative care and hospice registered nurses, physicians, advanced practice registered nurses, physician associates, chaplains, social workers, and counselors alike.

To foster inclusive care, the Five-Dimension Assessment Model incorporates questions about sex assigned at birth, current gender identity, sexual orientation, sexual behavior, and sexual health in the assessment process and places the primary focus on the patient as person. The five dimensions are:

- Dimension 1A: Patient as Person, Part 1
- Dimension 2: Illness/Treatment Summary
- Dimension 3: Functional Activities and Symptoms
- Dimension 4: Decision Making
- Dimension 5: Anticipatory Planning for Death
- Dimension 1B: Patient as Person, Part 2

When someone is diagnosed with a chronic or life-limiting illness, their life changes in countless ways. Their diagnosis is likely to force them to make adjustments to their daily routine, priorities, long-term goals, and how they choose to spend their limited time and energy. Fatigue—both physical and emotional—can also take its toll on a patient with a chronic or life-limiting illness. These changes can affect a patient's desire for intimacy with a partner or spouse. One of the gaps I observed in Knight and von Gunten's framework was the absence of a sexual health assessment, and I have incorporated sexual health questions into dimension 2 of the Five-Dimension Assessment Model. Sexuality is an important component of the social aspects of palliative care (Ferrell, Coyle, & Paice, 2015b; Ferrell & Paice, 2019).

April 24, 2019

GoFundMe post from Kathy Brandt:

I am so tired that anything could trigger tears. I'm tired in a way I have never been tired before. Moving my body takes more effort and I need more time to recover after doing something. And that's fine. I have time to rest between working to get the house ready to sell (Kim works, I rest). The problem is Kim is exhausted from

(continued on next page)

(continued from previous page)

> everything she has been doing. So when I randomly start crying it disrupts her ability to get stuff done and she feels bad she can't comfort me. But here's the thing, I'm not sad. My filter is just gone. Obliterated by exhaustion (and cancer) the loss of my filter means I might start crying while thinking about the nice lunch Kim and I had on Monday, or how proud I am of Greyson for all his hard work this semester. I guess the good thing is, I'm right there feeling whatever I'm feeling, not trying to hide my tears. And Kim, dear patient Kim, is getting used to the instant waterworks.
>
> kb

USING THE FIVE-DIMENSION MODEL

When you first meet a patient, there is a narrow window of opportunity in which you can communicate your commitment to honoring the patient's values, customs, and preferences. People—particularly those who have had negative experiences with health care professionals in the past—have an exquisitely fine-tuned radar for detecting health care professionals who are closed-minded or focused on their own agenda. To address this, I have incorporated into the Five-Dimension Assessment Model questions about values, customs, and preferences (Golley, 2012). Also, before you begin the assessment conversation outlined here, preface it by telling the patient how you plan to proceed and indicating that the patient will be in control of the process. You might say, for example, "I'm going to ask you a series of questions that I ask everyone. If you don't feel comfortable answering a particular question, just let me know and we can skip it." (Note: The following is based on the assumption that the questions "What sex were you assigned at birth, on your original birth certificate?" and "What gender do you identify as now?" were asked at the time of intake and the answers are documented in the patient's chart.) I've also included questions designed to yield an accurate record of the organs that an individual has currently.

An **organ inventory** "can improve care and safety of transgender patients to enhance clinical decision-making based on sex-based care guidelines, by neutralizing clinical assumptions about the organs a person has at a given point in time" (Lau et al., 2020).

A WORD ABOUT COMMON SENSE

Do not conduct an organ inventory or ask questions about a person's surgical history or sexual orientation unless your professional judgment is that you *absolutely* need to know this information in order to provide them with the best care possible. Before asking a patient a question, ask yourself two things: (1) how could being asked this question change the patient's experience of receiving care and (2) how could the patient's answer to this question change the plan of care? If you anticipate that a patient will die within a matter of days, you don't need to know whether they had top surgery or whether they are bisexual.

The order in which you ask the following questions may vary based on the norms in the communities and areas where you work. Keep local and cultural norms in mind when approaching these topics. At the same time, be aware of the extent to which your own discomfort may be influencing your assessment of whether patients and families might be offended or upset by certain questions.

DIMENSION 1A: PATIENT AS PERSON, PART 1

- What name would you like me to call you?
- What pronouns do you go by? (e.g., he/him, she/her, they/them, ze/zir)?
- How would you describe your sexual orientation?
- How would you describe your current quality of life?
- I'd like to learn more about the people you consider to be family. Many people have two kinds of families: the family they were born or adopted into (sometimes called their family of origin) and the

support group of close friends they have chosen to surround themselves with (what some people call their chosen family, family of choice, or lavender family).

- Who are the people you consider to be part of your family of origin? *For each person named, ask:*
    - How would you describe your relationship with _____?
    - Is your relationship with _____ generally a source of support or a source of stress?
    - Many people have unresolved differences or conflicts that they want to resolve before they die. What, if any, unresolved differences do you have with _____?
    - What role, if any, do you hope _____ will play in your care?
    - Under the HIPAA Privacy Rule (45 CFR 164.510b), I can generally share information directly relevant to your care with your family and friends only if I have your permission to do so. What information, if any, would you like me to share with _____ regarding your illness, condition, or care?
    - What information, if any, would you *not* want me to share with _____ regarding your illness, condition, or care?
- Who are the people you consider to be your family of choice? *For each person named, ask:*
    - How would you describe your relationship with _____?
    - Is your relationship with _____ generally a source of support or a source of stress?
    - Many people have unresolved differences or conflicts that they want to resolve before they die. What, if any, unresolved differences do you have with _____?
    - What role, if any, do you hope_____ will play in your care?
    - Under the HIPAA Privacy Rule (45 CFR 164.510b), I can generally share information directly relevant to your care with your family and friends only if I have your permission to do so. What information, if any, would you like me to share with _____ regarding your illness, condition, or care?
    - What information, if any, would you *not* want me to share with _____ regarding your illness, condition, or care?

- I'd like to learn about your connections and supports in your community. What groups or organizations do you belong to that are important to you?
    - What role do these groups play in your life?
    - What involvement, if any, have these groups or communities had in meeting your needs for care or support in the past?
    - What involvement would you like them to have in the future?
- I'd like to learn about the things that give your life meaning or give you strength:
    - "What gives your life meaning? Where do your find strength during difficult times?"
    - "Do you consider yourself to be spiritual? Is spirituality something important to you? Do you have spiritual beliefs, practices, or values that help you to cope with stress, difficult times, or what you are going through right now?"
    - "What importance does your spirituality have in your life? Has your spirituality influenced how you take care of yourself, particularly regarding your health? Does your spirituality affect your healthcare decision making?"
    - "Are you part of a spiritual community? Is your community of support to you, and how? Is there a group of people you really love or who are important to you?"
    - "How would you like me, as your healthcare provider, to address spiritual issues in your healthcare?" (Puchalski, 2022)

FICA SPIRITUAL HISTORY TOOL©

The acronym FICA can help to structure questions for health care professionals who are taking a spiritual history.

F—Faith, Belief, Meaning

"Do you consider yourself to be spiritual?" or "Is spirituality something important to you?"

(continued on next page)

(continued from previous page)

> "Do you have spiritual beliefs, practices, or values that help you to cope with stress, difficult times, or what you are going through right now?" *(contextualize to visit)*
>
> "What gives your life meaning?"
>
> ### I—Importance and Influence
>
> "What importance does spirituality have in your life?"
>
> "Has your spirituality influenced how you take care of yourself, particularly regarding your health?"
>
> "Does your spirituality affect your healthcare decision making?
>
> ### C—Community
>
> "Are you part of a spiritual community?"
>
> "Is your community of support to you and how?" For people who don't identify with a community consider asking "Is there a group of people you really love or who are important to you?" (Communities such as churches, temples, mosques, family, groups of like-minded friends, or yoga or similar groups can serve as strong support systems for some patients.)
>
> ### A—Address/Action in Care
>
> "How would you like me, as your healthcare provider, to address spiritual issues in your healthcare?" (With newer models, including the diagnosis of spiritual distress, "A" also refers to the "Assessment and Plan" for patient spiritual distress, needs and or resources within a treatment or care plan).
>
> ---
>
> © *Copyright Christina Puchalski, MD, and The George Washington University 1996 (updated 2022). All rights reserved. Adapted from Puchalski & Romer (2000).*

- I'd like to learn more about your informal social activities and hobbies. When you have free time, what are the kinds of things you like to do?
    o What role do these activities and/or hobbies play in your life?
    o What involvement would you like to have with these activities and/or hobbies in the future?

- I'd like to learn more about household supports and stressors. Many times, people find themselves experiencing difficulty as a result of their chronic or life-limiting illness.
    o Whom do you consider to be your primary caregiver?
    o Who else is available to help you with your everyday needs?
    o How are you managing financially in light of the illness you are currently facing?
    o Who is in charge of your banking and paying your bills?
    o How has your illness affected your ability to meet your other financial obligations, such as rent, mortgage, utility bills, and so on?
    o Who does the grocery shopping and cooking in your house?
    o Are there ever weeks when you are unable to afford enough groceries to meet your basic needs?
    o Are there ever weeks when you are unable to afford your medications?
    o How do you get to and from appointments?

DIMENSION 2: ILLNESS/TREATMENT SUMMARY

- What is the primary illness that brought you to [palliative care/hospice care]?
- How has that illness affected your life?
- What treatments, if any, have you received for that illness?
- How did those treatments affect your life?
- What is your understanding of your prognosis?
- How would you like us to share medical information with you? Would you prefer to get just the "big picture" or more detailed information? How would you like to receive this information: alone or with someone else—family, friends, etc.? Or would you rather not receive the information yourself and instead appoint someone else to receive it?
- What other illnesses or conditions do you have? *For each illness, ask:*
    o How has that illness affected your life?

- o What treatments, if any, did you receive for that illness?
- o How did those treatments affect your life?
- What prescription medications are you currently taking? *For each prescription medication, ask:*
  - o How often do you take it? (frequency)
  - o How much/how many do you take each time you take it? (dose)
  - o How often do you forget to take it?
  - o Why do you take this medication? (reason it was prescribed)
  - o Any adverse effects?
- What over-the-counter medications are you currently taking? *For each over-the-counter medication, ask:*
  - o How often do you take it? (frequency)
  - o How much/how many do you take each time you take it? (dose)
  - o Why do you take this medication?
  - o Any adverse effects?
- What vitamins, supplements, and/or complementary/alternative therapies are you currently taking? *For each vitamin, supplement, and/or complementary/alternative therapies, ask:*
  - o How often do you take it? (frequency)
  - o How much/how many do you take each time you take it? (dose)
  - o Why do you take this medication?
  - o Any adverse effects?
- What other drugs or hormones (either prescribed or obtained another way) are you currently taking? For each additional drug and/or hormone, ask:
  - o How often do you take it? (frequency)
  - o How much/how many do you take each time you take it? (dose)
  - o Why do you take this medication?
  - o Any adverse effects?
- Do you have any worries or concerns about your past or current substance use as it relates to your current care?
- Do you have any allergies or adverse reactions to any medications?
- *If the patient's sex assigned at birth differs from their current gender identity, conduct an organ inventory (Deutsch et al., 2013). This should be done only after rapport has been established and should not be done*

by more than one member of the care team. People may have a variety of different organs regardless of what sex they were assigned at birth or what gender they are now. Knowing which organs you have will help me provide the best care possible. As I read each item on the list, let me know if you have that organ and if so, the word you use to refer to that part of your body. If you're uncomfortable doing this right now, we can talk about it another time. Would you like me to ask you these questions now or another time? *Pause and give the person time to react. Proceed only if the person says it's alright to continue.*
- o   Penis?
- o   Testes?
- o   Prostate?
- o   Breasts?
- o   Vagina?
- o   Cervix?
- o   Uterus?
- o   Ovaries?
- Have you had any surgeries other than the ones you have already mentioned to me?
  - o   What was the reason for that surgery?
  - o   When did you have the surgery?
  - o   Were there any complications or problems after the surgery?
- One area of people's lives that rarely gets the attention needed from health care professionals is sexuality. Some individuals have never been asked questions like these before, so I want to let you know why I'm asking them. No matter a person's age or physical abilities or health conditions, sex and intimacy may be important aspects of that person's life. As a health care professional, I want to do whatever I can to ensure that this part of your life remains as fulfilling as possible, to the extent that this is something that's important to you. May I ask you a few questions about this?
- What questions or concerns do you have about sex and intimacy in your life?
- Is sex with a partner, or other forms of sexual expression—whether partnered or not—important to you?

- Do you have any physical or health concerns regarding the act of masturbation (self-love) and/or sex with a partner or partners, such as pain, bleeding, difficulty reaching orgasm?
- What do you wish could be better about sex for you?

DIMENSION 3: FUNCTIONAL ACTIVITIES AND SYMPTOMS

Functional activities are often referred to as activities of daily living (ADLs) and instrumental activities of daily living (IADLs).

- What kind of help do you currently need with bathing? For example:
    - Do you need help getting dressed and undressed?
    - Do you need help getting in and out of the tub or shower?
    - Do you need help washing yourself?
    - Do you need help drying yourself off after bathing?
- What kind of help do you currently need with dressing yourself? For example:
    - Do you need help getting your clothes in and/or out of your closet?
    - Do you need help buttoning shirts and pants?
    - Do you need help pulling shirts and sweaters over your head?
    - Do you need help bending down to put on your socks and shoes?
- What kind of help do you currently need with feeding yourself? For example:
    - Do you need help preparing your meals?
    - Do you need help carrying your meal to the table?
    - Do you need help cutting your food with a knife?
    - Do you need help using a spoon or fork?
- What kind of help do you currently need with changing positions or transferring your body from one location to another? For example:
    - Do you need help sitting down?
    - Do you need help getting up from a chair or sofa?
    - Do you need help sitting up in bed?
    - Do you need help getting in and/or out of bed?

- o Do you need help moving from your bed to a chair? What about from the chair to your bed?
  - o Do you need help moving from a chair to the bathroom? What about from the bathroom to a chair?
  - o Do you need help moving onto or off of the toilet?
  - o Do you need help getting in or out of a car?
- What kind of help do you currently need managing bladder or bowel continence (aka peeing and pooping)? For example:
  - o Do you sometimes have accidents in which you don't make it to the bathroom in time?
  - o Do these accidents happen frequently enough that you need to wear incontinence pads or adult diapers?
  - o Are you able to wipe yourself?
- What kind of help do you currently need getting to the bathroom? For example:
  - o Are you able to get to the bathroom without assistance?
  - o Do you use a urinal, bedpan, or bedside commode at night because of difficulties making it to the bathroom in time?

When assessing each symptom—**pain, breathlessness, weakness/fatigue, constipation, anxiety, confusion, depression, insomnia, nausea/vomiting,** and **weight loss**—ask:

- Have you experienced any _____ in the past week?
- Are you currently experiencing any_____?
- On a scale of 0 to 10, with 0 being no _____ and 10 being the worst you can imagine, how would you rate your current _____ ?
- How has your _____ interfered with your daily activities? With your sleeping? With your walking? With your relationships? With your libido (desire for sex)? With your ability to have satisfying sex with yourself or a partner?
- What do you think is causing your _____?
- What things seem to make your _____ worse?
- What things seem to make your _____ better?

ASSESSMENT INSTRUMENTS

Consider using a valid, reliable assessment instrument like the Edmonton Symptom Assessment System (Bruera et al., 1991) or the Memorial Symptom Assessment Scale (Portenoy et al., 1994) as part of your assessment process. Although both instruments were originally developed for use with individuals who have cancer, you may find them beneficial with other patient populations as well. The Edmonton and Memorial symptom assessments are available for download through the National Palliative Care Research Center (n.d.a, n.d.b). When assessing depression, use an appropriate clinical assessment instrument—for example, the Beck Depression Inventory or the Patient Health Questionnaire PHQ-9 (Kroenke, Spitzer, & Williams, 2001). Remember to assess for suicidal ideation when assessing depression. For information on assessing pain, the American Academy of Hospice and Palliative Medicine maintains a robust list of guidelines and resources on its website. When assessing functional status, use a tool like the Palliative Performance Scale Version 2 (Victoria Hospice Society, 2001), the Karnofsky Performance Scale (Cherny et al., 2015), or the Edmonton Functional Assessment Tool (Cherny et al., 2015). For other assessment tools, check out the Palliative Care Network of Wisconsin's "Palliative Care Fast Facts" (2022) and the PEACE Project's list of assessment instruments and quality measures addressing "domains of quality of care included in the National Consensus Project for Quality Palliative Care and endorsed by the National Quality Forum" (PEACE Project, 2016). Cancer-specific guidelines for assessment can be found online through the National Comprehensive Cancer Network's website (2022).

DIMENSION 4: DECISION MAKING

- When it comes to your health and prognosis, how direct or explicit do you want me to be? For example, if there comes a time when it seems as though you have weeks to live, would you want me to say to you, "My best guess is that you have about a week or two left to live"? or "Time is short . . . this might be a good time to begin saying your goodbyes to the people closest to you"? Or would you rather I not say anything to you at all.

- If there comes a time when you are too sick to make your wishes known regarding your care, whom do you want to make decisions on your behalf?
- Have you put that decision in writing? [*If the answer is yes, get a copy of the advance directive in question. If it's no, work with the patient to complete the appropriate advance directives. If it's within your scope of practice, you should also discuss the issue of resuscitation preferences with the patient and complete a do-not-resuscitate (DNR) order, do-not-attempt-resuscitation (DNAR) order, allow-natural-death (AND) order, or out-of-hospital provider/physician/medical order for life-sustaining treatment (POLST/MOLST), as appropriate.*]
- In addition to your legal decision maker, is there anyone you would like to have involved in the shared decision-making process?
- Do you have any worries or concerns about a specific person or persons trying to step in to make decisions for you?
- Have you discussed these concerns with that person or persons? What about with your chosen health care surrogate/decision maker?

DIMENSION 5: ANTICIPATORY PLANNING FOR DEATH

- Although it can be painful to talk about death when you are trying to focus on living, making plans for how you would like your final days to be can bring a sense of healing and peace to you and your family while you are alive.
- When you're days or hours from death . . .
  - Where would you like to be? In your bedroom? Somewhere else in your home? In an inpatient hospice house? Somewhere else?
  - Would you like silence? Music? Other sounds?
  - Are there certain scents you would like to be able to smell?
  - How would you like the room lit? Lights turned down low? Bright light from a nearby window? Soft natural light filtered through a curtain?
  - Who are the people you'd like to have at your bedside? Who would you like to have in the house but not at your bedside?

- Are there any pets you'd like to have at your bedside?
- Any pets you would like to have in the house but not at your bedside?
- Would you like to have a chaplain or spiritual leader at your bedside? In the house but not at your bedside?
- What would you like to be wearing? A favorite pair of pajamas? A nightshirt? Something else?
- Would you like your hair and/or makeup to be done in your final hours? If so, what would you like done?

- Immediately after you have died, what rituals, traditions, or preferences would you like us to honor?
  - Is bathing or cleansing important to you? If so, who should be involved in the bathing/cleansing process?
  - Would you like the care team (or someone else) to change your clothes? Do you have a particular outfit you'd like your body to be dressed in?
  - Would you like friends or family to spend time at your bedside after you've died? For how long?
  - Would you like a member of the clergy or other spiritual leader to be at your bedside after you've died? For how long?

- Would you like a funeral or memorial service? Does your family know this?
  - Have you decided on burial, cremation, or another option?
  - If you would like to have a funeral, have you decided on an open casket, closed casket, or no casket?
  - Have you selected a funeral home?
  - Have you discussed specific plans for a funeral or memorial service with your family?
  - Would you like to have any special music, songs, hymns, religious or spiritual readings, or other passages to be included in the service?
  - Have you chosen an outfit in which to be buried or cremated?
  - Have you drafted your obituary?
  - Have you written notes or recorded videos for your family members to view after you've died?

- o Have you written an "ethical will" so that you can pass down your values to your family?
- What questions do you have about the dying process and what it might be like for someone with your illness?

May 2, 2019

GoFundMe post from Kathy Brandt:

In case you haven't heard, we have a contract pending on our house with no contingencies in less than 48 hours, which was our goal. Kim's hard work paid off big time and now we can focus on the next step, moving to Charlottesville. We just found out that the offer we put in on a house was accepted so we'll be moving into our beautiful new house in June.

We accepted the offer on our house while we were in Oklahoma for the Barebones Film Festival in Oklahoma where Greyson won two awards for his film. He composed the music in 24 hours on his computer last November despite the fact that he can't read sheet music. It's crazy how talented Grey is. We'll post a link to his film, TIC, soon. All these incredibly happy events that we experienced in less than one week. We are so lucky.

And yet . . . my death is still right here in front of us. Grey's acceptance speech at the Film Festival filled me with pride and crushed me. Dedicating the film and award to me was the highlight of my life.

Witnessing Greyson watching me die is the hardest thing I'll ever do. I can't do anything to help him. Other than express my endless pride and love for him, hold him tight, and create positive memories with him before I go. I am so grateful that he has successfully completed his first year of college and that we'll have weeks, and hopefully months to spend as much time together as we can.

kb

(continued on next page)

(*continued from previous page*)

> GoFundMe post from Kim Acquaviva:
>
> Yesterday we put in an offer on a house in Charlottesville and it was accepted—an exciting day but at the same time, bittersweet. It's our dream house in a beautiful neighborhood in Charlottesville—it has literally every feature we were looking for. We were SO ecstatic the seller accepted our offer. But nothing dampens one's home-buying enthusiasm quite like realizing this is the house in which your spouse is going to die over the summer. Or worse—the house your spouse will never live in if they die before move-in day mid-June. I want to host Thanksgiving with Kathy and have a house full of family and a basket full of crescent rolls I burned because I was too busy laughing to pay attention to the oven timer. I want to sit next to Kathy on Christmas morning wearing dorky matching pajamas and opening stockings with Greyson. I want the house to be an envelope Kathy, Grey, and I stuff full of memories over the next twenty years. Knowing Kathy won't be with us a few months from now to stuff that envelope makes my heart hurt.
>
> Stuff your envelope with memories today. That's what we'll be doing today.
>
> Kim

DIMENSION 1B: PATIENT AS PERSON, PART 2

The purpose of dimension 1B is to bring the assessment back to a focus on the patient as person. These questions are intended to build on the first section of the assessment, dimension 1A, bookending the process with questions designed to elicit information and insights that will be helpful to you in meeting the patient's needs.

- What brings meaning and purpose to your life?
- When you think about your life up to this point, what are you proudest of?
- What is your biggest regret?
- What goals do you have for the remainder of your life?
- What things do you want to accomplish before you get sicker?
- What brings you joy or makes you happy?
- What brings you a feeling of control over your life?
- What are you most looking forward to in the coming days or weeks?
- What do you most want to avoid in the coming days or weeks?
- What values, beliefs, customs, and preferences would you like us to know about?
- What or who is your source of hope?
- Is there anything you're worried we might do or not do in the coming days or weeks?
- What else would you like me to know about you as a person? *Alternative wording:* "What should I know about you as a person to help me take the best care of you that I can?" (Chochinov, 2007).

ADDITIONAL QUESTIONS TO CONSIDER

The National Hospice and Palliative Care Organization (NHPCO) has outlined recommended outcomes for end-of-life care; these are reprinted in table 4.2 In the column to the right of each recommended outcome I have added questions you can ask the patient and family during your assessment, as appropriate. These questions are from the **Patient and Family Outcomes-Focused Inquiry for Developing Goals for Care**, a subset of the questions in the **Patient and Family Outcomes-Focused Inquiry for Interdisciplinary Teams**, which is described in chapter 6. Use your clinical judgment regarding if, when, and how to pose these questions to individuals and families during the assessment process.

TABLE 4.2 Patient and Family Outcomes-Focused Inquiry for Developing Goals for Care

Domain	Recommended outcomes[a]	Patient and family outcomes-focused inquiry	
		Questions to ask the patient	Questions to ask the family
Self-determined life closure	Staff will prevent problems associated with coping, grieving, and existential results related to imminence of death.	What are your goals for coping related to the imminence of death? What are your goals for grieving related to the imminence of death? What are your goals for existential issues related to the imminence of death?	What are your goals for coping related to the imminence of death? What are your goals for grieving related to the imminence of death? What are your goals for existential issues related to the imminence of death?
	Staff will support the patient in achieving the optimal level of consciousness.	How do you define your optimal level of consciousness? What are your goals for achieving the optimal level of consciousness?	How do you define the optimal level of consciousness for the patient? What are your goals for achieving the optimal level of consciousness?
	Staff will promote adaptive behaviors that are personally effective for the patient and family caregiver.	What are your goals related to adaptive behaviors that are personally effective for you? What are your goals related to adaptive behaviors that are personally effective for your caregiver?	What are your goals related to adaptive behaviors that are personally effective for the patient? What are your goals related to adaptive behaviors that are personally effective for the caregiver?
Safe and comfortable dying	Staff [will] appropriately treat and prevent extension of the disease and/or comorbidity. Staff [will] treat and prevent adverse effects of treatment.	What are your goals related to the treatment and prevention of extension of the disease and/or comorbidity? What are your goals related to the treatment and prevention of adverse effects of treatment?	What are your goals related to the treatment and prevention of extension of the disease and/or comorbidity? What are your goals related to the treatment and prevention of adverse effects of treatment?
	Staff [will] treat and prevent distressing symptoms in concert with patient's wishes.	What are your wishes regarding the treatment and prevention of distressing symptoms? What symptoms do you consider to be distressing?	What symptoms do you consider to be distressing? What are your goals related to the treatment and prevention of distressing symptoms?

		What are your goals related to the treatment and prevention of distressing symptoms?	
	Staff [will] tailor treatments to patient's and family's functional capacity.	What are your goals related to tailoring treatment to your functional capacity?	What are your goals related to tailoring treatment to your family's functional capacity? To the patient's functional capacity?
	Staff [will] prevent crises from arising due to resource deficits.	What are your goals related to preventing crises from arising due to resource deficits?	What are your goals related to preventing crises from arising due to resource deficits?
	Staff [will] respond appropriately to financial, legal, and environment problems that compromise care.	What are your goals related to addressing financial problems that may compromise care? What are your goals related to addressing legal problems that may compromise care?	What are your goals related to addressing financial problems that may compromise care? What are your goals related to addressing legal problems that may compromise care?
		What are your goals related to addressing environment problems that may compromise care?	What are your goals related to addressing environment problems that may compromise care?
	Staff [will] identify opportunities for family members' grief work.	What are your goals related to identifying opportunities for your family members' grief work?	What are your goals related to identifying opportunities for your family members' grief work?
	Staff [will] assess the potential for complicated grief and respond appropriately.	What are your goals related to having the staff assess and respond to complicated grief?	What are your goals related to having the staff assess and respond to complicated grief?
	Staff [will] assist the family in integrating the memory of their loved one into their lives.	What are your goals for your family's integration of your memory into their lives after you've died?	What are your goals for integrating the memory of the patient into your lives after the patient has died?
Effective grieving	Staff [will] treat and prevent coping problems.	What are your goals related to treating and preventing coping problems? What are your goals related to treating and preventing your family's coping problems?	What are your goals related to treating and preventing coping problems in the patient? What are your goals related to treating and preventing your family's coping problems?

(continued)

TABLE 4.2 (Countinued)

Domain	Recommended outcomes[a]	Patient and family outcomes-focused inquiry	
		Questions to ask the patient	Questions to ask the family
	Staff [will] treat and prevent adverse effects of treatment.	What are your goals related to the treatment and prevention of adverse effects of treatment?	What are your goals related to the treatment and prevention of adverse effects of treatment?
	Staff [will] coach the patient and family through normal grieving.	What are your goals related to being coached through normal grieving? What are your goals related to your family's being coached through normal grieving?	What are your goals related to the patient's being coached through normal grieving? What are your goals related to your family's being coached through normal grieving?
	Staff [will] assess and respond to anticipatory grief.	What are your goals related to staff assessing and responding to your anticipatory grief? What are your goals related to staff assessing and responding to your family's anticipatory grief?	What are your goals related to staff assessing and responding to the patient's own anticipatory grief? What are your goals related to staff assessing and responding to your family's anticipatory grief?
	Staff [will] prevent unnecessary premature death.	How do you define "unnecessary premature death"? What are your goals related to preventing unnecessary premature death?	How do you define "unnecessary premature death"? What are your goals related to preventing unnecessary premature death?

Source: Institute of Medicine and National Research Council, 2003.
[a]Text under "Recommended outcomes" ©. National Hospice and Palliative Care Organization and National Academy of Sciences. Reprinted with permission from the National Hospice and Palliative Care Organization and the National Academies Press.

DISTINGUISHING BETWEEN RELEVANT AND INTRUSIVE QUESTIONS

It is important to distinguish between questions that are relevant and necessary for your care toward a patient and questions that may stem primarily from your own personal curiosity. Transgender and gender-nonconforming individuals, in particular, are often subjected to intrusive questions that lack relevance to the clinical care they are seeking. Table 4.3 lists examples of intrusive questions along with questions that are relevant to patient care.

TABLE 4.3 Relevant versus intrusive, curiosity-driven questions

Questions that are relevant and necessary to patient care	Intrusive questions that stem from personal curiosity
• How has your pain interfered with your libido (desire for sex)? With your ability to have satisfying sex with yourself or a partner? • Have you had any surgeries other than the ones you've already mentioned to me? What was the reason for the surgery? When did you have the surgery? Were there any complications or problems after the surgery? • What other drugs or hormones (either prescribed or obtained another way) are you currently taking? Frequency? Dose? Reason for taking? Any adverse effects? • Many people have differences or conflicts that they want to resolve before they die. What, if any, unresolved differences do you have with——? • What sex were you assigned at birth? What gender do you identify as now? • What word or words would you use to describe your sexual orientation? What word or words would you use to describe your sexual behavior?	• How many sexual partners have you had in your lifetime? • Do you still have your penis? • Can I see your surgical scars? • When will you be "complete"? • Are your breasts "real"? • What did your parents say when you told them you were gay/lesbian/bisexual/trans? • When did you know you were gay/lesbian/bisexual/trans? • Have you ever tried having sex with someone of the other gender? • Your coming out must have been so hard for your partner. How did he/she decide to stay with you? • If you have only had sex with men, how do you know you're bisexual?

PROFESSIONAL PERSPECTIVE

I'd been serving as the home hospice chaplain for an eighty-year-old man, M., and his partner of forty-four years, G., for about five months when M. began the active dying process. He was brought to our hospice home, and G. kept an almost constant vigil at his bedside. G.'s sister and several friends came to sit with M. when G. had to go home to shower. During this time, my state's amendment specifically banning same-sex marriage was overturned by the Supreme Court as unconstitutional.

G. and M. were suddenly able to do the unthinkable: get legally married. G. got the necessary letter from our physician indicating M. was bedbound and could not go to the county clerk's office to get the marriage license but was able to sign the letter, then G. went to that office. It happened so soon after the decision was handed down that the form still said "groom's name" and "bride's name." The clerk's office staff member had crossed out "bride" where necessary, and G. and M. had a marriage certificate.

I quickly threw together a stripped-down wedding ceremony, emphasizing the lifetime of love they had already shared and pointing out the wedding as a legal recognition of their life together. I ran to a nearby florist to get them each a boutonniere. G. came back to the hospice house and gathered his sister and a couple of dear friends.

G. stood beside M.'s bed and took his hand. M. was weak and barely able to talk, but when the time came for him to speak his vows, he pledged his love in a voice strong and sure. They shared a kiss, and I had performed my first legal same-sex wedding—for men whose years together were drawing rapidly to an end. M. died just a few days later, with G. at his side, as he had been for forty-four years.

—*Reverend Holly Lux-Sullivan, MDIV*

THE PHYSICAL EXAMINATION

This book is intended to supplement rather than replace clinical texts. You should continue to use evidence-based best practice in conducting physical examinations, congruent with your clinical discipline, licensure, and role. For example, although the following section does not include content about auscultation, you should continue to use auscultation if it is considered to be best practice for the clinical discipline in which you hold an active license and for the role you currently hold.

When performing a physical examination of a palliative care or hospice patient, registered nurses, physicians, advanced practice registered nurses, and physician associates should conduct a neurological exam (including an assessment of the patient's mental status), along with a focused physical examination tailored to the individual patient's needs. Assess the patient's skin integrity and document your findings. Breast, pelvic/urogenital, rectal, and prostate exams should be performed only when appropriate and medically necessary to the care of the patient.

Individuals whose sex assigned at birth does not align with their gender, as well as individuals who have experienced sexual abuse, may feel particularly vulnerable during a physical examination. Great care should be taken to respect the privacy and dignity of every patient you examine. Explain what you are going to be doing—and why—before you examine any part of a person's body. Encourage them to let you know if anything you are doing is causing them physical or emotional pain or discomfort.

If, during the physical exam, a patient tells you to stop or expresses pain or discomfort, immediately stop what you're doing. Remove your hands from the patient, take a small step back, and acknowledge (in a reassuring tone) that you heard and respect the patient's wishes. It is appropriate to ask follow-up questions, but only to the extent the patient is comfortable with them. For example, if a patient who has vulvar cancer winces when you begin the pelvic/urogenital part of the exam, it is appropriate to say (after you have stopped and moved your hands away), "I noticed that you winced when I started examining your [vulva/vagina/anus]. Can you tell me more about what you were experiencing when you winced?" Asking an open-ended question like this is better than launching immediately into a pain assessment; not all discomfort is related to physical pain.

When providing care to transgender individuals, be cognizant of the fact that they may or may not feel uncomfortable with aspects of their body, whether or not those aspects are in alignment with their gender identity. The body is not always a source of shame or discomfort for transgender individuals. A patient who was assigned the female sex at birth, is a man, and has had **gender affirmation surgery** may feel indifferent about having you see the surgical scars on his chest or penis after phalloplasty. A patient who was assigned the female sex at birth, is a man, and has affirmed his gender identity without surgical intervention may feel a sense of shame when you examine his breasts or genitals. No matter what body parts a patient has or shares with you, always treat people according to their gender. You would never accidentally refer to a man with gynecomastia (male breast development) as "she." Working with transgender individuals is no different. If a patient is a man, the presence of breasts (or a vagina) doesn't change the fact he is a man and should be treated as a man.

KEY POINTS TO REMEMBER

- To elicit a complete and accurate history from a patient, you need to establish rapport and communicate a genuine openness to hearing the patient's answers to your questions.
- When you take a comprehensive history of a palliative care or hospice patient, ask questions in each of the five dimensions:
  o Dimension 1A: Patient as Person, Part 1
  o Dimension 2: Illness/Treatment Summary
  o Dimension 3: Functional Activities and Symptoms
  o Dimension 4: Decision Making
  o Dimension 5: Anticipatory Planning for Death
  o Dimension 1B: Patient as Person, Part 2
- When people are diagnosed with a chronic or life-limiting illness, their life changes in countless ways. These changes can have an effect on their desire for intimacy with their partner or spouse. When asking questions about symptoms and functional abilities, remember to assess the impact of symptoms on sexual function.
- When taking a patient's spiritual history, be aware that some individuals may have had negative past experiences with religion. When individuals are facing a chronic or life-limiting illness, they may struggle to reconcile their own spiritual beliefs with the messages they have heard from others.

DISCUSSION QUESTIONS

1. Of the five dimensions of a comprehensive history for individuals receiving palliative care or hospice care, which is the most important to the delivery of high-quality care for a given patient? Which is the least important? Of the five fingers on your right hand, which is the most important to you? Which is the least important to you? How do you think these two sets of questions relate to one another?
2. Imagine that you have just met a new patient whose assigned sex at birth differs from their gender identity and expression. What are the questions that pop into your head? Which questions are relevant to your care of the patient? Which of your questions are curiosity-driven, intrusive, and not relevant to your care of the patient?
3. How much information do you need about a patient's sexual behavior in order to provide the patient with high-quality palliative or hospice care? Do you need to know about specific sexual practices? How many sexual partners the patient currently has? Whether the patient uses condoms and/or dental dams? Why or why not?
4. What are the similarities and differences between a spiritual history and a spiritual assessment in the context of palliative care and hospice?
5. Imagine you have been asked by a health care professional about your "family of origin" and your "family of choice." Who are the people you consider to be your family of origin? Who are the people you consider to be your family of choice? If you were facing a life-threatening illness, what roles would you want members of those two families—your family of origin and your family of choice—to play in your care? How well does your family of origin know your family of choice and vice versa?

CHAPTER ACTIVITY

Use the Five-Dimension Assessment Model to take a comprehensive history of a patient (either real or simulated via role playing). Immediately afterward, write down what you were thinking and feeling during each step in the process. Did any of your thoughts or feelings surprise you? If you used the Five-Dimension Assessment Model in your work with everyone, do you think it would improve the quality of care you deliver? Why or why not?

May 9, 2019

GoFundMe post from Kathy Brandt:

The disease is progressing. I knew it was, but I couldn't tell. Now I can. Cancer is growing in my abdomen. Fluid is building up and causing my belly to swell and even though we have the tube to drain the fluid, because the fluid is loculated, the drain can't access all the fluid. Which is a bummer.

Right now my stomach doesn't hurt much, but I can feel the pressure and know that it will just continue to grow over time. I'm not scared of the pain. We have a meeting with palliative care to come up with a plan to address it. And I know that Kim and the team will keep me comfortable. It's what the pain represents, the ticking clock.

kb

5 Shared Decision Making and Family Dynamics

CHAPTER OUTCOMES

1. Facilitate shared decision making among the individuals and families you serve.
2. Understand the ethical imperative for shared decision making as you approach your work with individuals and families.
3. Coordinate and facilitate a family meeting focused on shared decision making.
4. Engage in shared decision making whenever palliative sedation is being considered by an individual and family.
5. Navigate challenging family dynamics when engaging in shared decision making with individuals and families.

Key Terms: autonomy, beneficence, compassionate sedation, continuous sedation until death, ethical principles, genogram, palliative sedation, sedation for intractable symptoms, self-determination, shared decision making

CHAPTER SUMMARY

Shared decision making is one of the cornerstones of quality palliative and hospice care; it is anchored in the ethical principles of autonomy and self-determination. Shared decision making is complex, and it may be made more challenging by complicated family dynamics and medically and ethically complex clinical situations. This chapter explains how to coordinate and facilitate a family meeting focused on shared decision making, how to use shared decision making for decisions surrounding **palliative sedation**, and how family dynamics may play a role in the shared decision-making process.

FACILITATING SHARED DECISION MAKING

A fundamental characteristic of both palliative care and hospice care is the central role that **shared decision making** (also referred to as collaborative decision making) plays in the care-planning process. Shared decision making is firmly rooted in the **ethical principles** of **self-determination** and **autonomy**:

> At its core, SDM [shared decision making] rests on accepting that individual self-determination is a desirable goal and that clinicians need to support patients to achieve this goal, wherever feasible. Self-determination in the context of SDM does not mean that individuals are abandoned. SDM recognizes the need to support autonomy by building good relationships, respecting both individual competence and interdependence on others" (Elwyn et al., 2012). Regarding the historical origins of shared decision making, Stark and Fins (2013) note that it "emerged as a compromise in the longstanding debate about the relative role of patient autonomy and provider beneficence in medical decision-making.

The phrase "shared decision making" appears frequently in the literature but, as Makoul and Clayman (2006) discovered in their review of 418 articles about shared decision making, there is little agreement among health care professionals as to how the concept is defined. One of the most widely cited articles frames the process as dyadic in nature, primarily between a physician and a patient (Charles, Gafni, & Whelan, 1999). This dyadic view has persisted, although interdisciplinary/interprofessional models have emerged in recent years (Sieck, Johansen, & Stewart, 2016). Today there is a rich and robust body of literature on shared decision making and its use in the clinical setting (Barry & Edgman-Levitan, 2012; Baik, Cho, & Masterson Creber, 2019; Bomhof-Roordink et al., 2019; Elwyn et al., 2014; Ferrer & Gill, 2013; Oliver et al., 2018; Washington et al., 2016, 2022) and a growing body of work focused on shared decision making with LGBTQIA+ individuals (Acree et al., 2020; DeMeester et al., 2016; McNulty et al., 2021; Peek et al., 2016; Baig et al., 2016; Ng, 2016; Tan et al., 2016; Chin et al., 2016; Margolies & Brown, 2019; Baca-Dietz, Wojnar, & Espina, 2021).

Given the interdisciplinary nature of the care provided in both palliative care and hospice settings, what does shared decision making mean within that context, and how can you facilitate the shared decision-making process? In hospice and palliative care, there are two sides to the equation, each of which plays an important role. On one side you have the patient and the patient's family. The patient and family bring with them their values, preferences, and goals. On the other side you have the palliative or hospice care team. The team members bring with them their knowledge, expertise, and scientific evidence. Notice that I said team rather than clinician. This is an important distinction. Each member of the interdisciplinary/interprofessional team brings to the process a unique perspective anchored in the evidence base of their discipline. While this collaborative, interdisciplinary approach to shared decision making may be logistically more challenging than dyadic decision making between just the patient and a single professional, individuals and families are likely to benefit from the involvement of the team as a whole (Legare, Stacey, & IP Team, 2014).

The *Clinical Practice Guidelines for Quality Palliative Care* asserts that, in palliative care, "promoting and facilitating open communication to foster patient- and family-centered shared decision-making, and advance care planning is essential. Ethnic and cultural differences should be acknowledged. Family members' decision-making strategies around options of care, location, and preferences should take into account cultural, ethnic, and religious preferences. The earlier these discussions can occur, the better, so when there are unexpected changes in a patient's condition, discussions have already happened, and decisions have been made" (National Consensus Project for Quality Palliative Care, 2018).

So what does shared decision making in palliative care and hospice care look like from an operational standpoint, and which team members should be involved in the process? The answer depends in part on the decision being considered, the number of possible options, and the potential risks and benefits for the patient. Some treatment decisions—for example, the decision to put a patient who is receiving opioids on a bowel regimen—are relatively straightforward. Shared decision making regarding a bowel regimen may involve the patient and the physician, registered nurse, advanced practice registered nurse, or physician associate without other members of the interdisciplinary/interprofessional team. However, if a patient is reluctant to commit to following a bowel regimen, the social worker or counselor might be brought in to talk with the patient, to explore where the reluctance is coming from, and to find out whether preventing constipation is one of the patient's goals.

Other treatment decisions, such as decisions regarding the management of delirium in a patient nearing the end of life, may be more complex and necessitate the involvement of multiple team members in the shared decision-making process. It's worth emphasizing, however, that all members of the interdisciplinary/interprofessional team share responsibility, within each member's scope of practice, for helping individuals achieve all of their goals.

FAMILY PERSPECTIVE

My husband had a very rare form of cancer and was in treatment for two years. He seemed to be getting better and then suddenly took a turn for the worse. Those final days were painful as I watched him deteriorate before my eyes. The day before he passed he was admitted back to the ICU and I was called and told to come up as soon as possible. After several tests confirmed he was not going to get better, I had to begin calling family and get his mother and brother up to the hospital as fast as possible, as they lived 3 hours away. I then had to make a decision about hospice care. My husband's wishes had been to be taken home on hospice and to be allowed to pass there. I communicated this to the doctors but they were honest with me that he could not withstand that kind of transport. So I made the decision to do in-hospital hospice care in the ICU. It was one of the hardest decisions of my life. After the decision had been made, the staff raced into gear to do all that they could for not only David but also for me and his family. They checked in often, made sure we were comfortable, answered any questions we had, brought us a courtesy kit with food and drinks, and reassured us that we were doing the right thing and that David was comfortable. The ICU Hospice Team at The Ohio State University James Cancer Hospital in Columbus Ohio made that hardest night as bearable as possible and put in all of the extra work and effort to help us. On top of that, no one called me his "friend" or "person," but his husband. No questions, no awkward conversations. I was his husband, and that was that. I cannot even begin to express how much that meant to me.

—Timothy Sandusky

WHAT IS PALLIATIVE SEDATION?

Palliative sedation—also referred to as **sedation for intractable symptoms, compassionate sedation,** *and* **continuous sedation until death**—*is "the monitored use of medications intended to induce varying degrees of unconsciousness, but not death, for relief of refractory and unendurable symptoms in imminently dying patents" (Dahlin & Lynch, 2003). It is considered to be "a treatment of last resort when symptom distress cannot be relieved using standard methods" and is rarely used "because the vast majority of patients get acceptable relief without sedation" (Center to Advance Palliative Care, 2010). Definitions of palliative sedation vary widely but, in general, "palliative sedation . . . is the intentional lowering of awareness towards, and including, unconsciousness for patients with severe and refractory symptoms" (American Academy of Hospice and Palliative Medicine, 2014). The literature on palliative sedation can be*

(continued on next page)

(*continued from previous page*)

> *difficult to navigate because of the absence of clear distinctions "between primary intended sedation and secondary sedation, or between light and deep, intermittent and continuous, progressive (proportionate) and precipitous (sudden) sedation" (Twycross, 2019). When palliative sedation consists of continuous sedation until death (as opposed to intermittent sedation), the line between palliative sedation and euthanasia may be seen as a blurry one (Papavasiliou et al., 2013a, 2013b; Twycross, 2019). However, the goals of palliative sedation and euthanasia are distinct, and continuous sedation until death, when used appropriately, is not euthanasia. When discussing the possible use of palliative sedation with a person receiving hospice or palliative care and their family, be very clear about what you mean by the term* palliative sedation *so that everyone is on the same page regarding the intended goal and likely outcome.*

SHARED DECISION-MAKING SCENARIO

Let's use a fictional case involving a patient with delirium to illustrate the shared decision-making process and the role of each member of the interdisciplinary team. While the treatment of delirium might be viewed as a strictly medical issue, there may be psychosocial and spiritual components of relevance to the decision-making process. Ross and Alexander (2001) write: "Hospice workers have noted that a changed mental status is more pronounced in patients who have been undergoing a significant psychosocial or spiritual struggle. They would argue that sedation is not appropriate in this setting. For families, however, the open, staring eyes and agitated movement of a patient may not be emotionally tolerable, resulting in a request for something to 'quiet' the patient."

Given that delirium may be seen near the end of life and that it can be emotionally upsetting for families to witness, shared decisions regarding its treatment may involve the patient's family (as defined by the patient), the registered nurse, physician, advanced practice registered nurse, physician associate, social worker, chaplain, and/or counselor, especially when palliative sedation is being considered as a treatment option.

May 17, 2019

GoFundMe post from Kathy Brandt:

I'm saving the "healthcare system" money—and yet my cancer is breaking our bank.

We are so appreciative of the hundreds of donations we've received from friends, family, and complete strangers. When Heather Wilson and Joy Barry set up the Go Fund Me after my operation we were floored. We were worried about how long I'd be able to keep up my consulting work (turns out, not very long) and manage our ongoing expenses. We hadn't considered the healthcare costs because we opted for palliative care. The problem is, my primary palliative care "treatment" isn't covered by insurance.

I take between 8–10 medical marijuana capsules a day ($5 per pill) to manage my pain and anxiety. That's $50 day, $350 a week. I also vape to supplement the pills as needed. All told we are spending about $2,000 a month on my pain/anxiety medication. I also take CBD pills, miscellaneous other medications, and take injections once a day, all of these except the CBD have co-pays. The CBD, which costs $1 a day, isn't covered. My drain supplies cost us $850 a month and office visits for the oncologist are $408 each time we go. I can't begin to untangle all the charges from my operation, scans and related visits. But needless to say, we paid thousands of dollars. All of these added costs arriving when I can't work, we are moving, and we still have our regular mortgage, car payments, etc.

I know that patients with more complicated or longer illnesses will pay tens of thousands more than Kim and I will, I guess I'm just a little resentful that our antiquated ideas about marijuana, combined with our rigid Federal bureaucracy, and payers that are wary about providing treatment that is a Schedule I substance, according to the Federal government.

I'm saving the healthcare system money by not having any more scans, no longer seeing my oncologist, doing everything possible to

(continued on next page)

(*continued from previous page*)

> avoid the ER through expert pain and symptom management. And yes, I'd do it even if it didn't save money because it's what's right for me. I just wish that our healthcare system could figure out a way to pay for those things which truly add value to patient quality of life, even if it means breaking out of its comfort zone.
>
> kb

ABOUT THE PATIENT AND FAMILY

In our scenario, the patient experiencing delirium is a fifty-six-year-old woman named Mary. Mary received palliative care for two years while she was seeking curative treatment for ovarian cancer. Mary transitioned from palliative care to in-home hospice care two weeks ago and, after a precipitous decline, now appears to be days from death. Her partner of twenty years and primary caregiver, Martha, is very distressed by Mary's delirium. Five years ago, Mary named Martha her durable power of attorney for health care.

Because of the intense need for round-the-clock symptom management in the past several days, the hospice team has put continuous-care nursing in place. Martha keeps asking the nurses to "do something" because she's worried that Mary is in pain. After searching online for information on ways to help Mary, Martha expresses interest in palliative sedation.

Mary's mother and father, estranged from Mary since she left home at age eighteen, are also at the bedside. Martha called Mary's parents a week ago because Mary said she wanted a chance to tell them good-bye. At that time, Mary was still alert and communicating clearly, and she didn't appear to be in any distress. When Mary's parents arrived, they told Mary they loved her but they were suffering deeply because they believed she was going to "burn in the fires of hell" if she didn't "accept Jesus Christ as her Lord and Savior" before she died. Mary tried to change the subject to something that wasn't so contentious, but her parents were adamant: they said if she didn't get "saved" before she died, she would suffer eternal damnation.

In the days following, Mary's level of consciousness changed, she stopped speaking, and she began intermittently moaning and thrashing.

Mary's parents are now convinced that her current distress is a sign that she's "trying to get right with the Lord" before she dies. For this reason, they are insisting that they don't want Mary to be sedated, and they have repeatedly asserted that, as Mary's parents, they should have been appointed as her legal decision makers. Martha (Mary's legal decision maker) does not share Mary's parents' belief about the cause of Mary's distress, and she feels strongly that Mary should be sedated to relieve her agitation. Martha says Mary told her many times that she wanted Martha to do whatever she could to make sure Mary didn't "suffer" in her last days.

WHO ARE THE DECISION MAKERS?

In this scenario, there are four individuals (the patient, the patient's partner, and the patient's two parents) whose needs the hospice interdisciplinary team must try to meet. Of central concern is Mary, the patient. Since Mary is unable to participate in the shared decision-making process owing to her delirium, her partner, Martha—who was appointed Mary's durable power of attorney for health care—is the individual with the legal right to make decisions on Mary's behalf. After their long period of estrangement, Mary's parents are seeking to reengage with their daughter, but their religious beliefs and lack of understanding about Martha's decision-making rights are causing distress—for Martha as well as for themselves. Although Martha is legally the decision maker, involving Mary's parents in the shared decision-making process to the extent that Martha is comfortable may help to decrease the emotional distress for all the parties involved.

Although Mary did not explicitly express her desire for palliative sedation prior to her recent decline, she told her partner (her legal decision maker) about her wishes regarding the alleviation of suffering at the end of life. Her preferences should drive the decision-making process:

> While it seems an ethical imperative to involve family members and other persons close to the patient when identifying the values of a patient

lacking capacity or, where relevant, to interpret any advance statement in terms of the decision about palliative sedation therapy, the role of family members as decision makers is restricted to those legally representing the patient. Even in such a case it seems important to stress that family members or other people who have taken up this task as representatives must base their decisions on the (presumed) will of the patient. (Schildmann & Schildmann, 2014)

Martha's advocacy for Mary is clearly anchored in what she believes to be the will of the patient, Mary.

FACILITATING THE SHARED DECISION-MAKING PROCESS

There are almost infinite possibilities for how the interdisciplinary team could facilitate the shared decision-making process in this case. The following scenario describes just one way the team might choose to proceed.

Team Discussion About Ethics, Risks, and Benefits

At the hospice interdisciplinary team meeting, the social worker raises the issue of Mary's delirium and asks the other team members for their thoughts regarding the possibility of using palliative sedation to alleviate Mary's delirium. The registered nurse says that, since Mary seems to be imminently dying and other efforts to manage her symptoms have been unsuccessful in addressing her delirium, palliative sedation seems an appropriate option to explore and would be consistent with the Hospice and Palliative Nurses Association's "Position Statement: Palliative Sedation at End of Life" (Dahlin & Lynch, 2003). The physician agrees and adds that, because Mary is no longer eating or drinking, no longer substantially interacting with those around her, and no longer making decisions regarding her own care, palliative sedation does not seem to raise any ethical concerns from her perspective (which is consistent with American Academy of Hospice and Palliative Medicine's "Palliative Sedation Position Statement";

see AAHPM, 2014). In her professional opinion, the use of palliative sedation to treat Mary's delirium would meet AAHPM's four criteria for ethical defensibility:

1. Palliative sedation will be used only "after careful interdisciplinary evaluation and treatment of the patient."
2. "Palliative treatments that are not intended to affect consciousness have failed or, in the judgment of the clinician, are very likely to fail."
3. The use of palliative sedation "is not expected to shorten the patient's time to death."
4. Palliative sedation will be used "only for the actual or expected duration of symptoms."

After hearing the physician read this list of criteria, the registered nurse comments on how different the AAHPM and HPNA (Hospice and Palliative Nurses Association) positions are regarding when palliative sedation is ethically defensible. According to the HPNA:

The use of medication to promote comfort and relieve pain in dying patients is supported by the American Nurses Association (ANA). . . ., [which states that] "achieving adequate symptom control, even at the expense of life, thus hastening death is ethically justified." This statement is reiterated in the ANA's Code of Ethics for Nurses[,] which also states that nurses may not act with the sole intent to end a patient's life even if motivated by compassion and concern for dignity and quality of life. Thus, palliative sedation with its intent to relieve suffering in dying patients but not to deliberately hasten death is seen as distinct from euthanasia or assisted suicide where the intent is solely to end life. These statements reflect the rule of double effect. (Dahlin & Lynch, 2003)

After a brief discussion about the evidence in the literature, the registered nurse and the physician agree that there does not appear to be a risk that palliative sedation would hasten Mary's death. Given that palliative sedation appears to be both clinically appropriate and ethically defensible, the team physician is supportive of palliative sedation and says she will contact Mary's primary care physician immediately after the meeting to discuss moving the plan forward, assuming the rest of the team agrees that this is the appropriate course of action. The team social worker expresses concern about the tension and conflict between Mary's parents and Martha and worries aloud that Mary's parents will become even more agitated if Mary is sedated. The team chaplain echoes the social worker's concerns and indicates that she is planning to visit the patient and family later that day to provide spiritual support. The chaplain adds that she suspects Mary's agitation stems from the frightening message of damnation that her parents have repeatedly conveyed to her. The interdisciplinary team as a whole comes to a consensus that the shared decision-making process needs to begin with a conversation among the hospice physician, registered nurse, social worker, chaplain, Martha, and Mary's parents. (Martha had previously expressed that she was not interested in meeting one on one with the chaplain, but she was supportive of the idea of the chaplain's supporting Mary's parents.)

In preparation for engaging in the shared decision-making process with Mary's partner and parents, the interdisciplinary team discusses the different dimensions of palliative sedation as a potential treatment for Mary's delirium, using something like the chart in table 5.1. Working from left to right, the team discusses each dimension and rates its level of potential risk

TABLE 5.1 Risk-benefit discussion tool for shared decision making in hospice and palliative care

Risk of exacerbation of physical symptoms	minimal	low	moderate	high
Potential for alleviation of physical symptoms	minimal	low	moderate	high
Risk of negative impact on quality of life	minimal	low	moderate	high
Potential for positive impact on quality of life	minimal	low	moderate	high
Risk of shortening length of life	minimal	low	moderate	high
Potential for extending length of life	minimal	low	moderate	high
Risk of exacerbation of psychosocial and/or spiritual issues	minimal	low	moderate	high
Potential for alleviation of psychosocial and/or spiritual issues	minimal	low	moderate	high

TABLE 5.2 Completed risk-benefit discussion tool for shared decision making in hospice and palliative care

Risk of exacerbation of physical symptoms	**minimal**	low	moderate	high
Potential for alleviation of physical symptoms	minimal	low	moderate	**high**
Risk of negative impact on quality of life	**minimal**	low	moderate	high
Potential for positive impact on quality of life	**minimal**	low	moderate	high
Risk of shortening length of life	minimal	low	moderate	high
Potential for extending length of life	**minimal**	low	moderate	high
Risk of exacerbation of psychosocial and/or spiritual issues	**minimal for patient**	low	**moderate for parents**	high
Potential for alleviation of psychosocial and/or spiritual issues	minimal	low	**moderate for partner**	high

or benefit. Table 5.1 is a template; table 5.2 shows a chart as completed by the team in this case study.

Quantifying the potential risks and benefits of a given treatment option is an evidence-based endeavor and should be grounded in the literature to the extent possible. Because each member of the interdisciplinary team is familiar with a different body of literature (the one anchored in their own discipline), disagreements may occur among team members about perceived degrees of risk or benefit along the various dimensions. The team members do not need to reach perfect consensus on the degrees of risk and benefit. What is important is that they have an open discussion about each dimension so that, when they meet with the patient and family, they have a shared understanding of how they plan to present the risks and benefits of a given treatment option.

Coordination with the Primary Care Professional

After the interdisciplinary team meeting, the hospice physician reaches out to Mary's primary care physician to begin discussing the possibility of palliative sedation. The primary care physician is supportive of the hospice physician's recommendation that palliative sedation be used to address Mary's delirium.

Setting Up the Family Meeting

After the hospice physician gets off the phone with Mary's primary care physician, she contacts the team social worker to request assistance with setting up a meeting at the patient's home later that day. The team social worker calls the team nurse and they find a block of time that works for all of the team members, including the chaplain. The social worker calls Martha, confirms that the time works for her as well as for Mary's parents, and briefly explains the purpose of the meeting. During the call, the social worker reiterates that the hospice team recognizes Martha as Mary's legal decision maker and explains that the chaplain will be coming to provide support for Mary's parents if Martha is comfortable with that. Martha says she's open to the chaplain's involvement if it will be helpful to Mary's parents.

The Family Meeting

At the designated time, the hospice physician, registered nurse, social worker, and chaplain arrive at Mary and Martha's home. When Martha opens the front door, her eyes are puffy and red from crying. It looks as though Mary's parents have been crying as well. The social worker asks Martha where she would feel most comfortable meeting with the team. Martha asks whether the meeting can take place in the room where Mary is, "so that it feels like she's part of the decision." Mary's mother says she'd like that—she doesn't want to leave Mary's bedside. The registered nurse, physician, social worker, and chaplain pull up chairs around Mary's bed so that everyone is seated in a circle around her. Because the registered nurse is the team member who has formed the strongest bond with the patient and family in the short time the patient has been receiving hospice care, the nurse starts the meeting. The registered nurse explains that the purpose of the meeting is to discuss options for making sure Mary is as comfortable as possible. The nurse frames the purpose of the meeting this way because ensuring Mary's comfort is the one thing that Martha and Mary's parents agree on. Thus, the registered nurse helps to lay the foundation for a shared decision-making session in which Martha and Mary's parents can work together toward that common goal.

The social worker asks Martha and Mary's parents what their goal or hope is for Mary's final days. Martha says her goal is for Mary "to be able to die peacefully without so much suffering." Mary's father says his hope is for his daughter to "be able to die a Christian." At hearing this, Mary's mother nods and begins weeping. The chaplain says gently that she thinks the hospice team can help Martha and Mary's parents ensure that Mary's final days are as peaceful as possible. She says that even though Mary is no longer speaking, her parents can pray for her and help Mary resolve unfinished business that may be causing her some distress. The chaplain suggests that four of the greatest gifts parents can give their dying child are unconditional love, apologies, forgiveness, and permission. The chaplain lets a brief silence hang in the air.

Mary's father asks the chaplain how to do that. The chaplain tells Mary's father and mother that there is no right or wrong way; the main idea is to:

1. Tell Mary that they love her the way she is—she doesn't need to change anything to be worthy of their love.
2. Tell Mary that they're sorry for any hurt they may have caused her over the years.
3. Tell Mary that they forgive her for any hurt she may have caused them over the years.
4. Tell Mary that it's all right for her to let go and die—she doesn't need to hang on for them.

On hearing the chaplain's words, Mary's parents visibly soften and Mary's father begins to weep. The hospice team sits with the family, providing a silent, supportive presence. After several minutes, the physician brings the issue of Mary's delirium into the conversation. She explains what delirium is and describes the treatments for Mary's delirium that have been tried so far. She asks first Martha and then Mary's parents how Mary's delirium is affecting them. All three agree that Mary's delirium is extremely upsetting to them and that being at Mary's bedside is, as Mary's father puts it, "almost more painful than not being there at all." The physician asks

Martha whether she can think of anything that might be causing Mary's distress. Martha says that her distress seemed to have started when Mary's parents arrived and began telling her she was going to go to hell when she died if she didn't accept Jesus before it was too late. Martha quickly turns to Mary's parents and says she's not trying to blame them—she knows they were just doing what they thought was best for their daughter. Martha pauses and then adds, "I wish you knew Mary like I do. She is the kindest, most compassionate human being you could ever imagine. If Mary's going to hell, there's not much hope for anybody." Martha begins to weep. Mary's mother reaches over tentatively and puts her arm around Martha's shoulder in support.

Next, the physician explains palliative sedation as an option for treating Mary's delirium. Using the risk-benefit chart that the interdisciplinary team explored prior to the family meeting, the physician walks Martha and Mary's parents through the potential risks and benefits of palliative sedation (see table 5.2). She talks about each dimension in the chart and asks questions of both Martha and Mary's parents to make sure they all understand the information she is presenting. When the physician gets to the assessment of the risk of shortening the length of Mary's life, Mary's parents say they are relieved to hear that palliative sedation is not euthanasia—before the meeting, they had thought it was. The physician affirms that this is a common misconception and that scientific evidence supports the finding that palliative sedation, when used appropriately, does not hasten death (Maltoni et al., 2009, 2012; Won et al., 2019; Herx, 2021; Bhyan et al., 2021).

After hearing about all of the potential risks and benefits, Martha says she thinks she wants to move forward with sedating Mary but she's not sure. Martha turns to Mary's parents and says she would like to have their help in making this difficult decision. Mary's father asks whether it would be possible for them to have some time "to say the things that need to be said" before Mary is sedated, if sedation is what Martha decides is the right thing to do. Martha nods and says she thinks that is a good idea. Mary's mother thanks Martha for being willing to do that. Martha turns to the hospice physician and says she would like to move forward with palliative sedation for Mary, starting the following morning. Martha signs an **informed**

consent form for the palliative sedation. The hospice physician (working in concert with the primary care physician) arranges for a prescription of continuous subcutaneous midazolam to be delivered to the home later that day. The plan is for the medication to be carefully titrated and Mary to be carefully monitored to ensure that a deep level of sedation in maintained (Periyakoil, n.d.). As the hospice social worker wraps up the meeting with the family, Mary's father asks if the chaplain can stay for a while. The chaplain agrees and the rest of the team leaves. A registered nurse remains in the home to provide continuous care.

That afternoon, the chaplain sits with Mary's parents at the bedside. Mary's parents pray with the chaplain and tell Mary all the things they wish they had said to her before she got sick. They tell her they're proud of her and that they see what a kind person Martha is. They apologize for saying hurtful things to Mary over the years, and they forgive Mary for the hurtful things she said to them. They tell Mary that it's okay for her to let go when she's ready. They tell Mary that they will do their best to support Martha in her grief and that they know Martha will do the same for them. Most important, they tell Mary that they love her unconditionally.

Ultimately Mary did not need to be sedated. Shortly after Mary's parents spoke to her at her bedside, Mary's delirium decreased significantly and she began resting comfortably. Mary died less than twenty-four hours later.

PALLIATIVE SEDATION DECISION-MAKING GUIDELINES

The extent to which interdisciplinary team members other than the physician have real decision-making power regarding the use of palliative sedation for a given patient is unclear. As Schildmann and Schildmann (2014) discovered in their analysis of eight sets of guidelines on palliative sedation:

> Guidelines on [palliative sedation therapy] differ also with regards to recommendations on the appropriate roles of the different health care professionals in decision making. The majority of guidelines

(continued on next page)

(*continued from previous page*)

> recommend involvement of nonphysician health care professionals.... While a consensus within the multiprofessional palliative care team in practice seems important especially in difficult situations of end-of-life care, it is not clear in the majority of guidelines how the stakeholders should proceed in the case of disagreement.
>
> Find out whether your organization/program has guidelines for how decision making and disagreements are handled with regard to palliative sedation. Your organization/program may have an ethics committee that consults on challenging cases such as those involving palliative sedation. When does the ethics committee get involved in a case, and what triggers its involvement? Can any member of the interdisciplinary team request an ethics consult? If no guidelines currently exist in your organization, talk with the medical director to express an interest in being part of an interdisciplinary effort to develop them. Registered nurses, physicians, advanced practice registered nurses, physician associates, chaplains, social workers, counselors, and pharmacists are ideally suited to work collaboratively—and proactively—to develop guidelines to smooth the way for their future interactions around difficult decisions like palliative sedation.

SHARED DECISION-MAKING SCENARIO DEBRIEFING

Reading this scenario, you may be thinking to yourself that in "real life" the hospice physician, registered nurse, social worker, and chaplain would never make a joint home visit for the purpose of shared decision making. How could a hospice program afford to send four members of an interdisciplinary team to a single patient's home for an hourlong shared decision-making session? Wouldn't it be more efficient to have just the physician or registered nurse meet with a family caregiver like Martha? And since the hospice team did not even end up using palliative sedation, what was the point of this whole scenario?

I used this scenario because it illustrates how complicated shared decision making can be, even when it's done well. Shared decision making is not easy or efficient. It takes time and effort to walk a patient and family through the options available to them, and sometimes the only real "intervention" you end up providing is the shared decision-making session itself. In the scenario I just described, four interdisciplinary team members spent fifteen minutes in a meeting prior to the visit and sixty minutes during the visit on the shared decision-making process. Five person-hours (plus travel time) were spent facilitating the shared decision making regarding Mary's delirium. In the grand scheme of things, this is not a large investment of time.

In the scenario described, there were complex family dynamics and spiritual/existential concerns. Had those factors not been understood and addressed by the team as a whole, the spiritual distress Mary's parents felt and the emotional distress experienced by Martha might have worsened, and the conflict in the home would have been exacerbated by the decision to move forward with palliative sedation. By working collaboratively with the patient and her family, the interdisciplinary team was able to give Martha and Mary's parents the tools they needed to alleviate Mary's suffering—and their own.

FAMILY PERSPECTIVE

They say you don't remember days, you remember moments. In 2014, eight inexplicable days turned into final moments. The woman who ushered me into this world had become my patient on hospice that I would have to usher out. Like a scene out of the Wizard of Oz, when you endure the nightmare of loss, you wake and realize you had everything you needed in that sacred journey. She started me on this path when she brought me to volunteer as a child to comfort elders in need. Teachable moments and humble lessons of grief, loss, but also of compassion and love. I carry those lessons like marbles in my pocket every day.

—Kris Helm

Kris Helm describes herself as "a white woman with a tapestry of lesbian authentic living who holds the space as a Hospice Massage Therapist."

FAMILY DYNAMICS AND SHARED DECISION MAKING

According to Bowen family systems theory, the family is "an emotional unit" that "so profoundly affect[s] their members' thoughts, feelings, and actions that it often seems as if people are living under the same 'emotional skin'" (Kerr, 2003). Kerr explains: "People solicit each other's attention, approval, and support and react to each other's needs, expectations, and upsets. The connectedness and reactivity make the functioning of family members interdependent. A change in one person's functioning is predictably followed by reciprocal changes in the functioning of others. Families differ somewhat in the degree of interdependence, but it is always present to some degree."

Sometimes an individual will try to reduce the tension associated with interacting with their family by using a strategy Bowen family systems theory calls "emotional cutoff":

> The concept of emotional cut off describes people managing their unresolved emotional issues with parents, siblings, and other family members by reducing or totally cutting off emotional contact with them. Emotional contact can be reduced by people moving away from their families and rarely going home, or it can be reduced by people staying in physical contact with their families but avoiding sensitive issues. Relationships may look 'better' if people cut off to manage them, but the problems are dormant and not resolved. (Kerr, 2003)

As a palliative care or hospice care professional, you are likely to encounter individuals who have been cut off emotionally from their families of origin, either voluntarily through their own actions or involuntarily through the actions of their family members. In the scenario presented in this chapter, two families—Mary's family of origin and her family of choice—came together at her bedside during an emotionally difficult time, each bringing a unique set of family dynamics that governed the families' respective interactions with Mary. To manage the tension surrounding Mary's sexual orientation and her parents' evangelical Christian religious beliefs, Mary and her parents had cut off contact with each other years before. The issues between them resurfaced as Mary was dying, leading to distress for the patient, her partner, and her parents.

Although you may see estrangement in families of LGBTQIA+ individuals in palliative and hospice care, you are also likely to see it in the families of heterosexual and cisgender people (Lawton, White, & Fromme, 2014; Mazanec & Panke, 2016). When you are working with LGBTQIA+ individuals, don't assume that their parents have disowned them, judged them, or shunned them, and don't assume they have not.

The same holds true when you are working with heterosexual or cisgender individuals: do not make any assumptions about individuals' relationships with their families of origin. Families are like snowflakes: no two are exactly the same. The only way to know what the dynamics in a particular patient's family are like is to ask the patient. Ask not only who their legal decision maker is (e.g., the person they have appointed to serve as their durable power of attorney for health care or is their health care proxy) but also about who they would like to have included—and excluded—from discussions surrounding decisions about their care.

> **AUTHOR'S NOTE**
>
> *My own family is a good example of why you should never make assumptions about a patient's family and the roles of those family members in the shared decision-making process. My mom and dad were a legally married, deeply religious couple, and I was their lesbian daughter living thousands of miles away. It would have been easy to make assumptions about my family and the roles that each of us would play in the decision-making process if one of my parents became ill, but those assumptions would have been wrong. When my mother was dying, I was in my mid-twenties, living in Philadelphia. I went home to Texas to help my father take care of her during the last six weeks of her life.*
>
> *Because my parents were married, my dad would have been the default decision maker for my mother's health care decisions.*

(continued on next page)

(*continued from previous page*)

> *However, my mom had named me as her durable power of attorney (DPOA) for health care because she didn't want my dad to have the burden of making tough decisions about things like forgoing medically administered nutrition and hydration. My dad was fully supportive of my mom's decision to name me as the DPOA for health care, but he wanted to remain involved in the decision-making process—and I really needed his involvement. When my mom became unable to make her own health care decisions, I made those decisions in consultation with my dad, and I made sure that he had a voice in all decisions that were made. Working together, my dad and I were able to ensure that my mom died comfortably and without any futile extraordinary measures. Unfortunately, my mom was on hospice care for only a few days before she died—a common problem. Often individuals get referred to hospice care far too late in the progression of their illness. Had my mom been on hospice care for a longer time, the hospice team would likely have played a role in supporting our family's shared decision-making efforts.*

MAPPING FAMILY DYNAMICS

When you begin working with a new patient, make note of any distinguishing features of the patient's relationships with members of their family of origin and family of choice. Creating a **genogram** is one way to map the emotional relationships within a patient's family constellation (Piasecka, Slusarska, & Drop, 2018; McGoldrick, Gerson, & Petry, 2020). Inexpensive software programs can help you create a genogram quickly and easily, but you can also compile a genogram using pen and paper. When indicating in a genogram that a patient or family member is male or female, record the person's gender rather than sex assigned at birth. Whether or not you draw up a genogram, take the time to ask individuals about the different emotional relationships in their family of origin and family of choice and the communication patterns between the two (Smolinski & Colón, 2011). This information will be incredibly helpful to you as you work to support individuals and families and facilitate effective shared decision making.

KEY POINTS TO REMEMBER

- A fundamental characteristic of both palliative care and hospice care is the central role that shared decision making plays in the care-planning process.
- Shared decision making is firmly rooted in the ethical principles of self-determination and autonomy.
- In hospice and palliative care, shared decision making is a two-sided equation, with the patient and family on one side and the palliative care or hospice care team on the other.
- Shared decision making is not easy or efficient. It takes time and effort to walk a patient and family through the options available to them, and sometimes the only real "intervention" you end up providing is the shared decision-making session itself.
- When working with LGBTQIA+ individuals, do not assume that their parents disowned them, judged them, or shunned them. Do not assume that they didn't. When working with heterosexual or cisgender individuals, the same holds true: do not make any assumptions about their relationships with their families of origin.
- The only way to know what the dynamics are like within a particular patient's family is to ask the patient. Ask questions not only about who will be the legal decision maker (i.e., who has their durable power of attorney for health care or their health care proxy) but also about who they would like to have included—and excluded—from discussions surrounding their health care decisions.
- When you begin working with a new patient, make note of any distinguishing features of the patient's relationship with members of their family of origin and their family of choice.

Creating a genogram is one way to do this. Regardless of whether you draw a genogram, always ask the patient about the different emotional relationships in their family of origin and family of choice.

DISCUSSION QUESTIONS

- Why is it important to think of the first patient encounter as a "family meeting," even if the patient decides not to (or in unable to) include family members in the visit?
- Describe how you would coordinate and facilitate a family meeting focused on shared decision making, starting from your very first meeting with the patient.
- What role does ethics play in shared decision making? Explain the ethical imperative for shared decision making.
- Explain the role of shared decision making in decisions surrounding palliative sedation. What role does your own discipline play in those decisions? If a patient expressed interest in palliative sedation, how do you think you would feel? How would you respond?
- How might shared decision making be made more challenging by family dynamics for LGBTQIA+ individuals?

CHAPTER ACTIVITY

Draw a genogram of the emotional relationships in your family, including members of both your family of origin and your family of choice. After you have drawn your genogram, reflect on what the diagram reveals about the relationships in your family. Would these emotional relationships be immediately apparent to a health care professional who had just met you? Would having an understanding of these relationships be helpful to a palliative care or hospice professional caring for you? Why or why not?

May 29, 2019

GoFundMe post from Kathy Brandt:

"Taco Tuesdays"

There is a saying going around Facebook "It's okay if you fall apart sometimes. Tacos fall apart and we still love them." It's a really great thing that Kim and Grey like tacos. Between the depressants (medical marijuana), steroids, emotional goodbyes we're saying to DC folks before the move, and navigating the depths of sadness I feel about leaving my family—I fall apart on a regular (multiple times a day) basis. It's gotten to the point where it's funny (sort of).

Kim and Grey were worried that the frequent tears were indicative of the fact that I was sad or suffering. Nothing could be farther from the truth. Every day I find joy and good things happen. Some recent examples include:

- Seeing close friends over the week for a DC goodbye
- A lovely send-off from our Quaker family at Friends Meeting of Washington
- Eating homemade cookies made with love from a dear friend
- An hour-long conversation with Grey last night about his record collection, as he played some of his favorite tunes for me
- A very silly conversation with my wife last night when I was feeling the effects of the MMJ pills I took before bed—she was quite amused by me

I think the tears reflect the need to release a bunch of emotions I've never accessed, let alone expressed until recent years. And the tears appear on the regular because that filter we all have that allows us to regulate our emotions has been obliterated by the MMJ. While I am definitely not suffering, the frequent, sudden, and at times random appearance of the tears is causing suffering . . . poor Kim never knows when I'll break down.

Last night, Kim mentioned Ting, a company that provides fiber cable services in Charlottesville and I started bawling—full-on

(continued on next page)

(continued from previous page)

guttural animal wailing. Not surprisingly, Kim was baffled, wondering what caused the floodgates to open this time. Over the past month I've spent way too much time researching cable, TV, and phone providers in Charlottesville and had found the best plan for Kim and Grey. I was ready to commit her to a two-year contract with Comcast but she didn't know any of this. It felt like she wanted to ditch this "gift" I wanted to leave for them—the perfect bundle of services. It really is a silly thing. Yet in that moment it felt huge to me and the emotions were overwhelming.

I don't enjoy all this crying, and I certainly hate traumatizing Kim and Grey with the unpredictability of my emotions, but I'm glad that I can express my feelings now to the ones I love in the time I have left. Tacos for everyone!

kb

6 | Care Planning and Coordination

CHAPTER OUTCOMES

1. Help individuals and their families formulate and track progress toward goals of care and expected outcomes.
2. Ask questions during interdisciplinary/interprofessional team meetings to keep the plan of care focused on patient- and family-centered outcomes.
3. Assess for environmental and safety risks and provide suggestions for modifying a patient's environment to minimize safety risks.

Key Terms: environmental and safety assessment, expected outcomes, goals of care, Patient and Family Outcomes-Focused Inquiry for Interdisciplinary Teams, plan of care

CHAPTER SUMMARY

In palliative care and hospice care, the patient and family (as defined by the patient) are the unit of care, and the plan of care is focused on the patient's and family's goals of care, values, and preferences. Helping individuals and families identify their own goals requires both skill and a commitment to avoiding the temptation to use the "drop-down menu" goals of care provided in many electronic health records. This chapter explains how to help individuals and families identify their own unique goals, how to use a set of key questions to refocus interdisciplinary/interprofessional team meetings on patient- and family-centered outcomes of care, and how to conduct an environmental and safety risk assessment.

In chapter 5 we explored the concept and practice of shared decision making. While it may seem odd to place the chapter about setting goals of care after the chapter on shared decision making, this sequence is intentional. Your work with individuals and families is not strictly linear or sequential—care planning and shared decision making occur contemporaneously; the two concepts are inextricably intertwined. However, having an understanding of shared decision making is foundational to understanding care planning and coordination.

PLAN OF CARE

When a patient begins receiving palliative care or hospice care, the interdisciplinary/interprofessional team puts together a **plan of care** built around the patient's and family's goals. The Five-Dimension Assessment Model (presented in detail in chapter 4) provides a comprehensive list of LGBTQIA-inclusive questions for use during the history-taking process, designed to help elicit the patient's and family's goals of care, values, and preferences. The plan of care should be based on information gathered during the initial assessment:

a. Patient and family understanding of the serious illness, goals of care, treatment preferences, and a review of signed advance directives, if available;

b. A determination of decision-making capacity or identification of the person with legal decision-making authority;

c. A physical examination including identification of current symptoms and functional status;
d. A thorough review of medical records and relevant laboratory and diagnostic test results;
e. A review of the medical history, therapies, recommended treatments, and prognosis;
f. The identification of comorbid medical, cognitive, and psychiatric disorders;
g. A medication reconciliation, including over-the-counter medications;
h. Social determinants of health, including financial vulnerability, housing, nutrition, and safety;
i. Social and cultural factors and caregiving support, including caregiver willingness and capacity to meet patient needs;
j. Patient and family emotional and spiritual concerns, including previous exposure to trauma;
k. The ability of the patient, family, and care providers to communicate with one another effectively, including considerations of language, literacy, hearing, and cultural norms;
l. Patient and family needs related to anticipatory grief, loss, and bereavement, including assessment of family risk for prolonged grief disorder. (National Consensus Project for Quality Palliative Care, 2018)

Essential elements of the care plan include documentation of the "patient's preferences, needs, values, expectations, and goals, as well as the family's concerns" and the ways the patient and family understand the patient's illness (National Consensus Project for Quality Palliative Care, 2018). Equally important to the care-planning process is identifying "the elements of quality of life" in the physical, social, spiritual, and psychological domains and then planning interventions "to alleviate stress in one or any of these domains." The result of the care-planning process is a "care plan . . . based on the identified and expressed preferences, values, goals, and needs of the patient and family and . . . developed with professional guidance and support for patient/family decision making" (National Consensus Project for Quality Palliative Care, 2013). By design, the care plan is not static and unchanging, nor is its development the work of the interdisciplinary team (IDT) alone. On the contrary:

> The IDT develops, implements, and coordinates the care plan in collaboration with the patient and family, other clinicians, and community providers, when indicated and possible. The care plan is always accessible to the patient, IDT, and other involved clinicians and, with the patient's consent, is shared with family, caregivers, and community providers. The care plan is updated and reviewed at regular intervals and when the patient experiences a significant change in status; changes are based on the evolving needs of the patient and family, with recognition of complex, competing, and shifting priorities in goals of care. (National Consensus Project for Quality Palliative Care, 2018)

June 3, 2019

GoFundMe post from Kathy Brandt:

"Coming in Hot"

    I started saying that a few weeks ago and now I can't stop. I picked up the phrase while re-watching the entire Battlestar Galactica (04) series. In the series the pilots often have to land during tricky situations where are flying too fast or be slightly off target. The phrase conveys to the ground crew that it's going to be a messy landing.

    While I generally avoid battle jargon, I can't stop using this phrase. I use it when I stand up and quickly head to the bathroom. Or if one of our dogs is freaking out because there is a fly in the house. Or we might be headed down an exit ramp a little quickly (in my opinion while high in the backseat) and I'll exclaim it in the car.

    Well, "coming in hot" definitely applies to getting us to Maine. The trip started off great, we left really early Friday, Kim did a great job driving and we ended up in Rhode Island as planned Friday afternoon. That's when things started falling apart . . .

I was constipated (which is common with ovarian cancer), the car ride was causing some pain issues in my back, and we realized when we got to the hotel that I had thrush. Yay! What we didn't know at that point was that Grey had picked up a stomach bug, which would hit the next day.

All this to say, Saturday we came into Maine hot! We went to Portland so Grey could find some used records (he did), and we got my haircut. Then we headed to Boothbay and a fun night of me drinking Mag Citrate (again). Kim was a wonder woman, driving the entire trek, providing care and support to Grey and I, getting the groceries, and medications for my thrush. My pacifist Quaker wife was as skilled as any of those combat pilots, getting us safely to our destination and then she also provided the ground support for a safe landing.

None of that matters. The pain, the constipation, etc. It's all a distant memory. We are in Maine. This is huge. For me, Maine is me running around in the sun by the lake as a child, painting someone's old barn as a middle schooler, having bonfires on the beach as a teenager, and enjoying Maine every summer as a "healthy" adult for the past ten years with my family. Maine is sunshine, fog, rain, stunning views, lobster, blueberries, ice cream, games, laughter, love, light, life.

Getting here was an important milestone. Last night I slept 8 straight hours for the first time in weeks. I woke up today in Maine feeling energized and alive.

I know there may be more "bad" days than good, physically, over the next few weeks. I may end up saying "coming in hot" so many times Kim and Grey will ban me from saying it. And if so, that's okay. As long as I am with my family, and I keep this time in Maine in my heart, I'll still be just fine.

Kb

GOALS OF CARE AND EXPECTED OUTCOMES

The patient's and family's **goals of care** and their **expected outcomes** serve as the cornerstones for each plan of care. Goals of care are straightforward, simple statements aligned with the hopes, values, priorities, and fears expressed by the patient and family (Vermont Ethics Network, 2011b). Once you have helped a patient or family member identify a goal, ask follow-up questions that will help them articulate what the successful achievement or outcome of that goal would look like. For example, Mr. Smith might express one of his goals as "I want to get a good night's sleep." Your follow-up questions to Mr. Smith might be:

- What does "a good night's sleep" mean to you? (Mr. Smith's answer: "Six hours without waking up.")
- Are you having trouble falling asleep, staying asleep, or both? (Mr. Smith's answer: "Staying asleep.")
- Is anything in particular waking you up? (Mr. Smith's answer: "Pain—the pain wakes me up every time.")

Expected outcomes—the outcomes of your interventions toward achieving the goal—should be measurable and time-limited; they should state what will happen, and when. To develop an expected outcome aligned with Mr. Smith's goal of a good night's sleep, for example, put together the following components (Austin Community College, n.d.):

- A subject ("Mr. Smith")
- A verb in future tense ("will sleep")
- A condition ("without pain waking him up")
- A criterion ("for at least six consecutive hours")
- A time ("tonight")

Here is how Mr. Smith's goal and expected outcome might align:

Patient's goal: To sleep soundly.
Expected outcome: Mr. Smith will sleep, without pain waking him up, for at least six consecutive hours tonight.

TABLE 6.1 Examples of expected outcomes

Subject	Verb (future tense)	Condition	Criteria	Time
Mr. Smith (the patient)	will sleep	without pain waking him up	for at least six consecutive hours	tonight
Mr. Jones (Mr. Smith's partner)	will attend his Thursday twelve-step meeting	with respite care in the home for Mr. Smith	for two hours (6:00 pm–8:00 pm)	this Thursday
Mr. Smith (the patient)	will urinate	without falling	using a bedside commode	tonight

Table 6.1 provides a few other examples of expected outcomes. As goals of care change over time, your task is to collaborate with the patient, family, and other members of the interdisciplinary/interprofessional team to modify the plan of care to facilitate achieving the revised goals and expected outcomes. If you have been working in the field of palliative care or hospice for a few years, you may have noticed that you are writing down similar goals for care for most of the individuals you work with: "live independently," "remain as pain-free as possible," "achieve remission or cure" (for individuals receiving palliative care), "spend quality time with family and friends," and so on.

While there are certainly some naturally occurring commonalities among individuals and families regarding goals of care, you should try to identify some unique goals for each patient and family you work with. It's easy to fall into a rut, charting the same goals of care over and over again, especially if you use an electronic health record that includes a menu of often-cited goals. Resist the urge to take shortcuts when it comes to goals of care.

When I first started working with individuals struggling with serious or life-limiting illnesses, I had the good fortune to work with mentors who encouraged me to craft patient- and family-specific goals of care in collaboration with the patient, family, and the rest of the interdisciplinary/interprofessional team. The piece that was missing, though, was a tool to help me brainstorm a broad range of goals with the patient and family, inclusive of their sexual orientation, gender identity, and sexual health. Almost twenty years later we still don't have a comprehensive tool like that for use

> **PROFESSIONAL PERSPECTIVE**
>
> *One of the most memorable patients that I took care of in palliative care and subsequently in hospice was a gay man with HIV/AIDS who willfully decided to stop taking antiretroviral therapy because he was "fed up with the world" and "ready to die." The biggest challenge in taking care of him was establishing good rapport. He was mistrustful of the healthcare system at large, owing to his feelings of abandonment and judgment. As an advocate and provider [of] LGBTQ+ medicine, I only wanted what was best for this community [which] collectively has been pushed to the sidelines and not necessarily receive[d] the best quality of care afforded to the general population.*
>
> *One night in the hospice unit, as he was dying, it was found out that not even his mother, his only known family, knew of his illness. Up to the last few moments of his life, he felt alone. I took refuge in hospice being there for him and in a sense became a surrogate support. I was moved by images of a mother grieving and crying at the bedside and a son who felt betrayed by society. I felt like there was a hint of vindication in that he at least received the best medical and psychosocial care possible at that stage of his life. But did he really? The truth is that there continue to be gaps in knowledge and skills in taking care of the palliative care and hospice needs of the seriously ill in the LGBTQ+ community.*
>
> —Noelle Marie Javier MD

by palliative care and hospice teams. With the wide variety of electronic health records in use, proposing a one-size-fits-all tool would be unrealistic. After you have taken a patient's comprehensive history using the questions in the Five-Dimension Assessment Model, revisit the patient's answers and discuss possible goals of care.

You may be thinking that using the Five-Dimension Assessment Model to help individuals and families identify their goals of care will be more time-consuming than the method you're currently using. I would not disagree. This approach to setting goals requires an investment of time on the part of both professional and patient. The result is a plan of care designed to help the interdisciplinary/interprofessional team facilitate the achievement

> **PROFESSIONAL PERSPECTIVE**
>
> *It's important to take the time to search for goals that people are actually motivated to achieve and start there. For example, a person might say that she injured her back and "wishes she had help." As the healthcare provider, we might say then that the goal is to get caregiver assistance. The patient might reply, "John would never allow anyone in the house but our daughter, and she has not been speaking to us lately." Our response: "Would you be willing/able to give her a call to speak with her about it?" Patient's response: "John might not like that." Our response: "Could you speak with John about it?" Patient's response: "Yes." So the goal is not to get a caregiver. The goal is for the patient to speak to her husband about possibilities. All too often we jump to "our end goal," setting people up for the dreaded "noncompliant" label by continuing to ask them, "Have you gotten a caregiver yet?"—overlooking the critical first steps . . . and setting them up for failure."*
>
> —Gary Gardia, LCSW, APHSW-C

of each patient's unique goals. Individuals and families are as unique as fingerprints: their goals of care should be unique as well.

HELPING INDIVIDUALS AND FAMILIES ASSESS PROGRESS

In chapter 4, we walked through the process of coordinating and facilitating the first meeting with a patient and family. The core principles for coordinating and facilitating family meetings remain the same throughout your work with that patient and family:

- The patient and the family (as identified by the patient) are the unit of care.
- Ask each patient, "Whom do you consider to be your family? Who are the people in your life who are sources of emotional support to

you?" Then invite and facilitate the inclusion of those individuals in family meetings.
- Once a patient has identified the people they would like to have present at a family meeting, ask whether any of the individuals need an interpreter or have mobility, hearing, or visual impairments that you should be aware of, so you can ensure their access to and full participation in the family meeting. Enlist the help of the social worker or counselor on your interdisciplinary/interprofessional team to make the necessary arrangements to accommodate the needs of the patient and the family.

During every visit with a patient, as well as during each family meeting, revisit the patient's and family's goals of care, values, and preferences, and assess the progress toward expected outcomes. In palliative care and hospice care, goals should evolve over time to address changes in symptoms, psychosocial and spiritual needs, and caregiving concerns. If you are a registered nurse, physician, advanced practice registered nurse, or physician associate, you're probably well versed in the practice of crafting new goals at each visit. Symptom management is a constantly moving target that requires both nimbleness and vigilance on the part of the clinician. If you are a social worker, counselor, or chaplain, though, you may notice from time to time that you are charting a fairly unchanged set of goals and expected outcomes over the course of weeks or months. If this happens, take a hard look at the way you are conducting assessments during your visits with the patient and family. As a patient's disease progresses, psychosocial and spiritual needs are likely to change—and goals of care should change too.

Interdisciplinary/interprofessional team meetings are the ideal forum in which to explore the evolving nature of the patient's and family's goals and expected outcomes. It is easy to fall into a routine, though, with the APRN, PA, or RN giving a report on the patient's condition and then other team members weighing in with their information. Instead of organizing team meetings around a discipline-by-discipline report on the patient and family, consider using the patient's and family's goals and expected outcomes as the framework for your team discussions. Another approach is to start the interdisciplinary/interprofessional team's discussion with a list of questions

June 9, 2019

GoFundMe post from Kathy Brandt:

I am not a patient person. That's been true my entire life. I have so many memories of sitting by the door as a child, so annoyed that once again I was having to wait for my mother. I've never been a patient driver, I seek opportunities to pass someone, speed up, or quickly turn right on red.

So, it shouldn't surprise me that I'm still impatient. Pretty much every hospice person I know abides by the saying that people "die how they lived." Meaning if someone is sweet and kind in life, they will likely act the same way until they die and if someone was mean and ornery, they'll continue to be that way until they die.

This is a problem. Because my impatience is even worse than it's been my entire life and it's hurting my family. After attending a family event this week—an event I really wanted to go to—Kim, Grey, and I arrived very late to a restaurant to finally eat. It was 9:30 at night—the place wasn't crowded but they were wrapping up a big event and had other patrons still eating. After a few minutes waiting at the hostess station, I asked Kim to check to see if they were still seating people, because no one on the staff said a word to us as we waited. Impatience was creeping onto the scene.

After approximately five minutes we were seated. It took at least 10 minutes before someone took our drink order. Another ten minutes later before the waitress acknowledged us and said she'd be right with us. If they were mobbed, great, then I get that. But she was bringing people their checks and boxing up food. She was chatting and casual and nothing about her was rushed. She could have taken 3 minutes to get our order, so I could eat and go to the hotel and sleep. I was annoyed, and I wasn't about to hide it.

I sound like a child. When did everything in the universe become about me, about fulfilling my immediate need? Kim and Grey just wanted to have a nice dinner. By the time we got back to the hotel the happy mood we had after seeing family was gone. Kim said that

(continued on next page)

> *(continued from previous page)*
>
> in situations like this, she feels like she's trying to control a toddler version of Kim Jong Un—one wrong move and the bomb goes off. The more she tries to control my behavior and reactions, though, the more upset I get. I've lost all control over my physical self. The only thing that's forever mine that cancer can't take away is my free will. Throw fatigue and anxiety and sorrow into the mix and "free will" sometimes looks a lot like a temper tantrum.
>
> This is but one example. Other examples include me yelling, crying, and generally being a brat. I wish I could tell you why I'm so much more impatient and reactive now. (I'm betting the psychosocial professionals in the audience have ideas.) But more than that, I wish I could stop hurting my family during these last precious weeks. They keep telling me they love me, and I know that they do. I just can't help thinking they would suffer a lot less if I could figure out a way to die differently than how I lived.
>
> kb

designed to keep the team focused on outcomes of care. You might also rotate which team member or discipline leads each meeting.

Chapter 4 discussed the Patient and Family Outcomes-Focused Inquiry for Developing Goals for Care, developed from the National Hospice and Palliative Care Organization's recommended outcomes for hospice and palliative care (Institute of Medicine and National Research Council, 2003). Here, table 6.2 builds on that model, providing a framework for discussing patient and family goals for care during interdisciplinary/interprofessional team meetings. If you are part of a palliative care team that uses the case presentation model, consider incorporating some or all of these questions into your team discussions following presentations, as appropriate. To the right of each of the recommended outcomes listed in the table are questions you can ask yourself and other members of the team as you revisit and

TABLE 6.2 Patient and Family Outcomes-Focused Inquiry for Interdisciplinary Teams

Recommended outcomes[a]	Questions to ask interdisciplinary team
Staff will prevent problems associated with coping, grieving, and existential results related to imminence of death [for patients near the end of life]	• What are we doing as a team to prevent problems associated with coping related to the imminence of death? • What, if any, are the patient's and family's goals and expected outcomes for coping with the imminence of death? • What are we doing as a team to prevent problems associated with grieving related to the imminence of death? • What, if any, are the patient's and family's goals and expected outcomes for grieving related to the imminence of death? • What are we doing as a team to prevent problems associated with existential issues related to the imminence of death? • What, if any, are the patient's and family's goals and expected outcomes for existential issues related to the imminence of death?
Staff will support the patient in achieving the optimal level of consciousness	• What are we doing as a team to support the patient in achieving the optimal level of consciousness? • How does the patient define the optimal level of consciousness? • How does the family define the optimal level of consciousness for the patient? • What, if any, are the patient's and family's goals and expected outcomes for achieving the optimal level of consciousness?
Staff will promote adaptive behaviors that are personally effective for the patient and family caregiver	• What are we doing as a team to promote adaptive behaviors that are personally effective for the patient? • What are the specific adaptive behaviors we are promoting? • What, if any, are the patient's and family's goals and expected outcomes related to these adaptive behaviors? • What are we doing to promote adaptive behaviors that are personally effective for the family caregiver? • What are the specific adaptive behaviors we are promoting? • What, if any, are the patient's and family's goals and expected outcomes related to these adaptive behaviors?
Staff will appropriately treat and prevent extension of disease and/or comorbidity **Staff will treat and prevent adverse effects of treatment**	• What are we doing as a team to treat and prevent extension of the disease and/or comorbidity? • What, if any, are the patient's and family's goals and expected outcomes related to the treatment and prevention of extension of disease and/or comorbidity? • What are we doing as a team to treat and prevent adverse effects of treatment? • What, if any, are the patient's and family's goals and expected outcomes related to the treatment and prevention of adverse effects of treatment?

(continued)

TABLE 6.2 *(continued)*

Recommended outcomes[a]	Questions to ask interdisciplinary team
Staff will treat and prevent distressing symptoms in concert with patient's wishes	• What are we doing as a team to treat and prevent distressing symptoms in concert with the patient's wishes? • What are the patient's wishes regarding the treatment and prevention of distressing symptoms? • What symptoms does the patient consider to be distressing? • What symptoms does the family consider to be distressing? • What, if any, are the patient's and family's goals and expected outcomes related to the treatment and prevention of distressing symptoms?
Staff will tailor treatments to patient's and family's functional capacity	• What are we doing as a team to tailor treatments to the patient's functional capacity? • What is the patient's functional capacity? • What are we doing as a team to tailor treatments to the family's functional capacity? • What is the family's functional capacity? • What, if any, are the patient's and family's goals and expected outcomes related to tailoring treatment to their functional capacity?
Staff will prevent crises from arising due to resource deficits	• What are we doing as a team to prevent crises from arising owing to resource deficits? • What are the existing resource deficits? What are the possible crises that may arise if these deficits are not addressed? • What, if any, are the patient's and family's goals and expected outcomes related to preventing crises arising owing to resource deficits?
Staff will respond appropriately to financial, legal, and environment problems that compromise care	• What are we doing as a team to respond appropriately to financial problems that compromise care? • What are the financial problems that could compromise care? • What, if any, are the patient's and family's goals and expected outcomes related to addressing financial problems that could compromise care? • What are we doing as a team to respond appropriately to legal problems that compromise care? • What are the legal problems that could compromise care? • What, if any, are the patient's and family's goals and expected outcomes related to addressing legal problems that could compromise care? • What are we doing as a team to respond appropriately to environmental problems that could compromise care? • What are the environmental problems that could compromise care? • What, if any, are the patient's and family's goals and expected outcomes related to addressing environmental problems that could compromise care?

Staff will treat and prevent coping problems	• What are we doing as a team to treat and prevent the patient's coping problems? • What coping problems exist currently? • What coping problems are anticipated? • What, if any, are the patient's and family's goals and expected outcomes related to treating and preventing the patient's coping problems? • What are we doing as a team to treat and prevent the family's coping problems? • What coping problems exist currently for the family? • What coping problems are anticipated for the family? • What, if any, are the patient's and family's goals and expected outcomes related to treating and preventing the family's coping problems?
Staff will coach the patient and family through normal grieving	• What are we doing as a team to coach the patient through normal grieving? • What, if any, are the patient's and family's goals and expected outcomes related to coaching the patient through normal grieving? • What are we doing as a team to coach the family through normal grieving? • What, if any, are the patient's and family's goals and expected outcomes related to coaching the family through normal grieving?
Staff will assess and respond to anticipatory grief	• What are we doing as a team to assess and respond to the patient's anticipatory grief? • What, if any, are the patient's and family's goals and expected outcomes related to assessing and responding to the patient's anticipatory grief? • What are we doing as a team to assess and respond to the family's anticipatory grief? • What, if any, are the patient's and family's goals and expected outcomes related to assessing and responding to the family's anticipatory grief?
Staff will prevent unnecessary premature death	• What are we doing as a team to prevent unnecessary premature death? • How does the team define "unnecessary premature death"? • How does the patient define it? • How does the family define it? • What, if any, are the patient's and family's goals and expected outcomes related to preventing unnecessary premature death?
Staff will identify opportunities for family members' grief work	• What are we doing as a team to identify opportunities for family members' grief work? • What, if any, are the patient's and family's goals and expected outcomes related to identifying opportunities for family members' grief work?

(continued)

TABLE 6.2 (*continued*)

Recommended outcomes[a]	Questions to ask interdisciplinary team
Staff will assess the potential for complicated grief and respond appropriately	• What are we doing as a team to assess the potential for complicated grief? • What are we doing as a team to respond appropriately to complicated grief? • What, if any, are the patient's and family's goals for assessing and responding to complicated grief?
Staff will assist the family in integrating the memory of their loved one into their lives	• What are we doing as a team to assist the family in integrating the memory of their loved one into their lives? • What, if any, are the patient's and family's goals for integrating the memory of their loved one into their lives?

Source: National Research Council, 2003.
[a] Text under "Recommended outcomes" © National Hospice and Palliative Care Organization and National Academy of Sciences. Reprinted with permission from the National Hospice and Palliative Care Organization and the National Academies Press.

refine the patient's and family's goals of care. These questions constitute the core of what I call the Patient and Family Outcomes-Focused Inquiry for Interdisciplinary Teams.

If you work at one of the rare palliative care or hospice programs that still conducts physician-led interdisciplinary/interprofessional team meetings centered on the physician's or nurse's report, it may take some effort (and patience) to make the switch to structuring team discussions around the Patient and Family Outcomes-Oriented Inquiry framework. When your interdisciplinary/interprofessional team decides to give this approach a try, consider having one member of the team serve as the person who puts the questions before the team. Where team meetings have traditionally been run by the registered nurse, physician, advanced practice registered nurse, or physician associate, try mixing things up a bit by asking the chaplain, social worker, or counselor to serve as the person posing the questions.

If you yourself are a registered nurse, physician, advanced practice registered nurse, or physician associate, you may be feeling a twinge of discomfort at this suggestion. That's understandable given the central role that your discipline has probably played in interdisciplinary/interprofessional team meetings to this point, but it is important to remember that your role will not be diminished by having a member of another discipline pose questions to the team. On the contrary, you may find yourself contributing more substantively to the team discussions because you'll be answering the outcomes-oriented inquiry questions rather than spending your time and energy trying to facilitate the meeting.

ASSESSING AND ADDRESSING ENVIRONMENTAL AND SAFETY RISKS

Risk assessment is easiest when you can view the environment in person, so I will walk you through the process for conducting an in-home risk assessment before explaining how to carry out a risk assessment for a patient you are unable to visit at home.

The purpose of an **environmental and safety assessment** is twofold: to prevent patient falls and other accidents and to facilitate continued independence. Before you begin an environmental and safety assessment, communicate to the patient, and to the family or others living in the home, if present, that you would like their permission to walk through their home in order to identify ways to help them make the home environment safer and easier for the patient to navigate. Make sure to let the patient and family know that you do this with everyone you work with. Once the patient gives you permission to walk through the home, evaluate each room of the house and make notes on an assessment form.

If your palliative care service or hospice program has a standard assessment tool it prefers, use that tool to complete and document your assessment. Otherwise, consider using an assessment tool like the Home Safety Self-Assessment Tool developed by the University of Buffalo (Tomita, 2011). This assessment is short and includes potential interventions for each problem identified. Once you have completed your environmental and safety assessment, circle your recommended interventions on the form and review them with the patient and family. To avoid overwhelming the patient and family, explain which of the interventions you and other members of the team will take care of for them, and when you will do so. Another environmental and safety assessment tool worth checking out is HESTIA (Home Evaluation System with a Triangulating Integrative Approach), a smartphone-based app being developed by a team of researchers with funding from the U.S. Department of Health and Human Services National Institute on Disability, Independent Living, and Rehabilitation Research (University of Wisconsin–Milwaukee, 2022; Pickens et al., 2020; Burns & Pickens, 2017).

Consider proactively reaching out to your organization's volunteer coordinator to see if the coordinator would be open to recruiting volunteer handypersons to help implement the recommended safety interventions in people's homes. Many of the interventions listed on the assessment form are simple tasks—for example, removing rugs, turning down the water heater temperature, and anchoring cords along baseboards. Recruiting and training a cadre of volunteers to address the potential safety risks in people's homes can give prospective volunteers a way to contribute their talents while also providing individuals with a valuable service—one that can facilitate their continued independence.

When you see individuals in a clinic and you are unable to assess their homes directly, you can use the University of Buffalo tool, HESTIA, or your program's preferred assessment tool as a framework for discussing safety risks. For example, you can ask the patient and family whether they have unsafe features in the home—rolling beds, slippery floors, loose throw rugs, and so on—and discuss potential interventions. Alternatively, you can give patients a copy of the assessment form and encourage them to complete it at home and share the results with you at your next meeting. (This is the least desirable of the options, however, because it places the burden of assessment on the person receiving care, and they may feel overwhelmed.)

Regardless of whether you conduct the environmental and safety assessment in person or through discussions with a patient, make sure to follow up with the patient to confirm that the safety risks you identified have been addressed. Assessing and documenting safety risks without later ensuring that those risks have been addressed is unwise; follow-through is essential.

A NOTE ABOUT OXYGEN USE IN THE HOME

When a person uses oxygen in the home, you must pay particular attention to assessing, documenting, and addressing any safety risks you identify. LGBTQIA+ individuals are more likely to be smokers than their cisgender and heterosexual counterparts, and this becomes an issue of particular concern when LGBTQIA+ individuals have oxygen tanks in the house. According to the Centers for Disease Control (2022), "smoking among lesbian, gay, and bisexual adults in the United States is much higher than among heterosexual/straight adults. Nearly 1 in 6 (16.1 percent) of lesbian, gay, and bisexual adults smoke cigarettes, compared with nearly 1 in 8 (12.3 percent) of heterosexual/straight adults. Cigarette smoking is also higher among transgender adults (35.5 percent), than among adults whose gender identity corresponds with their birth sex (cisgender)."

Many individuals, families, and even health care professionals are unaware of the specific precautions that need to be taken to prevent a fire. Every hospice and palliative care professional knows that a patient should not smoke while connected to an oxygen tank, but did you know that it's not enough for the patient to disconnect the oxygen and go into another room in order to smoke safely? It is recommended that individuals wait ten minutes after discontinuing their oxygen and then go outside to smoke—and "even these steps cannot guarantee a person's safety. The safest course of action is to not smoke" (Massachusetts Executive Office of Public Safety, n.d.).

Educate individuals and families about the following precautions, which they should take to ensure their safety (Massachusetts Executive Office of Public Safety, n.d.):

- Do not allow smoking in a home in which oxygen is being used. Smokers should go outside to smoke. If the patient is the smoker, they should wait ten minutes after turning off the oxygen before going outside and smoking. Keep electric razors, hair dryers, matches, candles, lighters, and gas stoves "at least 10 feet from the point where the oxygen comes out" because sparks can start a fire.

- Do not use aerosol sprays, petroleum jelly, lip balm, or oil-based lotions. These products can "spontaneously ignite when exposed to high oxygen concentrations."
- Put a sign on the front door of the home that reads "Oxygen in Use" so emergency responders (including firefighters) will know to take the proper precautions should they need to enter the home.
- Make sure there are working smoke alarms throughout the house and that they have fresh batteries.

PROFESSIONAL PERSPECTIVE

Cynthia was a forty-eight-year-old widowed female with a primary diagnosis of chronic airway obstruction. Cynthia had wounds on her head and forehead from a burn sustained one week prior to hospice admission while staying at her sister's home. Cynthia and family reported that her oxygen concentrator was located too close to the furnace in her sister's house and the tube ignited, burning Cynthia's face. Cynthia was a smoker but denied that she was smoking when her oxygen caught fire. She moved in with her daughter Lisa. Also living in the home were Lisa's partner Melinda, Melinda's mother Norma, and Norma's son Joshua. Approximately one month after her hospice admission, there was an explosion and fire at Cynthia's daughter's home, which resulted in the deaths of Cynthia and Joshua. In addition to the deaths of their family members, Melinda and Lisa lost all of their personal items, even the clothes they had been wearing.

With the support of the Red Cross, a hotel room was found for Lisa and Melinda and clothing was provided, along with counseling support at their hotel room. The hospice's spiritual coordinator, Laurie, who visited Lisa and Melinda at the hotel, recalled that in addition to offering trauma counseling, she affirmed the relationship challenges and other social challenges Lisa and Melinda spoke of in relation to society and their sexual orientation. Laurie also recalled that she affirmed the support and strength they had provided for each other in their individual and shared challenges and how this could be seen as a strength in moving forward.

In this case, a very complicated and traumatic situation could have been made far worse if Melinda and Lisa's relationship was not accepted and honored by the hospice staff. Melinda was an active member of Cynthia's care team and managed her medications while also supporting Lisa, who was struggling emotionally with her own grief and health issues. Our hospice continued support of this couple following the fire tragedy at their home and provided additional counseling to them which both respected and recognized their close relationship as well as their losses.

—Kunga Nyima Drotos, LMSW

KEY POINTS TO REMEMBER

- A plan of care should be "based on the identified and expressed preferences, values, goals, and needs of the patient and family and . . . developed with professional guidance and support for patient/family decision making" (National Consensus Project for Quality Palliative Care, 2013).
- The patient's and family's goals for care and expected outcomes serve as the cornerstones for each plan of care.
- Expected outcomes—the outcomes of your interventions—should be measurable and time-limited: What will happen, and by when?
- Goals and expected outcomes will change over time. Work in collaboration with the patient, family, and other members of the interdisciplinary/interprofessional team to modify the plan of care as needed.
- It's easy to fall into a rut, charting the same goals of care over and over again for every patient. Resist the urge to take shortcuts when it comes to goals of care.
- During every visit with a patient, as well as during each family meeting, revisit the patient's and family's goals of care and assess progress toward expected outcomes.
- Interdisciplinary/interprofessional team meetings are the ideal forum in which to explore the evolving nature of the patient's and family's goals and expected outcomes.

- The Patient and Family Outcomes-Focused Inquiry for Interdisciplinary Teams provides a framework for discussing patient and family goals for care during team meetings. Consider incorporating some or all of these questions into your team discussions, as appropriate.
- The purpose of an environmental and safety assessment is twofold: to prevent falls and other accidents and to facilitate the continued independence of the patient.
- Regardless of whether you conduct the environmental and safety assessment in person or through a discussion with the patient, make sure to follow up with the patient to make sure that risks have been addressed. Assessing and documenting safety risks without documenting that those risks have been addressed is unwise; follow-through is essential.
- If a patient is using oxygen in the home, pay particular attention to assessing, documenting, and addressing any safety risks. Because LGBTQIA+ individuals are more likely to be smokers than their cisgender and heterosexual counterparts, this is an issue of particular concern when working with LGBTQIA+ individuals who use oxygen in the home.
- It is not enough for someone to disconnect their oxygen and go into another room in order to smoke safely. Individuals must wait ten minutes after discontinuing their oxygen and then go outside to smoke—and even these precautions won't guarantee their safety (Massachusetts Executive Office of Public Safety, n.d.).
- Educate the patient and family about the precautions they should take to ensure their safety while using oxygen.

DISCUSSION QUESTIONS

1. What are the qualities of a well-crafted goal for care?
2. Imagine you are meeting with a patient to develop goals of care. Describe how you would help the patient and the patient's family formulate their goals of care and track progress toward expected outcomes.

3. Describe how an interdisciplinary/interprofessional team can stay focused on patient- and family-centered outcomes of care.
4. Imagine you are working with a new patient. How might you assess the patient's environmental and safety risks and provide suggestions for modifying the patient's environment to minimize safety risks?
5. Explain the precautions that individuals, families, and staff need to take when oxygen is being used in the home.

CHAPTER ACTIVITY

Imagine that you have just been diagnosed with a life-threatening illness. Ask a colleague to write down five goals for your care without asking you any questions or talking to you about it. While they are writing down their goals for your care, write down your own five goals of care using the information in this chapter. Compare your goals with the goals written by your colleague. How has this activity changed your thoughts and feelings about the importance of patient-driven goals for care?

June 13, 2019

GoFundMe post from Kathy Brandt:

The cancer is spreading in my abdomen. It's been growing for a while but now I can actually feel the tumors. The masses in my liver are causing increasing pain and discomfort. Fortunately, I've only had a few days with bad pain but when they happen, I'm pretty much glued to the couch all day, relying on my MMJ [medical marijuana] and the other tools in my pain control toolbox. I've decided I don't want to be completely "out of it," so I'll take a little pain if it means I can be fully present with my family.

(continued on next page)

(continued from previous page)

No matter what I do to control my symptoms, though, the underlying cause of those symptoms is increasingly evident: I'm dying. I'm jaundiced (yellow) from the masses in my liver, I get out of breath easily and need a hand as I climb steps or curb cuts. I have trouble getting up from a low sofa. I walk with my hands behind my back now in an attempt to counterbalance the big belly I'm hauling around. I can't walk around for more than 10 minutes without being completely exhausted and winded.

Sometimes I lose my balance because the weight of my abdomen is throwing off my center of gravity. My legs are skinny and my butt has disappeared and I'm rarely hungry and food doesn't taste the same anymore. I know it's a matter of weeks, not months. My family knows it too. I'm hoping to make it to late July, but I know that's a long shot.

I wanted you to know this because, while we post happy photos on social media, the inevitable is happening. Recently two dear friends visited me. They were shocked: I was sicker than they had expected. I don't want anyone else to feel that kind of shock so I'm laying it all out there in case people aren't clear: I'm dying—sooner rather than later. I don't say this because I want people to feel badly—I'm sharing it so that people aren't surprised when the inevitable happens.

kb

7 | Ethical and Legal Issues

CHAPTER OUTCOMES

1. Identify the ethical principles relevant to the provision of palliative care and hospice care.
2. Define and compare advance directive, advance care planning, living will, durable power of attorney for health care, will, POLST/MOLST, and do-not-resuscitate order.
3. List the particular ethical and legal issues that may affect LGBTQIA+ individuals.
4. Describe how to help LGBTQIA+ individuals and their families navigate the ethical and legal issues they may encounter.

Key Terms: advance care planning, advance directive, autonomy, beneficence, do-not-resuscitate order, durable power of attorney for health care, ethical principles, health care power of attorney, justice, living will, nonmaleficence, out-of-hospital/provider/physician/medical order for life-sustaining treatment (POLST/MOLST), will

CHAPTER SUMMARY

Palliative care and hospice professionals have a duty to the individuals and families they work with—of all sexual orientations, gender identities, and gender expressions—to adhere to a core set of ethical principles in carrying out their work. These ethical principles compel them to honor the autonomy of the people they serve. In health care, autonomy is "protected" through the advance care planning process. The surgeon and author Atul Gawande (2014) writes of the true meaning of autonomy in *Being Mortal*: "He moved his line in the sand. This is what it means to have autonomy—you may not control life's circumstances, but getting to be the author of your life means getting to control what you do with them." This chapter provides an overview of the ethical principles that guide practice, the elements of advance care planning, and the legal issues that may affect LGBTQIA+ individuals in particular as they navigate serious and life-threatening illness and seek to remain the authors of their own lives.

None of the following information is intended to constitute legal advice, nor is it my intent to encourage you to provide legal advice to the individuals and families you work with. The information in this chapter is designed to make you aware of some of the ethical and legal issues that LGBTQIA+ individuals and their families may encounter so that you can provide support and guidance within the scope of your professional discipline. For a deeper dive into ethics as they relate to health care delivery, I highly recommend Beauchamp and Childress's (2013) *Principles of Biomedical Ethics*.

ETHICAL PRINCIPLES AND THEIR RELEVANCE TO CARE DELIVERY

Your work as a hospice or palliative care professional should be shaped by the four principles that define your ethical duties to the individuals and families you serve (Beauchamp & Childress, 2013):

- **Autonomy**: Honor the right of individuals to make their own decisions.

- **Beneficence**: Do the best you can for the patient (in ways defined by each individual).
- **Nonmaleficence**: Do not harm individuals or their families.
- **Justice**: Ensure all individuals and families have equitable access to care and treatments.

It can be challenging—one might even argue that it's impossible—to uphold all four ethical principles in equal measure at all times. Imagine you are working with a man who has stage IV lung cancer, brain metastases, and mild cognitive impairment. The patient tells you during your first meeting that, given his limited life expectancy, he plans to continue smoking. The patient has been experiencing severe dyspnea for the past few weeks and uses oxygen at home. You have explained the risks associated with smoking while on oxygen, but the patient insists that he wants to continue to smoke until he dies. The patient assures you he will smoke only outside the home, and only after waiting for ten minutes after he has discontinued his oxygen use. You convey to the patient and his family caregiver that even those precautions will not eliminate the risk of fire, but the patient is unmoved.

In this scenario, there is a clear conflict between following the principles of autonomy and beneficence. Despite your best efforts to convince the patient of the dangers of smoking while on oxygen, the patient is asserting his right to make an autonomous choice to continue to smoke. The patient's cognitive impairment complicates things, however: Can a patient make an autonomous choice under a condition of mild cognitive impairment? Your duty of beneficence compels you to protect the patient and his family from harm. Further complicating things is the fact that your duty of nonmaleficence prevents you from discontinuing the patient's oxygen because that would cause the patient to suffer. How can you reconcile these conflicting principles in a way that meets the needs of the patient while also meeting your need to uphold the ethical principles? Unless a patient lacks the capacity for decision making, upholding the principle of autonomy should be your primary goal, followed closely by the other three ethical principles.

The patient in the scenario described has mild cognitive impairment, but in the opinion of the physician and the rest of the care team, he still has the capacity to make an autonomous decision to continue to smoke. The patient has indicated a willingness to take certain precautions to reduce the risk of fire in the home. In striving to uphold the principle of beneficence, you might meet with the patient and family caregiver together to review the safety concerns and recommended precautions so that everyone is on the same page regarding the risks and precautions being taken in the home. The safety precautions are not simply for the benefit of the patient and family: the principle of beneficence extends to the surrounding community as well. Home oxygen fires result in injuries, death, and loss of property, all of which are harms you should seek to prevent.

June 18, 2019

GoFundMe post from Kathy Brandt:

Family caregivers are heroes. They add the caregiving duties to their already busy lives, learning on the fly, and worrying that they are messing it all up.

I was my mother's caregiver for the last few years of her life. Many of you provided support to me during that time. I thought it was the 2nd hardest job besides being a mother.

For the record, I was a punk. Was it hard? Sure. I had to fly down for emergencies a few times. I had to manage her healthcare, coordinate private duty aides, handle her finances, etc. However, I will tell you that as soon as Tidewell Hospice admitted her, my life got immeasurably less stressed. I could focus more on being her daughter. But before we started hospice it was challenging. And I was a punk.

You know where this is headed, right? You've all seen our crazy updates re: moving, contractors, etc. I have no idea how it has come to pass that Grey and I are in C'Ville.

I married a force of nature. Kim has always been a hard worker, someone ready, willing, and able to take on the next challenge. Need someone to learn about and develop a huge online disaster preparedness curriculum or develop bylaws for a brand new school of nursing? Kim was all over these projects the minute she heard about them. Here's what you don't know about Kim these past few months:

- She's holding down a job while getting ready for her new one
- She has an autoimmune/chronic illness which exhausts her
- She hasn't gotten much sleep since I was diagnosed
- She is trying to learn her new roles on the fly in the middle of all this (a division of duties only works if there is someone to divide with)
- She has had to take over all of the chores by this point
- She hasn't lost her sense of humor
- She's providing incredible emotional support to Grey and I
- She's providing hands-on care to me, which I never had to do for mom

I don't know how she is still standing. And you might think, she should ask for/accept help from others. She literally had everything so scheduled/organized/mapped out, that having helpers would have caused her more stress than doing it herself. And that's what caregivers do: they coordinate details, they work hard, they worry they aren't doing a good enough job, and then they get up and do it all again. Kim is all that, on steroids. I was a punk. Luckily for Grey and I, Kim is not.

kb

[Author's Note: I don't agree with Kathy's choice to use the word *punk* here because it's often used as a homophobic slur. However, that's the word she used when she wrote this.]

ADVANCE CARE PLANNING

When a patient is facing a serious or life-limiting illness, they may be fearful of the uncertain future that lies ahead. Although you can't predict everything the patient is going to experience in the weeks, months, or years to come, you can increase the patient's feeling of control and reduce fear of the unknown by helping with advance care planning. **Advance care planning** is an overarching term used to describe the process of identifying, discussing, and executing plans for future health care decisions. The Institute of Medicine's (2015) report *Dying in America* notes the importance of advance care planning, asserting that "fundamental to the advance care planning process is clear empathetic communication between clinicians and patients, which can lead to shared decision-making." While experts encourage all adults

PROFESSIONAL PERSPECTIVE

Ben and Jeff were a couple who had been together for twenty years. Ben was an art collector and Jeff was a businessman. They lived in a condominium that they had renovated together. Ben was estranged from his family. Ben developed heart failure. He continued active treatment. However, one day he went into heart failure and was admitted to the medical intensive care unit. Jeff visited regularly. Ben's condition declined suddenly and he became unconscious.

Unfortunately, Ben and Jeff had never completed surrogate decision-maker paperwork. Therefore, Jeff was not legally able to make decisions. Contact was made with Ben's family. They came to the intensive care unit to visit Ben once. The healthcare team held a family meeting to discuss comfort measures. Ben's family stated that they had not agreed with Ben's "lifestyle" and they wanted him to suffer. The team stated that, ethically, they needed to treat his heart failure. Again Ben's family stated that they believed allowing him to suffer would help him atone for his sins. The healthcare team explained that their code of ethics mandated appropriate management of pain and symptoms. The family forbade Jeff to visit, stating he had made Ben sin. The team explained that Jeff was Ben's family and had been a support person over the course of his disease. Moreover, Ben had stated he wanted Jeff there.

The family left and never returned, even when Ben died. The team allowed Jeff to see Ben to say good-bye and offered support. As a team, we were united and committed to delivering patient-centered and compassionate care to Ben and Jeff. I think we were stunned by the family's departure.

—*Constance Dahlin, ANP-BC, ACHPN*

to engage in advance care planning conversations, when individuals have a serious or life-limiting illness the planning process can help them clarify and express their goals of care to family and care professionals.

YOUR ROLE IN ADVANCE CARE PLANNING

As a palliative care or hospice professional, your role (in collaboration with other members of the interdisciplinary/interprofessional team) in the advance care planning process consists of four core tasks: (1) identifying the patient's current understanding of the illness; (2) providing the patient with information about treatment options, benefits, and burdens; (3) facilitating discussions between the patient and family regarding the patient's treatment options, preferences, and decisions; and (4) assisting the patient in documenting preferences and decisions in writing. I have intentionally kept the first two tasks focused on the patient (as opposed to both the patient and family) because each patient should be given the opportunity to explore and express treatment options, preferences, and decisions with their health care professional without the presence or influence of family members or other caregivers. Since clinicians gained the ability in 2016 to bill for advance care planning under Medicare, palliative care professionals are well positioned to partner with social workers, counselors, and other members of the team in delivering this valuable service to the individuals and families they serve.

While the patient and family are considered to be the unit of care in hospice and palliative care, there is substantial value in providing individuals with a safe space in which to explore and express their own questions, concerns, and preferences before the patient's family is brought into the conversation. A patient may want to discontinue curative treatment or talk with you about forgoing resuscitation, but they may be reluctant to express that desire in front of their spouse, partner, adult child, or other family member. Whenever possible, talk with the patient one on one. Once you have a clear sense of the patient's wishes, you can facilitate a discussion between the patient and family toward the dual goal of supporting the patient's decisions and assisting the family in understanding and supporting the patient's wishes. The third task, facilitating patient-family discussions, depends on family dynamics and the patient's preferences.

Although there are four core tasks in the advance care planning process, the process is more iterative than linear. Advance care planning is intended to be an ongoing process, supporting patient-identified goals and decisions. It is not uncommon, for example, for individuals who were initially in favor of resuscitation to change their mind as their condition worsens. Likewise, individuals who were strongly opposed to receiving medically administered nutrition or hydration when they were first diagnosed may change their mind if there is a major life event (e.g., birth of a grandchild, wedding, graduation) they are trying to live long enough to witness. As conditions and circumstances change, patients' wishes and decisions may, and often do, evolve. (Note: When individuals state in their advance directive that they want to receive medically administered nutrition and hydration and a hospice program is unwilling or unable to provide that service, it would be unethical for that hospice to admit them.)

Palliative and hospice care professionals weave the first two tasks into regular goals-of-care discussions, to affirm the patient's understanding of the illness and provide treatment options. If a patient's goals of care or treatment choices change, then additional patient and family discussions may be needed.

_____ June 24, 2019

GoFundMe post from Kim Acquaviva:

I've always been a thank you note writer. My mom made me write thank you notes as soon as I could scribble words on paper. Kathy and I passed along the same tradition with Greyson, modifying it slightly because of the hand tics that make it painful for him to write with a pen or pencil. Now that he's 19, Greyson usually remembers to send Paperless Post thank you notes when he receives gifts.

> I don't think I've sent a single thank you note in the 5 months since Kathy's diagnosis—and I've felt guilty about that pretty much every day. Hundreds of people have donated to the GoFundMe or sent us ice cream or made us meals or shipped us cookies or knit Kathy a shawl or done a million other kind and loving things to support our family. And I haven't written a single thank you note. I couldn't find words to explain the feelings driving this lapse in manners until this morning.
>
> Every day for the past five months, I've felt like I've been treading water in the middle of a vast ocean. Rescue helicopters pass overhead daily, dropping cookies and ice cream and water and home-cooked meals directly into my mouth. The helicopter can't pull me out of the water, though—the seas are too rough. So I keep treading water, flutter-kicking my legs and churning my cupped hands through the choppy water. Periodically the helicopter drops waterproof blank note cards and a pen and I think to myself, "If I write a thank you note today I'll have to use both hands and then I'll drown." So I keep treading water and feeling guilty about not sending thank you notes. But I know I made the right choice because seriously—who wants a thank you note from someone who had to drown in order to write it?
>
> Thank you for your love and understanding. The absence of a thank you note in your mailbox isn't rudeness—it's evidence that our family is still afloat, thanks to your support. ♥
>
> Kim

ADVANCE CARE PLANNING DOCUMENTS

As a palliative care or hospice professional, you may already be familiar with the different kinds of documents and processes involved in advance care planning. Following is a quick refresher for professionals who are less familiar with advance care documents.

Advance directive "is both an umbrella term for defining and expressing how one wants to live and be treated and for state approved advance directive documents which allow you to specify those things and usually to appoint a person (healthcare power of attorney) to speak when you are unable to speak for yourself" (National Hospice and Palliative Care Organization, n.d.a).

State regulations guide the execution and implementation of advance directives, with some states detailing the specific content and format of each document. Some states—California is one—use the term *advance healthcare directive* to describe a document that combines a health care power of attorney and a living will.

A **health care power of attorney** (also called a **durable power of attorney for health care**) specifies the individual—sometimes referred to as the health care agent, health care proxy, or health care surrogate—authorized by the patient to make health care decisions in the event that the patient is no longer capable of communicating treatment decisions to health care professionals. The power of attorney (POA) document typically names a primary decision maker and also an alternate decision maker who is authorized to make decisions in the event the primary person is unable to fulfill that role. The decision maker can be the person's spouse, adult child, another relative, or a close friend. State laws govern the restrictions regarding who can serve as the POA, including prohibitions against health care professionals or paid caregivers serving in that role.

An individual appointed to serve as a health care POA is authorized to make medical decisions only in the event the patient is temporarily or permanently incapacitated owing to an illness or accident. Unlike a legal or financial power of attorney, the health care POA authorizes that individual to make only medical decisions on the patient's behalf. Similarly, a person holding legal or financial power of attorney is authorized to make only legal or financial decisions and does not have the authority to make medical decisions for a patient. When a patient does not have a documented health care POA, state law specifies the person authorized to make medical decisions for the patient—the default decision maker.

Each state delineates a list of default surrogate decision makers, in hierarchical order, so that health care professionals in that state can determine who is authorized to make decisions. (This person is sometimes referred to as the "next of kin.") Typically, the first default decision maker is the person's legally recognized spouse. In the absence of a spouse, the next person listed varies depending on state statutes but is typically a person related to the patient (Williamson, Lesandrini, & Kamdar, 2016; Wynn, 2014).

Having a health care POA is extremely important for unmarried LGBTQIA+ individuals, especially for those who are estranged from one or more family members. Unmarried life partners can be excluded from the decision-making process, or even prevented from seeing the patient, at the discretion of the default decision maker. Therefore, the ethical principles of autonomy and beneficence dictate that health care professionals must educate the patient and family of choice about the importance of executing a health care power of attorney.

A **living will** enables individuals to codify in writing the specific treatments they do or do not want to receive in the event they become unable to communicate their wishes. Although a written living will is the most commonly encountered form, the Institute of Medicine (2015) gives a broader definition: "A written or video statement about the kind of medical care a person does or does not want under certain specific conditions if no longer able to express those wishes." Several digital and video advance directive options are currently available (National Hospice and Palliative Care Organization, n.d.b). The types of treatments outlined in a living will may include, but are not limited to, cardiopulmonary resuscitation (CPR), medically administered nutrition or hydration, antibiotics, surgery, and use of a ventilator.

Individuals and families should be able to obtain forms for a living will from your palliative care or hospice program; they can also obtain them from their local area agency on aging (see, for example, www.eldercare.gov), from their state health department, from the organization Aging with Dignity (https://www.agingwithdignity.org/five-wishes), and from CaringInfo, a program of the National Hospice and Palliative Care Organization (www.caringinfo.org). The Conversation Project (www.theconversationproject.org) offers free, downloadable "starter kits" that can be helpful for individuals and families before they begin the process of completing a living will.

Many states allow individuals to include supplementary instructions about a particular treatment that they wish to allow only for a specified period of time. For example, a patient may opt to be placed on a ventilator for a short period of time in the event of an acute crisis so long as the ventilator is discontinued if the patient cannot survive without mechanical ventilation. Or they may specifically request palliative or hospice care in the living will so their health care professionals will make a referral to palliative or hospice care.

If a patient has a living will and a health care power of attorney, these must be documented in the medical record. In the absence of a living will, the health care professionals must rely on the individual designated in the health care power of attorney or a default decision maker to make decisions if the patient is incapacitated. If decision makers are unavailable, then health care professionals are required to provide life-sustaining treatments. Without a health care power of attorney and a living will, a patient may receive treatment that is unwanted and that can potentially lead to prolonged suffering. For example, individuals with dementia who are given medically administered nutrition and hydration while they are actively dying may suffer discomfort as the body works to process the nutrients when its systems are shutting down.

A **do-not-resuscitate (DNR) order**, sometimes called a **do-not-attempt-resuscitation (DNAR) order** or **allow-natural-death (AND) order**, is a signed medical order that instructs health care professionals not to perform cardiopulmonary resuscitation (CPR) if the patient stops breathing or the patient's heart stops beating. While individuals can request a DNR either verbally or in their living will, a health care practitioner must sign the order and place it in the patient's medical record. Congruent with the principle of autonomy, the health care practitioner should contact the patient or decision maker to confirm that a DNR is desired before writing the order.

An **out-of-hospital/provider/physician/medical order for life-sustaining treatment (POLST/MOLST)** varies from state to state in name, format, and powers, but in general it "provides medical orders for current treatment" for "persons with serious illness." The POLST form "complements the Advance Directive and is not intended to replace it. An Advance Directive is necessary to appoint a legal health care representative and provide instructions for future life-sustaining treatments" (National POLST Paradigm, n.d.).

Individuals and families are sometimes confused about the difference between a health care power of attorney and a legal or financial power of attorney. Again, the individual designated by a patient to serve as their health care power of attorney is authorized to make only health care decisions—decisions a person given legal or financial power of attorney would be unable to make. If a patient tells you they have completed a health care power of attorney, ask for a copy for the patient's chart or medical record and make sure that team members from all shifts are aware of the designated decision maker. If the document the patient gives you is actually a legal or financial power of attorney, return it and offer to walk the patient through completing a health care power of attorney.

Individuals and families also get confused about the difference between a living will and a **will** (or last will and testament). A living will is a document expressing a patient's health care treatment preferences. In contrast, a last will and testament is a financial document that allows individuals to plan who receives their financial assets and property (National Hospice and Palliative Care Organization, 2016).

As with a health care power of attorney, if a patient says they have a living will, ask to make a copy of it for the chart or medical record. If the document the patient gives you is actually a will, give it back and ask if you can help by walking the patient through the process of completing a living will.

HELPING LGBTQIA+ INDIVIDUALS NAVIGATE LEGAL ISSUES

Within the context of a serious or life-limiting illness, LGBTQIA+ individuals and their families may encounter difficulty with legal issues in three overarching areas: health care decision making, disposition of remains, property ownership, and permanency planning. These issues are not unique to LGBTQIA+ individuals, and you should be aware of them as you begin working with any new patient and family. LGBTQIA+ individuals who want to create legal documents without hiring an attorney can often do so online. However, individuals and families who have complex legal and/or financial issues and concerns should be encouraged to consult with an attorney for guidance.

Health Care Decision Making

In the absence of a properly executed advance directive such as a health care power of attorney, the right to make decisions for a patient who is incapable of making decisions autonomously generally falls to a legal spouse and then to other relatives, although the default hierarchy varies from state to state. Individuals may be in a long-term relationship that they consider to be a marriage, but in the absence of a marriage certificate, that relationship may not be legally recognized. This is true whether the relationship is between two men, two women, or a man and a woman.

Never assume that words like *married*, *spouse*, *husband*, and *wife* mean that a relationship has been formalized legally. When individuals use terms like these to refer to a person who is significant to them, follow up, in a way that is both nonjudgmental and affirming, to ascertain whether the relationship has been formalized legally. For example, you might say something like this to a patient: "I want to make sure you have the documents you need to

---

June 30, 2019

GoFundMe post from Kathy Brandt

Anytime a meeting is cancelled or ends early, someone typically makes a comment about being given "the gift of time." But can you really give or get time as a gift?

This week I met with the fabulous Dr Leslie Blackhall, Director of UVA's palliative care program. She did an assessment, we talked about my goals and symptoms, she tweaked a few medications, and she was great.

For the past month or so, Kim and I have been fairly certain I'm going to die around my birthday in mid-July. I'm weaker, I get short of breath easily, I'm coughing more, and I have to take more MMJ [medical marijuana] pills now to keep the pain under control. I need more assistance with my activities of daily living (ADLs) now, so

Kim helps me get dressed and she's installed a shower chair. Walking up the front stairs of our new home, I have to pull myself up by using the railing. And outings like a trip to the movie theatre require the use of a wheelchair.

I know how I feel these days but I was curious as to Leslie's "prediction" of how much longer I'd live based on my symptoms. A side note: Kim wondered before the visit why I cared how long Leslie thinks I have left. It's a valid question. Somehow hearing it from a palliative care physician felt more "official" than our musings. Anyway, Leslie told us she thought I had a few more months. Months?!! I was given the gift of time. Wow! Woo hoo!!! I'll have more time with Kim and Greyson and my family and friends. This is great! And then the reality hit. If I live longer:

- We have to arrange for my caregiving when Kim starts work on August 1st—Grey will be home during August, but depending on my symptoms it may be too much for him for manage alone while Kim's in the office.
- Grey goes back to college at the end of August—if I'm still alive, that means starting in September I'll be home with the dogs alone all day unless Kim comes home for lunch.
- How will we afford caregivers or other supports to keep me home while Kim works? I haven't worked in 5 months and one salary won't cover my care needs (medical supplies, co-pays, and MMJ) and our bills.
- What TV shows can I binge to fill the time each day? When Kim's working or walking I typically watch TV to pass the time. I'm done with The Blacklist (Thanks Pauline!), I need ideas!

In addition to the above, it's a mind-altering experience to be certain you'll be dead by August and then be told actually you might see September too. I'm happy, but as you can see from my list above, also stressed about what it all means. I'll take the time, if it really can be given to me, and I'll revel in it with Kim and Grey. We'll figure out the logistics, I'm sure. And I'll keep breathing and living, one day at a time, until I can't.

kb

protect your right to involve [name of individual] in your care. Sometimes couples choose to formalize their relationship through a legally recognized process such as a marriage or domestic partnership. If you have not done that, don't worry—there are easy ways I can help you put things in writing if you choose to, so that [name of individual] or someone else can act on your behalf if need be." Let the patient know you are asking about the relationship not out of curiosity but to help you better understand who the patient's default decision maker will be if there is no health care power of attorney on file.

Disposition of Remains

A patient's death can clearly be very upsetting to caregivers, other family members, and friends. Conflict over the patient's remains can compound the distress experienced by all those involved. A funeral directive or disposition-of-remains directive is a tool that can ensure that the wishes of the patient are honored after death. The potential consequences of forgoing a funeral directive for LGBTQIA+ individuals can be substantial:

> If [patients do] not record [their] wishes in a legal document, the law defaults to the person or people [their] state defines as [their] "next of kin" to make these decisions for [them]—usually a blood relative. If [patients have] a spouse or registered domestic partner legally recognized in [their] state or the state where the death occurs, that person probably will stand ahead of [the patient's] blood relatives. [Patients will] want to establish who will be in charge, and also make [their] wishes about the arrangements clear in writing so as to prevent arguments. If [patients do] not leave binding written instructions, someone [they] haven't chosen could decide everything from whether [their] organs will be donated to whether [they] will be buried or cremated, from what [their] memorial service will be to the clothing [they] will be buried in, from the language [on their] headstone to how [their] gender identity is listed in an obituary. (Lambda Legal, 2014).

When working with transgender individuals, it is vitally important that you encourage them to put their wishes in writing in the form of a funeral directive. Although this document may seem redundant if disposition of remains is covered in a durable power of attorney, will, or other legal document, legal complexities are such that redundancy may be wise in order to allay individuals' concerns about how they will be dressed, referred to, and honored after their death. Individuals do not need to hire a lawyer to draw up a funeral directive. A funeral directive can be written by the patient, then signed and dated in the presence of a notary public (Lambda Legal, 2014).

A few states have passed laws to make it easier for transgender individuals to ensure their identity will be respected on their death certificates. In 2014, California passed the Respect After Death Act (AB 1577) requiring that "the official responsible for completing a transgender person's death certificate to do so in a manner that reflects the person's gender identity if they are presented appropriate documentation, such as written instructions from the deceased person confirming their wishes, an updated birth certificate or driver's license, or evidence of medical treatment for gender transition" (Transgender Law Center, 2014). California passed legislation in 2021 that expanded the protections of the Respect After Death Act by "authoriz[ing] a person completing a death certificate to record the decedent's gender identity as female, male, or nonbinary" (Bautista, 2022). In January 2020, the New York City Department of Health started including "X" as an option on death certificates in an effort to "to make every possible attempt to record a gender identity on death certificates consistent with the wishes of the decedent . . . based on knowledge of the person or documentation including, but not limited to: an amended birth certificate indicating different sex than sex assigned at birth; a statement from the decedent during life requesting a change of birth certificate to different from sex assigned at birth; and medical records indicating self-identification as gender identity differing than sex assigned at birth, as well as other records" (New York City Department of Health, 2019).

Although laws like the ones in California and New York City are a move in the right direction, the documentation requirements may be a barrier for some transgender individuals:

> These reforms are a start, but they don't go far enough. Many trans and nonbinary people do not have the resources to legally change their identity on their driver's license, birth certificate or social security card. These

are the documents that many death investigators use—along with a physical examination—to determine the dead person's sex. Right now, there is no national requirement that death investigators learn how to capture gender identity. In many states, including Oregon, funeral directors enter the final sex designation on death certificates, but next of kin, who may not support the dead person's gender identity, have the final say and can tell funeral director what to enter. This process is known as "nonconsensual detransitioning." (Repp, 2022)

A study conducted by a Repp and colleagues in the Portland, Oregon metropolitan area found than more than half of the transgender and nonbinary people whose deaths were investigated by the medical examiner's office between January 2011 and September 2021 were misgendered on their death certificates (Walters, Mew, & Repp, 2023). Since conducting the study, Repp (2022) has called for several national reforms to address this issue:

- Laws that mandate recording of gender identity on death certificates.
- Fields on death certificates and case management systems that allow for gender identity to be recorded in place of, or in addition to, sex assigned at birth.
- Mandatory training for death investigators and funeral directors on how and why to collect gender identity information.
- Laws that give funeral directors the power to use gender identifying documentation enacted by the decedent prior to death, rather than relying solely on the opinion of the next of kin.

Find out about the laws in the state where you work and advocate for changes to protect the rights of patients to have their gender identity affirmed on their death certificate.

Property Ownership

The third area in which LGBTQIA+ individuals and their families may encounter legal issues is property ownership. If a patient shares a home with a partner or friend who is not their legal spouse, beneficiary, or joint tenant, upon the death of the patient there is nothing to protect the partner or friend from being put out on the street by the patient's biological family. A less extreme outcome, but still distressing to a grieving partner or friend, could be the removal of jewelry, mementos, artwork, furniture, photo albums, computers, and other personal property from the home by members of the patient's biological family. Unfortunately, a "same-sex partner or a friend not named as a beneficiary in a Will, or as a joint tenant on a property deed or in trust, could find all the property belonging to the deceased going to the deceased's children, parents, siblings or other biological family members against the deceased's intention" (Wenzel, 2015). When you are working with a person who is lesbian, gay, bisexual, transgender, nonbinary, gender nonconforming, queer, questioning, intersex, and/or asexual, be aware of the possibility that the individual and their caregiver may be anxious about something like this happening to them. Anticipatory grief can be complicated by worries about impending conflicts over property, so connect the patient and caregiver with the resources they need to put their legal affairs in order.

LAMBDA LEGAL'S CHECKLIST FOR FUNERAL PLANNING

- Who should have authority over your remains?
- Do you wish to be an organ donor? If so, have you indicated that on your driver's license? In your health care proxy and/or funeral directive? Do you wish to make any restrictions on the organs available for donation, and are those wishes documented?
- Who should have authority to make funeral-related decisions?
- Do you have wishes for a particular funeral home and how much money should be spent? Do you have particular wishes for a casket?
- Do you want a wake or "viewing"? If so, do you have preferences as to whether your casket is open or closed, or what clothing and makeup should be used?

(continued on next page)

(*continued from previous page*)

- Do you want cremation?
- Do you want burial, regardless of whether or not you are cremated?
- Do you have strong feelings about what should happen at your memorial service? Do you want your service to invoke a religious tradition?
- Do you have wishes about a particular cemetery, headstone, and maintenance of the plot, or about some alternative way that you wish to be remembered in the future?
- If you have a spouse or partner, how do you want that person described in your obituary? How would you like your gender identity described and what name and pronouns should be used? Do you have any other specific wishes for how you and your life are described?

From Lambda Legal 2014. Reprinted with permission. © 2014 Lambda Legal.

Permanency Planning

The fourth area in which LGBTQIA+ individuals and their families may encounter legal issues is permanency planning for minor children. If a patient is the legal parent or guardian of a child by birth, adoption, surrogacy, or fostering, plans need to be put in place sooner rather than later to ensure that the child will be cared for upon the death of the patient. If the patient is coparenting with someone who is not their legal spouse and/or who is not also a legal parent or guardian of the child, legal paperwork needs to be put in place to prevent the child from being removed from the home by the patient's biological family upon the patient's death.

WHO NEEDS TO KNOW? ENSURING CONFIDENTIALITY

During the care planning and coordination process, you will probably be communicating with a variety of professionals and laypeople outside your interdisciplinary/interprofessional team. In the course of providing

PROFESSIONAL PERSPECTIVE

The hospice where I work admitted Jim, an elderly married man with a primary diagnosis of a stroke. Jim lived at an independent living center and was supported by his spouse, Bob. Jim and Bob had been together for fifty-seven years but had just been married the week before Jim was admitted to hospice. Their marriage was made possible by the Supreme Court decision a few weeks earlier in support of same-sex marriages. Bob reported that Jim had grown up in Battle Creek, and they met when Jim's car broke down at a rest area off the highway and Bob gave him a ride home. Bob reported that getting married after fifty-seven years together was purely a business decision to protect their assets from family members who might not respect their relationship, or their wills. Specifically, Bob stated that there were several lawyers in the family who might try to contest Jim's will. Jim had a sister in a city a few hours away, but the couple had no local family support. Jim was unable to provide any personal information to hospice staff, owing to the effects of his stroke. Bob stated that he and his spouse used to enjoy having dinner with friends and throwing large parties several times a year. Since Jim's decline and the couple's relocation to an assisted living facility, Bob was mainly supported by phone contact with friends who lived out of town and by some local friends at the facility. Jim and Bob were at higher risk for bereavement issues because they had limited family support as well as stress related to concerns that family members would contest Jim's dying wishes. Their right to marry was a contested issue, and the media at the time were saturated with stories and opinions both in support of and against same-sex marriage. Bob and Jim lived in a small, conservative community where there were no bereavement support groups for same-sex couples.

—Kunga Nyima Drotos, LMSW

and coordinating care, you might interact with the patient's primary care professional, spiritual adviser, counselor or therapist, family members, friends, and neighbors, among others. The Health Insurance Portability and Accountability Act (known as HIPAA) prohibits you from disclosing a patient's "protected health information" (including sexual orientation, sex assigned at birth, and gender identity) without the patient's permission, except in certain situations outlined in the law. In general, you should not share such information outside the interdisciplinary/interprofessional team without the patient's permission, even if HIPAA allows such disclosures.

When individuals' sex assigned at birth and gender identity do not align, your use of their pronouns may inadvertently "out" them to friends and family. When individuals tell you which gender pronouns they prefer, ask them if there is anyone with whom you should avoid using those pronouns. For example, a patient who was assigned female at birth and is a man may not want to be referred to as "he" or "him" in front of his parents. Do not assume this is the case, however: a transgender patient's family of origin may be completely accepting of the patient's gender identity.

Information about sex assigned at birth should be shared only with individuals who have a clinical need to know that information. For example, a home health aide making a home visit to assist a patient with bathing should be informed if the patient's sex assigned at birth and gender identity do not align. Ideally, home health aides should be able to deliver high-quality patient care to transgender individuals without getting a heads-up before their interaction with the patient, but the reality is that not all home health aides have had the benefit of education regarding the care of transgender individuals. Transgender individuals should never be made to feel as though they are their health care professional's "teachable moment," nor should transgender individuals be subjected to care from a professional who acts shocked or flummoxed by the appearance of a patient's genitals. (This principle extends to the care of all individuals in palliative care and hospice care.)

It is difficult to imagine a situation in which it would be clinically relevant to share information about a patient's sexual orientation with individuals outside the interdisciplinary/interprofessional team. More likely to occur are inadvertent disclosures resulting from making reference to a patient's partner. If the patient self-identifies as lesbian, gay, or bisexual and is currently with a partner, ask if there is anyone with whom you should avoid making reference to that partner. Regardless of whether they are currently with a partner, if individuals self-identify as lesbian, gay, or bisexual, ask them if there are any significant individuals in their life who are unaware of their sexual orientation. It's important for individuals to be able to trust that you will maintain confidentiality and prevent information about their sexual orientation from being disclosed inappropriately.

When in doubt about whether a particular disclosure is both necessary and appropriate, ask yourself the following questions:

- Can the patient receive the best care possible without this information being disclosed?
- If I do not disclose this information to a professional, could the patient be subjected to insensitive or poor-quality care by that professional? If so, is there a way I can prevent the patient from being subjected to insensitive or poor-quality care without disclosing the information?
- Am I disclosing this information to meet my own needs or the needs of the patient?
- Does the patient want this information to be disclosed? How do I know that?

KEY POINTS TO REMEMBER

- Your duty to the individuals and families you work with—of all sexual orientations, gender identities, and gender expressions—is to adhere to a core set of ethical principles in carrying out your work. These ethical principles compel you to honor the autonomy of the people you serve. In health care, autonomy should be supported and protected through the advance care planning process.
- As a hospice or palliative care professional, your work should be shaped by the four principles that define your ethical duties to the individuals and families you serve: autonomy, beneficence, nonmaleficence, and justice.
- Although you can't predict everything a patient is going to experience in the weeks, months, or years to come, you can increase

individuals' sense of control and reduce their fear of the unknown by helping them with advance care planning.

- Advance care planning is intended to be an ongoing process, supporting patient-identified goals and decisions. As individuals' conditions and circumstances change, their wishes and decisions may, and often do, evolve.
- Appointing a health care POA is extremely important for unmarried LGBTQIA+ individuals, especially those who are estranged from one or more family members. The ethical principles of autonomy and beneficence dictate that health care professionals must educate the patient and family of choice about the importance of executing a health care power of attorney.
- Within the context of a serious or life-limiting illness, LGBTQIA+ individuals and their families may encounter difficulty with legal issues in four overarching areas: health care decision making, disposition of remains, and property ownership. These issues are not unique to LGBTQIA+ individuals and their families, and you should be aware of these issues as you begin working with any new patient and family.
- HIPAA prohibits you from disclosing a patient's "protected health information" (including sexual orientation, sex assigned at birth, and gender identity) without the patient's permission, except in certain situations outlined in the law. In general, you should not share such information outside the interdisciplinary/interprofessional team without the patient's permission, even if HIPAA allows such disclosures.
- When individuals' sex assigned at birth and gender identity do not align, your use of their pronouns may inadvertently "out" them to friends and family. When individuals tell you their pronouns, ask them if there is anyone with whom you should avoid using those pronouns.
- Information about sex assigned at birth should be shared only with individuals who have a clinical need to know that information.

DISCUSSION QUESTIONS

1. What are the ethical principles relevant to the provision of palliative care and hospice care? Which of these ethical principles do you think are the most important? Which do you think are the most difficult to uphold?
2. Advance directive documents can be confusing even to experienced health care professionals—it's not surprising that professionals new to the field might be confused. Imagine that you are working with a recent graduate in your discipline who has asked you to explain the following concepts: advance directive, advance care planning, living will, durable power of attorney for health care, POLST/ MOLST, and DNR order. What would you say?
3. What are some of the ethical and legal issues that may affect LGBTQIA+ individuals in particular in palliative and hospice care?
4. Describe how you would help an LGBTQIA+ patient and family navigate the ethical and legal issues they might encounter when facing a serious or life-threatening illness.
5. When is disclosing a patient's "protected health information" (including sexual orientation, sex assigned at birth, and gender identity) permitted? How might the use of gendered pronouns constitute a breach of HIPAA?

CHAPTER ACTIVITY

Complete a living will and a durable power of attorney for health care using free resources available on the internet. Make sure the forms you use are valid in the state in which you live. Share the documents with your primary care professional as well as with at least one member of your family. After you have completed the documents, reflect on what the process was like for you. Was it easier or harder than you had anticipated? How do you think your choices and preferences might change over the course of your lifetime? How often do you think you might revisit (and, if necessary, revise) these documents?

July 11, 2019

GoFundMe post from Kathy Brandt:

I'm ready.

Over the past few days I've decided I'm ready to die. That may sound like I've given up or want to die. That isn't the case. I'll try to describe it.

For me I think the transition started last week. We went to dinner and when we got home, I struggled mightily to get up the 5 steps to our front door. And to do so, I had to pull myself up using the banister, which was painful. I told Kim a few days later that I didn't think I'd leave the house again. Then I had another episode of having to drink Magnesium Citrate, reminding me that my bowels are still capable of bringing me down.

My pain is worse. My side hurts all the time and when I cough sometimes it hurts a lot. It's taking much higher doses of MMJ to keep my pain under control. I want to be awake enough to enjoy time with my family so I know I'm under-treating my pain. I started a new medicine on Friday—olanzapine—that's helped a lot with my nausea, anxiety, and emotionality. But weird new symptoms keep popping up. The latest one: genital lymphedema. (Kim has decided my drag queen name is "Puffy Pudenda"). Is this TMI [too much information]? Probably. But I want people to know that dying isn't like a Lifetime movie. It's weird and your body betrays you and you're constantly having to adjust.

Kim gives me a shower now and she does my nightly shots. I use a walker to go from the sofa to the bathroom and I keep a waterproof pad under me all the time because I keep feeling as though I'm going to pee myself but I never do. I'm constantly bracing myself for my body's betrayals.

The physical issues exist apart from and yet are linked to how I am experiencing my illness. Physically my symptoms can be managed and I can be kept comfortable. Emotionally each of the issues represents my march toward death. And while I've said "I'm ready" in the abstract when talking about my illness and death, now I really am.

I'm not ready to leave Greyson and Kim, and yet I am. I love them with all my heart and already feel some separation between us. I'm the outside observer at times watching them live their lives without me.

My ex-sister-in-law, Terri, and two nieces visited this week, [which] was wonderful. Before they left, Terri gave me the most amazing gift, through her goodbye "prayer" with me. I feel good about our goodbye.

I've been lucky enough to collect an odd assortment of friends. I've had visitors, calls, and messages from countless friends, from each area of my life. I feel the love and it is so appreciated. I'm not depressed. My symptoms are managed well. I'm just done being here.

I have no doubt that I could keep going, push to live longer. The question is for whom or why would I do that? Kim and Grey are ok. They'll be sad no matter [when] I die. You will all be ok when I die. So why linger, why not verbalize that I'm ready to go.

I'm ready.

kb

8 Patient and Family Education and Advocacy

CHAPTER OUTCOMES

1. Assess knowledge of patient care and teach patient-care skills.
2. Assess knowledge and teach individuals and caregivers about end-stage disease progression.
3. Assess knowledge and teach individuals and caregivers about pain and symptom management.
4. Assess knowledge and teach individuals and caregivers about medication management.
5. Assess knowledge and teach individuals and caregivers about disposal of supplies.
6. Assess knowledge and teach individuals and caregivers about the signs and symptoms of imminent death.

Key Terms: disposal of supplies, end-stage disease progression, medication management, medication reconciliation, pain and symptom management, patient-care skills, signs and symptoms of imminent death

CHAPTER SUMMARY

Patient and family education is an essential part of delivering quality care (Institute of Medicine, 2013). Education is an integral part of the work that advanced practice registered nurses, physician associates, physicians, registered nurses, chaplains, social workers, and counselors do with individuals and families. This chapter provides palliative care and hospice professionals with specific, actionable strategies for teaching individuals and families (including but not limited to those who are LGBTQIA+) about patient care, end-stage disease progression, **pain and symptom management**, medication management, the **disposal of supplies**, and **signs and symptoms of imminent death**.

HOW TO ASSESS PRIOR KNOWLEDGE AND TEACH PATIENT-CARE SKILLS

If you are a physician, advanced practice registered nurse, physician associate, or registered nurse and you're preparing to teach **patient-care skills** to a patient and a family caregiver, a good place to start is with the patient's answers to the questions about activities of daily living in dimension 3 of the Five-Dimension Assessment Model, discussed in chapter 4. The patient's answers to those questions will give you much of the information you need to provide focused education to the patient; the missing piece will be understanding the caregiver's knowledge and needs. Before you ask questions to assess the caregiver's knowledge about patient care, let the caregiver know that your questions are designed to help you provide better support, not to see whether the caregiver is doing a "good" or "bad" job caring for the patient.

In assessing a caregiver's knowledge of and need for particular patient-care skills, you should ask four key questions. The caregiver's answers will give you the information you need to teach the patient-care skills in question. Each question aligns with a teaching task, described in greater depth in table 8.1.

1. Walk me through how you help [patient] with _____.
- *Offer concrete praise to the caregiver regarding at least one aspect of the process they have been following to help the patient. Provide focused education to correct any tasks the caregiver has been performing incorrectly (based on the caregiver's description of the process).*
2. What tasks are the most difficult for you in terms of helping [patient] with _____?
- *Provide focused education for each task the caregiver identifies as having been difficult.*
3. What challenges or problems have you encountered helping [patient] with _____?
- *Provide specific strategies for overcoming or addressing the challenges the caregiver has encountered.*
4. What questions or concerns do you have regarding helping [patient] with _____?
- *Answer the caregiver's questions and address the caregiver's concerns.*

TABLE 8.1 Assessing and teaching patient-care skills

Questions for assessing patient and caregiver knowledge and needs	Addressing knowledge and needs when teaching patient-care skills
BATHING	
Walk me through how you [help patient] bathe. What tasks are the most difficult for you in terms of bathing [patient]? What challenges or problems have you encountered in bathing [patient]? What questions or concerns do you have regarding bathing [patient]?	Offer concrete praise to the patient and caregiver regarding at least one aspect of the process they've been using for bathing. Provide focused education for any bathing tasks that the patient or caregiver has been performing incorrectly (based on their description of the bathing process). Provide focused education for each bathing task the patient or caregiver identifies as having been difficult. Provide specific strategies for overcoming or addressing the challenges the patient or caregiver has encountered in the bathing process. Answer the patient's and caregiver's questions and address their concerns regarding bathing.

GETTING DRESSED

Walk me through how you help [patient] get dressed.
What tasks are the most difficult for you in terms of dressing [patient]?
What challenges or problems have you encountered in dressing [patient]?
What questions or concerns do you have regarding dressing [patient]?

Offer concrete praise to the patient and caregiver regarding at least one aspect of the dressing process they've been using.
Provide focused education for any dressing tasks that the patient or caregiver has been performing incorrectly (based on their description of the process).
Provide focused education for each dressing task the patient or caregiver identifies as having been difficult.
Provide specific strategies for overcoming or addressing the challenges the patient or caregiver has encountered when dressing the patient.
Answer the patient's and caregiver's questions and address their concerns regarding dressing the patient.

MEALS AND EATING

What challenges or problems have you encountered preparing meals and eating [feeding patient]?
What questions or concerns do you have regarding preparing meals and eating [feeding patient]?

Provide focused education for each meal prep and feeding task the patient or caregiver identifies as having been difficult.
Provide specific strategies for overcoming or addressing the challenges the patient or caregiver has encountered when preparing meals for and feeding the patient.
Answer the patient's and caregiver's questions and address their concerns regarding preparing meals for and feeding the patient

GETTING OUT OF BED

Walk me through how you help [patient] get out of bed.
What tasks are the most difficult for you in terms of getting [patient] out of bed?
What challenges or problems have you encountered getting [patient] out of bed?
What questions or concerns do you have regarding getting [patient] out of bed?

Offer concrete praise to the patient and caregiver regarding at least one aspect of the process they've been using to get the patient out of bed.
Provide focused education for any tasks that the patient or caregiver has been performing incorrectly (based on their description of the process).
Provide focused education for each task the patient or caregiver identifies as having been difficult in terms of getting the patient out of bed.
Provide specific strategies for overcoming or addressing the challenges the patient or caregiver has encountered when getting the patient out of bed.
Answer the patient's and caregiver's questions and address their concerns regarding getting the patient out of bed.

MOVING FROM BED TO CHAIR

Walk me through how you help patient] move from the bed to the chair.

Offer concrete praise to the patient and caregiver regarding at least one aspect of the process they've been using to move the patient from the bed to the chair.

(continued)

TABLE 8.1 (*continued*)

Questions for assessing patient and caregiver knowledge and needs	Addressing knowledge and needs when teaching patient-care skills
What tasks are the most difficult for you in terms of moving [patient] from the bed to the chair? What challenges or problems have you encountered moving [patient] from the bed to the chair? What questions or concerns do you have regarding moving [patient] from the bed to the chair?	Provide focused education for any tasks that the patient or caregiver has been performing incorrectly (based on their description of the process). Provide focused education for each task the patient or caregiver identifies as having been difficult in terms of moving the patient from the bed to the chair. Provide specific strategies for overcoming or addressing the challenges the patient or caregiver has encountered when moving the patient from the bed to the chair. Answer the patient's and caregiver's questions and address their concerns regarding moving the patient from the bed to the chair.
MOVING FROM CHAIR TO BATHROOM	
Walk me through how you help [patient] move from the chair to the bathroom. What tasks are the most difficult for you in terms of moving [patient] from the chair to the bathroom? What challenges or problems have you encountered moving [patient] from the chair to the bathroom? What questions or concerns do you have regarding moving [patient] from the chair to the bathroom?	Offer concrete praise to the patient and caregiver regarding at least one aspect of the process they've been using to move the patient from the chair to the bathroom. Provide focused education for any tasks that the patient or caregiver has been performing incorrectly (based on their description of the process). Provide focused education for each task the patient or caregiver identifies as having been difficult in terms of moving the patient from the chair to the bathroom. Provide specific strategies for overcoming or addressing the challenges the patient or caregiver has encountered when moving the patient from the chair to the bathroom. Answer the patient's and caregiver's questions and address their concerns regarding moving the patient from the chair to the bathroom.
MOVING ON/OFF TOILET	
Walk me through how you help [patient] get onto and off of the toilet. What tasks are the most difficult for you in terms of moving [patient] onto and off of the toilet?	Offer concrete praise to the patient and caregiver regarding at least one aspect of the process they've been using to move the patient onto and off of the toilet. Provide focused education for any tasks that the patient or caregiver has been performing incorrectly (based on their description of the process).

What challenges or problems have you encountered moving [patient] onto and off of the toilet?	Provide focused education for each task the patient or caregiver identifies as having been difficult in terms of moving the patient onto and off of the toilet.
What questions or concerns do you have regarding moving [patient] onto and off of the toilet?	Provide specific strategies for overcoming or addressing the challenges the patient or caregiver has encountered when moving the patient onto and off of the toilet. Answer the patient's and caregiver's questions and address their concerns regarding moving the patient onto and off of the toilet.

GETTING IN/OUT OF CAR

Walk me through how you [help patient] get into and out of the car. What tasks are the most difficult for you in terms of getting [patient] into and out of the car?	Offer concrete praise to the patient and caregiver regarding at least one aspect of the process they've been using to get the patient into and out of the car. Provide focused education for any tasks that the patient or caregiver has been performing incorrectly (based on their description of the process).
What challenges or problems have you encountered getting [patient] into and out of the car?	Provide focused education for each task the patient or caregiver identifies as having been difficult in terms of getting the patient into and out of the car.
What questions or concerns do you have regarding getting [patient] into and out of the car?	Provide specific strategies for overcoming or addressing the challenges the patient or caregiver has encountered when getting the patient into and out of the car. Answer the patient's and caregiver's questions and address their concerns regarding getting the patient in and out of the car.

MANAGING INCONTINENCE

Walk me through how you [help patient] manage incontinence of urine or stool (accidents, leakage, etc.). What tasks are the most difficult for you in terms of helping [patient] manage incontinence of urine or stool?	Offer concrete praise to the patient and caregiver regarding at least one aspect of the process they've been using to help manage incontinence of urine or stool. Provide focused education for any tasks that the patient or caregiver has been performing incorrectly (based on their description of the process). Provided hands-on instruction to the patient and caregiver regarding the correct use of universal precautions.
What challenges or problems have you encountered helping [patient] manage incontinence of urine or stool?	Provide focused education for each task the patient or caregiver identifies as having been difficult in terms of managing incontinence of urine or stool.
What questions or concerns do you have regarding helping [patient] manage incontinence of urine or stool?	Provide specific strategies for overcoming or addressing the challenges the patient or caregiver has encountered in managing incontinence of urine or stool. Answer the patient or caregiver's questions and address their concerns regarding managing incontinence of urine or stool.

(continued)

TABLE 8.1 (*continued*)

Questions for assessing patient and caregiver knowledge and needs	Addressing knowledge and needs when teaching patient-care skills
NIGHTTIME BATHROOM NEEDS	
Walk me through how you [help patient] with nighttime bathroom needs. What tasks are the most difficult for you in terms of [helping patient with] nighttime bathroom needs? What challenges or problems have you encountered [helping patient] with nighttime bathroom needs? What questions or concerns do you have regarding [helping patient with] nighttime bathroom needs?	Offer concrete praise to the patient and caregiver regarding at least one aspect of the process they've been using to help with nighttime bathroom needs. Provide focused education for any tasks that the patient or caregiver has been performing incorrectly (based on their description of the process). Provide focused education for each task the patient or caregiver identifies as having been difficult in terms of helping the patient with nighttime bathroom needs. Provide specific strategies for overcoming or addressing the challenges the patient or caregiver has encountered when helping the patient with nighttime bathroom needs. Answer the patient's and caregiver's questions and address their concerns regarding helping the patient with nighttime bathroom needs.

HOW TO ASSESS KNOWLEDGE AND TEACH ABOUT END-STAGE DISEASE PROGRESSION

When assessing the patient's and caregiver's knowledge regarding a particular aspect of **end-stage disease progression**, keep things simple by asking just one question. For example: "What have you heard about recurrent infections in someone with [patient's] diagnosis and what they mean in terms of the progression of the disease?" The patient's and caregiver's answers will give you a good jumping-off point for focused education. Table 8.2 walks you through the process of assessing patient and caregiver knowledge and addressing knowledge gaps related to end-stage disease progression. Because the particulars of end-stage disease progression will depend on the patient's primary diagnosis, you should omit or add questions, depending on your professional judgment as a registered nurse, physician, advanced practice registered nurse, or physician associate.

TABLE 8.2 Assessing and teaching about end-stage disease progression

End-stage disease progression	Questions for assessing patient and caregiver knowledge and needs	Addressing knowledge and needs when teaching about end-stage disease progression
CLINICAL STATUS		
Repeated or intractable infections, such as pneumonia, sepsis, or upper urinary tract infection	What have you heard about repeated infections in someone with [patient's] diagnosis and what they mean in terms of the progression of the disease?	Provide focused education to address myths, misinformation, and knowledge gaps about repeated infections and their significance as indicators of end-stage disease progression.
Weight loss not due to reversible causes such as depression or use of diuretics	What have you heard about weight loss in someone with [patient's] diagnosis and what it means in terms of the progression of the disease?	Provide focused education to address myths, misinformation, and knowledge gaps about weight loss and its significance as an indicator of end-stage disease progression.
Dysphagia leading to recurrent aspiration and/or inadequate oral intake documented by decreasing food portion consumption	What have you heard about swallowing problems (dysphagia) in someone with [patient's] diagnosis and what that means in terms of the progression of the disease?	Provide focused education to address myths, misinformation, and knowledge gaps about swallowing problems and their significance as indicators of end-stage disease progression.
SYMPTOMS		
Dyspnea with increasing respiratory rate	What have you heard about shortness of breath or breathlessness (dyspnea) in someone with [patient's] diagnosis and what it means in terms of the progression of the disease?	Provide focused education to address myths, misinformation, and knowledge gaps about shortness of breath or breathlessness and its significance as an indicator of end-stage disease progression.
Intractable coughing	What have you heard about coughing that won't go away in someone with [patient's] diagnosis and what it means in terms of the progression of the disease?	Provide focused education to address myths, misinformation, and knowledge gaps about intractable coughing and its significance as an indicator of end-stage disease progression.
Nausea/vomiting poorly responsive to treatment	What have you heard about nausea/vomiting that won't go away in someone with [patient's] diagnosis and what it means in terms of the progression of the disease?	Provide focused education to address myths, misinformation, and knowledge gaps about nausea/vomiting that won't go away and its significance as an indicator of end-stage disease progression.

(continued)

TABLE 8.2 *(continued)*

End-stage disease progression	Questions for assessing patient and caregiver knowledge and needs	Addressing knowledge and needs when teaching about end-stage disease progression
Intractable diarrhea	What have you heard about diarrhea that won't go away in someone with [patient's] diagnosis and what it means in terms of the progression of the disease?	Provide focused education to address myths, misinformation, and knowledge gaps about intractable diarrhea and its significance as an indicator of end-stage disease progression.
Pain requiring increasing doses of major analgesics more than briefly	What have you heard about pain that requires increasing doses of pain medication in someone with [patient's] diagnosis and what it means in terms of the progression of the disease?	Provide focused education to address myths, misinformation, and knowledge gaps about pain that requires increasing doses of pain medication and its significance as an indicator of end-stage disease progression.

SIGNS

Decline in systolic blood pressure to below 90, or progressive postural hypotension	What have you heard about low blood pressure or dizziness when standing up in someone with [patient's] diagnosis and what it means in terms of the progression of the disease?	Provide focused education to address myths, misinformation, and knowledge gaps about low blood pressure or dizziness when standing up and its significance as an indicator of end-stage disease progression.
Ascites	What have you heard about abdominal swelling (ascites) in someone with [patient's] diagnosis and what it means in terms of the progression of the disease?	Provide focused education to address myths, misinformation, and knowledge gaps about abdominal swelling and its significance as an indicator of end-stage disease progression.
Venous, arterial, or lymphatic obstruction due to local progression or metastatic disease	What have you heard about obstructions in veins, arteries, or the lymphatic system in someone with [patient's] diagnosis and what they mean in terms of the progression of the disease?	Provide focused education to address myths, misinformation, and knowledge gaps about obstructions in veins, arteries, or the lymphatic system and their significance as indicators of end-stage disease progression.
Edema	What have you heard about swelling (edema) in someone with [patient's] diagnosis and what it means in terms of the progression of the disease?	Provide focused education to address myths, misinformation, and knowledge gaps about swelling (edema) and its significance as an indicator of end-stage disease progression.

Pleural/pericardial effusion	What have you heard about pleural/pericardial effusion in someone with [patient's] diagnosis and what it means in terms of the progression of the disease?	Provide focused education to address myths, misinformation, and knowledge gaps about pleural/pericardial effusion and its significance as an indicator of end-stage disease progression.
Weakness	What have you heard about weakness in someone with [patient's] diagnosis and what it means in terms of the progression of the disease?	Provide focused education to address myths, misinformation, or knowledge gaps about weakness and its significance as an indicator of end-stage disease progression.
Change in level of consciousness	What have you heard about changes in the level of consciousness in someone with [patients] diagnosis and what they mean in terms of the progression of the disease?	Provide focused education to address myths, misinformation, and knowledge gaps about changes in the level of consciousness and their significance as indicators of end-stage disease progression.

OTHER INDICATORS

Increasing emergency room visits, hospitalizations, or physician's visits related to primary diagnosis	What have you heard about repeated emergency room visits or hospitalizations in someone with [patient's] diagnosis and what they mean in terms of the progression of the disease?	Provide focused education to address myths, misinformation, and knowledge gaps about repeated emergency room visits or hospitalizations and their significance as indicators of end-stage disease progression.
Progression to dependence on assistance with additional activities of daily living	What have you heard about increased dependence on help for activities of daily living in someone with [patient's] diagnosis and what it means in terms of the progression of the disease?	Provide focused education to address myths, misinformation, and knowledge gaps about increased dependence on help for activities of daily living and its significance as an indicator of end-stage disease progression.
Progressive stage 3–4 pressure ulcers in spite of optimal care	What have you heard about pressure ulcers in someone with [patient's] diagnosis and what they mean in terms of the progression of the disease?	Provide focused education to address myths, misinformation, and knowledge gaps about pressure ulcers and their significance as indicators of end-stage disease progression.

Note: Text under "End-stage disease progression" is from Centers for Medicaid and Medicare Services, 2022.

HOW TO ASSESS KNOWLEDGE AND TEACH ABOUT PAIN AND SYMPTOM MANAGEMENT

When you teach a patient and caregiver about pain and symptom management, start by reviewing the patient's answers to questions in dimension 3 of the Five-Dimension Assessment Model. Table 8.3 explains how to assess the patient's and caregiver's prior knowledge of pain and symptom management and then teach them what they need to know.

TABLE 8.3 Assessing and teaching about pain and symptom management

Questions for assessing patient and caregiver knowledge and needs	Addressing knowledge and needs when teaching about pain and symptom management
ANXIETY	
How can you tell when [patient] is experiencing anxiety?	Provide focused education on preventing and addressing anxiety using both nonpharmacologic and pharmacologic approaches, as prescribed by the patient's primary care professional.
What have you tried in the past to help [patient] with anxiety?	
What challenges or problems have you encountered in helping [patient] with anxiety?	Provide specific strategies for overcoming or addressing challenges the patient and caregiver have encountered in helping the patient with anxiety.
What questions or concerns do you have regarding [patient's] anxiety?	Answer the patient's and caregiver's questions and address their concerns regarding helping the patient with anxiety.
BREATHLESSNESS	
How can you tell when [patient] is experiencing breathlessness?	Provide focused education on preventing and addressing breathlessness using both nonpharmacologic and pharmacologic approaches, as prescribed by the patient's primary care professional.
What have you tried in the past to help [patient] with breathlessness?	
What challenges or problems have you encountered in helping [patient] with breathlessness?	Provide specific strategies for overcoming or addressing challenges the patient and caregiver have encountered in helping the patient with breathlessness.
What questions or concerns do you have regarding [patient's] breathlessness?	Answer the patient's and caregiver's questions and address their concerns regarding helping the patient with breathlessness.

CONFUSION	
How can you tell when [patient] is experiencing confusion? What have you tried in the past to help [patient] with confusion? What challenges or problems have you encountered in helping [patient] with confusion? What questions or concerns do you have regarding [patient's] confusion?	Provide focused education on preventing and addressing confusion using both nonpharmacologic and pharmacologic approaches, as prescribed by the patient's primary care professional. Provide specific strategies for overcoming or addressing challenges the patient and caregiver have encountered in helping the patient with confusion. Answer the patient's and caregiver's questions and address their concerns regarding helping the patient with confusion.
CONSTIPATION	
How can you tell when [patient] is experiencing constipation? What have you tried in the past to help [patient] with constipation?	Provide focused education regarding preventing and addressing constipation using both nonpharmacologic and pharmacologic approaches, as prescribed by the patient's primary care professional.
What challenges or problems have you encountered in helping [patient] with constipation? What questions or concerns do you have regarding [patient's] constipation?	Provide specific strategies for overcoming or addressing challenges the patient and caregiver have encountered in helping the patient with constipation. Answer the patient's and caregiver's questions and address their concerns regarding helping the patient with constipation.
DEPRESSION	
How can you tell when [patient] is experiencing depression? What have you tried in the past to help [patient] with depression? What challenges or problems have you encountered in helping [patient] with depression? What questions or concerns do you have regarding [patient's] depression?	Provide focused education regarding preventing and addressing depression using both nonpharmacologic and pharmacologic approaches, as prescribed by the patient's primary care professional. Provide specific strategies for overcoming or addressing challenges the patient and caregiver have encountered in helping the patient with depression. Answer the patient's and caregiver's questions and address their concerns regarding helping the patient with depression.

(continued)

TABLE 8.3 (*continued*)

Questions for assessing patient and caregiver knowledge and needs	Addressing knowledge and needs when teaching about pain and symptom management
INSOMNIA	
How can you tell when [patient] is experiencing insomnia? What have you tried in the past to help [patient] with insomnia? What challenges or problems have you encountered in helping [patient] with insomnia? What questions or concerns do you have regarding [patient's] insomnia?	Provide focused education on preventing and addressing insomnia using both nonpharmacologic and pharmacologic approaches, as prescribed by the patient's primary care professional. Provide specific strategies for overcoming or addressing challenges the patient and caregiver have encountered in helping the patient with insomnia. Answer the patient's and caregiver's questions and address their concerns regarding helping the patient with insomnia.
NAUSEA/VOMITING	
How can you tell when [patient] is experiencing nausea or vomiting? What have you tried in the past to help [patient] with nausea or vomiting? What challenges or problems have you encountered in helping [patient] with nausea or vomiting? What questions or concerns do you have regarding [patient's] nausea or vomiting?	Provide focused education on preventing and addressing nausea/vomiting using both nonpharmacologic and pharmacologic approaches, as prescribed by the patient's primary care professional. Provide hands-on instruction to the patient and caregiver in the correct universal precautions to follow when there is a risk of exposure to blood or body fluids. Provide specific strategies for overcoming or addressing challenges the patient and caregiver have encountered in helping the patient with nausea/vomiting. Answer the patient's and caregiver's questions and address their concerns regarding helping the patient with nausea/vomiting.
WEAKNESS/FATIGUE	
How can you tell when [patient] is experiencing weakness or fatigue? What have you tried in the past to help [patient] with weakness or fatigue?	Provide focused education on preventing and addressing weakness or fatigue using both nonpharmacologic and pharmacologic approaches, as prescribed by the patient's primary care professional. Provide specific strategies for overcoming or addressing challenges the patient and caregiver have encountered in helping the patient with weakness or fatigue.

What challenges or problems have you encountered in helping [patient] with weakness or fatigue? What questions or concerns do you have regarding [patient's] weakness or fatigue?	Answer the patient's and caregiver's questions and address their concerns regarding helping the patient with weakness or fatigue. |//
WEIGHT LOSS	
How can you tell when [patient] is experiencing weight loss? What have you tried in the past to address [patient's] weight loss? What challenges or problems have you encountered in addressing [patient's] weight loss? What questions or concerns do you have regarding [patient's] weight loss?	Provide focused education on preventing and addressing weight loss using both nonpharmacologic and pharmacologic approaches, as prescribed by the patient's primary care professional. Provide specific strategies for overcoming or addressing challenges the patient and caregiver have encountered in helping the patient with weight loss. Answer the patient's and caregiver's questions and address their concerns regarding helping the patient with weight loss.
PAIN	
How can you tell when [patient] is experiencing pain? What have you tried in the past to help [patient] with pain? What challenges or problems have you encountered in helping [patient] with pain? What questions or concerns do you have regarding [patient's] pain?	Provide focused education on preventing and addressing pain using both nonpharmacologic and pharmacologic approaches, as prescribed by the patient's primary care professional. Provide specific strategies for overcoming or addressing challenges the patient and caregiver have encountered in helping the patient with pain. Answer the patient's and caregiver's questions and address their concerns regarding helping the patient with pain.

HOW TO ASSESS KNOWLEDGE AND TEACH ABOUT MEDICATION MANAGEMENT

To manage medications effectively, individuals and caregivers need to have a core set of skills: "management skills such as the ability to store, organize, and discard medications, and technical skills such as the ability to recognize symptoms and administer different types of medications" (Lau et al., 2009). Teaching these core skills to individuals and caregivers not only facilitates safe and effective **medication management** but also helps you comply with insurance and regulatory requirements. When you document in the patient's medical record the education and training you have provided, you give others a clear picture of the actions taken to ensure that both patient and family are equipped to administer the medications prescribed.

Before you can begin teaching the patient and caregiver how to manage the patient's medications, you need to have a clear understanding of what those medications are and, in the case of a recent or impending care transition, any changes in the medications. This understanding can by attained through the process of **medication reconciliation**, which involves "creating the most accurate list possible of all medications a patient is taking—including drug name, dosage, frequency, and route—and comparing that list against the [clinician's] admission, transfer, and/or discharge orders, with the goal of providing correct medications to the patient at all transition points" (Institute for Healthcare Improvement, n.d.). For a detailed guide to medication reconciliation, see Medications at Transitions and Clinical Handoffs (MATCH) Toolkit for Medication Reconciliation (Gleason et al., 2012).

Table 8.4 covers how to assess the patient's and caregiver's knowledge of medication management and address any knowledge gaps. Because the particulars of medication management will depend on the patient's diagnosis, you should omit or add questions as necessary, following your professional judgment as a physician, advanced practice registered nurse, physician associate, or registered nurse.

HOW TO ASSESS KNOWLEDGE AND TEACH ABOUT DISPOSAL OF SUPPLIES

Table 8.5 walks you through the process of assessing individuals' and caregivers' knowledge about how to dispose of medical supplies. It discusses how to address their knowledge gaps and teach them proper procedures related to disposing of supplies such as used syringes and lancets, soiled incontinence pads, and used gauze and bandages.

TABLE 8.4 Assessing and teaching about medication management

Skill area	Questions for assessing patient and caregiver knowledge and needs	Addressing knowledge and needs when teaching about medication management
Storing medication	Have you ever used this medication before? If so, where did you keep the medicine? What have you been told about how to store this medication? What questions or concerns do you have about storing this medication?	Provide focused education on how and where to store the medication. Ensure that patient and family understand the precautions they need to take to keep the medication out of reach of children, pets, and others who should not have access to it. Address myths, misinformation, and knowledge gaps about how and where to store the medication. Answer the patient's and caregiver's questions and address their concerns about how and where to store the medication.
Organizing medication	What have you tried in the past to help organize and keep track of [patient's] medications? What challenges or problems have you encountered in organizing and keeping track of [patient's] medications in the past? What questions or concerns do you have regarding organizing and keeping track of [patient's] medications?	Provide focused education on how to organize and keep track of the patient's medications. Consider the patient's and caregiver's literacy level, visual acuity, and cognitive abilities when suggesting tools and strategies. Provide specific strategies for overcoming or addressing challenges the patient and caregiver have encountered in organizing and keeping track of medications. Answer the patient's and caregiver's questions and address their concerns about organizing.
Discarding medication	How have you discarded unused medication in the past? What challenges or problems have you encountered in discarding [patient's] medications? What questions or concerns do you have regarding discarding [patient's] medications?	Provide focused education on the proper way to discard medications. Address misinformation and knowledge gaps about safe medication disposal. Ensure that patient and family understand the precautions they need to take to keep discarded medication out of reach of children, pets, and others who should not have access to it.
Administering breakthrough medication	Walk me through/show me the process you use to administer [patient's] breakthrough medication for pain.	Provide focused education for any tasks that the patient or caregiver has been performing incorrectly (based on their description of the process).

(*continued*)

TABLE 8.4 (*continued*)

Skill area	Questions for assessing patient and caregiver knowledge and needs	Addressing knowledge and needs when teaching about medication management
	What challenges or problems have you encountered in administering [patient's] breakthrough medication for pain? What questions or concerns do you have about administering [patient's] breakthrough medication for pain?	Provide specific strategies for overcoming or addressing the challenges the patient or caregiver has encountered in giving breakthrough medication for pain. Answer the patient's and caregiver's questions and address their concerns about administering breakthrough medication for pain.
Administering medication patches	Walk me through/show me the process you use to administer (give patient) a medication patch. What challenges or problems have you encountered in using (giving patient) a medication patch? What questions or concerns do you have regarding using (giving patient) a medication patch?	Provide focused education for any tasks that the patient or caregiver has been performing incorrectly (based on their description of the process). Provide specific strategies for overcoming or addressing challenges the patient or caregiver has encountered with medication patches in the past. Answer the patient's and caregiver's questions and address their concerns regarding medication patch use.
Using a syringe	Walk me through/show me the process you use to administer [patient's] medication using a syringe. What challenges or problems have you encountered in administering [patient's] medication using a syringe? What questions or concerns do you have about administering [patient's] medication using a syringe?	Provide focused education for any tasks that the patient or caregiver has been performing incorrectly (based on their description of the process). Provide hands-on instruction in the correct universal precautions to follow when there is a risk of exposure to blood or body fluids. Provide specific strategies for overcoming or addressing challenges the patient or caregiver has encountered in administering medication using a syringe. Answer the patient's and caregiver's questions and address their concerns regarding administering medication using a syringe.

Using a dropper	Walk me through/show me the process you use to administer [patient's] medication using a dropper.	Provide focused education for any tasks that the patient or caregiver has been performing incorrectly (based on their description of the process).
	What challenges or problems have you encountered in administering [patient's] medication using a dropper? What questions or concerns do you have regarding administering [patient's] medication using a dropper?	Provide specific strategies for overcoming or addressing challenges the patient or caregiver has encountered in administering medication using a dropper. Answer the patient's and caregiver's questions and address their concerns regarding giving medication using a dropper.
Administering pills and capsules	Walk me through/show me the process you use when you administer [patient's] pills or capsules.	Provide focused education for any tasks that the patient or caregiver has been performing incorrectly (based on their description of the process).
	What challenges or problems have you encountered in administering [patient's] pills or capsules?	Provide specific strategies for overcoming or addressing challenges the patient or caregiver has encountered in administering pills or capsules.
	What questions or concerns do you have regarding administering [patient's] pills or capsules?	Answer the patient's and caregiver's questions and address their concerns regarding administering pills and capsules.

HOW TO ASSESS KNOWLEDGE AND TEACH ABOUT SIGNS AND SYMPTOMS OF IMMINENT DEATH

Think back to the first time you saw a person die. In the minutes before they took their last breath, did you know what to expect? Or did you have questions you wished you could have asked someone? Were there moments when the person made a noise or a facial expression or movement that frightened or confused you? Your answers to these questions will likely differ depending on whether the first person you saw die was a patient or a close friend or family member.

TABLE 8.5 Assessing and teaching about disposal of supplies

Skill area	Questions for assessing patient and caregiver knowledge and needs	Addressing knowledge and needs when teaching about disposal of supplies
Disposing of used incontinence pads, diapers, and other supplies soiled with urine and/or stool	How have you disposed of used supplies soiled with urine and/or stool? What challenges or problems have you encountered in disposing of used supplies soiled with urine and/or stool? What questions or concerns do you have about disposing of used supplies soiled with urine and/or stool?	Provide focused education and address knowledge gaps regarding the proper disposal of used supplies soiled with urine and/or stool. Ensure that patient and family understand the precautions they need to take in handling and disposing of used supplies soiled with urine and/or stool. Provide patient and family with the supplies needed for proper disposal.
Disposing of gauze, bandages, and other supplies soiled with blood or body fluids	How have you disposed of supplies soiled with blood or body fluids? What challenges or problems have you had encountered in disposing of supplies soiled with blood or body fluids? What questions or concerns do you have regarding the disposal supplies soiled with blood or body fluids?	Provide focused education and address knowledge gaps regarding the proper disposal of gauze, bandages, and other supplies soiled with blood or body fluids. Ensure that patient and family understand the precautions they need to take in handling and disposing of supplies soiled with blood or body fluids. Provide patient and family with the supplies needed for proper disposal.
Disposing of used syringes, lancets, and other sharps	How have you disposed of used syringes, lancets, and other sharps? What challenges or problems have you encountered in disposing of used syringes, lancets, and other sharps? What questions or concerns do you have about disposing of used syringes, lancets, and other sharps?	Provide focused education and address knowledge gaps regarding the proper disposal of used syringes, lancets, and other sharps. Ensure that patient and family understand the precautions they need to take in handling and disposing of used syringes, lancets, and other sharps. Provide patient and family with the supplies needed for proper disposal.

July 15, 2019

GoFundMe post from Kim Acquaviva

Lately I've been thinking a lot about why Kathy and I don't want hospice despite spending our entire careers advocating for earlier access to hospice care. At first I told myself it was because we didn't need hospice care to meet Kathy's needs at home. We know who to ask and what to ask for when it comes to symptom management, and hands-on care (showering, bandage changes, dressing, etc) are intimate acts of love that I enjoy doing for Kathy. I told myself it was because we're introverts and we have crazy dogs who bark at strangers and we'd rather not be bothered by regulatory-required nurse visits that we don't need. All of these things are true. But there's a bigger reason—one that I'm ashamed to admit. I don't want hospice because I know what good hospice care is supposed to look like and I don't want to spend these last weeks with Kathy feeling disappointed, frustrated, or enraged by less-than-optimal care. Kathy spent her entire career advocating for exceptional end-of-life care and so have I. Nothing would increase her suffering (or mine) more than getting shitty hospice care. And shitty hospice care is a very real possibility, especially for us as a lesbian couple: Gary Stein [and Cathy Berkman]'s survey of almost 900 hospice professionals revealed that things are even worse than I had imagined: "Most providers surveyed said LGBT people received discriminatory care, he said. For transgender patients, two-thirds said that was true." (https://www.washingtonpost.com/health/for-the-stonewall-generation-turning-to-others-for-care-could-make-them-uniquely-vulnerable/2019/05/31/cd313748-80b1-11e9-933d-7501070ee669_story.html?noredirect=on&utm_term=.64aaa366a32f)

I write this with a heavy heart. I love hospice—if I knew that our family would receive the world's best hospice care, I'd say "sign us up." I'm sure I could make some calls and get the very best hospice team assigned to our family. The local hospices here have great reputations and amazing professionals at their helm. A local hospice would send us the most LGBTQ-friendly, dog-loving professionals

(continued on next page)

(continued from previous page)

> and we'd get the best care in the world. But if I weren't me and Kathy weren't her, would we have the same certainty that we'd get exceptional care? Would we know who to call or what to say or what to ask for so that we'd receive what hospice is truly meant to be? The answers to those questions make me sad. They make Kathy sad. And if you're a hospice professional, they should make you sad, too. Channel that sadness into action: do whatever you can to ensure that ALL LGBTQ+ people—not just those who know who to call or what to ask for—have access to hospice care provided by professionals who will treat them with dignity, respect, and clinical competence. There is no room in hospice care for homophobia or transphobia or biphobia. There is no room in hospice care for heterosexism or cissexism. And until those things are eradicated? There is no room in hospice care for my family.
>
> Kim

When individuals and families are dealing with a life-limiting illness, fear of the unknown, especially regarding the signs of imminent death, can be distressing. By demystifying the dying process and providing concrete information about what to expect, you can reduce the family's fear and help the patient and family prepare themselves emotionally for the end of life. Table 8.6 is designed to help you assess patient and caregiver knowledge of the signs and symptoms of imminent death and then offer information to address their knowledge gaps.

Depending on the patient's primary diagnosis, you may want to provide additional information about what to expect when the patient is dying. For example, if a patient is likely to experience exsanguination or hemoptysis, explain to the patient and family what to expect and consider giving the family several red towels. (Using red towels for cleaning up during and after bleeding can help caregivers avoid or minimize the

TABLE 8.6 Assessing and teaching about signs and symptoms of imminent death

System	Questions for assessing patient and caregiver knowledge and needs	Addressing knowledge and needs when teaching about signs and symptoms of imminent death
Neurological	What have you heard about how a person's alertness, awareness, or thinking might change as death becomes imminent? What questions, concerns, or worries do you have regarding changes in [patients] alertness, awareness, or thinking as death becomes imminent?	Provide focused education to address myths, misinformation, or knowledge gaps about neurological changes and their significance as indicators of imminent death. Answer the patient's and caregiver's questions and address their concerns about neurological changes.
Integumentary (skin)	What have you heard about how a person's skin might change as death becomes imminent? What questions, concerns, or worries do you have regarding changes in [patient's] skin as death becomes imminent?	Provide focused education to address myths, misinformation, or knowledge gaps about skin changes and their significance as indicators of imminent death. Answer the patient's and caregiver's questions and address their concerns regarding skin changes.
Respiratory	What have you heard about how a person's breathing might change as death becomes imminent? What questions, concerns, or worries do you have regarding changes in [patient's] breathing as death becomes imminent?	Provide focused education to address myths, misinformation, or knowledge gaps about respiratory changes and their significance as indicators of imminent death. Answer the patient's and caregiver's questions and address their concerns regarding respiratory changes.
Cardiovascular and circulatory	What have you heard about how a person's heart function and circulation might change as death becomes imminent? What questions, concerns, or worries do you have regarding changes in [patient's] heart function or circulation as death becomes imminent?	Provide focused education to address myths, misinformation, or knowledge gaps about cardiac and circulatory changes and their significance as indicators of imminent death. Answer the patient's and caregiver's questions and address their concerns regarding cardiac and circulatory changes.

(continued)

TABLE 8.6 (*continued*)

System	Questions for assessing patient and caregiver knowledge and needs	Addressing knowledge and needs when teaching about signs and symptoms of imminent death
Excretory	What have you heard about how a person's excretion of urine and/or feces might change as death becomes imminent? What questions, concerns, or worries do you have regarding changes in [patient's] excretion of urine and/or feces as death becomes imminent?	Provide focused education to address myths, misinformation, or knowledge gaps about excretory changes and their significance as indicators of imminent death. Answer the patient's and caregiver's questions and address their concerns regarding excretory changes.
Digestive	What have you heard about how a person's desire and ability to eat and drink might change as death becomes imminent? What questions, concerns, or worries do you have regarding changes in [patient's] eating and drinking as death becomes imminent?	Provide focused education to address myths, misinformation, or knowledge gaps about changes in food and fluid intake and their significance as indicators of imminent death. Answer the patient's and caregiver's questions and address their concerns regarding changes in food and fluid intake.

distressing sight of their loved one's blood.) Be alert to the possibility of exsanguination in individuals with ear, nose, or throat tumors; neck metastases; leukemia; bladder tumors; disseminated intravascular coagulation (DIC); or gastrointestinal tumors. While massive hemoptysis is relatively rare, it is a possibility with some types of cancer (Akinola, Baru, & Marks, 2015).

KEY POINTS TO REMEMBER

- Patient and family education is an essential part of the delivery of quality care (Institute of Medicine, 2013).

- Patient-care skills are the skills needed by a patient and/or caregiver to support the patient in meeting bathing, dressing, feeding, transferring, toileting, and transportation needs.
- When assessing the caregiver's knowledge of and need for a particular patient-care skill, ask four key questions:
    1. Walk me through how you help [patient] with ____.
    2. What tasks are the most difficult for you in terms of helping [patient] with ____?
    3. What challenges or problems have you encountered in helping [patient] with ____?
    4. What questions or concerns do you have regarding helping [patient] with ____?
- Pain and symptom management requires skills on the part of a patient and/or caregiver to assess and address symptoms including, but not limited to, anxiety, breathlessness, confusion, constipation, depression, insomnia, nausea/vomiting, pain, weakness/fatigue, and weight loss. Teaching individuals and families how to manage pain and other symptoms is usually the role of the registered nurse, physician, advanced practice registered nurse, or physician associate, but other members of the team may provide education regarding nonpharmacologic interventions, such as relaxation techniques, mindfulness, meditation, and so on.
- Disposing of supplies—such as used syringes and lancets, soiled incontinence pads, and used gauze and bandages—safely and effectively requires skills on the part of the patient and/or caregiver. Teaching individuals and families how to dispose of supplies is generally the role of the registered nurse, physician, advanced practice registered nurse, or physician associate.
- When individuals and families are dealing with a life-limiting illness, fear of the unknown regarding end-stage disease progress and signs of imminent death can be distressing. Patient and family education can reduce fear and help the patient and family prepare themselves emotionally for the end of life.

DISCUSSION QUESTIONS

1. How would you assess knowledge of and teach *patient-care skills* to a patient and caregiver? Describe the questions you would ask and explain how your process would vary depending on whether you met with the patient and caregiver together or separately.
2. How would you assess knowledge and teach about *end-stage disease progression*? Describe the questions you would ask a patient and caregiver and explain how your process would vary depending on whether you met with the patient and caregiver together or separately.
3. How would you assess knowledge and teach about *pain and symptom management*? Describe the questions you would ask and explain how your process would vary depending on whether you met with the patient and caregiver together or separately.
4. How would you assess knowledge and teach about *medication management*? Describe the questions you would ask a patient and their caregiver and explain how your process would vary depending on whether you met with the patient and caregiver together or separately.
5. How would you assess knowledge and teach about the *disposal of supplies*? Describe the questions you would ask a patient and caregiver and explain how your process would vary depending on whether you met with the patient and caregiver together or separately.
6. How would you assess knowledge and teach about the *signs and symptoms of imminent death*? Describe the questions you would ask a patient and caregiver and explain how your process would vary depending on whether you met with the patient and caregiver together or separately.

CHAPTER ACTIVITY

Using the information in this chapter, assess a patient's knowledge and teach the patient about pain and symptom management. (You may work with either a real patient or a simulated patient via role playing.) Immediately afterward, write down your reflections on the process. If you used this process in your work with all individuals, do you think it would improve the quality of care you deliver? Why or why not?

July 15, 2019

GoFundMe post from Greyson Acquaviva:

The day my mom Kathy found out she had ovarian cancer it was a rainy day in Boston and it was my mom Kim's birthday. (I'm going to call them Kim and Kathy in this update to make it easier for people reading this to follow). The first thing I thought of when Kim told me what the doctors in the emergency room found on the scans was that I hoped Kathy's cancer was treatable. Based on what showed up in those scans, though, both of my moms were clear that Kathy's cancer was probably at least a Stage III. I cried myself to sleep the next few nights in my dorm room. When Kathy told me she didn't want to have chemo for a cancer that would end up killing her anyway, I understood. It would've been hard for me to see her in a place she dreaded so much.

 I knew my mom would die before the year was over and I told my friends at college this. I never felt like I was saying something shocking: it was the truth. It felt like someone else was saying it, though—it was hard for me to truly accept that I was going to lose my mom. I found out my mom was dying at the end of January, so I did my best to hold it together for the remaining 3 months of spring semester. It was rough for me and my tics (from Tourette Syndrome) got a lot worse because of the stress. When I came home to DC at the end of freshman year, things didn't feel right at all. Our house was about to be listed for sale so I knew my home wasn't going to be home for very long. My life was changing and there was nothing I could do about it. I hated that feeling, that loss of control.

 The past two months have been even harder for me. It's painful watching Kathy decline so fast and not be able to do the things she loves. It was as much of a loss of control for her as it was for me, even more so. We went to Maine the beginning of June and she had very little energy but she could still go out to dinner. By the time we moved to Charlottesville on June 22, Kathy had a lot less energy to go out and do things. We went out to eat a few times with her

(continued on next page)

(continued from previous page)

in a wheelchair but by the beginning of July, she couldn't leave the house anymore because she was too weak to climb the stairs up to the front door of our house.

In the past few days, she's gotten so much weaker. She hasn't left her bedroom since her birthday, so I hang out with her in a chair next to the bed whenever I can. She's nauseous a few times a day and sometimes she's confused. I've noticed something change within me, though: I'm finally able to see past the weakness of her body to her strength and perseverance as a human being. She truly is an amazing mother. The strength it takes to face the daily struggles of dying is enormous but she faces it with honesty and laughter and tears and love. Every. Single. Day.

I'm so happy to have had almost 20 years of her being in my life, and I'm so grateful for all that she's taught me. I will never forget the impact she has had on my life. When she dies, I will feel grief, sorrow, and loss—that much is true. But I know that her lessons, care, and love towards me knows no bounds, and I will cherish the memories that we've spent our lives together making. Although I wish she could see me graduate from college, get my first job, get married, and have kids, I know that the lessons she's taught me will live on within me. I'd like to think she'll still be there in spirit to guide me on my path through life as well as be there in spirit to view these life-changing moments.

Mom, you'll forever be my mother, and I, your son. Thank you for all that you've taught me in life, and I hope that if there's some kind of afterlife, that you'll find it to be as peaceful and loving as the family you and Ma created has been for me. I love you to the moon and back, to the edge of the universe, and to infinity and beyond.

Love,

Greyson

9 | Psychosocial and Spiritual Issues

CHAPTER OUTCOMES

1. Use psychosocial assessment and supportive techniques in your role as an interdisciplinary/interprofessional team member.
2. Recognize and assess emotional distress.
3. Recognize the developmental tasks involved in life completion and life closure.
4. Understand despair, hope, and meaning in the context of chronic and life-limiting illness.
5. Conduct a spiritual/existential assessment in your role as an interdisciplinary/interprofessional team member.
6. Anticipate common experiences of distress around spiritual/existential issues for individuals and families facing chronic and life-limiting conditions.

Key Terms: despair, emotional distress, hope, life completion and life closure, meaning, psychosocial assessment, spiritual/existential assessment, spiritual/existential distress

CHAPTER SUMMARY

Assessing and addressing psychosocial and spiritual issues is as important to the delivery of quality care as assessing and addressing pain and other physical symptoms. This chapter explains the developmental tasks of life completion and life closure as well as the roles that despair, hope, and meaning play in the context of advanced illness. The chapter describes LGBTQIA-inclusive assessment skills and supportive techniques for addressing psychosocial and spiritual issues and explains how a spiritual/existential history and a spiritual/existential assessment differ. Finally, the chapter examines the ways the members of the interdisciplinary/interprofessional team collaborate to support the patient and family in achieving their goals for care in the psychosocial and spiritual/existential domains.

PSYCHOSOCIAL ASSESSMENT AND SUPPORTIVE TECHNIQUES

Clinical Practice Guidelines for Quality Palliative Care provides guidance regarding the essential elements of psychosocial assessment and support in two areas: the psychological and psychiatric domain (domain 3 in the guidelines), and the social domain (domain 4) (National Consensus Project for Quality Palliative Care, 2013). The Five-Dimension Assessment Model described in chapter 4 translates many of the core elements from *Clinical Practice Guidelines for Quality Palliative Care* into a clear and comprehensive list of questions to ask individuals and families when taking an initial history. Psychosocial assessment questions are interwoven throughout the five dimensions to reinforce the practice among interdisciplinary/interprofessional team members of recognizing the interrelated nature of physical and psychosocial issues. Although **psychosocial assessment** is a term used to describe "an evaluation of a person's mental health, social status, and functional capacity within the community, generally conducted by . . . social workers" (*Mosby's Medical Dictionary*, 2009), physicians, advanced practice registered nurses, physician associates, registered nurses, and chaplains may also assess and document the patient's and family's psychosocial issues, stressors, strengths, and goals. Similarly, while supportive psychotherapy is considered to be the domain of licensed mental health practitioners, supportive techniques can be used appropriately and effectively by all members of the patient's interdisciplinary/interprofessional team. As is the case with all care provided by members of the team, any psychosocial assessments and interventions you use should be guided by the scope of practice for your discipline.

Supportive techniques are valuable in developing a positive therapeutic relationship with individuals and families. To infuse supportive techniques into your work, maintain a focus on each patient and family and see them as the owners and drivers of their plan of care. This will reinforce the collaborative nature of your relationship with the patient and family and convey your respect for and acceptance of their goals and preferences.

DOCUMENTING PSYCHOSOCIAL ASSESSMENTS

When individuals are receiving palliative care or hospice care they interact with and are assessed by multiple members of the interdisciplinary/interprofessional team, each of whom documents their assessment using the lens and language of their discipline. Within hospice, this may lead to seemingly contradictory documentation that can raise questions in the minds of the Centers for Medicare and Medicaid Services (CMS) employees and contractors who conduct medical reviews of claims submitted for payment. When documenting your psychosocial assessment of individuals in hospice care, consider including a notation of your "observations related to the patient's hospice eligibility within the scope of [your] practice" (Hilliard, 2012). Hilliard suggests following what he calls the **DAROP format** for psychosocial documentation, referring to the format's components: data, action, results, observations, and plan (see box).

DAROP FORMAT FOR PSYCHOSOCIAL DOCUMENTATION

D—Data: *Write what you observed at the beginning of the session and relate it to the hospice diagnosis. Write your assessment of need in this session and the care plan you are addressing. Sentences in this section should start with "patient" or "family," as you are documenting what you saw at the beginning of the session. For example, "Patient was received sitting up in the living room watching television with his wife. He appeared melancholic as evidenced by his flat affect and downcast eyes. He denied pain and stated, "I'm just kind of tired today." Care plans being addressed: altered mood (depression) and anticipatory grief.*

A—Action: *Write what you did in the session to address the needs you assessed. Sentences in this section should start with your position (e.g., chaplain, social worker, music therapist), as you are documenting your interventions for the patient and/or family. For example, "Social worker assessed patient's mood as depressed and provided supportive counseling, empathetic listening, and validation. Social worker introduced the concept of a legacy project and offered to work with patient and family on documenting the patient's life story. Encouraged life review and reminiscence. Contacted RN case manager, Betty Smith, and reported observations of patient's depression."*

R—Results: *Write observable outcomes of your actions or interventions. Sentences in this section should start with "patient" or "family," as you are documenting what you observed as the result of your interventions. For example, "While the patient was relatively guarded when asked about his depression and current situation, his affect significantly brightened during life review. His wife shared stories of their courtship 30 years ago, and he joined in the discussion with additional stories. While reminiscing, they held hands and laughed. Overall, the patient continues to struggle with his depressed mood, and when the wife walked the social worker outside at the end of the visit, she shared her concerns for her husband. There were no signs of suicidal ideation. She agreed to a legacy project with him as a coping skill to lift his mood."*

O—Observations: *Write all observations of physical decline related to the diagnosis. You are answering the question: "Within your scope of practice, what do you see that makes this patient hospice-eligible today?" Sentences in this section should start with "patient," as you are describing your objective and subjective observations of his hospice eligibility. For example, "Patient was utilizing oxygen throughout the visit today, whereas on previous visits he would take it on and off. His*

> *feet were swollen and he had them raised on a footstool. He said he gets dizzy when he stands, so he rises slowly. Due to his increased weakness, he said he avoids any activities other than moving from his bed to the living room."*
>
> **P—Plan:** *Document your plan for further addressing the patient's needs. For example, "Social worker will visit patient next week to further facilitate a legacy project and will continue to assess his and his wife's needs."*
>
> From Hilliard, 2012. Reprinted with permission of Russell Hilliard, © 2012 Russell Hilliard. Permission also obtained from the National Hospice and Palliative Care Organization.

EMOTIONAL DISTRESS AND STRATEGIES FOR ASSESSING IT

Emotional distress denotes "an emotional . . . state of pain, sorrow, misery, suffering, or discomfort" (*Mosby's Medical Dictionary*, 2009). Emotional distress is sometimes referred to as psychological distress: "a set of painful mental and physical symptoms that are associated with normal fluctuations of mood in most people" (American Psychological Association, n.d.).

When a patient or family member appears to be experiencing emotional distress, first assess for clinically significant depression and suicidal ideation, document the results of your assessment, and take the appropriate actions based on your discipline's scope of practice. Clinically significant depression differs from situational depression and may benefit from pharmacologic intervention. Individuals and families receiving palliative care and hospice care may be experiencing significant stressors and thus awareness and assessment are prudent.

Although registered nurses, physicians, advanced practice registered nurses, physician associates, chaplains, social workers, and counselors may each assess emotional distress within their respective scope of practice, it is good practice to coordinate with the other members of the interdisciplinary/interprofessional team so that everyone is on the same page. Individuals and family members receiving palliative care and hospice services are already dealing with a flood of information—and feelings—that come with a diagnosis of a serious or life-limiting illness. Having three members of the team each conduct a comprehensive assessment of emotional distress on the same day could be overwhelming. Joint assessment visits are one strategy to address this. For example, a chaplain and a social worker or counselor might meet with a patient or family member together to assess and address emotional distress. When joint visits are conducted skillfully, individuals and families feel as though they are part of a conversation rather than the objects of an assessment.

When assessing emotional distress in a patient or family member, be sensitive to the fact that the perceived source of emotional distress may be a long-standing issue—one that may seem to have nothing to do with the seriousness of the patient's life-limiting illness. Lesbian, gay, bisexual, transgender, nonbinary, gender nonconforming, queer, questioning, intersex, and/or asexual individuals (or *any* individual, really) may indicate that relationships with their family of origin are the most distressing aspects of their life. Just because an issue has a long history does not mean it cannot (or should not) be addressed by the palliative care or hospice professional. Ask follow-up questions to discern how you might be able to support the patient or family member with their distress over challenging family relationships.

In providing psychosocial support to individuals and families, however, it is important to focus on providing support rather than "therapy" surrounding LGBTQIA+ issues. PFLAG (the organization previously known as Parents, Families, and Friends of Lesbians and Gays) is an excellent resource for individuals and families seeking information and support. Its website, www.pflag.org, contains a directory of local chapters as well as a list of helpful resources.

Conversely, do not assume that all lesbian, gay, bisexual, transgender, nonbinary, gender nonconforming, queer, questioning, intersex, and/or asexual individuals will be experiencing emotional distress in their relationships with their families of origin. Many LGBTQIA+ individuals have positive, supportive family relationships.

DESPAIR, HOPE, AND MEANING IN THE CONTEXT OF ADVANCED ILLNESS

When you ask individuals how they cope with distress, you will probably hear the word *hope* quite a bit. Despair, hope, and meaning all play important roles in individuals' and families' experiences of growth in the context of advanced illness. **Hope** is "the belief that what is desired is also possible and that events will turn out for the best . . . [and] the feeling that what one believes will occur" (Gladding, 2011). Individuals receiving palliative care and their families may hope for a cure, for remission, for symptom relief, and/or for continued independence. Individuals receiving hospice care and their families may have similar hopes, although it is normal to see a shift from hope for a cure to hope for the best possible quality of life. Individuals and families (families of origin and families of choice) may hope for an affirmation of their relationship with and the presence of God, the Creator, a spirit, or whatever they call the source to which they look for support and guidance. It is up to each patient and family to define what hope means for them. Your role is to offer information, choices, and support, not the permission to hope for a given outcome.

The converse of hope is **despair,** "an inability . . . to find meaning in one's life. A complete loss of hope" (Gladding, 2011). Despair is a state of existential angst that arises from the void where hope and meaning used to be. When individuals and families experience despair, it's very painful. When a person finds **meaning** in their life, they feel as though their life has "significance and purposefulness" (Gladding, 2011). Part of your role is to help individuals and families find hope, find meaning, and, ultimately, complete the developmental tasks associated with life completion and life closure.

July 28, 2019

GoFundMe post from Kim Acquaviva:

I haven't posted an update in a while because I've only had the time and energy to post "micro" updates via social media (Twitter Facebook, and Instagram). Kathy hasn't been able to get out of bed for almost a week and she's sleeping 99 percent of the time now. When she's awake, she's very confused but there are brief flickers of lucidity. In those moments when her head is clear, she tells Greyson

(continued on next page)

(continued from previous page)

and me that she loves us. I read cards, texts, emails, and social media messages to her and she cries happy tears.

Kathy's sleeping as I type this on my phone. It's 4am and I'm laying awake next to her, listening to her breathe. Thinking about the moment when my nighttime sound machine of 18 years will fall silent makes my heart hurt.

Everything about this feels surreal. Kathy's too weak to get out of bed now but her walker and shower chair still sit accusatorially in our bedroom and bathroom. A never-used bedside commode sits 6 feet away from the bed, its basin turned into a handy receptacle for soapy water and its arms turned into towel racks for washcloths. I should probably put the walker and the shower chair in the garage but doing that before Kathy dies means acknowledging that Kathy will never leave this bed again and I'm not quite ready for that.

I've never felt closer to Kathy and Greyson than I do right now. Strip away the ordinariness of daily family life and we're left with something extraordinary. With adult diapers and emesis bags and pads on the bed to catch errant urine comes humility, realness, and humor. Greyson and I have had to learn how to cut through the parent-child noise so that we can focus on the signal. I don't want you to get the wrong impression, though: none of us is doing this perfectly. Kathy, Greyson, and I are still perfectly imperfect human beings. There are no heroes or saints or angels in our house—just people doing their best moment by moment. My new job at UVA starts in 4 days and I have to confess: there are moments when I wish Kathy would hurry up and die. That sounds monstrous to admit but in a way, that's end-of-life caregiving in a nutshell: feeling torn between dreading the loss of a loved one and eagerly anticipating a life beyond loss.

I don't think I'll ever be able to convey what a difference your support has meant to Kathy, Greyson, and me over the past 6 months. The emotional support has kept our spirits afloat; the financial support has kept our family afloat. It'd made it possible for us to afford the medications and equipment to keep Kathy comfortable and cared for at home. It made it possible for us to spend time in Maine saying goodbye to family and friends. It's making it possible for me to pay Kathy's debts and avoid going into more debt. Most importantly, it's making it possible for Greyson and I to breathe knowing we're going to be OK.

When we have Kathy's memorial service, I hope I can thank many of you in person for your support. The service will be held on Saturday, October 26th at 2pm ET at Friends Meeting of Washington. All are welcome. ♥

Much love -

Kim

LIFE COMPLETION AND LIFE CLOSURE: DEVELOPMENTAL TASKS

Individuals facing serious or life-limiting conditions continue to have opportunities for personal growth and fulfillment. Whether you are a physician, social worker, counselor, chaplain, advanced practice registered nurse, physician associate, or registered nurse, there are things you can do to support individuals and families in completing the developmental tasks associated with **life completion and life closure**. Byock's (1994) chart "Developmental Landmarks and Taskwork for the End of Life," reprinted in table 9.1, is a seminal resource that provides a clearly articulated model for the developmental tasks associated with life completion and life closure.

Because Byock's developmental tasks are presented as a list, it can be tempting to imagine them as easily defined tasks on a linear checklist of sorts. However, most of the developmental tasks have no discrete beginning or end point. Individuals may move in and out of accepting their own worthiness or feeling comfortable with chaos. There is no right or wrong way to progress through these developmental tasks—every patient is unique in how, when, and even if they tackle them. Remember, your role is to be a supportive guide, not a taskmaster.

Using these developmental tasks as a framework, Byock and Merriman developed the Missoula-VITAS Quality of Life Index (MVQOLI), a

TABLE 9.1 Byock's developmental landmarks and taskwork for the end of life

Landmarks	Taskwork
Sense of completion with worldly affairs	• Transfer of fiscal, legal, and formal social responsibilities
Sense of completion in relationships with community	• Closure of multiple social relationships (employment, commerce, organizational, congregational); components include: expressions of regret, expressions of forgiveness, acceptance of gratitude and appreciation • Leave taking; the saying of good-bye
Sense of meaning about one's individual life	• Life review • The telling of "one's stories" • Transmission of knowledge and wisdom
Experienced love of self	• Self-acknowledgment • Self-forgiveness
Experienced love of others	• Acceptance of worthiness
Sense of completion in relationships with family and friends	• Reconciliation, fullness of communication, and closure in each of one's important relationships; components include: expressions of regret, expressions of forgiveness and acceptance, expressions of gratitude and appreciation, acceptance of gratitude and appreciation, expressions of affection • Leave-taking; the saying of good-bye
Acceptance of the finality of life—of one's existence as an individual	• Acknowledgment of the totality of personal loss represented by one's dying, and experience of personal pain of existential loss • Expression of the depth of personal tragedy that dying represents • *Decathexis* (emotional withdrawal) from worldly affairs and *cathexis* (emotional connection) with an enduring construct • Acceptance of dependency
Sense of a new self (personhood) beyond personal loss	• Developing self-awareness in the present
Sense of meaning about life in general Surrender to the transcendent, to the unknown—"letting go"	• Achieving a sense of awe • Recognition of a transcendent realm • Developing/achieving a sense of comfort with chaos • In pursuit of this landmark, the doer and "taskwork" are one. Here, little remains of the ego except the volition to surrender.

Source: Byock, 1994. Reprinted with permission from Ira Byock, MD, © 1994.

PROFESSIONAL PERSPECTIVE

So often I hear people say, "Hospice is not about giving up hope," and my response is, "Says who?!" I get that the notion of hope changes, yet I also think that letting go of hope for continued life is something we should be offering to address with individuals and families, and that it is likely we do not do this enough. Just because we are not doing psychotherapy based on a clinical diagnosis does not mean we are not using many of the same interventions we would use in psychotherapy or "counseling" sessions. We can be using things like motivational interviewing to create person-centered plans of care; mindfulness techniques to address pain/symptom management, stress, agitation; the dual process model for grief and loss; and much of cognitive behavioral therapy (CBT) can be used by us to help address suffering at all levels. Social workers, counselors, and chaplains can use mindfulness, guided imagery, "combat breathing," and many of the CBT interventions. One of my mantras is, "How do we get beyond active listening and emotional support?" And as Kübler-Ross said, "People are dying here. There is no time for funny business!"

—Gary Gardia, LCSW, APHSW-C

validated, widely used instrument designed to assess quality of life along the following dimensions:

Symptoms (S): Experience of physical discomfort associated with progressive illness and the resulting level of physical distress; Functional (F): Perceived ability to perform accustomed functions and activities of daily living experienced in relation to the person's expectations, and the associated emotional response; Interpersonal (IP): Degree of investment in personal relationships and the perceived quality of one's relations/interactions with family and friends; Well-being (WB): Self-assessment of a person's internal condition. A subjective sense of wellness or disease, contentment or lack of contentment; Transcendent (T): Experienced degree of connection with an enduring construct; degree of experienced meaning and purpose of one's life. (Byock & Merriman, 1998)

Although the MVQOLI was originally developed for use with individuals facing a terminal, life-limiting illness, "the MVQOLI has been used with palliative care and hospice patients in a variety of settings including hospice, hospital, home health, long-term care (including assisted living), outpatient palliative care, and pre-hospice programs . . . [and] is appropriate for any patient population facing advanced, chronic, progressive illness" (Byock & Merriman, n.d.). Consider using the MVQOLI to gain a better understanding of patients' quality of life from a holistic perspective.

SPIRITUAL/EXISTENTIAL ASSESSMENT: WHOSE JOB IS IT?

In palliative care and hospice care, chaplains are the members of the interdisciplinary/interprofessional team with the most training and experience in providing a **spiritual/existential assessment**, "an informed judgment concerning treatment options based on the spiritual [or existential] history" (LaRocca-Pitts, 2007). However, other members of the team may conduct spiritual histories or support the patient and family in achieving their goals of care related to spirituality or existential concerns.

All too often, team members ask individuals and families only a single screening question in the spiritual arena: "Would you like to see a chaplain?" Instead of asking such a narrow question, consider saying something like this: "Many people I work with say they worry about what will happen to them after they die. Is that something that you've been thinking about?" If the patient's answer is yes, you can respond by saying, "There's someone on our team who's really good with those conversations. Can I have that person call you?" Another way you could open the conversation might include asking, for example, "In times when you experience challenges such as serious illness, what are some ways that you cope and find strength?"

There's a difference between a spiritual/existential history and a spiritual/existential assessment, although the two terms are often used interchangeably or indistinctly. In the first edition of this book, I noted that the third edition of the *Clinical Practice Guidelines for Quality Palliative Care* (2013) did not articulate a distinction between spiritual assessment and spiritual history, nor did it distinguish between which members of the team should be able to take such a history and which should be able to design and implement treatment and interventions to address issues identified during the history. A reference was made to people operating only within their scope of practice, but I noted that this should be made more explicit. The fourth edition (2018) does exactly that:

> The spiritual assessment process has three distinct components—spiritual screening, spiritual history, and a full spiritual assessment. The spiritual screening is conducted with every patient and family to identify spiritual needs and/or distress. The history and assessment identify the spiritual background, preferences, and related beliefs, values, rituals, and practices of the patient and family. Symptoms, such as spiritual distress and spiritual strengths and resources, are identified and documented. . . . All aspects of the screening, history, and assessment are conducted using standardized tools. . . . Spiritual screening is completed as part of every clinical assessment to identify spiritual distress and the need for urgent referral to a professional chaplain. Screening is designed to evaluate the presence or absence of spiritual needs and spiritual distress . . . IDT members also include a spiritual history as part of the clinical evaluation in the initial assessment process. A spiritual history identifies patient preferences and values that may affect medical decision-making. . . . A spiritual assessment is triggered based upon the results of the spiritual screening and history. It is an in-depth and ongoing process of evaluation of spiritual needs, results in a plan of care, and is conducted by a professional chaplain as the spiritual care specialist, in collaboration with the faith community, based upon patient wishes. (National Consensus Project for Quality Palliative Care, 2018)

A description of the terms *spiritual history* and *spiritual assessment* can be found in "Improving the Quality of Spiritual Care as a Dimension of Palliative Care: The Report of the Consensus Conference":

> Spiritual history-taking is the process of interviewing a patient in order to come to a better understanding of their spiritual needs and resources.

A spiritual history can be integrated into existing formats such as the social history section of the clinical database. The information from the history permits the clinician to understand how spiritual concerns could either complement or complicate the patient's overall care. It also allows the clinician to incorporate spiritual care into the patient's overall care plan. Those doing a spiritual history should have some education in and comfort with issues that may emerge and knowledge of how to engage patients comfortably in this discussion. (Puchalski et al., 2009)

In contrast to a spiritual history, which may be completed by a physician, registered nurse, advanced practice registered nurse, physician associate, social worker, or chaplain, among others, a spiritual assessment (also called a spiritual/existential assessment) refers to

> a more extensive process of active listening to a patient's story conducted by a board-certified chaplain that summarizes the needs and resources that emerge in that process. The chaplain's summary should include a spiritual care plan with expected outcomes that is then communicated to the rest of the treatment team. Unlike history-taking, the major models for spiritual assessment are not built on a set of questions that can be used in an interview. Rather, the models are interpretive frameworks that are based on listening to the patient's story as it unfolds. Because of the complex nature of these assessments and the special clinical training necessary to engage in them, this assessment should be done only by a board-certified chaplain or an equivalently prepared spiritual care provider. (Puchalski et al., 2009)

Figure 9.1, which comes from Puchalski et al. (2009), "Improving the Quality of Spiritual Care as a Dimension of Palliative Care," illustrates how the spiritual history, spiritual assessment, and spiritual interventions and treatment fit together in an inpatient setting. The diagram outlines an approach that would be appropriate in both palliative care and hospice care, regardless of setting.

Note: As you conduct a spiritual history of a patient, remember the mitigation plan discussed in chapter 1. It is important that you prevent your

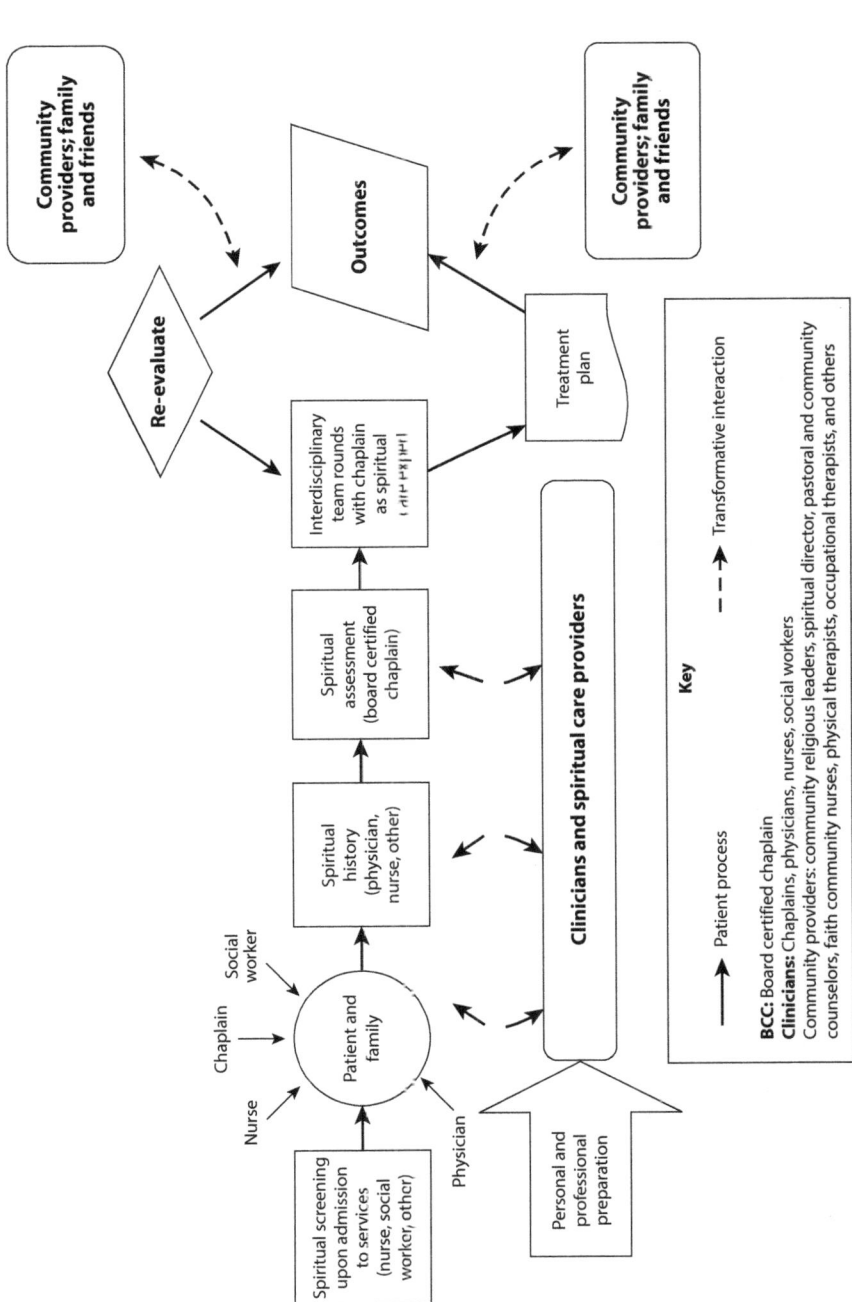

FIGURE 9.1 Collaboration of spiritual history, spiritual assessment, and spiritual interventions and treatment in patient care

unconscious biases from having a negative impact on the care you provide to that patient.

THE IMPORTANCE OF INCLUSIVE LANGUAGE

When you ask a patient or patient's family about their spiritual/existential needs, you are asking them to enter into a very personal dialogue with you about a part of their life that may be very important to them. As is the case with every aspect of an assessment, the words you use in opening that conversation can either build a bridge or burn one. Table 9.2 offers a few examples of how the words you use may not convey the message you intend.

The language you use with individuals and families should be inclusive enough that they should not be able to guess your own spiritual or religious beliefs. Ask questions in a way that conveys that you are open to all possible answers. The spiritual history questions in dimension 1-A of the Five-Dimension Assessment Model are examples of open-ended, inclusive questions (see the box "FICA Spiritual History Tool" in chapter 4).

Inclusive language and open-ended questions are essential to conducting an effective spiritual/existential history (Knight, n.d.). If you struggle to think outside the box of your own spiritual or religious beliefs, strive to learn more about other spiritual and religious beliefs and traditions. The more you learn about other ways of making sense of the world spiritually

TABLE 9.2 Intent versus impact

What You Say	What You Imply
"Are you part of a church?"	I can't imagine you'd be anything other than Christian.
"Do you believe in God?"	I have a traditional, narrowly defined concept of spirituality. If you have a more expansive concept of a higher power, I'm probably not going to be receptive to talking with you about it.
"Would you like me to call a priest?"	You're dying—like, soon. And obviously you're Catholic, right?
"I'm guessing from your last name that you're Jewish?"	I'm super awkward when it comes to asking questions about spirituality.

and existentially, the more comfortable you will be eliciting spiritual/existential histories from individuals and families.

COMMON EXPERIENCES OF SPIRITUAL/EXISTENTIAL DISTRESS

Feelings of **spiritual/existential distress** may consist of "discomfort related to religious, intellectual, or cultural concerns" or "a disruption in the life principle that pervades a person's entire being and that integrates and transcends his or her biological and psychosocial nature." When patients or family members experience spiritual/existential distress, they may voice "concern[s] with the meaning of life and death, question the meaning of suffering or of [their] own existence, verbalize inner conflict about beliefs, express anger toward God or other Supreme Being (however defined), or actively seek spiritual assistance" (*Miller-Keane Encyclopedia and Dictionary of Medicine*, n.d.).

Any patient or family member may experience spiritual/ existential distress, including individuals who have had very negative experiences with religion in the past. A transgender patient raised in an Orthodox Jewish family, for example, may have spent her life hearing messages that the male sex she was assigned at birth will be her "halachic gender"— her gender according to Jewish law—for life (Kaleem, 2016). When this patient is facing a chronic or life-limiting illness, she may struggle with those messages replaying on a loop in her head and feel conflicted about her decision to stop wearing tefillin when she transitioned to her true gender. She may struggle to reconcile her own beliefs with the beliefs she was taught as a child. This is not only the case with LGBTQIA+ individuals—heterosexual and cisgender individuals may struggle with these issues as well.

Spiritual distress may manifest itself in a variety of ways, many of which may seem to overlap with indicators of psychosocial or emotional distress. In "Improving the Quality of Spiritual Care as a Dimension of Palliative Care," Puchalski and colleagues (2009) illustrate the connections between specific spiritual "diagnoses" and the way they are manifested through a patient's or family member's history and statements (see table 9.3).

TABLE 9.3 Spiritual concerns

Diagnosis (primary)	Key feature from history	Sample statements
Existential concerns	Lack of meaning Questions the meaning about one's own existence Concern about afterlife Questions the meaning of suffering Seeks spiritual assistance	"My life is meaningless." "I feel useless."
Abandonment by God or others	Lack of love, loneliness Not being remembered No sense of relatedness	"God has abandoned me." "No one comes by anymore."
Anger at God or others	Displaces anger toward religious representatives Inability to forgive	"Why would God take my child... it's not fair."
Concerns about relationship with deity	Desires closeness to God, deepening relationship	"I want to have a deeper relationship with God."
Conflicted or challenged belief systems	Verbalizes inner conflicts or questions about beliefs or faith Conflicts between religious beliefs and recommended treatments Questions moral or ethical implications of therapeutic regimen Expresses concern with life/death or belief system	"I am not sure if God is with me anymore."
Despair/hopelessness	Hopelessness about future health, life Despair as absolute hopelessness No hope for value in life	"Life is being cut short." "There is nothing left for me to live for."
Grief/loss	The feeling and process associated with the loss of a person, health, relationship	"I miss my loved one so much." "I wish I could run again."
Guilt/shame	Feeling that one has done something wrong or evil Feeling that one is bad or evil	"I do not deserve to die pain-free."
Reconciliation	Need for forgiveness or reconciliation from self or others	"I need to be forgiven for what I did." "I would like my wife to forgive me."

Isolation	Separated from religious community or others	"Since moving to the assisted living I am not able to go to my church anymore."
Religious-specific	Ritual needs Unable to perform usual religious practices	"I just can't pray anymore."
Religious/spiritual struggle	Loss of faith or meaning Religious or spiritual beliefs or community not helping with coping	"What if all that I believe is not true."

Source: Puchalski et al., 2009. Reprinted with permission of Mary Ann Liebert, Inc., © 2009 Mary Ann Liebert, Inc. The publisher for this copyrighted material is Mary Ann Liebert, Inc.

PROFESSIONAL PERSPECTIVE

There they were. The old church lady and the young man with the purse. Sitting next to each other at the Sunday afternoon worship service I coordinated at the hospice home. "This will never work," I thought. She, a conservative Christian of many years; he, a lapsed Catholic of many fewer years. Her gray hair was adorned by a little hat with a veil, all black and gray, like her attire. His head was bare, but his outfit was brightly colored. The only thing similar about them was that they both smelled of floral perfume—hers understated, his discernible across the room. Quietly I prayed for a miracle: that they would get along, just this once, as they sat together. I needn't have worried. Every week they came to service, and sat next to each other. In fact, they became the best of friends. Sure, the differences were many. But what they had in common was that they were both dying, or—better said—living until they died. They both sought God in their own way and found him to be bigger, together, than I had imagined possible. As they shared that experience, they formed a bond of friendship that taught me that important lesson.

—Steve Shick, MDiv, MA Rel, BCC

SUPPORTING THOSE IN SPIRITUAL/EXISTENTIAL DISTRESS

Physician Daniel Sulmasy argues that there are three "pressing categories of spiritual questions that serious illness raises—questions of meaning, value, and relationship" (Sulmasy, 2006). To help individuals and families make meaning of their experience, Sulmasy suggests that clinicians ask them questions in each of the three areas. Sulmasy's final question—"If you're a religious person, how are things between you and God?"—represents a somewhat narrow conceptualization of what it means to be a "religious person." People may consider themselves to be religious and yet not believe in the existence of a solitary deity named "God." Rather than posing the question Sulmasy suggests, try asking something like, "If you believe in a higher power—a guiding force, deity, god, goddess, gods, the divine, or the sacred—how are things between you and that power?" Although grammatically awkward, using such inclusive language will communicate to the individuals and families you work with that you have an open mind regarding their spiritual, existential, and religious beliefs.

A NOTE ABOUT BEREAVEMENT CARE

After a patient dies, their family of choice, family of origin, or both will likely benefit from bereavement care. Bereavement care should address the psychosocial and spiritual needs of the family and should be delivered in a manner that is sensitive to the unique needs of the individuals. In delivering bereavement care, it is important to remember the historical context of LGBTQIA+ individuals' reluctance to access care and acknowledge the effect that may have on bereavement outcomes. "Those occupying the position of overt exclusion may be at increased risk of adverse bereavement outcomes due to the additional barriers and stressors they experience and, therefore, may need additional support. In addition, for some individuals, due to historical factors, such as having lived through a period when homosexuality was illegal, there may be an expectation of homophobia or assumption of overt exclusion, even if this is not actualized in interactions with healthcare professionals" (Bristowe, Marshall, & Harding, 2016).

When recommending a bereavement group to an individual, give careful thought to whether the individual's needs are likely to be met by that particular group. Consider the following factors:

- A man may not feel comfortable in an all-female bereavement group.
- A woman whose female partner just died may feel as though her loss is seen as "less than" the loss experienced by women whose husbands have died.
- A nonbinary person may not feel comfortable in a single-gender bereavement group.
- A transgender individual in a bereavement group with cisgender persons may feel as though their gender identity and expression is the focal point of the group's attention rather than their experience of grief and loss.
- A bisexual individual may feel as though group members' misconceptions about bisexuality make it difficult for them to recognize the significance of the individual's loss.
- A heterosexual individual may not feel comfortable in a bereavement group comprised entirely of LGB individuals.
- A cisgender individual may not feel comfortable in a bereavement group made up entirely of transgender individuals.
- Heterosexual, cisgender support-group members may not behave in a welcoming way to an LGBTQIA+ person.

In short, every grieving individual is just that—an individual. Never make assumptions about where a person will be most comfortable. Ask questions to determine the bereavement group or groups in which the individual is most likely to feel a sense of safety and support.

KEY POINTS TO REMEMBER

- If a patient or family member appears to be experiencing emotional distress, assess for clinically significant depression and suicidal ideation, document the results of your assessment, and take the appropriate actions, based on your discipline's scope of practice.

- When assessing emotional distress in a patient or family member, be sensitive to the fact that the perceived source of distress could be a long-standing issue that would seem to have nothing to do with the seriousness of the patient's life-limiting illness.
- Don't assume that all lesbian, gay, bisexual, transgender, nonbinary, gender nonconforming, queer, questioning, intersex, and/or asexual individuals will be experiencing emotional distress regarding relationships with their family of origin. Many LGBTQIA+ individuals have a positive, supportive relationship with their family of origin.
- Despair, hope, and meaning all play important roles in individuals' and families' experiences of growth in the context of advanced illness. It is up to each patient and family to define what hope means for them. Your role is to offer them information, choices, and support, not permission to hope for a particular outcome.
- There is a difference between a spiritual history and a spiritual assessment. Any member of the team may conduct a spiritual history but only a board-certified chaplain or spiritual care professional with equivalent training should complete a spiritual assessment.
- When you ask a patient or patient's family about their spiritual/existential needs, the language you use should be neutral, open, and inclusive; they should not be able to guess your own spiritual or religious beliefs based on your questions.
- As you take a patient's spiritual history, remember the mitigation plan discussed in chapter 1. It is important to prevent your unconscious biases from having a negative impact on the care you provide.
- Spiritual distress may manifest itself in a variety of a ways, many of which may seem to overlap with indicators of psychosocial or emotional distress.
- In delivering bereavement care, it is important to remember the historical context of LGBTQIA+ individuals' reluctance to access care and acknowledge the effect this may have on bereavement outcomes. When recommending a bereavement group to an individual, give careful thought to whether the individual's needs are likely to be met by that particular group.

DISCUSSION QUESTIONS

1. In palliative care and hospice, each member of the interdisciplinary/interprofessional team plays a role in ensuring that the psychosocial needs of individuals and families are assessed and addressed. Describe a psychosocial assessment and supportive techniques. What is the role of your discipline in using these tools?
2. What are the similarities and differences between emotional distress and spiritual/existential distress in terms of presentation and assessment? Which members of the interdisciplinary/interprofessional team address each type of distress?
3. What are the developmental tasks involved in life completion and life closure? What roles do despair, hope, and meaning play in the context of serious and life-threatening illness?
4. Within the context of palliative care and hospice, what is a spiritual/existential assessment and what role, if any, does your discipline play in conducting such an assessment?
5. Describe common experiences of spiritual/existential distress for individuals and families facing chronic and life-limiting conditions.

CHAPTER ACTIVITY

Contact a palliative care or hospice chaplain and ask to meet at their workplace for about an hour to learn more about the chaplain's role on the interdisciplinary/interprofessional team. During your meeting, ask the chaplain about spiritual distress and how it presents in individuals receiving palliative care or hospice care. Ask about the chaplain's experiences working with LGBTQIA+ individuals and families and the ways the chaplain has supported these individuals and families. Afterward, reflect on your meeting. Were you surprised by anything you learned? Do you think working in collaboration with a chaplain would improve the care you deliver to individuals in palliative care or hospice? Why or why not?

August 4, 2019

GoFundMe post from Kim Acquaviva:

Kathy died at 4:51 this morning. I had fallen asleep with my hand on her arm—both dogs were in the bedroom with us. I woke up around 3:30 am when I noticed her breathing change. I could tell she was close so I talked softly to her about her favorite beach and ocean waves and cobalt blue sea glass. She sighed deeply and that was it—she was gone. I washed her and contemplated putting a different outfit on her but then remembered how pragmatic she was. Instead, I pulled the covers up to tuck her in one last time, and then I brushed my teeth and took a shower. No idea why . . . maybe I just wanted the day to have something normal in it. I don't know.

 Mitzi was still laying in the bed watching over Kathy when I was done showering. I took both dogs out, brought them back inside, then went upstairs to wake up Greyson. Grey came downstairs and kissed Kathy goodbye. Then I turned on the oven and made cinnamon rolls. Kathy always made Greyson cinnamon rolls on the first day of school. It seemed like the right thing to do so I did it.

 While the cinnamon rolls were in the oven, I started making calls. I called Kathy's palliative care doc and our close family and friends. Pretty much everyone had their ringer off so I tried to think of other things to do while I was waiting for people to wake up. Greyson and I ate breakfast and talked about how weird it felt being sad and relieved simultaneously. We're both kind of numb.

 I pulled out the checklist that Kathy and I had put together of things I needed to do when she died. Her last wish was an obit in the New York Times with very specific wording, so Greyson and I placed the ad and laughed at what she had written. Kathy has planned for us to use her tiny life insurance policy to pay for the ad, so I charged it to my credit card. And then an awful thought hit me: her life insurance policy was through GW. My last day of work was July 31. I'm praying the policy will still be valid but am sick at the thought that it might not be. My new job at UVA started August 1 but I haven't been able to elect benefits yet. HR said benefits will be retroactive to August 1 but I have a bad feeling about whether that's true for life insurance. Ugh. [Author's note, July 29, 2022: In a miraculous twist of fate, Kathy's small life insurance policies at both GW and UVA were active the day she died].

As I type this, it's 11:41 am. Dr. Blackhall, the palliative care doc from UVA, came out earlier to pronounce Kathy's death. She was wonderful and spent a long time talking with Greyson and me in the breakfast room while we waited for the funeral home to arrive. She left once she knew we were OK, then two men from the funeral home pulled up in minivans. A large stag and a baby deer were together in front of the house as they pulled up. While Greyson was outside with the dogs, they transferred Kathy onto a gurney. One of them asked me if there were "any valuables other than your wife." It was the kindest phrasing possible—I had trouble answering because my throat felt so tight. Greyson and I then came into the bedroom to say a final goodbye to Kathy before they drove her to the crematorium.

I'm sorry for the rambling post. I wanted all of you to know that Kathy had a peaceful death and your love and support is what made that possible. Our family has felt your love and we can't begin to tell you how much it's meant to us. Thank you ♥

Love,

Kim & Greyson

10 | Ensuring Institutional Inclusiveness

CHAPTER OUTCOMES

1. Strengthen the inclusion of LGBTQIA+ individuals and families in the palliative care or hospice institution/facility/program in which you work.
2. Assess the inclusiveness of wording on the intake or admission forms your institution/facility/program uses.
3. Assess marketing and outreach materials for inclusive language and imagery.
4. Recognize five policies or benefits that demonstrate an employer's commitment to being LGBTQIA-inclusive.
5. List one action you will take in the next month as an individual health care professional to strengthen the inclusion of LGBTQIA+ individuals and their families in your institution/facility/program.

Key Terms: employee benefits, orientation, and training; intake forms and processes; marketing and community engagement

CHAPTER SUMMARY

The first nine chapters of this book describe how individual health care professionals can deliver high-quality palliative care and hospice care that is inclusive of LGBTQIA− individuals and their families. For palliative care and hospice professionals to have the best opportunity to put this knowledge into practice, however, they need to take a few steps at the institutional level to ensure that LGBTQIA+ individuals and their families feel welcome and safe coming to them for care. The care that individual health care professionals provide is a bit like a clinic on an offshore island. The care provided on that island may be the best in the world, but if individuals and families can't reach it, those health care professionals lose out on the opportunity to serve them. This chapter explains how to assess the structural integrity of an institution's bridge to LGBTQIA+ individuals and how to extend and strengthen that bridge to reach, welcome, and serve LGBTQIA+ individuals and their families.

YOUR ROLE IN STRENGTHENING INSTITUTIONAL INCLUSION OF LGBTQIA+ INDIVIDUALS AND FAMILIES

Whether you are an advanced practice registered nurse, physician associate, physician, registered nurse, chaplain, social worker, or counselor, your profession's code of ethics and accompanying interpretive statements compel you to advocate for changes at the institutional level to ensure that LGBTQIA+ individuals and their families have access to the same high-quality care available to others:

- **Chaplains**
    - Members shall seek to represent the best interests of those whom they serve[,] giving voice to the vulnerable whenever possible. (Association of Professional Chaplains, 2000)

- **Social Workers**
  - The primary mission of the social work profession is to enhance human well-being and help meet the basic human needs of all people, with particular attention to the needs and empowerment of people who are vulnerable, oppressed, and living in poverty. Social workers promote social justice and social change with and on behalf of clients. "Clients" is used inclusively to refer to individuals, families, groups, organizations, and communities. Social workers are sensitive to cultural and ethnic diversity and strive to end discrimination, oppression, poverty, and other forms of social injustice. These activities may be in the form of direct practice, community organizing, supervision, consultation administration, advocacy, social and political action, policy development and implementation, education, and research and evaluation. Social workers seek to enhance the capacity of people to address their own needs. Social workers also seek to promote the responsiveness of organizations, communities, and other social institutions to individuals' needs and social problems. (National Association of Social Workers, 2021)
- **Nurses**
  - Ethics, human rights, and nursing converge as a formidable instrument for social justice and health diplomacy that can be amplified by collaboration with other health professionals. Nurses understand that the lived experiences of inequality, poverty, and social marginalization contribute to the deterioration of health globally.
  - Nurses collaborate with others to change unjust structures and processes that affect both individuals and communities. Structural, social, and institutional inequalities and disparities exacerbate the incidence and burden of illness, trauma, suffering, and premature death.
  - Nurses must recognize that health care is provided to culturally diverse populations in this country and around the globe. Nurses should collaborate to create a moral milieu that is sensitive to

diverse cultural values and practices. (American Nurses Association, 2015)
- **Physicians**
  - A physician shall support access to medical care for all people. (American Medical Association, 2001)
- **Physician Associates**
  - "The principal value of the PA profession is to respect the health, safety, welfare, and dignity of all human beings. (American Academy of Physician Associates, 2018)

Each discipline's code of ethics contains language about the importance of advocating for institutional change to ensure access to care, but how do you translate what's written in your discipline's code of ethics into specific actions you can take? If your primary role in your institution involves direct practice with individuals and families, you may be unfamiliar or uncomfortable with advocating for institutional-level change. Even the word *advocacy* can sound a bit strident to health care professionals accustomed to focusing on direct patient care in the palliative care and hospice environment. Advocacy does not have to be confrontational, though—in fact, when done well, advocacy feels more collaborative than confrontational to all parties involved. Following are concrete steps you can take within your institution to advocate for greater inclusion of LGBTQIA+ individuals and families.

ASSESSING YOUR BRIDGE TO LGBTQIA+ INDIVIDUALS AND FAMILIES

As a palliative care or hospice professional, you have an interest in providing LGBTQIA-inclusive care. But before LGBTQIA+ individuals and their families can benefit from your knowledge and skills, they need to seek out the services of your program. The bridge between you and the individuals and families you hope to serve is made up of four main "planks," each essential to the structural integrity of the bridge as a mechanism for reaching, welcoming, and serving everyone.

266 | Ensuring Institutional Inclusiveness

- Plank 1: Nondiscrimination statement
- Plank 2: Employee benefits, orientation, and training
- Plank 3: Intake forms and processes
- Plank 4: Marketing and community engagement

When I speak to hospice and palliative care programs on this topic, participants are often surprised by my heavy focus on employee benefits, policies, orientation, and training. All too often, palliative care and hospice programs approach the challenge of reaching LGBTQIA+ individuals and their families primarily through marketing. Although marketing is an important plank, the bridge won't be strong enough unless the other planks are in place.

PLANK 1: NONDISCRIMINATION STATEMENT

Of all the planks in your program's bridge, your organization's nondiscrimination statement is the most important. Your nondiscrimination statement needs to be two things—inclusive and visible—if it is going to be an effective tool for reaching and welcoming LGBTQIA+ individuals and their families.

An LGBTQIA-inclusive nondiscrimination statement will include the phrases *gender identity*, *gender expression*, *sexual orientation*, *intersex status*, *intersex traits*, *differences of sex development*, and *diversity in sex characteristics* (National LGBTQIA+ Health Education Center, 2020) in addition to the other phrases that commonly appear in nondiscrimination statements. It's not enough to list "sex" and "sexual orientation"—the statement needs to be specific in conveying a commitment not to discriminate against transgender individuals. Lambda Legal (2010) recommends an even broader and more inclusive approach, urging organizations to "establish nondiscrimination, fair visitation[,] and other policies that prohibit bias and discrimination based on sexual orientation, gender identity and expression[,] and HIV status, recognize families of LGBTQ[IA+] people and their wishes[,] and provide a process for reporting and redressing discrimination if it occurs."

Imagine that you are a transgender individual trying to choose a palliative care or hospice program. What would you think about the following nondiscrimination statements (based on actual statements found online), and how would they make you feel? What about if you were bisexual? Gay or lesbian?

- **Statement 1:** It is the policy of _____ that no person shall, on the grounds of race, color, national origin, ancestry, age (over 40), sex, genetic information, handicap or disability (including AIDS, HIV infection, or AIDS- related condition), or religious creed, be excluded from participation in, be denied benefits of, or otherwise be subject to discrimination or harassment in the provision of any care or service or employment.
- **Statement 2:** No person shall be discriminated against based on the grounds of race, color, religion, age, sex, sexual orientation, gender identity, national origin, ancestry, marital status, protected veteran status, pregnancy, or disability, or any other categories protected by federal or state law.
- **Statement 3:** _____ does not discriminate against any person on the basis of race, color, creed, national origin, gender, age, sexual orientation, religion, veteran status, or disability.
- **Statement 4:** _____ is committed to a policy of nondiscrimination for patients, employees, and visitors. No person shall be subjected to discrimination in the provision of any care or service on the grounds of race, color, national origin (including limited English proficiency), ancestry, age, sex, religion, handicap, disability, or other legally protected basis. Applicants for staff positions shall not be denied membership or particular privileges/duties on the basis of race, color, national origin (including limited English proficiency), ancestry, religion, or sex.
- **Statement 5:** Patient services are provided without regard to race, religion, age, gender, gender identity, gender expression, sexual orientation, mental or physical disability, communicable disease, or place of national origin.
- **Statement 6:** We care for all people regardless of ability to pay, race, disability, color, creed, religion, gender, age, sexual orientation, gender expression, national origin, ancestry, citizenship, or veteran status.

The variability in the wording of these nondiscrimination statements is striking. How do you think your organization's nondiscrimination statement should read? Your organization should revise its nondiscrimination statement until you can answer yes to all of the following questions:

- Does the statement include all language required under the Federal Civil Rights Act of 1964?
- Does the statement include all language required under the Equal Pay Act of 1963?
- Does the statement include all language required under the Age Discrimination in Employment Act of 1967?
- Does the statement include all language required under the Rehabilitation Act of 1973?
- Does the statement include all language required under the Americans with Disabilities Act of 1991?
- Does the statement include all language required under other federal labor and employment laws?
- Does the statement include all language required under your state's human relations, labor, and employment laws?
- Does the statement include all language required under your city's human relations, labor, and employment laws?
- Does the statement include the phrases *sexual orientation*, *gender identity*, and *gender expression*?

It is important to point out that if your organization is not formally committed to a policy of nondiscrimination based on sexual orientation, gender identity, gender expression, intersex status, intersex traits, differences of sex development, and diversity in sex characteristics in its employment practices, you should not expect lesbian, gay, bisexual, transgender, nonbinary, gender nonconforming, queer, questioning, intersex, and/or asexual individuals and families to feel safe seeking out your services.

Your organization's nondiscrimination statement should be a highly visible manifestation of its commitment to inclusion. Unfortunately, many palliative care and hospice programs have nondiscrimination statements that are, at best, difficult to find online and, at worst, completely absent from the organization's website. So how should your organization disseminate its nondiscrimination statement? When the nondiscrimination statement is put forth correctly, your organization should be able to answer yes to all of the following questions:

- Is the nondiscrimination statement on the organization's home page online (not buried somewhere else on the website)?
- When a visitor to the organization's website types the term *gay, lesbian, bisexual, transgender, discrimination, gender identity, gender expression,* or *sexual orientation* into any search boxes embedded on your website, does the search yield a link to the nondiscrimination statement?
- When someone enters the name of your organization and the word *discrimination* in the Google search box, does the search yield a link to your organization's nondiscrimination statement?
- Is your organization's nondiscrimination statement included in every brochure and flyer?
- If someone calls your organization's main phone number and asks about your nondiscrimination policy, will the caller be read the nondiscrimination statement directly, without being transferred to someone else?
- When someone asks you what the organization's nondiscrimination policy is, do you know what to say?

If aspects of your organization's nondiscrimination statement need to be revised or strengthened, set up a meeting with the most senior administrator you have access to and say you wish to discuss an easy, low-cost way the organization can attract and serve more people in the community. When you pitch the nondiscrimination policy as a way to increase patient access and enrollment at little cost to the organization, you may stand a greater chance of getting that meeting.

It can take years of gentle but persistent advocacy to get an organization to change its nondiscrimination statement, so don't give up. Your persistence, politeness, and professionalism will go a long way toward transforming your organization into one that clearly articulates its commitment to inclusion and nondiscrimination. Once your organization's nondiscrimination statement is both inclusive and visible, you will be ready to move on to strengthening and extending other aspects of your bridge to LGBTQIA+ individuals and their families.

PLANK 2: EMPLOYEE BENEFITS, ORIENTATION, AND TRAINING

For your organization to be a place where LGBTQIA+ individuals and their families feel safe and comfortable accessing services, it needs to be a place where LGBTQIA+ employees feel safe, comfortable, and valued. If your organization can answer yes to all of the following questions, this plank is likely to be a strong part of your bridge to LGBTQIA+ individuals and their families.

- Does your organization provide "equivalency in same- and different-sex spousal medical and soft benefits"?
- Does your organization provide "equivalency in same- and different-sex domestic partner medical and soft benefits"?
- Does your organization provide "equivalency in spousal and domestic partner family formation benefits regardless of sex"?
- Does your organization provide "equal health coverage for transgender individuals without exclusion for medically necessary care"?
- Does your organization provide coverage for "hair removal . . . tracheal shave/reduction, facial feminization surgeries, voice modification surgery, voice modification therapy, lipoplasty/filling for body masculinization or feminization, [and] travel and lodging expenses"?
- Does your organization have "gender transition guidelines with supportive restroom, dress code[,] and documentation guidance"?

- Does your organization give benefits-eligible employees, "upon hire and annually, a guide on plan benefits specific to family formation, transgender-inclusive healthcare, and HIV treatment/prevention?" If so, does the guide "include details on benefits, services, and treatment offered, the process for using those benefits (such as preauthorization requirements), information on the appeals process if applicable, and contact information for a benefits advocate or other relevant contact"? (Human Rights Campaign Foundation, 2022)
- Does your organization "require health profession students and health professionals to undergo significant cultural competency training about sexual orientation, gender identity[,] and expression"?
- Does your organization's new-employee orientation "include training about the specific ways LGBTQIA+ people and people living with HIV who are also people of color, low income, seniors[,] or members of other underserved populations may experience discrimination in health care settings and establish policies to prevent them" (Lambda Legal, 2010)?
- Does your organization include optional questions on sexual orientation, sex assigned at birth, current gender identity, and pronouns on its employee data collection forms?
- Does your organization currently have any LGTBQIA+ employees? Are there any LGBTQIA+ employees in management or leadership positions?
- Do the orientation and training materials for new employees include the nondiscrimination policy?

Convincing your organization to be inclusive in its approach to employee benefits, orientation, and training may seem like a steep hill to climb, given concerns about potential cost, but in reality the steepest climb is getting an inclusive nondiscrimination statement. After that, employee policies fall into place more easily. Once the first two planks of your organization's bridge to LGBTQIA+ individuals and their families are in place, you are ready to focus on intake processes.

PROFESSIONAL PERSPECTIVE

I have faced discrimination in the workplace everywhere I've worked since I came out as trans publicly, but nothing compared to what I face as a hospice and palliative care nurse. The idea of nursing is separated between men taking care of men and women taking care of women and men. Where does that leave space for myself as a trans non-binary person? I'm almost invisible to the system I work for, there's nothing that HR can change for me, and I still face harassment, questions, and remarks from my coworkers daily. The patients love me because I provide fast and efficient care and because I listen with my heart. I care for patients everyday with deep compassion yet in the workplace I have to question if anyone can give me respect, compassion, or care back. I hope this system can change to provide a safe space for anyone by trans people becoming visible and respected publicly. Trans and non-binary people are nurses and we deserve respect. Queer, trans, and non-binary people have been working to provide for care for others for centuries. We all deserve care and respect especially in the workplace and in the last of our days.

—Vaiana Morgan

Vaiana Morgan describes themself as "a trans non-binary person who is white passing, indigenous, and a TNA becoming a CNA."

PLANK 3: INTAKE FORMS AND PROCESSES

When a potential patient or family member contacts your organization, the first interaction they have with an employee or volunteer can have a profound effect on whether they feel welcome and safe in seeking your organization's services. Think about who those crucial first points of contact are in your organization. They might be phone or switchboard operators, website administrators, social media directors, administrative assistants, members of the admissions team, volunteers, or all of the above. If a potential client called any of the people in these positions and asked whether your organization has the training and experience needed to care for a bisexual individual, for example, what would they be told? What if someone called and asked, "Are you comfortable taking care of gay people?" or "Has your program ever cared for a transgender woman?" If you are not sure how your organization's gatekeepers would answer, have a friend call and ask some of these questions. I am a big fan of the "mystery shopper" approach when it comes to getting an accurate sense of what individuals and families experience when they call an organization. Every employee in your organization who is a potential first point of contact with the public should be taught how to answer such questions warmly and accurately.

When individuals are in the process of being admitted to your program or service, you have an opportunity to communicate your commitment to honoring their values, customs, and preferences. Thus, the intake forms your organization uses need to be inclusive. Consider incorporating the following questions on the forms and in the intake process:

- What name would you like to be called?
- What are your pronouns (e.g., he/him, she/her, they/them, ze/zir)?
- What sex were you assigned at birth, on your original birth certificate?
- What gender are you now?
- What word or words would you use to describe your sexual orientation?

Once your organization has revised its nondiscrimination statement; strengthened its employee benefits, orientation, and training; and revised its intake forms and processes, it will be ready to begin marketing its services to LGBTQIA+ individuals and their families.

PLANK 4: MARKETING AND COMMUNITY ENGAGEMENT

With your organizational house in order, it's time to reach out directly, through marketing and community engagement, to welcome LGBTQIA+ individuals and their families. Interestingly, if your organization has put the first three planks of the bridge to LGBTQIA+ individuals and their families in place, it won't need to spend much money on marketing. A visible commitment to equality, inclusion, and nondiscrimination will yield tremendous word-of-mouth benefits.

Let's start by taking a look at your marketing materials. Placing a transgender pride flag on your marketing materials is not enough—in fact, that may even be harmful if staff members haven't been taught how to provide LGBTQIA-inclusive care. If your only data sources were the photographs on your organization's website and brochures, what would you conclude about the types of people your organization serves? Would LGBTQIA+ individuals see themselves reflected in the images they see? Do any of the images show same-gender dyads, or are they all photos of male-female couples? Are all the people in the images white? Do the photos depicting patient or staff diversity appear awkward or forced? (My personal pet peeve: photographs that seem like crayon-box lineups: one person of each race, gender, age, and so on.) Your organization's website and brochures should feature images that reflect the communities you already serve and the communities you are striving to serve.

Where does your organization spend its advertising and outreach dollars? If you are not doing so already, you may want to consider advertising in a local LGBTQIA+ newspaper. Putting up an information booth at an LGBTQIA+ pride festival can help to familiarize members of the community with your organization and the services it offers. Your organization could also offer an LGBTQIA-specific bereavement group as a community engagement tool.

WHAT NOW?

The path to creating and sustaining an LGBTQIA-inclusive palliative care or hospice program is not a linear one with a clear beginning and end. The journey requires an ongoing commitment to reassessing and strengthening your organization's policies, programs, services, and outreach efforts, and as such, it is an iterative process in which your organization will continually be engaged. You have the knowledge and skills to be a catalyst for change, and in reading this book you have demonstrated a commitment to providing LGBTQIA-inclusive palliative and hospice care. So what are you going to do to strengthen the inclusion of LGBTQIA+ individuals and their families at your workplace? Decide on one action you will take in the next month, write it down, and make it happen.

KEY POINTS TO REMEMBER

- Whether you are an advanced practice registered nurse, physician, registered nurse, physician associate, chaplain, social worker, or counselor, your profession's code of ethics compels you to advocate for changes at the institutional level to ensure that LGBTQIA+ individuals and families have access to the same high-quality care available to others.
- The bridge between you and the individuals and families you hope to serve is made up of four main planks, each essential to the structural integrity of the bridge as a mechanism for reaching, welcoming, and serving LGBTQIA+ individuals and families:
  - Plank 1: Nondiscrimination statement
  - Plank 2: Employee benefits, orientation, and training
  - Plank 3: Intake forms and processes
  - Plank 4: Marketing and community engagement
- Your organization's nondiscrimination statement needs to be two things—inclusive and visible—if it is going to be an effective tool for reaching and welcoming LGBTQIA+ individuals and their families.
- An inclusive nondiscrimination statement is one that includes the phrases *gender identity*, *gender expression*, and *sexual orientation*, in addition to the other phrases that commonly appear in nondiscrimination statements.
- If your organization is not formally committed to a policy of nondiscrimination based on sexual orientation, gender identity, and gender expression or gender presentation in its employment practices, you should not expect lesbian, gay, bisexual, transgender, nonbinary, gender nonconforming, queer, questioning, intersex, and/or asexual individuals and families to feel safe seeking out your services.

- Your organization's nondiscrimination statement should be a highly visible manifestation of its commitment to inclusion.
- For your organization to be a place where LGBTQIA+ individuals and their families feel safe and comfortable receiving services, it needs to be a place where LGBTQIA+ employees feel safe, comfortable, and valued.
- When individuals are being admitted to your program or service, you have an opportunity to communicate your commitment to honoring their values, customs, and preferences. Thus, the intake forms and processes used by your organization need to be inclusive.
- A visible commitment to equality, inclusion, and nondiscrimination will yield tremendous word-of-mouth benefits.
- Make sure your website, brochures, and other marketing materials depict images inclusive of LGBTQIA+ individuals and families.

DISCUSSION QUESTIONS

1. Can individual palliative care or hospice professionals improve the inclusion of LGBTQIA+ individuals and families in the programs where they work? Why or why not? Do individual professionals have an ethical obligation to advocate for institutional change in order to facilitate the inclusion of LGBTQIA+ individuals and families? Why or why not?
2. Describe five policies and/or employee benefits that demonstrate an employer's commitment to being LGBTQIA-inclusive. How do inclusive policies and employee benefits strengthen the inclusion of LGBTQIA+ individuals and families?
3. What does the wording on your program's intake or admission forms (or those of a program in your community) say about the program's commitment to recognizing and serving LGBTQIA+ individuals and families? What changes could be made to the wording to make it more inclusive?
4. What do the word and imagery on your program's website and brochures (or those of a program in your community) say about the

program's commitment to recognizing and serving LGBTQIA+ individuals and families? What changes could be made to the wording and imagery to make them more inclusive?
5. Describe one action you will take in the next month as an individual health care professional to strengthen the inclusion of LGBTQIA+ individuals and their families in your program (or in a program in your community).

CHAPTER ACTIVITY

List at least ten actions your program or organization could take to improve its inclusion of LGBTQIA+ individuals and families. Share your list of recommendations with someone who has the power to implement them and then ask them what you can do to help with the implementation process.

11 | Advocating for Change Beyond the Institution

CHAPTER OUTCOMES

1. Advocate for change regarding LGBTQIA+ inclusion beyond the program or organization where you work.
2. List one action you will take in the next thirty days to advocate for changes to a textbook, curriculum, or conference to ensure that current and future hospice and palliative care professionals have access to the content they need in order to provide exceptional LGBTQIA-inclusive care to individuals and families.

CHAPTER SUMMARY

The previous chapter explained how to assess the structural integrity of an institution's bridge to LGBTQIA+ individuals and how to extend and strengthen that bridge to reach, welcome, and serve LGBTQIA+ individuals and their families. This chapter builds on that foundation and provides specific strategies you can use to advocate for change beyond the organization or program where you provide hospice and/or palliative care. You will learn how to advocate for changes to textbooks, curricula, and conferences to ensure that current and future hospice and palliative care professionals have access to the content they need in order to provide exceptional LGBTQIA-inclusive care to individuals and families. Most importantly, you'll learn *why* you should advocate for change beyond the program or organization where you work.

CHANGE HOW YOUR DISCIPLINE WRITES ABOUT LGBTQIA+ PEOPLE

Textbooks

In the introduction to this book, I told you why I stopped writing stand-alone chapters about LGBTQIA+ people: it's time for hospice and palliative care professionals to move beyond thinking of LGBTQIA+ people as a "special population." When LGBTQIA+ people are relegated to a single chapter in a book, it reinforces the idea that they are the "other." Whether you're someone who borrows textbooks, buys textbooks, or writes textbooks (or chapters in them), there are things you can do to change the way we collectively write about LGBTQIA+ people. Here are two simple ways you can make a difference:

1. Take a close look at a hospice and palliative care textbook in your discipline *without looking at the stand-alone chapter on LGBTQIA+ people*. Pretend the chapter on LGBTQIA+ people was ripped out of the copy of the book you're looking at. What do the rest of the chapters tell you about how to welcome, affirm, and care for LGBTQIA+ individuals and families? If the chapter on LGBTQIA+ people were ripped out of the book, would the content in the other chapters still provide a clear road map for LGBTQIA-inclusive care? If not, consider writing the editor of the textbook to suggest ways they can make the other chapters of the book more inclusive the next time the textbook is revised.

2. If you're asked to write a stand-alone chapter about LGBTQIA+ people in a textbook, it will probably be hard to say no. It's an honor to be asked to write a chapter in a book, especially since the person asking you will most likely be a luminary in the field. However, until hospice and palliative care professionals take a unified approach to responding to requests for stand-alone chapters about LGBTQIA+ people, we're unlikely to see LGBTQIA+ content woven throughout the chapters of the seminal texts in the field. If you're willing to pass up a chance to write a book chapter, here are some sample replies you can use to decline the invitation politely:

Sample 1

Thanks so much for your kind words and for your invitation to contribute to your book. On principle, I don't write stand-alone chapters on LGBTQIA+ issues for textbooks because I strongly believe the content should be woven throughout every chapter. Grouping textbook content by population runs the risk of further marginalizing an already marginalized group in the eyes of readers. If you're in need of another editor, I'd be happy to review all the chapter drafts and provide detailed feedback to authors about any edits needed to make their chapters LGBTQIA+ inclusive. I know this isn't what you were looking for, but I'm offering it in the spirit of helping you move the field forward.

Sample 2: If they insist on moving forward with a stand-alone chapter approach

Thanks, [name of Editor]. I greatly appreciate your commitment to LGBTQIA+ inclusion and I know that you have good intentions in having a stand-alone chapter about the care needs of LGBTQIA+ people. The problems with such an approach far outweigh the benefits, though. Readers pick and choose the chapters they want to read in a nonlinear textbook: putting marginalized populations in stand-alone chapters further marginalizes them. I know there are LGBTQIA+ scholars who disagree with my perspective and that's okay: my goal isn't to be in step with other academics. Instead, I'm focused on social change to make palliative care better for LGBTQIA+ people. In order for that change to happen, we need to change how we teach health care professionals. Textbooks are a key piece of that puzzle. As much as it pains me to turn down opportunities to write chapters like this, the best way for me to push for a change in how we approach the topic in textbooks is to refuse to participate in book projects that are structured in ways that marginalize LGBTQIA+ people.

There's probably no shortage of scholars who would be happy to write a stand-alone chapter for you. There's tremendous prestige that comes along with being the author of a chapter in your book—it's an opportunity that few scholars would pass up. I've cc:ed [emerging scholar in the field] in case they might be interested in the project. Not everyone feels the way I do about stand-alone LGBTQIA+ book chapters: if they are interested and available, they would be a great contributor to your textbook.

I'm not naive enough to believe that textbook editors are going to ditch "special population" stand-alone chapters just because of my opposition to that kind of approach. It's going to take years of work to turn the slow-moving behemoth that is textbook publishing into something more inclusive. In the meantime, there's absolutely nothing wrong with your choosing to write stand-alone chapters for these books if you have the expertise and the will to do so. I'm going to push for change from the outside using one set of strategies—you're welcome to push for change from within using another set of strategies as a chapter author. Together we're bound to make headway eventually.

CHANGE HOW YOUR DISCIPLINE TEACHES ABOUT LGBTQIA+ PEOPLE

Each professional on the hospice and palliative care team attended school to learn the fundamentals of their discipline, but very few hospice and palliative care professionals learned how to provide LGBTQIA-inclusive care to individuals and families when they were in school. This is because curricula in the health professions are typically designed to prepare students to pass certification and/or licensing exams, and there is minimal LGBTQIA+ content on the existing certification and licensing exams in the health professions. Each discipline "teaches to the test" because the licensing and certification exams serve as gatekeepers to their respective professions. Before you can make meaningful changes to what your discipline teaches about LGBTQIA+ people, you need to change what your discipline is *required* to teach about LGBTQIA+ people. There are three points at which you can make this change: accreditation, licensing, and certification (see table 11.1). Here are three simple ways you can make a difference:

1. Take a close look at the accreditation standards and/or competencies for academic/degree programs in your discipline. Do the standards

TABLE 11.1 Ways to change how a discipline teaches about LGBTQIA+ people

Discipline	Discipline-specific accrediting body	Discipline-specific licensing exam	Discipline-specific specialty certification in hospice and palliative care
Medicine	Liaison Committee on Medical Education (LCME)	United States Medical Licensing Examination® (USMLE®)	The American Board of Medical Specialties administers the hospice and palliative medicine subspecialty for physicians. The Hospice Medical Director Certification Board administers the Hospice Medical Director Certification.
Osteopathy	American Osteopathic Association Commission on Osteopathic College Accreditation (COCA)	Comprehensive Osteopathic Medical Licensure Exam (COMLEX-USA)	The American Osteopathic Association's Bureau of Osteopathic Specialists administers the Certificate of Added Qualification in hospice and palliative medicine for osteopathic physicians.
Advanced practice registered nursing	Commission on Collegiate Nursing Education (CCNE)	The American Association of Nurse Practitioners is the certifying board for the AANP exam.	The Hospice and Palliative Credentialing Center administers the Advanced Certified Hospice and Palliative Nurse credential.

Field	Accreditation	Exam	Certification
	Accreditation Commission for Education in Nursing (ACEN) Commission for Nursing Education Accreditation (CNEA)	The American Nurses Credentialing Center (ANCC) Certification Program offers several specialty certifications including Pain Management Nursing Certification (PMGT-BC), Family Nurse Practitioner Certification (FNP-BC), and Adult-Gerontology Primary Care Nurse Practitioner Certification (AGPCNP-BC), among others. The American Nurses Association (ANA) is the governing body behind the ANCC.	
Registered nursing	Commission on Collegiate Nursing Education (CCNE) Accreditation Commission for Education in Nursing (ACEN) Commission for Nursing Education Accreditation (CNEA)	National Council Licensure Examination (NCLEX®) The National Council of State Boards of Nursing (NCSBN) develops the NCLEX exam for practice as an RN.	The Hospice and Palliative Credentialing Center administers the Certified Hospice and Palliative Nurse credential.
Physician associate	Accreditation Review Commission on Education for the Physician Assistant (ARC-PA)	Physician Assistant National Certification Exam (PANCE)	The National Commission on Certification of Physician Assistants administers the Certificate of Added Qualifications in Palliative Medicine and Hospice Care.
Chaplaincy	ACPE: The Standard for Spiritual Care and Education		The Board of Chaplaincy Certification administers the Certified Hospice and Palliative Care Chaplain credential.
Social Work and Counseling	Council on Social Work Education (CSWE)'s Commission on Accreditation	Association of Social Work Boards (ASWB) exams	The National Association of Social Workers Specialty Certification Program administers the Certified Hospice and Palliative Social Worker credential and the Advanced Certified Hospice and Palliative Social Worker credential.

and/or competencies explicitly address LGBTQIA-inclusive care? If not, consider writing the accrediting body in your discipline to suggest ways they can make the standards and/or competencies more inclusive the next time they are revised.
2. Look at the content outline for the licensing exam(s) in your discipline. Does the content outline address LGBTQIA-inclusive care? If not, consider writing the governing body responsible for developing the exam to suggest ways they can make the exam more inclusive moving forward.
3. Review the content outline for your discipline's specialty certification in hospice and palliative care. If the content outline doesn't address LGBTQIA-inclusive care, consider writing the organization that administers the certification to suggest ways they can make the specialty certification more inclusive.

Glossary

access to care Availability of care and "the timely use of personal health services to achieve the best health outcomes" (Institute of Medicine, 1993).

advance care planning "Advance care planning is a process, not an event, and is planning for future care based on a person's values, beliefs, preferences, and specific medical issues. An advance directive is the record of that process" (National Hospice and Palliative Care, n.d.a). Advance care planning as facilitated by palliative care and hospice professionals entails four core components: (1) educating individuals about their illness; (2) providing individuals with information about treatment options, benefits, and burden; (3) facilitating discussions between individuals and families regarding treatment options, preferences, and decisions; and (4) assisting individuals in documenting their preferences and decisions in writing.

advance directive "A general term that describes two types of legal documents: (1) Living will, and (2) Healthcare power of attorney. These documents allow [individuals] to instruct others about [their] future healthcare wishes and appoint a person to make healthcare decisions if [they] are not able to speak for [themselves]" (National Hospice and Palliative Care Organization, 2016).

affirmation Acknowledging the accuracy of a patient's statement or encouraging individuals' efforts to make sense of their experience.

agender a term used by individuals who don't identify as any gender to describe themselves (Refinery29, 2018).

aliagender A term used by individuals who identify as a gender other than male or female to describe themselves "without appropriating the term Third Gender from other cultures" (Refinery29, 2018).

anger "A strong feeling of annoyance, displeasure, antagonism, irritation, or rage" (Gladding, 2011).

anxiety "A normal reaction to stress [that] can be beneficial in some situations. It can alert us to dangers and help us prepare and pay attention" (American Psychological Association, n.d.).

asexual Some individuals "do not experience sexual attraction" toward anyone (National Academies of Sciences, Engineering, and Medicine, 2022). These individuals may refer to themselves as asexual or ace. Some asexual people experience romantic attraction without sexual attraction and describe their orientation using terms like *heteroromantic* ("romantically attracted to/desires romantic relationships with the opposite gender"), *homoromantic* ("romantically attracted to/desires romantic relationships with the same gender"), *biromantic* ("romantically attracted to/desires romantic relationships with multiple genders"), *panromantic* ("romantically attracted to/desires romantic relationships without gender being a factor"), and *aromantic* ("not romantically attracted to or desiring of romantic relationships at all") (Asexual Visibility and Education Network, n.d.).

assumption "A willingness to accept something as true without question or proof" (*Cambridge Dictionary Online*, n.d.).

attitude "A relatively stable and enduring predisposition to respond positively or negatively to a person, object, situation, institution, or event. An attitude carries a strong emotional component; when generalized, it becomes a stereotype" (Gladding, 2011).

autonomy One of the four ethical principles specifying the duties of health care professionals to their patients. Autonomy refers to individuals' right to make choices for themselves so long as they have the capacity to make those choices (Beauchamp & Childress, 2013).

barriers to care Factors that make it difficult for LGBTQIA+ individuals to seek and/or accept hospice and palliative care. Barriers to care generally fall into three categories: **financial barriers to care**, **institutional barriers to care**, and **perceptual barriers to care**.

belief "Conviction of the truth of some statement or the reality of some being or phenomenon especially when based on examination of evidence" (*Merriam-Webster Dictionary*, 2015).

beneficence One of the four ethical principles specifying the duties of health care professionals to their patients. Beneficence means "to help the patient advance his/her own good" (Vermont Ethics Network, n.d.c) or to help the patient benefit, as defined by that patient (Beauchamp & Childress, 2013).

bereavement "The condition of having lost a loved one to death" (American Psychological Association, n.d.).

bisexual A term that refers to "people whose attraction, behavior, or both is toward people of both the same and different genders" (National Academies of Sciences, Engineering, and Medicine, 2022). Often abbreviated as "bi."

breathlessness (shortness of breath, dyspnea) "Few sensations are as frightening as not being able to get enough air. Although shortness of breath—known medically as dyspnea—is likely to be experienced differently by different people, it's often described as an intense tightening in the chest or feeling of suffocation" (Mayo Foundation for Medical Education and Research, n.d.b).

CAMPERS A mnemonic device developed by the author to facilitate greater self-awareness among professionals. The letters stand for clear purpose, attitudes and beliefs, mitigation plan, patient, emotions, reactions, and strategy.

care coordination "An approach in which all members of the [interdisciplinary] team work together to plan for a patient's care" (Center to Advance Palliative Care, n.d.).

chosen family *See* **family of choice**

cisgender A term used to describe "a person whose gender identity corresponds to the sex they were assigned at birth" (National Academies of Sciences, Engineering, and Medicine, 2022)

clinical note "A notation of a contact with the patient and/or the family that is written and dated by any person providing services and that describes signs and symptoms, treatments and medications administered, including the patient's reaction and/or response, and any changes in physical, emotional, psychosocial or spiritual condition during a given period of time" (Centers for Medicaid and Medicare Services, 2020).

compassion "A response to the perceived suffering of others that requires listening intently and acting in a concerned, kind, and empathic way" (Gladding, 2011).

compassionate sedation *See* **palliative sedation**

competence "Competence is a legal term that is determined by a judge, and it is typically an all-or-nothing assessment. In other words, a patient is either competent or incompetent. . . . Decision-making capacity [DMC], on the other hand, is a clinical determination made by a medical professional. DMC is decision-dependent, meaning that a patient might have sufficient DMC to make a relatively straightforward decision, but not enough to make a complex medical decision. In general, higher levels of DMC are required for decisions that are complex, have potentially grave consequences, or when a patient is making a decision contrary to what most people would opt for" (Vermont Ethics Network, n.d.a).

comprehensive assessment In the hospice context, "a thorough evaluation of the patient's physical, psychosocial, emotional and spiritual status related to the terminal illness and related conditions. This includes a thorough evaluation of the caregiver's and family's willingness and capability to care for the patient" (Centers for Medicaid and Medicare Services, 2020).

comprehensive history A complete history that generally includes the patient's birth sex and true gender identity; the patient's understanding of his or her illness and prognosis; information about the patient's advance directives; the patient's goals for care; a history of the patient's illness and physical symptoms; a psychosocial history and spiritual/existential/cultural history; the patient's sexual orientation and sexual behavior; a surgical history; an assessment of the patient's activities of daily living; an assessment of the patient's quality of life; a depression screening; a list of pharmacologic, nonpharmacologic, and complementary/alternative therapies; a list of allergies and drug interactions; and information regarding substance abuse or dependency. In palliative care and hospice care, the Five-Dimension Assessment Model provides a framework for taking a comprehensive history.

confidentiality "The obligation of confidentiality prohibits the healthcare provider from disclosing information about the patient's case to others without permission and encourages the providers and health care systems to take precautions to ensure that only authorized access occurs" (De Bord, Burke, & Dudzinski, n.d.).

confusion (disorientation) When a patient cannot remember or is unclear "about the time of day, date, or season (time); where one is (place); or who one is (person)" (American Psychological Association, n.d.).

constipation "a change in normal bowel habits with decreased frequency of defecation or passage of hard dry feces" (Miller-Keane, n.d.).

continuous sedation until death *See* **palliative sedation**

coping skills "The skills and behaviors people use to adjust to their environments and avoid stress" (Gladding, 2011).

DAROP format A psychosocial documentation format developed by Russell Hilliard, DAROP stands for data, action, results, observations, and plan.

decision-making capacity "Patients with decision-making capacity (DMC) have the right to refuse any treatment, even one that is life-sustaining. They also have the right to choose between treatment options, based on the principle of informed consent. Generally only when a patient lacks DMC does their Advance Directive or health care proxy have a role in medical decision-making. For these reasons it's very important to determine whether a patient has DMC, which sometimes is a difficult determination to make, especially in cases of delirium or progressive dementia. DMC is not the same as 'competence'" (Vermont Ethics Network, n.d.a).

denial "A defense mechanism in which a person ignores or disavows unacceptable thoughts or acts as if an experience does not exist or never did" (Gladding, 2011).

depression "A negative affective state, ranging from unhappiness and discontent to an extreme feeling of sadness, pessimism, and despondency, that interferes with daily life. Various physical, cognitive, and social changes also tend to co-occur, including altered eating or sleeping habits, lack of energy or motivation, difficulty concentrating or making decisions, and withdrawal from social activities. It is symptomatic of a number of mental health disorders" (American Psychological Association, n.d.).

despair "An inability to find meaning in one's life. A complete loss of hope" (Gladding, 2011).

differences of sex development *See* **intersex**

discrimination In the context of this book's focus on LGBTQIA+ individuals and families, this term is used to describe "the negative treatment of sexual and gender diverse people compared to their heterosexual or cisgender counterparts. Discrimination can be interpersonal, such as denial of services based on sexual orientation or gender identity, and it can also be structural, such as laws or policies that systematically disadvantage sexual or gender diverse individuals in such areas as employment and education" (National Academies of Sciences, Engineering, and Medicine, 2022).

disposal of supplies Items such as used syringes and lancets, soiled incontinence pads, and used gauze and bandages must be disposed of safely and effectively; refers to the skills that individuals and their caregivers require to carry this out.

do-not-resuscitate order (do-not-attempt-resuscitation order, allow-natural-death order) "A do-not-resuscitate order, or DNR order, is a medical order written by a doctor. It instructs health care providers not to do cardiopulmonary resuscitation (CPR) if a patient's breathing stops or if the patient's heart stops beating. Ideally, a DNR order is created, or set up, before an emergency occurs. A DNR order allows you to choose whether or not you want CPR in an emergency. It is specific about CPR. It does not have instructions for other treatments, such as pain medicine, other medicines, or nutrition. The doctor writes the order only after talking about it with the patient (if possible), the proxy, or the patient's family" (National Library of Medicine, 2020).

durable power of attorney for health care *See* **health care power of attorney**

emotion "A strong feeling or affect of any kind. The so-called Big Four feelings are anger, sadness, fear, and joy" (Gladding, 2011).

emotional distress "An emotional . . . state of pain, sorrow, misery, suffering, or discomfort" (*Mosby's Medical Dictionary*, 2009). Sometimes referred to as **psychological distress**.

empathic behaviors Things caregivers say or do to convey to individuals that they care about them and are committed to understanding their perspectives or experiences.

empathy "The [health care professional's] ability to see, be aware of, conceptualize, understand, and effectively communicate back to a [patient] the [patient's] feelings, thoughts, and frame of reference in regard to a situation or points of view" (Gladding, 2011). (Note: I have replaced Gladding's terms *counselor* and *client* with the terms *health care professional* and *patient*.)

employee benefits, orientation, and training The ways an organization orients, trains, and supports its employees, ideally in a manner consistent with the organization's mission, vision, and values.

employment discrimination Consists of "bias in hiring, promotion, job assignment, termination, compensation, retaliation, and various types of harassment" (Legal Information Institute, n.d.).

endosex. A term used to describe "people whose reproductive or secondary sex characteristics align with medical binaries, just as the term *cisgender* is used in parallel with the term *transgender*" (National Academies of Sciences, Engineering, and Medicine, 2022).

end-stage disease "A disease condition that is essentially terminal because of irreversible damage to vital tissues or organs" (*Mosby's Medical Dictionary*, 2009).

end-stage disease progression Clinical status, symptoms, and other signs and indicators suggestive of progression of end-stage disease.

environmental and safety assessment An assessment undertaken of the patient's living environment to prevent accidents and falls and to facilitate the continued independence of the patient.

ethical principles "In the U.S., four main principles define the ethical duties that health care professionals owe to patients. They are: Autonomy: to honor the patient's right to make their own decision; Beneficence: to help the patient advance his/her own good; Nonmaleficence: to do no harm; and Justice: to be fair and treat like cases alike" (Vermont Ethics Network, n.d.c).

expected outcomes Projected outcomes that align with stated goals of care. A statement of expected outcome will contain a subject ("Mr. Jones"), a verb in future tense ("will sleep"), a condition ("without a sleeping pill"), a criterion ("for at least four consecutive hours"), and a time ("tonight"): Mr. Jones will sleep without a sleeping pill for at least four consecutive hours tonight.

eye contact "Looking at someone in the eye when interviewing them" (Gladding, 2011).

eye-level approach Entering into an interaction with a patient in a manner that ensures the caregiver's eyes are level with those of the patient. For example, if a patient is in bed, you would pull up a chair and sit next to the bed so that your eyes were as close to level as possible with those of the patient. This helps to minimize the power imbalance between professional and patient and facilitates rapport.

facilitating behaviors The things said or done to foster open communication with a patient.

family of choice (or **chosen family**) The "persons or group of people an individual sees as significant in their life. It may include none, all, or some members of their family of origin. In addition, it may include individuals such as significant others, domestic partners, friends, and coworkers" (Gender Equity Resource Center, 2019).

family of origin The family (by birth, adoption, or informal kinship care) in which a person was raised as a child.

fatigue "A state of tiredness and diminished functioning. Fatigue is typically a normal, transient response to exertion, stress, boredom, or inadequate sleep but also may be unusually prolonged and indicative of disorder" (American Psychological Association, n.d.).

fear "A basic, intense emotion aroused by the detection of imminent threat, involving an immediate alarm reaction that mobilizes the organism by triggering a set of physiological changes. These include rapid heartbeat, redirection of blood flow away from the periphery toward the gut, tensing of the muscles, and a general mobilization of the organism to take action" (American Psychological Association, n.d.).

FICA Spiritual History Tool Developed by Christina Puchalski, the FICA Spiritual History Tool © is widely used for assessing and addressing spiritual issues with individuals. FICA stands for faith or belief, importance, community, and address in care (Puchalski, 1996).

financial barriers to care Financial concerns (actual or perceived) regarding the degree to which an individual can afford to receive palliative care or hospice care.

Five-Dimension Assessment Model A practical framework for taking a comprehensive history of individuals receiving palliative care and hospice care. The Five-Dimension Assessment Model incorporates questions about birth sex, gender identity, sexual orientation, sexual behavior, and sexual health into the assessment process and places the primary focus on the "patient as person." The five dimensions in the model are: Patient as Person (Part 1); Illness/Treatment Summary; Functional Activities and Symptoms;

Decision-Making; Anticipatory Planning for Death; and Patient as Person (Part 2). The model, developed by the author, is based on a synthesis of the extant literature on patient and family assessment in palliative and hospice care.

focused history (history of present illness) A patient history narrowly focused on the presenting symptom, problem, or illness.

gay "An adjective used to describe a person whose enduring physical, romantic, and/or emotional attractions are to people of the same sex. . . . Sometimes lesbian (n. or adj.) is the preferred term for women. Avoid identifying gay people as 'homosexuals,' an outdated term considered derogatory and offensive to many lesbian and gay people. Ask people how they describe themselves before labeling their sexual orientations" (GLAAD, n.d.)

gender "A multidimensional construct that links gender identity, which is a core element of a person's individual identity; gender expression, which is how a person signals their gender to others through their behavior and appearance (such as hair style and clothing); and cultural expectations about social status, characteristics, and behavior that are associated with sex traits" (National Academies of Sciences, Engineering, and Medicine, 2022).

gender affirmation surgery "Surgery to change primary and/or secondary sex characteristics to affirm a person's gender identity. Sex reassignment surgery can be an important part of medically necessary treatment to alleviate gender dysphoria" (World Professional Association for Transgender Health, 2012).

gender diverse "A term used to describe people with gender identities and/or expressions that are different from social and cultural expectations attributed to their sex assigned at birth. This may include, among many other culturally diverse identities, people who identify as nonbinary, gender expansive, gender nonconforming, and others who do not identify as cisgender" (Coleman et al., 2022).

gender dysphoria "A marked incongruence between one's experienced/expressed gender and their assigned gender . . . associated with clinically significant distress or impairment in social, occupational, or other important areas of functioning" (American Psychiatric Association, 2022)

gender euphoria "A distinct enjoyment or satisfaction caused by the correspondence between the person's gender identity and gendered features associated with a gender other than the one assigned at birth" (Ashley & Ells, 2018).

gender expression "How a person signals their gender to others through their behavior and appearance (such as hair style and clothing)" (National Academies of Sciences, Engineering, and Medicine, 2022). Also called **gender presentation**.

gender fluid A term that describes someone who does not identify with a fixed or static gender.

gender identity "A person's deeply felt, inherent sense of being a boy, a man, or male; a girl, a woman, or female; or an alternative gender (e.g., genderqueer, gender nonconforming, gender neutral) that may or may not correspond to a person's sex assigned at birth or to a person's primary or secondary sex characteristics" (American Psychological Association, 2015).

gender incongruence "A diagnostic term used in the ICD-11 that describes a person's marked and persistent experience of an incompatibility between that person's gender identity and the gender expected of them based on their birth-assigned sex" (Coleman et al., 2022).

gender nonconforming "An umbrella term to describe people whose gender expression or gender identity differs from gender norms associated with their assigned birth sex" (American Psychological Association, 2015). You should only use the term *gender nonconforming* to describe someone if it's a term they use to describe themselves. Some gender nonconforming individuals use the acronym **GNC**.

gender presentation *See* **gender expression**

genderqueer "A term to describe a person whose gender identity does not align with a binary understanding of gender (i.e., a person who does not identify fully as either a man or a woman). People who identify as genderqueer may redefine gender or decline to define themselves as gendered altogether. For example, people who identify as genderqueer may think of themselves as both man and woman (bigender, pangender, androgyne); neither man nor woman (genderless, gender neutral, neutrois, agender); moving between genders (genderfluid); or embodying a third gender" (American Psychological Association, 2015).

genogram A diagram that shows the emotional relationships among individuals in a family.

GNC *See* **gender nonconforming**

goals of care "The goals of care are determined by a patient's priorities and values, their hopes and fears. Goals can be described in plain language without reference to procedures or medical interventions. Possible goals include wanting to live independently, to be able to read books, to play with one's grandchildren, to recognize the people one loves, or simply to live as long as possible. Goals often change over time and should be revisited regularly with one's [clinicians] and loved ones" (Vermont Ethics Network, n.d.b).

grief "An intense emotional response to a loss characterized by sorrow and distress" (Gladding, 2011).

guilt "An emotional response to having done something wrong or having failed to do something" (Gladding, 2011).

health care ethics "Health care ethics (a/k/a 'medical' ethics or 'bioethics'), at its simplest, is a set of moral principles, beliefs and values that guide us in making choices about medical care. At the core of health care ethics is our sense of right and wrong and our beliefs about rights we possess and duties we owe others All 4 principles are considered to be in effect at all times. In theory, each is of equal weight or importance. In practice, however, at least in the US, respect for patient autonomy often takes priority over the others" (Vermont Ethics Network, n.d.c).

health care power of attorney (also **durable power of attorney for health care**) "A healthcare power of attorney . . . permits the appointed person to make medical decisions for [the patient] if [the patient] cannot make those decisions [him- or herself]. It does not authorize the person to handle financial affairs, and normally does not empower him or her to make decisions while [the patient] can still make them. Most healthcare powers of attorney go into effect when [the patient's] physician concludes that [the patient is] unable to make [his or her] own decisions. If [the patient] regain[s] the ability to make decisions, [the] agent cannot continue to act for [him or her]. Many states have additional requirements that apply only to decisions about life-sustaining medical treatments" (National Hospice and Palliative Care Organization, 2016).

health care proxy "Similar to a durable power of attorney for healthcare: a document that designates the person you trust to make medical decisions on your behalf if you are unable" (Center to Advance Palliative Care, n.d.).

heterosexual A heterosexual woman is primarily attracted to men and a heterosexual man is primarily attracted to women; both are commonly referred to as "straight."

homosexual A man whose sexual orientation is homosexual (a man who is "gay") is primarily attracted to men. A woman whose sexual orientation is homosexual (who is "lesbian" or "gay") is primarily attracted to women. This term is outdated and should not be used unless a person chooses to use this word to describe themself.

hope "The belief that what is desired is also possible and that events will turn out for the best . . . [and] the feeling that what one believes will occur" (Gladding, 2011).

hospice "Hospice is based on prognosis. It focuses on providing palliative care for people with a life expectancy of months. It is covered by the hospice Medicare benefit. Hospice involves a team-approach to expert medical care, pain and symptom management, and emotional and spiritual support. It is considered a model of quality health care. The emphasis is on comfort. In most cases, hospice care is provided to a patient in his or her own home. It also can be provided in freestanding hospice facilities, hospitals, nursing homes and other long-term care facilities" (Center to Advance Palliative Care, n.d.). "Hospice care means a comprehensive set of services described in Section 1861(dd)(1) of the Act, identified and coordinated by an interdisciplinary group (IDG) to provide for the physical, psychosocial, spiritual, and emotional needs of a terminally ill patient and/or family members, as delineated in a specific patient plan of care" (Centers for Medicaid and Medicare Services, 2020).

housing discrimination Discriminatory practices that interfere with an individual's ability to rent or purchase housing.

humor "The ability to laugh at oneself and one's circumstances in a healthy, therapeutic, and nondefensive way" (Gladding, 2011).

informed consent "The process by which a patient learns about and understands the purpose, benefits, and potential risks of a medical or surgical intervention, including clinical trials, and then agrees to receive the treatment or participate in the trial. Informed consent generally requires the patient or responsible party to sign a statement confirming that they understand the risks and benefits of the procedure or treatment" (MedicineNet, 2021).

insomnia "abnormal wakefulness; a sleep disorder consisting of an inability to fall asleep easily or to remain asleep throughout the night. The frequency of persistent insomnia is high; epidemiologic data indicate that it is the most common sleep disorder in the industrialized world. The causes may be physical, psychological, psychiatric, or presence of a specific sleep disorder" (Miller-Keane, n.d.).

institutional barriers to care Barriers erected (often unintentionally) by palliative care and hospice care programs that prevent LGBTQIA+ individuals and their families from accessing services. Institutional barriers may include discriminatory admission and/or employment policies; lack of marketing and outreach materials; and lack of or inadequate orientation and training for health care professionals, staff, and volunteers.

intake forms and processes The human, electronic, and paper mechanisms by which an organization or program communicates a sense of welcoming, safety, and inclusion to new individuals and families. Includes both official mechanisms, like admissions processes and forms, and unofficial mechanisms, like interactions with phone or switchboard operators, administrative assistants, volunteers, and so on. When official mechanisms such as intake forms are not LGBTQIA-inclusive, LGBTQIA+ individuals and families may be reluctant to seek or accept services.

interdisciplinary/interprofessional team In the context of hospice care, the team generally consists of "physicians, nurses, hospice aides, social workers, counselors, chaplains, therapists, and trained volunteers. The Medicare Hospice regulations use the term 'interdisciplinary group' in the regulatory text, but the term 'interdisciplinary team' can be substituted" (National Hospice and Palliative Care Organization, n.d.c). In the context of palliative care, the team generally consists of "palliative care doctors, nurses and social workers. . . . Chaplains, massage therapists, pharmacists, nutritionists, and others might also be part of the team" (Center to Advance Palliative Care, 2008).

intersectionality An analytic framework for understanding the ways in which the combination of an individual's identities, experiences, and characteristics—each of which may be either oppressing or empowering when looked at in isolation—results in oppression or privilege. The term was coined by legal scholar Kimberlé Crenshaw in the late 1980s.

intersex "Intersex and differences of sex development are terms that describe people born with primary or secondary sex characteristics that do not fit binary medical definitions of male or female reproductive or sexual anatomy. Intersex traits are widely heterogeneous and include variations in number of sex chromosomes, structure or function of gonadal tissue, synthesis or action of sex hormones, appearance of external genitalia, and patterns of secondary sex traits" (National Academies of Sciences, Engineering, and Medicine, 2022).

justice One of the four ethical principles specifying the duties of health care professionals to their patients. Refers to treating individuals in a fair and equitable way (Beauchamp & Childress, 2013).

lesbian A woman whose sexual orientation is homosexual ("lesbian" or "gay") and who is primarily attracted to women.

life completion and life closure The facilitation of ongoing personal growth and fulfillment throughout the remainder of a person's life. Byock's (1994) "developmental taskwork" provides a clearly articulated model for the developmental tasks associated with life completion and life closure.

life review "The review of one's life . . . to find themes, meaning, understanding, and acceptance of what one has done" (Gladding, 2011).

listening "Listening involves hearing not only the content of a [patient's] words but also the tone and inflection of what is being said" (Gladding, 2011). (Note: I have replaced Gladding's term *client's* with *patient's*.)

living will "A written or video statement about the kind of medical care a person does or does not want under certain specific conditions"; designed for use when or if the person is unable to express those wishes (Institute of Medicine, 2015).

marketing and community engagement The ways an organization or program promotes its services (through marketing) and engages in mutually beneficial relationships with people and entities in the community (via community engagement).

meaning A sense of "having significance and purposefulness" (Gladding, 2011).

medication management The skills needed by a patient and/or caregiver to store, organize, administer, and discard the patient's medications safely and effectively.

medication reconciliation Involves "creating the most accurate list possible of all medications a patient is taking—including drug name, dosage, frequency, and route—and comparing that list against the [clinician's] admission, transfer, and/or discharge orders, with the goal of providing correct medications to the patient at all transition points" (Institute for Healthcare Improvement, n.d.). For a detailed guide to medication reconciliation, see Medications at Transitions and Clinical Handoffs (MATCH) Toolkit for Medication Reconciliation (Agency for Healthcare Research and Quality, 2012; Gleason et al., 2012).

men who have sex with men (MSM) A term that refers to men who have male sexual partners (National Academies of Sciences, Engineering, and Medicine, 2022). Men who have sex with men may identify as any sexual orientation: straight, gay, bisexual, pansexual, queer, etc.

mitigation plan A term used in the business world to describe an aspect of risk management. In the context of the CAMPERS self-awareness process, the term refers to the actions you plan to take to prevent the attitudes and beliefs identified in step 2 from having an impact on your interactions with an individual receiving hospice care or palliative care.

nausea/vomiting "Nausea is feeling an urge to vomit. It is often called 'being sick to your stomach.' Vomiting or throwing-up is forcing the contents of the stomach up through the esophagus and out of the mouth" (National Library of Medicine, n.d.).

nonbinary "Refers to those with gender identities outside the gender binary. People with nonbinary gender identities may identify as partially a man and partially a woman or identify as sometimes a man and sometimes a woman, or identify as a gender other than a man or a woman, or as not having a gender at all. Nonbinary people may use the pronouns they/them/theirs instead of he/him/his or she/her/hers. Some nonbinary people consider themselves to be transgender or trans; some do not, because they consider transgender to be part of the gender binary. The shorthand NB or "enby" is sometimes used as a descriptor for nonbinary. Examples of nonbinary gender identities are genderqueer, gender diverse, genderfluid, demigender, bigender, and agender" (Coleman et al., 2022).

nonmaleficence One of the four ethical principles specifying the duties of health care professionals to their patients. Nonmaleficence means to do no harm (Beauchamp & Childress, 2013).

nonverbal communication "The use of nonverbal behaviors such as eye contact, body position, and physical distance in building a . . . relationship" (Gladding, 2011).

normalization Conveying to individuals that "they are not alone in their difficulty (e.g., [that] most people have experienced mild depression in the course of their lives)" (Gladding, 2011).

open posture "Positioning the body with the torso leaning toward the person being addressed, the arms at one's sides, and the chest, abdomen, and lower extremities easily seen. This form of body positioning during communication implies that one is actively listening and emotionally available to the client or patient. By contrast, a closed posture (in which one leans back, crosses one's arms on the chest and crosses the legs) implies that a person is less receptive to the other person" (*Mosby's Medical Dictionary*, 2009).

organ inventory A record of the organs that a person currently has.

out-of-hospital/provider/physician/medical order for life-sustaining treatment (POLST/MOLST) A document that varies from state to state in format, name, and powers but that, in general, "provides medical orders for current treatment" for "persons with serious illness" (National POLST Paradigm, 2015).

pain "An unpleasant sensory and emotional experience associated with, or resembling that associated with, actual or potential tissue damage. . . . Pain is always a personal experience that is influenced to varying degrees by biological, psychological, and social factors. Pain and nociception are different phenomena. Pain cannot be inferred solely from activity in sensory neurons. Through their life experiences, individuals learn the concept of pain. A person's report of an experience as pain should be respected. Although pain usually serves an adaptive role, it may have adverse effects on function and social and psychological well-being. Verbal description is only one of several behaviors to express pain; inability to communicate does not negate the possibility that a human or a nonhuman animal experiences pain" (Raja et al., 2020).

pain and symptom management The process of assessing and addressing symptoms including but not limited to anxiety, breathlessness, confusion, constipation, depression, insomnia, nausea/vomiting, pain, weakness/fatigue, and weight loss. Individuals and families can be taught skills to manage pain and other symptoms at home.

pain management The use of "pharmacological, nonpharmacological, and other approaches to prevent, reduce, or stop pain sensations" (*Gale Encyclopedia of Medicine*, 2008).

palliative care "Beneficial at any stage of a serious illness, palliative care is an interdisciplinary care delivery system designed to anticipate, prevent, and manage physical, psychological, social, and spiritual suffering to optimize quality of life for patients, their families and caregivers. Palliative care can be delivered in any care setting through the collaboration of many types of care professionals. Through early integration into the care plan of seriously ill people, palliative care improves quality of life for both the patient and the family" (National Consensus Project for Quality Palliative Care, 2018). "Palliative care means patient- and family-centered care that optimizes quality of life by anticipating, preventing, and treating suffering. Palliative care throughout the continuum of illness involves addressing physical, intellectual, emotional, social, and spiritual needs and [facilitating] patient autonomy, access to information, and choice" (Centers for Medicaid and Medicare Services, 2020).

palliative sedation (also referred to as **sedation for intractable symptoms, compassionate sedation,** and **continuous sedation until death.**) "The intentional lowering of awareness towards, and including, unconsciousness for patients with severe and refractory symptoms" (American Academy of Hospice and Palliative Medicine, 2014). Also defined as "the use of specific sedative medications to relieve intolerable suffering from refractory symptoms by a reduction in patient consciousness, using appropriate drugs carefully titrated to the cessation of symptoms" (de Graeff & Dean, 2007).

pansexual An attraction to other people regardless of gender.

Patient and Family Outcomes-Focused Inquiry for Developing Goals for Care A model for eliciting goals of care from individuals and families based on the National Hospice and Palliative Care Organization's recommended outcomes for hospice and palliative care (Institute of Medicine and National Research Council, 2003).

Patient and Family Outcomes-Focused Inquiry for Interdisciplinary Teams A model for structuring interdisciplinary/interprofessional team meetings around a list of questions designed to keep the team focused on outcomes of care; based on the National Hospice and Palliative Care Organization's recommended outcomes for hospice and palliative care (Institute of Medicine and National Research Council, 2003).

patient-care skills The skills needed by a patient and/or caregiver to support the patient in meeting bathing, dressing, feeding, transferring, toileting, and transportation needs.

patient centered An approach in which the patient rather than the health care professional directs the goals and focus of care.

perceptual barriers to care Fears, perceptions/misperceptions, and concerns about palliative care and hospice care, either in general or specifically as they relate to one's status as an LGBTQIA+ individual.

physical examination "A physical examination is conducted by a healthcare provider and typically includes: "Inspection (looking at the body); Palpation (feeling the body with fingers or hands); Auscultation (listening to sounds); [and] Percussion (producing sounds, usually by tapping on specific areas of the body)" (National Library of Medicine, 2021).

plan of care "A [clinician's] written plan describing the type and frequency of services and care a particular patient needs" (Medicare Interactive, n.d.). A plan "based on the identified and expressed preferences, values, goals, and needs of the patient and family and . . . developed with professional guidance and support for patient/family decision making" (National Consensus Project for Quality Palliative Care, 2013).

power imbalance "An unequal relationship, such as between a [health care professional] and [patient], due to more power or prestige from one party, making the other party less free or more dependent in regard to initially making independent choices" (Gladding, 2011). (Note: I have replaced Gladding's terms *counselor* and *client* with the terms *health care professional* and *patient*.)

presence "(1) A mode of being available in a situation with the wholeness of one's individual being; a gift of self that can be given freely, invoked, or evoked. (2) [A] nursing intervention from the Nursing Interventions Classification (NIC) defined as being with another, both physically and psychologically, during times of need" (*Mosby's Medical Dictionary*, 2009).

prognosis "A forecast of the probable course and/or outcome of a disease" (*Segen's Medical Dictionary*, n.d.).

psychological distress "A set of painful mental and physical symptoms that are associated with normal fluctuations of mood in most people." (American Psychological Association, n.d.).

psychosocial assessment "An evaluation of a person's mental health, social status, and functional capacity within the community, generally conducted by . . . social workers" (*Mosby's Medical Dictionary*, 2009).

psychosocial history A patient history "involving both psychological and social aspects; age, education, [relational] and related aspects of a person's history" (*Stedman's Medical Dictionary*, 2006). (Note: I have replaced the term *marital* with the more inclusive term *relational*.)

quality of life "A patient's general well-being, including mental status, stress level, sexual function, and self-perceived health status" (*Stedman's Medical Dictionary*, 2006).

queer "An umbrella term for belonging to the LGBTQI+ community that can also refer to a nonbinary gender identity" (National Academies of Sciences, Engineering, and Medicine, 2022).

rapport "A conscious feeling of harmonious accord, trust, empathy, and mutual responsiveness between two or more people (healthcare provider and patient) that fosters the therapeutic process" (*Stedman's Medical Dictionary*, 2006).

reflection A technique in which the health care professional rephrases or verbalizes what the patient appears to be feeling in an effort to convey empathy (Gladding, 2011).

right to self-determination Under the 1990 Patient Self-Determination Act, the federal government formally recognized that individuals have a right "to decide ahead of time about the types and extent of medical care they want to accept or refuse if they become unable to make those decisions due to illness" (American Cancer Society, 2019).

same-gender-loving A term that "is often used in Black communities to describe non-heterosexual relationships" (National Academies of Sciences, Engineering, and Medicine, 2022).

scope of practice "A practitioner's scope of practice refers to what a health professional can and cannot do to or for a patient, and is defined by state professional regulatory boards—typically with the guidance or instruction of the state's legislature" (National Conference of State Legislatures, 2022).

sedation for intractable symptoms *See* **palliative sedation**

self-awareness "An ongoing process in life of recognizing thoughts, emotions, senses, and behaviors that influence a person on multiple levels" (Gladding, 2011).

self-determination "The Patient Self-Determination Act (PSDA) is a law that was passed in 1990. The PSDA reaffirms the common-law right of self-determination as guaranteed by the Fourteenth Amendment of the United States Constitution. Basically, this means that you, as the person receiving care, have the right to make choices and decisions about the type of medical care and the extent of medical care that you would or would not want" (National Hospice and Palliative Care Organization, n.d.d.).

self-disclosure "A conscious, intentional technique in which clinicians share information about their lives outside the counseling relationship" (Gladding, 2011).

sex A person is born with a "cluster of anatomical and physiological traits that include external genitalia, secondary sex characteristics, gonads, chromosomes, and hormones" (National Academies of Sciences, Engineering, and Medicine, 2022). Whether that cluster of traits is assigned the label "male" or "female" depends on the sociocultural context into which that baby has been born.

sexual behavior Acts engaged in by an individual toward the goal of sexual pleasure, reproduction, or both. Sometimes referred to as **sexual practices**.

sexual expression The way individuals express their sexual desires alone and with partners. It is more than "sex": "Sexual expression is a form of communication through which we give and receive pleasure and emotion. It has a wide range of possibilities—from sharing fun activities, feelings and thoughts, warm touch or hugs, to physical intimacy. It is expressed both individually and in relationships throughout life" (McKinley Health Center, 2009).

sexual health "A state of physical, emotional, mental and social well-being in relation to sexuality; it is not merely the absence of disease, dysfunction or infirmity. Sexual health requires a positive and respectful approach to sexuality and sexual relationships, as well as the possibility of having pleasurable and safe sexual experiences, free of coercion, discrimination and violence. For sexual health to be attained and maintained, the sexual rights of all persons must be respected, protected and fulfilled" (World Health Organization, 2006, 2010).

sexual orientation "A multidimensional construct encompassing emotional, romantic, and sexual attraction, identity, and behavior. . . . Sexual attraction refers to the gender(s) of the people to whom someone feels physically or romantically attracted. The delineation between sexual orientation and sexual attraction is often particularly important for people who may not be sexually active. Sexual behavior refers to the gender(s) of one's sexual partners. Self-identification refers to how people describe their own sexual orientation" (National Academies of Sciences, Engineering, and Medicine, 2022)

sexual practices *See* **sexual behavior**

sexuality "A central aspect of being human throughout life encompasses sex, gender identities and roles, sexual orientation, eroticism, pleasure, intimacy and reproduction. Sexuality is experienced and expressed in thoughts, fantasies, desires, beliefs, attitudes, values, behaviors, practices, roles and relationships. While sexuality can include all of these dimensions, not all of them are always experienced or expressed. Sexuality is influenced by the interaction of biological, psychological, social, economic, political, cultural, legal, historical religious and spiritual factors" (World Health Organization, 2006, 2010).

shared decision making "A collaborative process that allows patients and their providers to make health care decisions together, considering the best scientific evidence available and the patient's values and preferences. [Shared decision making] honors both the provider's expert knowledge and the patient's right to be fully informed of all care options and the potential harms and benefits. This process provides patients with the support they need to make the best individualized care decisions, while allowing providers to feel confident in the care they prescribe" (Washington State Health Care Authority, 2022).

signs and symptoms of imminent death Changes seen in a patient's eating and drinking as well as in their neurological, integumentary (skin), respiratory, excretory, cardiac, and circulatory systems indicative of approaching death.

silence A purposeful absence of speaking on the part of the health care professional that is designed to encourage the patient or family member to feel, reflect, and, if they choose to do so, speak.

sodomy laws Laws that make anal and/or oral sex between two adults illegal.

SOGI data Questions about sexual orientation, sex assigned at birth, and gender identity are often referred to collectively as SOGI (sexual orientation and gender identity) data.

spiritual/existential assessment "Refers to a more extensive process of active listening to a patient's story conducted by a board-certified chaplain that summarizes the needs and resources that emerge in that process. The chaplain's summary should include a spiritual care plan with expected outcomes that is then communicated to the rest of the treatment team" (Puchalski et al., 2009).

spiritual/existential distress "(1) Discomfort related to religious, intellectual, or cultural concerns; (2) a nursing diagnosis approved by the North American Nursing Diagnosis Association, defined as disruption in the life principle that pervades a person's entire being and that integrates and transcends his or her biological and psychosocial nature. The person experiencing spiritual distress may express concern with the meaning of life and death, question the meaning of suffering or of his or her own existence, verbalize inner conflict about beliefs, express anger toward God or other Supreme Being (however defined), or actively seek spiritual assistance" (*Miller-Keane Encyclopedia and Dictionary of Medicine, Nursing, and Allied Health*, n.d.).

spiritual/existential/cultural history "Spiritual history-taking is the process of interviewing a patient in order to come to a better understanding of [his or her] spiritual needs and resources. A spiritual history can be integrated into existing formats such as the social history section of the clinical database. The information from the history permits the clinician to understand how spiritual concerns could either complement or complicate the patient's overall care" (Puchalski et al., 2009). Dahlin et al. (2022) consider spiritual and cultural histories to be intertwined, noting that "normalizing culture in health may include reminding patients that it is common for people to find strength in their spiritual and religious belief."

suicidal ideation (suicidal ideas) "Thoughts about or a preoccupation with killing oneself, often as a symptom of a major depressive episode. Most instances of suicidal ideation do not progress to attempted suicide" (American Psychological Association, n.d.).

symptom "Any deviation from normal functioning that is considered indicative of physical or mental pathology" (American Psychological Association, n.d.).

symptom management "An approach to palliative care that treats the symptoms rather than the cause of a condition. Its focus includes confusion, dizziness, fatigue, incontinence, nausea, shortness of breath, vomiting, and weakness" (*Medical Dictionary*, 2009).

touch The use of physical contact by a health care professional to convey support to a patient. Touch should be used only with the express consent of the patient and should be offered in an effort to meet the patient's needs, not the needs of the health care professional.

transgender A term used to describe "a person whose gender identity is different from the sex they were assigned at birth." The word is used as an adjective (e.g., "He is a transgender man"), never as a noun (e.g., "He is a transgender"). People who identify as something other than female or male may use terms like *genderqueer, genderfluid, nonbinary, bigender*, and/or *gender nonconforming* to describe themselves and "may or may not identify as transgender" (National Academies of Sciences, Engineering, and Medicine, 2022). Often abbreviated as "trans."

transgender experience "When someone currently identifies with a gender identity that is different from their sex assigned at birth" (National Academies of Sciences, Engineering, and Medicine, 2022).

transgender identity "When someone currently identifies oneself as transgender" (National Academies of Sciences, Engineering, and Medicine, 2022).

transition "The process whereby people usually change from the gender expression associated with their assigned sex at birth to another gender expression that better matches their gender identity. People may transition socially by using methods such as changing their name, pronoun, clothing, hairstyles, and/or the ways they move and speak. Transitioning may or may not involve hormones and/or surgeries to alter the physical body. Transition can be used to describe the process of changing one's gender expression from any gender to a different gender. People may transition more than once in their lifetimes" (Coleman et al., 2022).

transsexual A term that some individuals whose sex assigned at birth does not align with their gender identity use to describe themselves. Transsexual is "an older term that originated in the medical and psychological communities [and is] still preferred by some people who have permanently changed—or seek to change—their bodies through medical interventions, including but not limited to hormones and/or surgeries" (Refinery29, 2018).

unconscious bias An attitude or preference that a health care professional feels toward or against an individual or group of people without consciously choosing to feel that way.

weakness "Weakness may be all over the body or in only one area. Weakness is more noticeable when it is in one area. [When] you . . . feel weak but have no real loss of strength, this is called subjective weakness. Or, you may have a loss of strength that can be noted on a physical exam. This is called objective weakness" (National Library of Medicine, n.d.).

weight loss "Unexplained weight loss is a decrease in body weight, when you did not try to lose the weight on your own. Unintentional weight loss is loss of 10 pounds OR 5 percent of your normal body weight over 6 to 12 months or less without knowing the reason" (National Library of Medicine, n.d.).

will "A will (last will and testament) [is a] financial document [that] allow[s] [individuals] to plan who receives [their] financial assets and property" (National Hospice and Palliative Care Organization, 2016).

Supplemental Reading List

Acquaviva, K. D., & Marshall, D. (2022). Introducing the special collection on "Palliative Care for LGBTQ2S+ Individuals and Families." *Palliative Care and Social Practice, 16*, 26323524211073409.

Almack, K. (2019). "I didn't come out to go back in the closet": Ageing and end-of-life care for older LGBT people. In A. King, K. Almack, Y.-T. Suen, & S. Westwood (Eds.), *Older lesbian, gay, bisexual and trans people* (pp. 158–171). New York: Routledge.

American Psychiatric Association. (2022). What is gender dysphoria? https://psychiatry.org/patients-families/gender-dysphoria/what-is-gender-dysphoria.

Bharani, A., Weiss, T., Rabner, M., & Javier, N. M. (2022). Rainbow connection and collection: Creating partnership between academic medicine and community-based hospice to collect sexual orientation and gender identity (SOGI) in the electronic medical record (FR225). *Journal of Pain and Symptom Management, 63*(5), 810–811.

Blotner, C., & Dotolo, D. (2022). LGBTQ patient palliative care. In T. Altilio & S. Otis-Green, & J. G. Cagle (Eds.), *The oxford textbook of palliative social work* (2nd ed.), 153–163. New York: Oxford University Press.

Bristowe, K., Hodson, M., Wee, B., Almack, K., Johnson, K., Daveson, B. A., et al. (2018). Recommendations to reduce inequalities for LGBT people facing advanced illness: ACCESSCare national qualitative interview study. *Palliative Medicine, 32*, 23–35.

Campbell, C. L., & Catlett, L. (2019). Silent illumination: A case study exploring the spiritual needs of a transgender-identified elder receiving hospice care. *Journal of Hospice & Palliative Nursing, 21*(6), 467–474.

Candrian, C., O'Mahony, S., Stein, G. L., Berkman, C., Javier, N. M., Godfrey, D., et al. (2021). Let's do this: Collecting sexual orientation and gender identity data in hospice and palliative care. *Journal of Palliative Medicine, 24*(8), 1122–1123.

Chen, J., McLaren, H., Jones, M., & Shams, L. (2022). The aging experiences of LGBTQ ethnic minority elders: A systematic review. *Gerontologist, 62,* e162–e177.

Cloyes, K. G., Hull, W., & Davis, A. (2018). Palliative and end-of-life care for lesbian, gay, bisexual, and transgender (LGBT) cancer patients and their caregivers. In *Seminars in Oncology Nursing, 34*(1), 60–71.

Cloyes, K. G., Jones, M., Gettens, C., Wawrzynski, S. E., Bybee, S., Tay, D. L., et al. (2023). Providing home hospice care for LGBTQ+ patients and caregivers: Perceptions and opinions of hospice interdisciplinary care team providers. *Palliative & Supportive Care, 21*(1), 3–11.

Cloyes, K. G., Tay, D. L., Iacob, E., Jones, M., Reblin, M., & Ellington, L. (2020). Hospice interdisciplinary team providers' attitudes toward sexual and gender minority patients and caregivers. *Patient Education and Counseling, 103*(10), 2185–2191.

de Vries, B., Gutman, G., Humble, Á., Gahagan, J., Chamberland, L., Aubert, P., et al. (2019). End-of-life preparations among LGBT older Canadian adults: The missing conversations. *International Journal of Aging and Human Development, 88*(4), 358–379.

Dhawan, N., Ovalle, A. A., & Yeh, J. C. (2021). The role of hospice and palliative care in supporting and fostering trust among the LGBTQ+ population. *Palliative Care and Social Practice, 15,* 26323524211042637.

Farmer, D. F., & Yancu, C. N. (2015). Hospice and palliative care for older lesbian, gay, bisexual and transgender adults: The effects of history, discrimination, health disparities and legal issues on addressing service needs. *Palliative Medicine and Hospice Care Open Journal, 1,* 36–43.

Haviland, K., Burrows Walters, C., & Newman, S. (2021). Barriers to palliative care in sexual and gender minority patients with cancer: A scoping review of the literature. *Health & Social Care in the Community, 29*(2), 305–318.

Higgins, A., & Hynes, G. (2019). Meeting the needs of people who identify as lesbian, gay, bisexual, transgender, and queer in palliative care settings. *Journal of Hospice & Palliative Nursing, 21*(4), 286–290.

Hinrichs, K. L., & Christie, K. M. (2019). Focus on the family: A case example of end-of-life care for an older LGBT veteran. *Clinical Gerontologist, 42*(2), 204–211.

Javier, N. M. (2021). Palliative care needs, concerns, and affirmative strategies for the LGBTQ population. *Palliative Care and Social Practice, 15,* 26323524211039234.

Liantonio, J., Tapper, C., Spina, E., Danielewicz, M., & Javier, N. M. (2022). Creating LGBTQ+ competencies for hospice and palliative medicine (HPM) fellowship programs (FR238). *Journal of Pain and Symptom Management, 63*(5), 814–815.

Lintott, L., Beringer, R., Do, A., & Daudt, H. 2022. A rapid review of end-of-life needs in the LGBTQ+ community and recommendations for clinicians. *Palliative Medicine, 36*(4), 609–624.

Lutz, G., & Ehrlich, M. (2022). Barriers to LGBTQIA-inclusive palliative care. *American Journal of Hospice and Palliative Medicine®,* 10499091221127990.

Maingi, S., Bagabag, A., & O'Mahony, S. (2018). Current best practices for sexual and gender minorities in hospice and palliative care settings. *Journal of Pain and Symptom Management, 55,* 1420–1427.

Maingi, S., Radix, A., Candrian, C., Stein, G., Berkman, C., & O'Mahony, S. (2021). Improving the hospice and palliative care experiences of LGBTQ patients and their caregivers. *Primary Care: Clinics in Office Practice, 48*(2), 339–349.

National Academies of Sciences, Engineering, and Medicine. (2020). *Understanding the well-being of LGBTQI+ populations*. Washington, DC: National Academies Press.

Reynaga, M., Bybee, S., Gettens, C., Tay, D. L., Reblin, M., Ellington, L., & Cloyes, K. G. (2022). "We treat everyone equally": Hospice care team members' language use regarding sexual and gender minority patients and caregivers. *American Journal of Hospice and Palliative Medicine®*, 10499091221116634.

Rosa, W. E., Roberts, K. E., Braybrook, D., Harding, R., Godwin, K., Mahoney, C., et al. (2022). Palliative and end-of-life care needs, experiences, and preferences of LGBTQ+ individuals with serious illness: A systematic mixed-methods review. *Palliative Medicine*, 02692163221124426.

Rosa, W. E., Shook, A., & Acquaviva, K. D. (2020). LGBTQ+ inclusive palliative care in the context of COVID-19: Pragmatic recommendations for clinicians. *Journal of Pain and Symptom Management, 60*(2), e44–e47.

Ryerson, L. M. (2022). Prioritizing health equity in palliative and end-of-life care. *Generations, 46*(3), 1–9.

Schneider, J. S., Silenzio V. M. B., & Erickson-Schroth, L. (2019). *The GLMA handbook on LGBT health*. Westport, CT: Praeger.

Sprik, P., & Gentile, D. (2020). Cultural humility: A way to reduce LGBTQ health disparities at the end of life. *American Journal of Hospice and Palliative Medicine, 37*(6), 404–408.

Stein, G. L., & Berkman, C. (2019). Palliative and end-of-life care to the LGBT community. *Innovation in Aging, 3*(Suppl. 1), S623–S623.

Stevens, E. E., & Abraham, J. L. (2019). Adding silver to the rainbow: Palliative and end-of-life care for the geriatric LGBTQ patient. *Journal of Palliative Medicine, 22*(5), 602–606.

Stinchcombe, A., Smallbone, J., Wilson, K., & Kortes-Miller, K. (2017). Healthcare and end-of-life needs of lesbian, gay, bisexual, and transgender (LGBT) older adults: A scoping review. *Geriatrics, 2*(1), 13.

Tobin, J., Rogers, A., Winterburn, I., Tullie, S., Kalyanasundaram, A., Kuhn, I., & Barclay, S. (2022). Hospice care access inequalities: A systematic review and narrative synthesis. *BMJ Supportive & Palliative Care, 12*(2), 142–151.

Valenti, K. G., Jen, S., Parajuli, J., Arbogast, A., Jacobsen, A. L., & Kunkel, S. (2020). Experiences of palliative and end-of-life care among older LGBTQ women: A review of current literature. *Journal of Palliative Medicine, 23*(11), 1532–1539.

WAKE Education. 2022. Louisiana LGBTQ+ End-of-Life Guide. https://www.wake.education/_files/ugd/b20ea6_f4ffeaf5b785416a95cf051f5166cb8.pdf

Wakefield, D., Kane, C. E., Chidiac, C., Braybrook, D., & Harding, R. (2021). Why does palliative care need to consider access and care for LGBTQ people? *Palliative Medicine, 35*(10), 1730–1732.

About the Content Expert Reviewers

Note: Reverend Vonshelle J. Beneby, MDiv served as a content expert reviewer for my first book but not the second. The following individuals joined the content expert review team in 2022 and reviewed only the second book: Charlie Blotner, MSW, APHSW-C; Reverend Dr. Danielle J. Buhuro; Alex Kemery, PhD, RN; and Shail Maingi, MD.

Each expert who reviewed and validated the content in this book provided a brief biographical statement incorporating the name, pronouns, and honorific of their choice. This practice is intended to model the way we should support individuals and families as they define and present themselves to the world.

Charlie Blotner, MSW, APHSW-C (he/him) is a hospice social worker at EvergreenHealth Hospice in Seattle, WA. Intercommunity knowledge serves as an access point to guide his practice interfacing with chronic illness communities. Charlie is a patient advocate who is dedicated to helping people be better informed about their health, research, policy, and the future implications of their disease. He served as a Stanford Medicine X student adviser, advocate for LGBTQIA+ health disparities, and cofounder and comoderator of #BTSM (Brain Tumor Social Media) Chats.

Rev. Dr. Danielle J. Buhuro (she/her) is the founder, executive director, and ACPE-certified educator at Sankofa CPE Center, LLC. She has been certified by the Association for Clinical Pastoral Education (ACPE) and board certified in the Association of Professional Chaplains (APC). Rev. Dr. Buhuro is an ordained clergy with ministerial standing in the Illinois Conference's Chicago Metropolitan Association of the United Church of Christ (UCC). Throughout her career, Rev. Dr. Buhuro has served as an ACPE associate supervisor and staff chaplain at Advocate Illinois Masonic Medical Center in Chicago, Illinois. Additionally, she has served as an ACPE-certified educator at Advocate Good Shepherd, South Suburban, Trinity, and Christ Hospitals in Illinois. Rev. Dr. Buhuro's has served as a chaplain at Mercy Hospital in Chicago, the University of Illinois at Chicago Medical Center, and the University of Chicago Medical Center. Rev. Dr. Buhuro is passionate about issues of race, gender, and sexuality. She is the author of *Spiritual Care in an Age of #BlackLivesMatter: Examining the Spiritual and Prophetic Needs of African Americans Living in a Violent America* (Wipf and Stock, 2019) and *Is There a Heaven for a "G"? A Pastoral Care Approach to Gang Violence* (Wipf and Stock, 2017). Rev. Dr. Buhuro attended Chicago Theological Seminary, where she earned her master of divinity (MDiv) and doctor of ministry (DMin) degrees. She is currently working on her PhD, studying social media identity, violence, and pastoral theology. Rev. Dr. Buhuro serves on the national board of directors of the Association of Clinical Pastoral Education. She also serves as adjunct faculty, teaching DMin and MDiv courses in spiritual care and chaplaincy at United Theological Seminary of the Twin Cities in Minneapolis, Minnesota and Eden Theological Seminary in St. Louis, Missouri. Rev. Dr. Buhuro facilitates numerous workshops nationwide on African American pastoral care and African-centered psychology. Rev. Dr. Buhuro is same-gender-loving and excited to be currently engaged to her life partner, Christina. Together they parent a son, Ezekiel. Rev. Dr. Buhuro is committed to excellence and community partnership. Her philosophy of education embraces a pedagogy of helping students enhance their pastoral identity and pastoral competence while improving their pastoral reflection.

Constance Dahlin, ANP-BC, ACHPN, FPCN, FAAN (she/her) has extensive hospice and palliative care experience in administration, clinical practice, and academia across the health continuum. She is a consultant to the Center to Advance Palliative Care (CAPC) in community-based care and education. She continues clinical practice as a palliative nurse practitioner, and she codirects the Palliative APP Externship. She is national faculty for the End of Life Nursing Education Consortium (ELNEC) and a member of the American Hospital Association Circle of Life Committee, the Massachusetts Serious Illness Coalition Nursing Taskforce, and the Massachusetts Comprehensive Cancer Steering Committee. She has served on many editions of the NCP Clinical Practice Guidelines as well as other national work on quality palliative care. She has authored peer-reviewed books, articles, chapters, and curricula and presented nationally and internationally. Ms. Dahlin has focused on access to quality palliative care throughout her career and is now focused on health equity in palliative care. Given the ever-changing social context and language, she is committed to the ongoing dialogue and education working toward diversity, equity, and inclusion within all aspects of palliative care.

Gary Gardia, LCSW, APHSW-C (he/him) is a frequent presenter and keynote speaker at state and national conferences and works as a consultant for various businesses and health care organizations. More than forty years ago, Gary began his hospice journey as a volunteer. Gary received the National Hospice and Palliative Care Organization's (NHPCO) Heart of Hospice Award for developing innovative programs to meet the needs of caregivers and the bereaved.

Judi T. Haberkorn, PhD, MSW, MBA, MPH (she/her) is a health care practitioner with more than twenty years of experience in health care and social services. Dr. Haberkorn has served as both an assistant professor and a health care training executive. Dr. Haberkorn has spent nearly ten years in the hospice field and considers it an honor to work with patients in end-of-life care.

Noelle Marie C. Javier, MD (she/her) is a trained internist, geriatrician, and hospice and palliative care specialist who also serves as a faculty member at the Icahn School of Medicine at Mount Sinai in New York. She is a longtime advocate and champion for the provision of high-quality and holistic medical care to the marginalized members of society, including older adults, the indigent population, and members of the LGBTQIA+ population. As an empowered minority woman of Asian descent and transgender experience, she also understands firsthand the unique set of care needs affecting this population. She has taken part in and continues to promote culturally sensitive health care education and training in local and regional settings.

Alex Kemery, PhD, RN (he/they) is a partner to three and parent to six and works as an associate professor at the University of Indianapolis. He obtained a BA in nursing from Indiana University–Purdue University Indianapolis; an MS in nursing, with a specialization in education, from the University of Indianapolis; and a PhD from the Catholic University of America. He is currently studying to become an adult gerontology primary care nurse practitioner. His primary research interests are end-of-life care for the LGBTQ+ community and developing LGBTQ+-competent health care professionals. Alex describes himself as a queer, polyamorous, trans man.

Shail Maingi, MD (she/her) is a medical oncologist, hematologist, and palliative care physician at the Dana-Farber Cancer Institute Network at their South Shore location. In addition to seeing patients with solid tumors and blood diseases, she is the inaugural DFCI Network health equity and inclusion liaison. She has been a health equity advocate and clinical researcher for years with a focus on health care disparities in oncology and end-of-life settings, particularly for sexual and gender minority people with a focus on intersectionality. She is an advocacy champion for the American Society of Clinical Oncology (ASCO). She served as track leader for the Survivorship and Symptom Management scientific program for ASCO's 2021 annual conference. She also currently serves on ASCO's Diversity and Inclusion Committee, Practice Health Task Force, and as the cochair of their Sexual and Gender Minority Task Force. In addition, she was the founding chair of the American Academy of Hospice and Palliative Medicine's (AAHPM) LGBT Special Interest Group. She serves on the GLMA:

Health Professionals Advancing LGBTQ Equality board and heads their Racial Justice Task Force.

Sam Mullen (he/him) ministered in an interfaith capacity in hospice chaplaincy with VITAS Healthcare, where he served as a staff chaplain. After serving fifteen years as an evangelical pastor, Sam came out as gay and is now actively involved in advocacy for the LGBTQIA+ community. Sam leads bereavement support groups for LGBTQIA+ people in his area.

Martha Rutland, DMin (she/her) is director of clinical pastoral education at VITAS Healthcare. She is a certified supervisor with the Association for Clinical Pastoral Education and a certified chaplain with the Association of Professional Chaplains; she holds a doctor of ministry from Chicago Theological Seminary. Martha is also an ordained minister in the United Methodist Church.

References

Acree, M. E., McNulty, M., Blocker, O. Schneider, J., & Williams, H. H. S. (2020). Shared decision-making around anal cancer screening among Black bisexual and gay men in the USA. *Culture, Health & Sexuality, 22*(2), 201–216.

Advanced Palliative Hospice Social Worker Certification Board. (2022). Frequently asked questions. https://aphsw-c.org/faq/.

Agency for Healthcare Research and Quality. (2012). Medications at Transitions and Clinical Handoffs (MATCH) Toolkit for Medication Reconciliation. Content last reviewed April 2023. https://www.ahrq.gov/patient-safety/settings/hospital/match/index.html.

Akinola, O., Baru, J., & Marks, S. (2015). Fast facts and concepts #297: Terminal hemorrhage preparation and management. https://www.mypcnow.org/fast-fact/terminal-hemorrhage-preparation-and-management/.

Aleccia, J. (2019a). Kathy Brandt, a hospice expert who invited the world into her own last days with cancer, dies. *Kaiser Health News*, August 5, 2019. https://khn.org/news/until-her-last-breath-hospice-expert-live-tweets-about-her-death-to-teach-others/.

Aleccia, J. (2019b). Palliative care power couple faces cancer at home. *NBC News*, May 15, 2019. https://www.nbcnews.com/health/cancer/palliative-care-power-couple-facescancer-Home-n1005516.

Almack, K., Yip, A., Seymour, J., Sargeant A., Patterson, A., & Makita, M. (2014). The last outing: Exploring end of life experiences and care needs in the lives of older LGBT people. https://www.nottingham.ac.uk/research/groups/ncare/documents/projects/srcc-project-report-last-outing.pdf.

Altilio, T., & Otis-Green, S. (Eds.). (2011). *Oxford textbook of palliative social work*. New York: Oxford University Press.

References

Altilio, T., Otis-Green, S., & Cagle, J. (Eds.). (2022). *Oxford textbook of palliative social work* (2nd ed.). New York: Oxford University Press.

Altilio, T., Otis-Green, S., & Dahlin, C. (2008). Applying the national quality forum preferred practices for palliative and hospice care: A social work perspective. *Journal of Social Work in End-of-Life and Palliative Care, 4*(1): 3–16.

American Academy of Family Physicians. (n.d.). Recommended curriculum guidelines for family medicine residents: Lesbian, gay, bisexual, transgender, queer/questioning, and asexual health. Retrieved December 13, 2022, from https://www.aafp.org/dam/AAFP/documents/medical_education_residency/program_directors/Reprint289D_LGBT.pdf.

American Academy of Hospice and Palliative Medicine. (2009). Hospice and palliative medicine core competencies, version 2.3. http://aahpm.org/uploads/education/competencies/Competencies%20v.%202.3.pdf.

American Academy of Hospice and Palliative Medicine. (2014). Statement on palliative sedation. http://aahpm.org/positions/palliative-sedation.

American Academy of Hospice and Palliative Medicine. (n.d.a). Certification for hospice and palliative medicine specialists. Retrieved August 4, 2022, from http://aahpm.org/education/certification.

American Academy of Hospice and Palliative Medicine. (n.d.b). Tools to address opioid prescribing. AAHPM. Retrieved August 9, 2022, from http://aahpm.org/education/opioid-resource-hub.

American Academy of Physician Associates. (2018). Guidelines for ethical conduct for the PA profession. https://www.aapa.org/download/56983/.

American Academy of Physician Associates. (2019). Q and A on PA reimbursement for hospice Medicare services. https://www.aapa.org/news-central/2019/03/q-pa-reimbursement-medicare-hospice-services/.

American Academy of Physician Associates. (2022). Title change implementation. https://www.aapa.org/title-change/.

American Cancer Society. (2019). The Patient Self-Determination Act. https://www.cancer.org/treatment/treatments-and-side-effects/planning-managing/advance-directives/what-is-an-advance-health-care-directive.html.

American Civil Liberties Union. (n.d.). Getting rid of sodomy laws: History and strategy that led to the *Lawrence* decision. Retrieved August 4, 2022, from https://www.aclu.org/getting-rid-sodomy-laws-history-and-strategy-led-lawrence-decision.

American Medical Association. (2001). Code of medical ethics of the American Medical Association. https://www.ama-assn.org/topics/ama-code-medical-ethics.

American Nurses Association. (2015). Code of ethics for nurses with interpretive statements. https://www.nursingworld.org/practice-policy/nursing-excellence/ethics/code-of-ethics-for-nurses/coe-view-only/.

American Psychiatric Association. (2013a). Gender dysphoria. https://www.psychiatry.org/file%20library/psychiatrists/practice/dsm/apa_dsm-5-gender-dysphoria.pdf.

American Psychiatric Association. (2013b). Glossary of technical terms. In *Diagnostic and Statistical Manual of Mental Disorders* (5th ed.). Arlington, VA: Author.

American Psychiatric Association. (2022). Gender dysphoria. https://psychiatry.org/File%20Library/Psychiatrists/Practice/DSM/DSM-5-TR/APA-DSM5TR-GenderDysphoria.pdf.

American Psychological Association. (2008). Answers to your questions: For a better understanding of sexual orientation and homosexuality. http://www.apa.org/topics/lgbt/orientation.pdf.

American Psychological Association. (2015). Guidelines for psychological practice with transgender and gender nonconforming people. *American Psychologist, 70*(9), 832–864.

American Psychological Association. (n.d.). *APA dictionary of psychology.* https://dictionary.apa.org/.

Asexuality Visibility and Education Network. (n.d.). Overview. Accessed April 26, 2023 at http://www.asexuality.org/?q=overview.html

Ashley, F., & Ells, C. (2018). In favor of covering ethically important cosmetic surgeries: Facial feminization surgery for transgender people. *American Journal of Bioethics, 18*(12), 23–25.

Association of American Medical Colleges. (2014). Implementing curricular and institutional climate changes to improve health care for individuals who are LGBT, gender nonconforming, or born with DSD: A resource for medical educators. https://store.aamc.org/downloadable/download/sample/sample_id/129/.

Association of Professional Chaplains. (2000). Code of ethics. https://www.apchaplains.org/wp-content/uploads/2022/06/APC-Code-of-Ethics.pdf.

Austin Community College. (n.d.). Nursing process: Planning outcome oriented care. Retrieved February 18, 2016, from http://www.austincc.edu/adnlev1/rnsg1413online/mod_nursing_process/outcome.html. Site no longer available.

Baca-Dietz, D., Wojnar, D. M., & Espina, C. R. (2021). The shared decision-making model: Providers' and patients' knowledge and understanding in clinical practice. *Journal of the American Association of Nurse Practitioners, 33*(7), 529–536.

Baig, A. A., Lopez, F. Y., DeMeester, R. H., Jia, J. L., Peek, M. E., & Vela, M. B. (2016). Addressing Barriers to Shared Decision Making Among Latino LGBTQ Patients and Healthcare Providers in Clinical Settings. *LGBT health, 3*(5), 335–341. https://doi.org/10.1089/lgbt.2016.0014

Baik, D., Cho, H., & Masterson Creber, R. M. (2019). Examining interventions designed to support shared decision making and subsequent patient outcomes in palliative care: A systematic review of the literature. *American Journal of Hospice and Palliative Medicine, 36*(1), 76–88.

Barry, M., & Edgman-Levitan, S. (2012). Shared decision making: The pinnacle of patient-centered care. *New England Journal of Medicine, 366*, 780–781.

Bautista, N. (2022). Dignity in life and in death: California expands protections for non-binary individuals in death certificate laws. Golden State Lawyer. https://www.goldenstatelawyer.com/2022/03/dignity-in-life-and-in-death-california-expands-protections-for-nonbinary-individuals-in-death-certificate-laws/.

Beauchamp, T., & Childress, J. (2013). *Principles of biomedical ethics* (7th ed.). New York: Oxford University Press.

Beischel, W. J., Gauvin, S. E. M., & van Anders, S. M. (2021). "A little shiny gender breakthrough": Community understandings of gender euphoria. *International Journal of Transgender Health, 23*(3), 274–294.

Benbassat, J., & Baumal, R. (2005). Enhancing self-awareness in medical students: An overview of teaching approaches. *Academic Medicine, 80*(2): 156–161.

Bhyan, P., Pesce, M. B., Shrestha, U., & Goyal, A. (2021). *Palliative sedation in patients with terminal illness.* Treasure Island, FL: StatPearls.

Blotner, C., & Dotolo, D. (2022). LGBTQ patient palliative care. In T. Altilio, S. Otis-Green, & J. Cagle (Eds.), *Oxford textbook of palliative social work* (2nd ed.). New York: Oxford University Press.

Board of Chaplaincy Certification. (n.d.). Competencies of the certified hospice and palliative care chaplain. Retrieved August 4, 2022, from http://bcci.professionalchaplains.org/content.asp.

Bomhof-Roordink, H., Gärtner, F. R., Stiggelbout, A. M., & Pieterse, A. H. (2019). Key components of shared decision making models: A systematic review. *BMJ Open, 9*(12), e031763.

Breder, K., & Bockting, W. (2022). Social networks of LGBT older adults: An integrative review. *Psychology of Sexual Orientation and Gender Diversity.*

Bristowe, K., Marshall, S., & Harding, R. (2016). The bereavement experiences of lesbian, gay, bisexual and/or trans people who have lost a partner: A systematic review, thematic synthesis and modelling of the literature. *Palliative Medicine, 30*(8), 730–744.

Bruera, E., Kuehn, N., Miller, M. J., Selmser, P., & Macmillan, K. (1991). The Edmonton Symptom Assessment System (ESAS): A simple method for the assessment of palliative care patients. *Journal of Palliative Care, 7*(2), 6–9.

Burns, S. P., & Pickens, N. D. (2017). Embedding technology into inter-professional best practices in home safety evaluation. *Disability and Rehabilitation: Assistive Technology, 12*(6), 585–591.

Byock, I. R. (1994). A working set of landmarks and developmental task-work. http://www.mywhatever.com/cifwriter/content/18/dw53.html.

Byock, I. R., & Merriman M. P. (1998). Measuring quality of life for patients with terminal illness: The Missoula-VITAS Quality of Life Index. *Palliative Medicine, 12,* 231–244.

Byock, I. R., & Merriman, M. P. (n.d.). The Missoula-VITAS Quality of Life Index (MVQOLI)©: An outcome measure for palliative care: Guide to using the MVQOLI. Retrieved August 4, 2022, from http://www.npcrc.org/files/news/missoula_vitas_quality_of_life_index.pdf.

Cahill, S., Singal, R., Grasso, C., King, D., Mayer, K., Baker, K., & Makadon, H. (2014). Do ask, do tell: High levels of acceptability by patients of routine collection of sexual orientation and gender identity data in four diverse American community health centers. *PloS One, 9*(9), e107104.

Candrian, C., & Lum, H. (2015). Lesbian, gay, bisexual, and transgender communication. In E. Wittenberg, B. Ferrell, J. Goldsmith, T. Smith, M. Glajchen, & G. Handzo (Eds.), *Textbook of palliative care communication.* New York: Oxford University Press.

Center to Advance Palliative Care. (2008). What should you know about palliative care? https://www-tc.pbs.org/wgbh/pages/frontline/facing-death/educational-module/support-for-the-dying/know-about-palliative-care.pdf.
Center to Advance Palliative Care. (2010). Palliative sedation: Myth vs. fact. https://www.capc.org/about/press-media/press-releases/2010-1-6/palliative-sedation-myth-vs-fact/.
Center to Advance Palliative Care. (2019). Get palliative care: Handouts for patients and families. https://getpalliativecare.org/handouts-for-patients-and-families/.
Center to Advance Palliative Care. (n.d.). Get palliative care: Glossary. Retrieved August 4, 2022, from https://getpalliativecare.org/whatis/glossary/.
Centers for Disease Control. (2022). Tips from former smokers: Lesbian, gay, bisexual, and transgender (LGBT). http://www.cdc.gov/tobacco/campaign/tips/groups/lgbt.html.
Centers for Medicare and Medicaid Services. (2018). Manual updates related to payment policy changes affecting the hospice aggregate cap calculation and the designation of hospice attending physicians. https://www.cms.gov/Outreach-and-Education/Medicare-Learning-Network-MLN/MLNMattersArticles/Downloads/MM10517.pdf.
Centers for Medicare and Medicaid Services. (2019). 42 CFR parts 403, 409, 410, 411, 414, 415, 416, 418, 424, 425, 489, and 498. https://www.federalregister.gov/public-inspection/2019/12/05.
Centers for Medicaid and Medicare Services. (2020). State operations manual: Appendix M—Guidance to surveyors: Hospice. https://www.cms.gov/Regulations-and-Guidance/Guidance/Manuals/downloads/som107ap_m_hospice.pdf.
Centers for Medicaid and Medicare Services. (2022). Local coverage determination: Hospice determining TERMINAL status—L34538. https://www.cms.gov/medicare-coverage-database/view/lcd.aspx?LCDId=34538.
Chai, E., Meier, D., Morris, J., & Goldhirsch, S. (Eds.). (2014). *Geriatric palliative care*. New York: Oxford University Press.
Charles, C., Gafni, A., & Whelan, T. (1999). Decision-making in the physician-patient encounter: Revisiting the shared treatment decision-making model. *Social Science & Medicine, 49*(5), 651–661.
Cherny, N., Fallon, M., Kaasa, S., Portenoy, R., & Currow, D. (Eds.). (2015). *Oxford textbook of palliative medicine* (5th ed.). New York: Oxford University Press.
Chin, M. H., Lopez, F. Y., Nathan, A. G., & Cook, S. C. (2016). Improving shared decision making with LGBT racial and ethnic minority patients. *Journal of general internal medicine, 31*, 591–593.
Chochinov, H. M. (2007). Dignity and the essence of medicine: The A, B, C, and D of dignity conserving care. *BMJ (Clinical research ed.), 335*(7612), 184–187.
City of Orlando. (2016). Victims' names. www.cityoforlando.net/blog/victims/.
Coble, C. (2015). Do sodomy laws still exist? FindLaw. http://blogs.findlaw.com/blotter/2015/09/do-sodomy-laws-still-exist.html.
Coleman, E., Radix, A. E., Bouman, W. P., Brown, G. R., de Vries, A. L. C., Deutsch, M. B., et al. (2022). Standards of care for the health of transgender and gender diverse people, version 8. *International Journal of Transgender Health, 23*(Suppl. 1), S1–S259.

C-TAC. (2019). *In their own words: Kathy Brandt and Kim Acquaviva.* https://www.youtube.com/watch?v=acF53M04ytY&t=5s.

C-TAC. (2022, May 1). *Kathy Brandt and Kimberly Acquaviva: Quality of life.* https://thectac.org/asset/stories/kathy-brandt-and-kimberly-acquaviva-quality-of-life/.

Dahlin, C., & Coyne, P. (Eds.). (2023). *Advanced practice palliative nursing* (2nd ed.). New York: Oxford University Press.

Dahlin, C., Coyne, P., & Ferrell, B. (Eds.). (2016). *Advanced practice palliative nursing.* New York: Oxford University Press.

Dahlin, C., DePace, N., Ford, J., Maani-Fogelman, P., & Chow, K. (2022). Promoting health equity: Palliative nurses on the frontlines. *Journal of Hospice and Palliative Nursing, 24*(4), 218–224.

Dahlin, C., & Lynch, M. (2003). HPNA position statement: Palliative sedation at end of life. Hospice and Palliative Nurses Association. https://journals.lww.com/jhpn/Citation/2003/10000/HPNA_Position_Paper__Palliative_Sedation_at_the.22.aspx.

De Bord, J., Burke, W., & Dudzinski, D. (n.d.). Ethics in medicine: Confidentiality. Retrieved August 12, 2022, from https://depts.washington.edu/bhdept/ethics-medicine/bioethics-topics/detail/58.

de Graeff, A., & Dean, M. (2007). Palliative sedation therapy in the last weeks of life: A literature review and recommendations for standards. *Journal of Palliative Medicine, 10,* 67–85.

DeMeester, R., Lopez, F., Moore, J., Cook, M., & Chin, M. (2016). A model of organizational context and shared decision-making: Application to LGBT racial and ethnic minority patients. *Journal of General Internal Medicine, 31*(6), 651–662.

Deutsch, M. B., Green, J., Keatley, J., Mayer, G., Hastings, J., Hall, A. M., & World Professional Association for Transgender Health EMR Working Group. (2013). Electronic medical records and the transgender patient: Recommendations from the World Professional Association for Transgender Health EMR Working Group. *Journal of the American Medical Informatics Association: JAMIA, 20*(4), 700–703.

Dimitrov, N., & Kemle, K. (Eds.). (2022). *Palliative and serious illness patient management for physician assistants.* New York: Oxford University Press.

Eisenhower, D. (1953). Television report to the American people by the President and members of the Cabinet, June 3, 1953. The American Presidency Project. https://www.presidency.ucsb.edu/documents/television-report-the-american-people-the-president-and-members-the-cabinet.

Elwyn, G., Dehlendorf, C., Epstein, R. M., Marrin, K., White, J., Frosch, D. L., et al. (2014). Shared decision-making and motivational interviewing: Achieving patient-centered care across the spectrum of health care problems. *Annals of Family Medicine, 12*(3), 270–275.

Elwyn, G., Frosch, D., Thomson, R., Joseph-Williams, N., Lloyd, A., Kinnersley, P., et al. (2012). Shared decision-making: A model for clinical practice. *Journal of General Internal Medicine, 27*(10), 1361–1367.

Emanuel, L., von Gunten, C., Ferris, F., & Hauser, J. (Eds.). (1999–2011). The Education in Palliative and End-of-Life Care (EPEC) Curriculum. © The EPEC Program, 1999–2011. http://www.epec.net.

Erickson-Schroth, Laura. (2022). *Trans bodies, trans selves: A resource by and for transgender communities* (2nd ed.). New York: Oxford University Press.
Ferrell, B. (Ed.). (2015). *Pediatric palliative care*. New York: Oxford University Press.
Ferrell, B., Coyle, N., & Paice, J. (Eds.). (2015a). *Oxford textbook of palliative nursing* (4th ed.). New York: Oxford University Press.
Ferrell, B., Coyle, N., & Paice, J. (Eds.). (2015b). *Social aspects of palliative care*. New York: Oxford University Press.
Ferrell, B. & Paice, J. (Eds.). (2019). *Oxford textbook of palliative nursing* (5th ed.). New York: Oxford University Press.
Ferrer, R., & Gill, J. (2013). Shared decision-making, contextualized. *Annals of Family Medicine, 11*, 303–305.
Fleishman, J., Kamsky, H., & Sundborg, S. (2019). Trauma-informed nursing practice. *OJIN: The Online Journal of Issues in Nursing, 24*(2), manuscript 3.
Gale Encyclopedia of Medicine. (2008). http://medical-dictionary.thefreedictionary.com/.
Gawande, A. (2014). *Being mortal: Medicine and what matters in the end*. New York: Metropolitan/Holt.
Gardia, G. (2022). Personal Communication.
Gender Equity Resource Center. (2019). Definition of terms. http://ejce.berkeley.edu/geneq/resources/lgbtq-resources/definition-terms.
Gendered Innovations. (n.d.). "Gender." Retrieved August 12, 2022, from https://genderedinnovations.stanford.edu/terms/gender.html.
Gibson, S. (2016). The advanced practice registered nurse in hospice. In C. Dahlin, P. Coyne, & B. Ferrell (Eds.), *Advanced practice palliative nursing*. New York: Oxford University Press.
GLAAD (n.d). Glossary of Terms. Accessed April 26, 2023 at https://www.glaad.org/reference/terms?gclid=CjwKCAjwl6OiBhA2EiwAuUwWZXdbR6f5b5NJ9GeZpn33nsTwOx-wnChXa0fTbkyoxZNgTxS1BOmf1RoCr4oQAvD_BwE
Gladding, S. (2011). *The counseling dictionary: Concise definitions of frequently used terms* (3rd ed.). Upper Saddle River, NJ: Pearson Education.
Gleason, K. M., Brake, H., Agramonte, V., & Perfetti, C. (2012). Medications at Transitions and Clinical Handoffs (MATCH) toolkit for medication reconciliation. Rev. ed. Prepared by the Island Peer Review Organization, under Contract No. HHSA290200900013C. AHRQ Publication No. 11(12)-0059. Rockville, MD: Agency for Healthcare Research and Quality. https://www.ahrq.gov/patient-safety/settings/hospital/match/index.html.
Golley, L. (2012). Cultural issues around end of life. University of Washington Medical Center, Interpreter Services. http://www.uwmedicine.org/uw-medical-center/documents/Cultural-Issues-around-End-of-Life.pdf. Site is no longer available.
Grant, J., Mottet, L., Tanis, J., Harrison, J., Herman, J., & Keisling, M. (2011). Injustice at every turn: A report of the national transgender discrimination survey. Washington, DC: National Center for Transgender Equality and National Gay and Lesbian Task Force. https://transequality.org/sites/default/files/docs/resources/NTDS_Report.pdf.
Griebling, T. (2016). Sexuality and aging: A focus on lesbian, gay, bisexual, and transgender (LGBT) needs in palliative and end of life care. *Current Opinion in Supportive & Palliative Care, 10*(1), 95–101.

Harding, R., Epiphaniou, E., & Chidgey-Clark, J. (2012). Needs, experiences, and preferences of sexual minorities for end-of-life care and palliative care: A systematic review. *Journal of Palliative Medicine, 15*(5), 602–611.

Hay, A., & Johnson, S. (2001). Fundamental skills and knowledge for hospice and palliative care social workers: Competency-based education for social workers. Arlington, VA: National Hospice and Palliative Care Organization.

Herx, L. M. (2021). Continuous palliative sedation therapy. In S. MacDonald, L. Herx, & A. Boyle (Eds.), *Palliative medicine: A case-based manual* (4th ed., pp. 219–227). Oxford: Oxford University Press.

Hilliard, R. (2012, June). Psychosocial documentation: A plan to support ADRs." NHPCO Newsline. https://www.nxtbook.com/nxtbooks/nhpco/newsline_201206/index.php?startid=1#/p/Intro

Hospice and Palliative Credentialing Center. (n.d.a). Advanced Certified Hospice and Palliative Nurse. Retrieved August 12, 2022, from https://advancingexpertcare.org/HPNA/HPCC/CertificationWeb/ACHPN.aspx.

Hospice and Palliative Credentialing Center. (n.d.b). Certified Hospice and Palliative Nurse. Retrieved August 12, 2022, from https://advancingexpertcare.org/HPNA/HPCC/CertificationWeb/CHPN.aspx.

Hospice Medical Director Certification Board. (2013). Eligibility requirements. http://www.hmdcb.org/about-the-exam/default/eligibility.html.

HPNA. (2003). HPNA Position Paper: Palliative Sedation at the End of Life. *Journal of Hospice & Palliative Nursing 5*(4), 235–237.

Hughes, M., & Cartwright, C. (2015). Lesbian, gay, bisexual and transgender people's attitudes to end-of-life decision-making and advance care planning. *Australasian Journal on Ageing, 34*(S2), 39–43.

Human Rights Campaign. (2022). 2023 Corporate equality index criteria evolution: Toolkit and FAQs. https://www.hrc.org/resources/2023-cei-criteria-evolution-toolkit-and-faq.

Human Rights Campaign. (n.d.a). Glossary of terms. Retrieved August 31, 2022, from https://www.hrc.org/resources/glossary-of-terms.

Human Rights Campaign. (n.d.b). Hate crimes timeline. Retrieved August 12, 2022, from http://www.hrc.org/resources/hate-crimes-timeline.

Indian Health Service. (n.d.). Two-spirit. Retrieved September 1, 2022, from https://www.ihs.gov/lgbt/health/twospirit/.

Institute for Healthcare Improvement. (n.d.). Medication reconciliation to prevent adverse drug events. Retrieved August 12, 2022, from https://www.ihi.org/topics/adesmedicationreconciliation/Pages/default.aspx.

Institute for Patient- and Family-Centered Care. (n.d.). Patient- and family-centered care. Retrieved August 12, 2022, from https://www.ipfcc.org/about/pfcc.html.

Institute of Medicine. (1993). *Access to health care in America*. Washington, DC: National Academies Press.

Institute of Medicine. (2011). *The health of lesbian, gay, bisexual, and transgender (LGBT) people: Building a foundation for better understanding*. Washington, DC: National Academies Press.

Institute of Medicine. (2013). Delivering high-quality cancer care: Charting a new course for a system in crisis. Washington, DC: National Academies Press.

Institute of Medicine. (2015). *Dying in America: Improving quality and honoring individual preferences near the end of life.* Washington, DC: National Academies Press.

Institute of Medicine and National Research Council. (2003). *Describing death in America: What we need to know.* Washington, DC: National Academies Press.

Intersex Society of North America. (2008). "What is intersex?" https://isna.org/faq/what_is_intersex/.

Joint Commission. (2011). Advancing effective communication, cultural competence, and patient- and family-centered care for the lesbian, gay, bisexual, and transgender (LGBT) community: A field guide. https://www.jointcommission.org/-/media/tjc/documents/resources/patient-safety-topics/health-equity/lgbtfieldguide_web_linked_verpdf.pdf.

Kaiser Health News. (2019). *Inclusive care at the end of life: The LGBTQ+ experience.* https://www.youtube.com/watch?v=o1YZL5zuD8I.

Kaleem, J. (2016). Orthodox rabbi addresses transgender issues. http://www.jewishjournal.com/religion/article/orthodox_rabbi_addresses_transgender_issues.

Kerr, M. E. (2003). *One family's story: A primer on Bowen theory.* Washington, DC: Bowen Center for the Study of the Family.

Kim, S., & Feyissa, I. F. (2021). Conceptualizing "family" and the role of "chosen family" within the LGBTQ+ refugee community: A text network graph analysis. *Healthcare (Basel), 9*(4), 369.

Knight, S. (n.d.). EndLink: An internet-based end of life care education program. Part I: How to assess spirituality. Retrieved April 11, 2016, from http://endlink.lurie.northwestern.edu/religion_spirituality/part_one.pdf. Site no longer available.

Knight, S., & von Gunten, C. (2004). Module 3: Whole-patient assessment: Nine dimensions. http://www.endoflife.northwestern.edu/whole_patient_assessment/step1.cfm. Site no longer available.

Kroenke, K., Spitzer, R., & Williams, J. (2001). The PHQ-9: Validity of a brief depression severity measure. *Journal of General Internal Medicine, 16*, 606–613.

Lambda Legal. (2010). When health care isn't caring: Lambda Legal's survey of discrimination against LGBT people and people with HIV. http://www.lambdalegal.org/health-care-report.

Lambda Legal. (2014). Tools for protecting your wishes for your funeral. http://www.lambdalegal.org/sites/default/files/final_pp_ttp-2014-07_protecting-your-wishes-for-your-funeral.pdf.

LaRocca-Pitts, M. (2007). A spiritual history tool. https://www.professionalchaplains.org/files/resources/reading_room/spiritual_history_tool_fact_larocca_pitts.pdf

Lau, D. T., Kasper, J. D., Hauser, J. M., Berdes, C., Chang, C. H., Berman, R. L., et al. (2009). Family caregiver skills in medication management for hospice patients: A qualitative study to define a construct. *Journals of Gerontology Series B, 64,* 799–807.

Lau, F., Antonio, M., Davison, K., Queen, R., & Devor, A. (2020). A rapid review of gender, sex, and sexual orientation documentation in electronic health records. *Journal of the American Medical Informatics Association, 27*(11), 1774–1783.

Lawton, A., White, J., & Fromme, E. (2014). End-of-life and advance care planning considerations for lesbian, gay, bisexual, and transgender patients #275. *Journal of Palliative Medicine, 17*(1), 106–107.

League of Women Voters. (2022). Explaining SCOTUS' abortion decision in *Dobbs v. Jackson Women's Health Organization*. https://www.lwv.org/blog/explaining-scotuss-abortion-decision-dobbs-v-jackson-womens-health-organization.

Legal Information Institute. (n.d.). Employment discrimination: An overview. Cornell University Law School. Retrieved August 12, 2022, from https://www.law.cornell.edu/wex/employment_discrimination.

Legare, F., D. Stacey, & IP Team. (2014). IP-SDM model. https://decisionaid.ohri.ca/docs/develop/IP-SDM-Model.pdf.

Leonard, K. (2018). Examples of a mitigation plan. *Chron*. http://smallbusiness.chron.com/examples-mitigation-plan-24507.html.

Limbo, R., & Davies, B. (2015). Grief and bereavement in pediatric palliative care. In B. Ferrell (Ed.), *Pediatric palliative care*. New York: Oxford University Press.

Makoul, G., & Clayman, M. L. (2006). An integrative model of shared decision-making in medical encounters. *Patient Education and Counseling, 60*(3), 301–312.

Maltoni, M., Pittureri, C., Scarpi, E., Piccinini, L., Martini, F., Turci, P., et al. (2009). Palliative sedation therapy does not hasten death: Results from a prospective multi-center study. *Annals of Oncology, 20*(7), 1163–1169.

Maltoni, M., Scarpi, E., Rosati, M., Derni, S., Fabbri, L., Martini, F., et al. (2012). Palliative sedation in end-of-life care and survival: A systematic review. *Journal of Clinical Oncology, 30*(12), 1378–1383.

Margolies, L., & Brown, C. G. (2019). Increasing cultural competence with LGBTQ patients. *Nursing2020, 49*(6), 34–40.

Massachusetts Executive Office of Public Safety. (n.d.). A firefighter's guide to educating occupant(s) on the hazards of smoking and home oxygen use. Retrieved August 12, 2022, from https://www.mass.gov/doc/a-firefighters-guide-to-educating-occupants-on-the-hazards-of-home-oxygen-use/download.

Matzo, M. (2015). Sexuality. In B. Ferrell, N. Coyle, & J. Paice (Eds.), *Oxford textbook of palliative nursing* (4th ed.). New York: Oxford University Press.

Mayo Foundation for Medical Education and Research. (n.d.a). Stress relief from laughter? It's no joke. Healthy Lifestyle: Stress Management. Retrieved August 12, 2022, from http://www.mayoclinic.org/healthy-lifestyle/stress-management/in-depth/stress-relief/art-20044456.

Mayo Foundation for Medical Education and Research. (n.d.b). Symptoms: Shortness of breath: Definition. Retrieved August 12, 2022, from www.mayoclinic.org/symptoms/shortness-of-breath/basics/definition/sym-20050890.

Mazanec, P., & Panke, J. T. (2016). Cultural considerations in palliative care. In B. R. Ferrell (Ed.), *Spiritual, religious, and cultural aspects of care*. New York: Oxford University Press.

McGoldrick, M., Gerson, R., & Petry, S. (2020). *Genograms: Assessment and treatment*. New York: Norton.

McKinley Health Center. (2009). Healthy sexuality. University of Illinois at Urbana-Champaign. Retrieved May 17, 2016, from http://www.mckinley.illinois.edu/handouts/healthy_sexuality.htm. Site no longer available.

McNulty, M. C., Acree, M. E., Kerman, J., Williams, H. H. S., & Schneider, J. A. (2021). Shared decision making for HIV pre-exposure prophylaxis (PrEP) with Black transgender women. *Culture, Health & Sexuality, 24*(8), 1033–1046.

Medical Dictionary. (2009). http://medical-dictionary.thefreedictionary.com.

Medicare Interactive. (n.d.). Glossary. Retrieved August 12, 2022, from http://www.medicareinteractive.org/glossary.

MedicineNet. (2021). Definition of informed consent. http://www.medicinenet.com/script/main/art.asp?articlekey=22414.

Merriam-Webster Dictionary. (2015). http://www.merriam-webster.com/dictionary/.

Miller-Keane Encyclopedia and Dictionary of Medicine, Nursing, and Allied Health (7th ed.). (n.d.). https://medical-dictionary.thefreedictionary.com/.

Moriichi, R. S., Dapper, A., & Vorpahl, M. (2020). Dispelling myths: Common misconceptions around hospice. *CSA Journal, 81*(4), 11–17. http://progressally6yogf8hc32ioroi.s3.amazonaws.com/list/Journal/81/Moriichi.pdf.

Mosby's Medical Dictionary (9th ed.). (2009). http://medicaldictionary.thefreedictionary.com.

Movement Advancement Project. (2016). Non-discrimination laws. Archived at https://web.archive.org/web/20160131020211/http://www.lgbtmap.org/equality-maps/non_discrimination_laws.

Movement Advancement Project. (2022). Nondiscrimination laws. http://www.lgbtmap.org/equality-maps/non_discrimination_laws.

Naierman, N., & Turner, J. (2012). Debunking the myths of hospice. American Hospice Foundation. https://americanhospice.org/learning-about-hospice/debunking-the-myths-of-hospice/.

Nasrallah, H. A. (2020). We are physicians, not providers, and we treat patients, not clients! *Current Psychiatry, 19*(2), 5–7, 29.

National Academies of Sciences, Engineering, and Medicine. (2022). *Measuring sex, gender identity, and sexual orientation*. Washington, DC: National Academies Press.

National Association of Social Workers. (2004). NASW standards for social work practice in palliative and end of life care. https://www.socialworkers.org/LinkClick.aspx?fileticket=xBMd58VwEhk%3d.

National Association of Social Workers. (2015). Standards and indicators for cultural competence in social work practice. https://www.socialworkers.org/LinkClick.aspx?fileticket=7dVckZAYUmk%3d.

National Association of Social Workers. (2021). Code of ethics of the National Association of Social Workers. https://www.socialworkers.org/About/Ethics/Code-of-Ethics/Code-of-Ethics-English.

National Commission on Certification of Physician Assistants. (2019). 2018 Statistical profile of certified physician assistants: An annual report of the National Commission on Certification of Physician Assistants. https://prodcmsstoragesa.blob.core.windows.net/uploads/files/2018StatisticalProfileofCertifiedPhysicianAssistants.pdf.

National Commission on Certification of Physician Assistants. (2021). 2020 Statistical profile of certified physician assistants: An annual report of the National Commission on Certification of Physician Assistants. https://www.nccpa.net/wp-content/uploads/2022/04/Statistical-Profile-of-Certified-PAs-2020.pdf

National Commission on Certification of Physician Assistants. (2022). Specialty certificates. https://www.nccpa.net/specialty-certificates/#palliative-medicine-hospice.

National Comprehensive Cancer Network. (2022). NCCN guidelines. https://www.nccn.org/professionals/physician_gls/f_guidelines.asp.

National Conference of State Legislatures. (2022). Scope of practice overview. https://scopeofpracticepolicy.org/practitioners-overview/.

National Consensus Project for Quality Palliative Care. (2013). *Clinical practice guidelines for quality palliative care* (3rd ed.). https://www.nationalcoalitionhpc.org/wp-content/uploads/2017/04/NCP_Clinical_Practice_Guidelines_3rd_Edition.pdf.

National Consensus Project for Quality Palliative Care. (2018). *Clinical practice guidelines for quality palliative care* (4th ed.). Richmond, VA: Author. https://www.nationalcoalitionhpc.org/wp-content/uploads/2020/07/NCHPC-NCPGuidelines_4thED_web_FINAL.pdf.

National Hospice and Palliative Care Organization. (2016). End-of-life decisions. https://www.nhpco.org/wp-content/uploads/2019/04/End-of-Life_Decisions.pdf.

National Hospice and Palliative Care Organization. (n.d.a). Advance directives. Retrieved August 10, 2022, from https://www.caringinfo.org/planning/advance-directives/.

National Hospice and Palliative Care Organization. (n.d.b). Digital and video advance directives. Retrieved August 11, 2022, from https://www.caringinfo.org/planning/advance-directives/digital-video-advance-directives/.

National Hospice and Palliative Care Organization. (n.d.c). Interdisciplinary team and care planning. Retrieved August 12, 2022, from https://www.nhpco.org/.

National Hospice and Palliative Care Organization. (n.d.d.) Your right to care that honors your wishes. Retrieved April 25, 2023, from https://www.caringinfo.org/planning/your-rights/your-rights-to-care/

National Institutes of Health Clinical Center. (2022). Pain and palliative care: Palliative care truths and myths. https://www.cc.nih.gov/palliativecare/truths_myths.html.

National LGBT Health Education Center. (2015). Collecting sexual orientation and gender identity data in electronic health records. https://www.lgbtqiahealtheducation.org/wp-content/uploads/Collecting-Sexual-Orientation-and-Gender-Identity-Data-in-EHRs-2016.pdf.

National LGBTQIA+ Health Education Center. (2020). Affirming primary care for intersex people. https://interactadvocates.org/wp-content/uploads/2020/10/Affirming-Primary-Care-for-Intersex-People-2020.pdf.

National Library of Medicine. (2020). Do-not-resuscitate order. In *MedlinePlus Medical Encyclopedia*. https://medlineplus.gov/ency/patientinstructions/000473.htm.

National Library of Medicine. (2021). Physical examination. In *MedlinePlus Medical Encyclopedia*. https://medlineplus.gov/ency/article/002274.htm.

National Library of Medicine. (n.d.). *MedlinePlus Medical Encyclopedia*. https://medlineplus.gov/encyclopedia.html.
National Palliative Care Research Center. (n.d.a). Guidelines for using the Edmonton Symptom Assessment Scale. Retrieved August 9, 2022, from http://www.npcrc.org/files/news/edmonton_symptom_assessment_scale.pdf.
National Palliative Care Research Center. (n.d.b). Memorial Symptom Assessment Scale. Retrieved August 9, 2022, from http://www.npcrc.org/files/news/memorial_symptom_assessment_scale.pdf.
National POLST Paradigm. (2016). "What Is POLST?" http://www.polst.org/.
National POLST Paradigm. (n.d.). POLST and advance directives. Retrieved August 11, 2022, from http://www.polst.org/advance-care-planning/polst-and-advance-directives/.
National Quality Forum. (2012). Palliative Care and End-of-Life Care—A Consensus Report. http://www.qualityforum.org/Publications/2012/04/Palliative_Care_and_End-of-Life_Care%E2%80%94A_Consensus_Report.aspx.
National Research Council. (2003). Describing Death in America: What We Need to Know: Executive Summary. Washington, DC: The National Academies Press. https://doi.org/10.17226/10619.
Neville, S., & Henrickson, M. (2009). The constitution of "lavender families": A LGB perspective. *Journal of Clinical Nursing, 18*(6), 849–856.
New York City Department of Health. (2019, December 17). Health Department will add third, non-binary gender category to New York City death certificates. https://www.nyc.gov/site/doh/about/press/pr2019/non-binary-gender-category-to-nyc-death-certificates.page.
Ng, H. H. (2016). Intersectionality and shared decision making in LGBTQ health. *LGBT health, 3*(5), 325.
O'Connor, A., Stacey, D., & Jacobsen. M. (2015). Ottawa personal decision guide. Ottawa Hospital Research Institute. https://decisionaid.ohri.ca/docs/das/OPDG.pdf.
Oliver, D. P., Washington, K., Demiris, G., Wallace, A., Propst, M. R., Uraizee, A. M., Craig, K., Clayton, M. F., Reblin, M., & Ellington, L. (2018). Shared decision making in home hospice nursing visits: A qualitative study. *Journal of Pain and Symptom Management, 55*(3), 922–929.
Palliative Care Network of Wisconsin. (2022). Palliative care fast facts and concepts. http://www.mypcnow.org/fast-facts.
Papavasiliou, E. S., Brearley, S. G., Seymour, J. E., Brown, J., & Payne, S. A. (2013a). From sedation to continuous sedation until death: how has the conceptual basis of sedation in end-of-life care changed over time? *Journal of Pain and Symptom Management, 46*(5), 691–706.
Papavasiliou, E., Payne, S., Brearley, S., Brown, J., & Seymour, J. (2013b). Continuous sedation (CS) until death: Mapping the literature by bibliometric analysis. *Journal of Pain and Symptom Management, 45*(6), 1073–1082.e10.
Paul, R., & Adamson, K. (1993). Critical thinking and the nature of prejudice. In R. Paul, *Critical thinking: What every person needs to survive in a rapidly changing world*. Santa Rosa, CA: Foundation for Critical Thinking.

PEACE Project. (2016). PEACE hospice and palliative care quality measures. https://www.med.unc.edu/pcare/resources/PEACE-Quality-Measures.

Peek, M., Lopez, F., Williams, H., Xu, L., McNulty, M., Acree, M., & Schneider, J. (2016). Development of a conceptual framework for understanding shared decision-making among African-American LGBT patients and their clinicians. *Journal of General Internal Medicine, 31*(6), 677–687.

Periyakoil, V. J. (n.d.). Palliative care case study: Palliative sedation. Stanford School of Medicine. Archived at https://www.acrrm.org.au/docs/default-source/all-files/stanford-case-study.pdf?sfvrsn=6904fffc_2.

Physician Assistants in Hospice and Palliative Medicine. (n.d.). PAs and hospice: Updates from CMS 2019–2020. Retrieved August 8, 2022, from https://pahpm.org/page-18267.

Piasecka, K., Slusarska, B., & Drop, B. (2018). Genograms in nursing education and practice a sensitive but very effective technique: A systematic review. *Journal of Community Medicine & Health Education, 8*(6), 1–5.

Pickens, N. D., Mendonca, R., Burns, S. P., & Smith, R. O. (2020). Home safety evaluation—getting it right. *Disability and Rehabilitation: Assistive Technology, 17*(6), 652–657.

Portenoy, R., Thaler, H., Kornblith, A., Lepore, J., Friedlander-Klar, H., Kiyasu, E., et al. (1994). The Memorial Symptom Assessment Scale: An instrument for the evaluation of symptom prevalence, characteristics and distress. *European Journal of Cancer, 30A*(9), 1326–1336.

Prendergast, J. (2020). Holding and letting go. *Pennsylvania Gazette*. http://thepenngazette.com/holding-and-letting-go/.

Puchalski, C. (2022). FICA Spiritual History Tool. GW Institute for Spirituality and Health. https://gwish.smhs.gwu.edu/sites/g/files/zaskib1011/files/2022-08/v2_fica_pdf_2_final_updated_6.29.22.pdf

Puchalski, C. (2014). The FICA Spiritual History Tool #274. *Journal of Palliative Medicine, 17*(1): 105–106.

Puchalski, C. (2021). Spiritual care in health care: Guideline, models, spiritual assessment and the use of the© FICA Spiritual History Tool. In Arndt Büssing (Ed.), *Spiritual needs in research and practice* (pp. 27–45). Cham, Switzerland: Palgrave Macmillan.

Puchalski, C., Ferrell, B., Virani, R., Otis-Green, S., Baird, P., Bull, J., et al. (2009). Improving the quality of spiritual care as a dimension of palliative care: The report of the consensus conference. *Journal of Palliative Medicine, 12*(10), 885–904.

Puchalski, C., & Romer, A. L. (2000). Taking a spiritual history allows clinicians to understand patients more fully. *Journal of Palliative Medicine, 3*(1), 129–137.

Raja, S. N., Carr, D. B., Cohen, M., Finnerup, N. B., Flor, H., Gibson, S., et al. (2020). The revised International Association for the Study of Pain definition of pain: Concepts, challenges, and compromises. *Pain, 161*(9), 1976–1982.

Rawlings, D. (2012). End-of-life care considerations for gay, lesbian, bisexual, and transgender individuals. *International Journal of Palliative Nursing, 18*(1), 29–34.

Redelman, M. (2008). Is there a place for sexuality in the holistic care of patients in the palliative care phase of life? *American Journal of Hospice and Palliative Medicine, 25*, 366–371.

Refinery29. (2018). Gender nation glossary. https://www.refinery29.com/en-us/lgbtq-definitions-gender-sexuality-terms.

Repp, K. (2022, December 14). Death certificates often misgendered transgender and nonbinary people, first-of-a-kind study finds. Retrieved December 31, 2022. https://jphmpdirect.com/2022/12/14/death-certificates-often-misgendered-transgender-and-nonbinary-people-first-of-a-kind-study-finds/.

Rosa, W. E., Banerjee, S. C., & Maingi. S. (2022). Family caregiver inclusion is not a level playing field: Toward equity for the chosen families of sexual and gender minority patients. *Palliative Care and Social Practice, 16.*

Ross, D., & Alexander, C. (2001). Management of common symptoms in terminally ill patients, part II: Constipation, delirium, and dyspnea. *American Family Physician, 64*(6): 1019–1026.

Saenger, P. (2006). Jewish pediatricians in Nazi Germany: Victims of persecution. *Israel Medical Association Journal, 8*(5), 324–328.

Scarff, J. R. (2021). What's in a name? The problematic term "provider." *Federal Practitioner, 38*(10), 446–448.

Schildmann, E., & Schildmann, J. (2014). Palliative sedation therapy: A systematic literature review and critical appraisal of available guidance on indication and decision making. *Journal of Palliative Medicine, 17*(5), 601–611.

Segen's Medical Dictionary. (n.d.). http://medical-dictionary.thefreedictionary.com/.

Serano, J. (2019, June 19). Julia Serano: The science of gender is rarely simple. *New York Times.* https://www.nytimes.com/2019/06/19/us/julia-serano-gender-science-lgbtq.html.

Serano, J. (2022). Julia's trans, gender, sexuality, and activism glossary. https://www.juliaserano.com/terminology.html.

Sieck, C., Johansen, M., & Stewart, J. (2016). Interprofessional shared decision-making: Increasing the "shared" in shared decision-making. *International Journal of Healthcare, 2*(1).

Sinclair, C., Kalender-Rich, J., Griebling, T., & Porter-Williamson, K. (2015). Palliative care of urologic patients at end of life. *Clinics in Geriatric Medicine, 31,* 667–678.

Smolinski, K., & Colón, Y. (2011). Palliative care with lesbian, gay, bisexual, and transgender persons. In T. Altilio & S. Otis-Green (Eds.), *Oxford textbook of palliative social work.* New York: Oxford University Press.

Stark, M., & Fins, J. J. (2013). What's not being shared in shared decision-making? *Hastings Center Report, 43*(4), 13–16.

Stein, G. L., Berkman, C., O'Mahony, S., Godfrey, D., Javier, N. M., & Maingi, S. (2020). Experiences of lesbian, gay, bisexual, and transgender patients and families in hospice and palliative care: Perspectives of the palliative care team. *Journal of Palliative Medicine, 23*(6), 817–824.

Steinmetz, K. (2014). "This is what 'cisgender' means." *Time.* http://time.com/3636430/cisgender-definition/.

Stripling, J. (2019). "Death is this professor's life's work. When it hit close to home, she invited everyone to watch." *Chronicle of Higher Education,* August 7, 2019. www.chronicle.com/article/Death-Is-This-Professor-s/246904.

Sulmasy, D. (2006). Spiritual issues in the care of dying patients: ". . . It's okay between me and God." *Journal of the American Medical Association, 296*(1), 1385–1392.

Tan, J., Xu, L., Lopez, F., Jia, J., Pho, M., Kim, K., & Chin, M. (2016). Shared decision-making among clinicians and Asian American and Pacific Islander sexual and gender minorities: An intersectional approach to address a critical care gap. *LGBT Health, 3*(5), 327–334.

Tate, C., Ledbetter, J., & Youssef, C. (2013). A two-question method for assessing gender categories in the social and medical sciences. *Journal of Sex Research, 50*(8), 767–776.

Tomita, M. (2011). Home Safety Self-Assessment Tool V.3. https://www.tompkinscountyny.gov/files2/cofa/documents/hssat_v3.pdf.

Torres, V. (n.d.). Gay events timeline: 1970–1999. Sexual Orientation Issues in the News. Archived at https://web.archive.org/web/20160303221541/ https://www.usc.edu/schools/annenberg/asc/projects/soin/enhancingCurricula/timeline.html#1972.

Trans Student Educational Resources. (2016). Gender pronouns. Designed by L. Pan. https://transstudent.org/graphics/.

Transgender Law Center. (2014, September 26). CA governor signs Respect After Death Act. https://transgenderlawcenter.org/archives/11140.

Twycross, R. (2019). Reflections on palliative sedation. *Palliative Care: Research and Treatment, 12*.

University of Wisconsin–Milwaukee, Rehabilitation Research Design & Disability Center. (2022). HESTIA: Home evaluation system with a triangulating integrative approach (A home evaluation app). https://uwm.edu/r2d2/projects/hestia/.

U.S. Department of Health and Human Services. (2003). HIPAA privacy rule at 45 CFR 164.510(b). https://www.gpo.gov/fdsys/pkg/CFR-2003-title45-vol1/xml/CFR-2003-title45-vol1-sec164-510.xml.

U.S. Department of Justice. (2009). The Matthew Shepard and James Byrd, Jr., Hate Crimes Prevention Act of 2009. http://www.justice.gov/crt/matthew-shepard-and-james-byrd-jr-hate-crimes-prevention-act-2009-0.

U.S. Supreme Court. (2003). *Lawrence et al. v. Texas*, No. 02–102. http://caselaw.findlaw.com/us-supreme-court/539/558.html.

Vermont Ethics Network. (n.d.a). Decision-making capacity. Retrieved August 12, 2022, from http://www.vtethicsnetwork.org/decisionmaking.html.

Vermont Ethics Network. (n.d.b). Goals of care. Retrieved August 10, 2022, from https://vtethicsnetwork.org/palliative-and-end-of-life-care/goals-of-care-conversations

Vermont Ethics Network. (n.d.c). Health care ethics: Overview and basics. Retrieved August 12, 2022, from http://www.vtethicsnetwork.org/ethics.html.

Victoria Hospice Society. (2001). Palliative Performance Scale Version 2 (PPSv2). http://www.npcrc.org/files/news/palliative_performance_scale_PPSv2.pdf.

Walters, J. K., Mew, M. C., & Repp, K. K. (2023). Transgender and nonbinary deaths investigated by the state medical examiner in the Portland, Oregon, metro area and their concordance with vital records, 2011–2021. *Journal of Public Health Management and Practice, 29*(1), 64–70.

Washington, K. T., Demiris, G., White, P., Mathis, H. C., Forsythe, J. E., & Parker Oliver, D. (2022). A goal-directed model of collaborative decision making in hospice and palliative care. *Journal of Palliative Care, 37*(2), 120–124.

Washington, K. T., Parker Oliver, D., Gage, L. A., Albright, D. L., & Demiris, G. (2016). A multimethod analysis of shared decision-making in hospice interdisciplinary team meetings including family caregivers. *Palliative Medicine, 30*(3), 270–278.

Washington State Health Care Authority. (2022). Engaging health consumers through shared decision making. https://www.hca.wa.gov/assets/program/sdm-fact-sheet.pdf.

Wenzel, H. (2015). Legal issues for LGBT caregivers. Family Caregiver Alliance, National Center on Caregiving. https://www.caregiver.org/legal-issues-lgbt-caregivers.

WGBH Educational Foundation. (2011). Timeline: Milestones in the American gay rights movement. Produced in connection with the *American Experience* television series. http://www.pbs.org/wgbh/americanexperience/features/timeline/stonewall/.

White, P. (2013). Use of "cisgender" perpetuates problematic dichotomy. *Kansas State Collegian*. http://www.kstatecollegian.com/2013/04/15/use-of-cisgender-perpetuates-problematic-dichotomy/.

Williamson, D., Lesandrini, J., & Kamdar, J. (2016). Incapacitated and surrogateless patients: Decision making for the surrogateless patient: An attempt to improve decision making. *American Journal of Bioethics, 16*(2), 83–85.

Wittenberg, E., Ferrell, B. Goldsmith, J. Smith, T. Glajchen, M., & Handzo, G. (Eds.). (2015). *Textbook of palliative care communication.* New York: Oxford University Press.

Won, Y. W., Chun, H. S., Seo, M., Kim, R. B., Kim, J. H., & Kang, J. H. (2019). Clinical patterns of continuous and intermittent palliative sedation in patients with terminal cancer: A descriptive, observational study. *Journal of Pain and Symptom Management, 58*(1), 65–71.

World Health Organization. (2006). Defining sexual health: Report of a technical consultation on sexual health, 28–31 January 2002, Geneva. https://www.who.int/teams/sexual-and-reproductive-health-and-research/key-areas-of-work/sexual-health/defining-sexual-health.

World Health Organization. (2010). Developing sexual health programmes: A framework for action. http://apps.who.int/iris/bitstream/10665/70501/1/WHO_RHR_HRP_10.22_eng.pdf.

World Health Organization. (2020). Genomic resource centre: Gender and genetics. Archived at https://web.archive.org/web/20201106060742/https://www.who.int/genomics/gender/en/index1.html

World Health Organization. (n.d.). Gender and health. Retrieved August 22, 2022, from https://www.who.int/health-topics/gender#tab=tab_1.

World Professional Association for Transgender Health. (2012). Standards of care for the health of transsexual, transgender, and gender nonconforming people. https://www.wpath.org/media/cms/Documents/SOC%20v7/SOC%20V7_English.pdf.

Wynn, S. (2014). Decisions by surrogates: An overview of surrogate consent laws in the United States. *Bifocal: A Journal of the American Bar Association Commission on Law and Aging, 36*(1), 10–14.

Yennurajalingam, S., & Bruera, E. (Eds.). (2016). *Oxford American handbook of hospice and palliative medicine and supportive care.* New York: Oxford University Press.

Zeitlin, D. (2020). Finding life in death. *Penn Gazette*. https://thepenngazette.com/finding-life-in-death/.

Index

access to care, 285; discrimination regarding, 76, 77; discussion questions on, 91–92; employment discrimination regarding, 79–80; eviction discrimination regarding 82–83; hate crimes regarding, 83–86; history regarding, 76, 77–78, 79–80; key points for, 91; key terms for, 75. labeling of homosexuality as mental illness regarding, 82. *See also* barriers to care
accreditation, 282, 284
ACHP-SW. *See* Advanced Certified Hospice and Palliative Social Worker credential
Acquaviva, Greyson, 34, 35, 81, 121, 197, 235–236, 260, 261
action, DAROP format, 240
activities of daily living (ADLs), 116
advance care planning, 206, 285; core tasks of, 189–190; documents, 191–195; family regarding, 189–190; legal issues regarding, 187–188, 189–190, 191–195; patient regarding, 189–190

Advanced Certified Hospice and Palliative Nurse credential, 17
Advanced Certified Hospice and Palliative Social Worker credential (ACHP-SW), 17
advance directive, 192, 285; discussion question on, 207; POLST/MOLST regarding, 194
Advanced Palliative Hospice Social Work Certification (APHSW-C), 17
Advanced Practice Palliative Nursing (Dahlin and Coyne), 7–8
Advanced Practice Palliative Nursing (Gibson), 6
advanced practice registered nursing education, *282–283*
advance healthcare directive, 192
advocacy: discussion questions on, 234; institutional inclusiveness regarding, 265, 269–270; key points for, 232–233; key terms for, 210
affirmation, 285
agender, 60, 285
Aging with Dignity, 193

Aleccia, JoNel, xix
aliagender, 60, 285
Almack, Kathryn, 68, 87
Altilio, T., 7
American Academy of Hospice and Palliative Medicine, 142–143
American Board of Medical Specialties, 16
American Nurses Association (ANA), 143
American Psychiatric Association (APA): gender identity disorder label of, 82; homosexuality mental illness label of, 82
ANA. *See* American Nurses Association
anger, *254*, 286
anticipatory grief, 90, *126*, *173*, 201
Anticipatory Planning for Death dimension, 119–121
antidiscrimination ordinances, 80
anxiety, 117, *220*, 286
APA. *See* American Psychiatric Association
APHSW-C. *See* Advanced Palliative Hospice Social Work Certification
APHSW Certification Board, 17
aromantic, 66
arrests, 83
asexual, 65, 286
asexual persons, 66
assessment instruments, 118
assigned sex, 54, 55, 70, 154; discussion question on, 71–72; gender affirmation surgery regarding, 58–59, 71; SOGI data question collecting, 62, 63–64. *See also* gender; gender expression; gender identity
assumption, 27, 99, 286
attitude, 286; CAMPERS, 27, 28–29, 30, 46; about death, 29; discussion questions on, 91–92; key points for, 91; key terms for, 75; about patient visits, 28–29; self-awareness regarding, 27–30
autonomy, 185, 205, 206, 286; Gawande on, 184; in shared decision-making, 134

Baird, P., 249–250, *251*, 253, *254–255*
Barebones Film Festival, 121
barriers to care, 20, 76, 77, 86, 286; discussion question on, 92; financial barriers, 87, 89, 91, *172*, 290. *See also* access to care; institutional barriers to care; perceptual barriers to care
behavior: adaptive, *171*; discussion questions on, 71–72; empathic, 40, *40*, 289; key points for, 70–71; key terms for, 50. *See also* sexual behavior
Being Mortal (Gawande), 184
Beischel, W. J., 58
belief, 286; CAMPERS, 27, 28–29, 30, 46; about death, 29; about patient visits, 28–29; self-awareness regarding, 27–30
beneficence, 185, 205, 206, 286
bereavement, 203, 286
bereavement care: bereavement groups regarding, 257; discrimination regarding, 256, 258
Bipartisan Budget Act (2018), 11
biphobia, 230
biromantic, 66
bisexual, 65, 68, 286
bisexual persons, nondiscrimination statement regarding, 267
Blackhall, Leslie, 196, 197
Board of Chaplaincy Certification, 18
bowel regimen, 136
Bowen family systems theory, 152
Brandt, Kathy, 10, 13, 18; Acquaviva relationship with, 34, 35, 81, 121, 197, 235–236, 260, 261; on cancer, xv, xvi–xix, 3–4, 23, 132, 181–182; Celiac Disease of, 53; daily life of, 73; death regarding, 182, 196–197, 208–209, 260–261; emotions of, 61, 74, 80–81, 93–94, 98–99, 107–108, 157–158; end-of-life caregiving for, 243–245; Facebook presence of, xv, xvi–xix, 3–4, 13–14, 18, 23–24; on family caregivers,

186–187; fatigue of, 107–108; financial support for, 34–35, 44–45, 49, 74, 81, 139, 244–245; gynecologic oncologist of, 34; help for, xviii–xix; home-buying of, 121, 122; on impatience, 169–170; life insurance of, 260–261; "The Long Goodbye" post by, 93–94; on Maine trip, 162–163; nausea/vomiting of, 13–14; *New Yorker* documentary comments regarding, xx–xxi; pain experienced by, 78–79, 181; pathology report results of, 23; quality of life prioritized by, 3–4; support network for, 81; surgery of, 3; symptoms and care for, 13–14, 33–34, 44, 53; treatment costs of, 139–140; weight loss of, 39, 44, 48, 52–53
breathlessness, 117, *220*, 286–287
Bull, J., 249–250, *251*, 253, *254–255*
Byock, Ira: developmental landmarks and taskwork for the end of life by, 245, *246*; MVQOLI by, 245, 247–248

Cagle, J., 7
California, transgender persons death certificate laws in, 199
CAMPERS, 287; attitudes and beliefs regarding, 27, 28–29, 30, 46; chapter activity, 48; emotion, 36, 47; mitigation plan, 31, 32, 46; patient, 32–33, 37, 47; purpose, 26–27, 46; reactions, 36, 37–38; self-awareness regarding, 26, 31, 38, 40, 46, 47, 48; strategy, 38
cancer, Brandt regarding, xv, xvi–xix, 3–4, 23, 132, 181–182
CAQ. *See* Certificate of Added Qualification
care coordination, 287; discussion questions on, 180–181; environmental and safety assessment regarding, 175–176; key points for, 179–180; key terms for, 159
caregivers: family, 186–187; primary, 90; questions assessing, 211–212, *212–216*

CaringInfo, 193
CDC. *See* Centers for Disease Control
Celiac Disease, of Brandt, 53
Centers for Disease Control (CDC): on smoking, 177; on SOGI data collection, 63–64
Centers for Medicare and Medicaid Services (CMS), 239
Certificate of Added Qualification (CAQ), 16–17
certifications, 16–17, 18, 284
Certified Hospice and Palliative Care Chaplain credential, 18
Certified Hospice and Palliative Nurse credential, 17
Certified Hospice and Palliative Social Worker credential (CHP-SW), 17
chaplain: Board of Chaplaincy Certification, 18; Certified Hospice and Palliative Care Chaplain credential, 18; chapter activity regarding, 259; discipline competencies, 16; education, *283*; ethics code and interpretive statement of, 263; shared decision-making scenario involvement of, 144, 147, 149; spiritual/existential assessment regarding, 248, 250, 258. *See also* interdisciplinary/interprofessional team
chapter activity: CAMPERS, 48; chaplain regarding, 259; on discrimination, 92; on durable power of attorney, 207; on Five-Dimension Assessment Model, 131–132; on genograms, 156; on goals of care, 181; on institutional inclusiveness, 277; on living will, 207; on pain and symptom management, 234; regarding sexual orientation, 72
children, permanency planning for, 202
chosen family. *See* family of choice
CHP-SW. *See* Certified Hospice and Palliative Social Worker credential
chromosomes, 55
cisgender, 56, 57, 287

cisgender patient, 92
civil rights, discrimination of, 22–23
Civil Rights Act, Title VII, 80
clinical note, 287
Clinical Practice Guidelines for Quality Palliative Care (National Consensus Project), 8–9, 70; comprehensive history domains delineated by, 96, 97, 104–105; on psychosocial assessment and support, 238; on shared decision-making, 135–136; spiritual/existential assessment and spiritual/existential/cultural history in, 248–249
CMS. *See* Centers for Medicare and Medicaid Services
Coalition to Transform Advanced Care (C-TAC), xix, xxi
Colby, Bill, 93
coming out: as bisexual, 68; discussion question on, 72, 91–92; safety of, 86
communication, 38; discussion questions on, 47–48; empathic behaviors regarding, 40; humor regarding, 45, 48; key points for, 46–47; key terms for, 25–26; nonverbal, 32, 47, 296; self-disclosure regarding, 41, 42, 48; techniques, 26; touch regarding, 42–43, 48
community support, 111, 112
comorbidity, *171*
compassion, 287
competence, 287
competencies, 16–17
comprehensive assessment, 287
comprehensive history, 20, 287–288; assessment model for, 103–107; components of, 103–104; discussion questions on, 131; evidence-based approach for, 96, *97*, 97–98; family presence regarding, 101, 102; FICA Spiritual History Tool regarding, 106, 111–112; inclusive language for, 105; key points for, 130; key terms for, 95–96;

rapport for, 97, 98; relevant questions and intrusive questions regarding, 127, *127*, 131. *See also* family meeting; Five-Dimension Assessment Model
confidentiality, 207, 288; HIPAA regarding, 203–204; legal issues regarding, 202, 203–205; pronouns regarding, 204, 206; sexual orientation regarding, 204–205
confusion, 117, *221*, 288
consciousness, optimal, *171*
consent, for touch, 42–43
constipation, 117, *221*, 288
Conversation Project, 193
coping: problems, *173*; skills, 288
counseling education, *283*
Coyne, P., 7–8
(C-TAC). *See* Coalition to Transform Advanced Care
cultural competency employee training, 271
cultural norms: Five-Dimension Assessment Model regarding, 109; shared decision-making regarding, 135

Dahlin, Constance, 7–8, 142, 188
DAROP format, 239–241, 288
data, DAROP format, 240
Davies, B., 6
death: attitudes and beliefs about, 29; Brandt regarding, 182, 196–197, 208–209, 260–261; certificates, 199–200; emotions regarding, 36; final days before, 119–120, 147; from home oxygen use, 178–179; prematurity of, *173*; rituals and traditions after, 120; safety and comfort for, *124–125*; self-determined life closure regarding, *124*
decision-making capacity (DMC), 288
Decision Making dimension, 118–119
delirium, shared decision-making scenario regarding, 138, 140–142, 147–148
denial, 31, 288
depression, 117, *221*, 241, 257, 288
despair, 242–243, *254*, 258, 288

developmental tasks, 245, *246*
Diagnostic and Statistical Manual of Mental Disorders (DSM), 82
difference of sex development (DSD), 83
Dimitrov, N., 11
discipline: competencies, 16–17; education, 281–282, *282–283*, 284; scope of practice, 15; textbooks, 5–6, 7, 8, 9–10, 279–281
discrimination, 2, 229, 288; access to care regarding, 76, 77; antidiscrimination ordinances regarding, 80; bereavement care regarding, 256, 258; chapter activity on, 92; of civil rights, 22–23; employee training on, 271; eviction, 82–83; of Family and Medical Leave Act, 22–23; fear of, 76; hate crimes, 83–86; housing, 293; institutional barriers to care regarding, 90, 91; institutional level change regarding, 19; intersectionality of oppression compounding, 77–78; of mental illness label, 82; against nonbinary persons, 272; sodomy laws, 83, 300 against transgender persons, 89, 272; trauma of, 77. *See also* employment discrimination; nondiscrimination statement
discussion questions: on access to care, 91–92; on advocacy, 234; on attitude, 91–92; on behavior, 71–72; on care coordination, 180–181; on communication, 47–48; on comprehensive history, 131; on education, 234; on ethical issues, 207; on family dynamics, 156; on gender, 71–72; on health, 71–72; on institutional inclusiveness, 276–277; on legal issues, 207; on physical examination, 131; on plan of care, 180–181; on psychosocial issues, 259; on self-awareness, 47–48; on sex, 71–72; on sexual orientation, 71–72, 92;

on shared decision-making, 156; on spiritual issues, 259
disease extension, *171*
disposal of supplies, 211, 233, 289; discussion question on, 234; education regarding, 224, *228*
disposition of remains: legal issues, 198–200; next of kin regarding, 198
DMC. *See* decision-making capacity
DNR. *See* do-not-resuscitate order
Dobbs v. Jackson Women's Health Organization, 83
do-not-resuscitate order (DNR), 194, 289
Drotos, Kunga Nyima, 178–179, 203
DSD. *See* difference of sex development
DSM. *See* Diagnostic and Statistical Manual of Mental Disorders
durable power of attorney: chapter activity on, 207; in shared decision-making, 153–154; in shared decision-making scenario, 140, 141–142
Dying in America (Institute of Medicine), 6, 188
dyspnea management consensus standards, *97*

education: discipline, 281–282, *282–283*, 284; discussion questions on, 234; disposal of supplies regarding, 224, *228*; end-stage disease progression regarding, 216, *217–219*; key points for, 232–233; key terms for, 210; medication management regarding, 223–224, *225–227*; pain and symptom management regarding, 220, *220–223*; patient-care skills regarding, 211–212, *212–216*; questions regarding, 234; signs and symptoms of imminent death regarding, 227, 230, *231–232*, 232
Education in Palliative and End-of-Life Care (EPEC), 104
Eisenhower, Dwight, 79–80

emotion, 289; asexual persons needs of, 66; of Brandt, 61, 74, 80–81, 93–94, 98–99, 107–108, 157–158; CAMPERS, 36, 47; denial, 31, 288; depression, 117, *221*, 241, 257, 288; despair, 242–243, *254*, 258, 288; hope, 242–243, 247, 258, 293; self-awareness regarding, 36. *See also* fear

emotional cutoff: family dynamics regarding, 152–153, 155; of shared decision-making scenario, 152–153

emotional distress, 257, 259; family of origin regarding, 242, 258; interdisciplinary/interprofessional team regarding, 241–242; psychosocial issues, 241–242, 289; strategies assessing, 241–242

empathic behaviors, 40, *40*, 289

empathy, 40, 289

employee benefits, orientation, and training, 266, 289; discussion question on, 276; institutional inclusiveness regarding, 270–271

employment discrimination, 289; access to care regarding, 79–80; history regarding, 79–80; legality of, 80

Employment of Homosexuals and Other Sex Perverts in Government U.S. Senate report, 79

end-of-life caregiving: for Brandt, 243–245; EPEC regarding, 104; Patient and Family Outcomes-Focused Inquiry for Interdisciplinary Teams regarding, *171*; standards for, 96, *97*

endosex, 289

end-stage disease, 289

end-stage disease progression, 211, 289; clinical status, *217*; discussion question on, 234; education regarding, 216, *217–219*; signs, *218–219*; symptoms, *217–218*

environmental and safety assessment, 180, 181, 289; assessment tools for, 175–176; care coordination regarding, 175–176; oxygen use regarding, 177–178

environment issues, *172*

EPEC. *See* Education in Palliative and End-of-Life Care

Erickson-Schroth, Laura, 52

ethical defensibility, of palliative sedation, 142–143

ethical issues: discussion questions on, 207; key points for, 205–206; key terms for, 183

ethical principles, 205, 289–290; care delivery regarding, 184–186; conflict amongst, 185–186; discussion question on, 207; of shared decision-making, 134

ethics code, 275, 276; of chaplain, 263; of hospice physician, 265; of physician associates, 265; of registered nurse, 264–265; of social worker, 264

ethics committee, 150

euthanasia, palliative sedation distinguished from, 138, 143, 148

eviction discrimination, 82–83

Executive Order 10450, 79–80

expected outcomes, 164–165, *165*, 179, 290

eye contact, 290

eye-level approach, 290

Facebook, xv, xvi–xix, 3–4, 12, 13–14, 18, 23–24

facilitating behaviors, 40, *40*, 290

family: advance care planning regarding, 189–190; Bowen family systems theory, 152; caregivers, 186–187; comprehensive history regarding, 101, 102; formation employee benefits, 271; goals of care identified by, 160; lavender, 100; permanency planning for, 202; physical examination regarding, 101, 102. *See also* education

Family and Medical Leave Act (FMLA), 22–23

family dynamics: discussion questions on, 156; emotional cutoff regarding, 152–153, 155; genogram mapping, 154–156, 292; key points for, 155–156; key terms for, 133; shared decision-making regarding, 152–154

family meeting: coordination and facilitation of, 100–101, 102, 156, 167–168; discussion questions on, 156; needs accommodated in, 102; for progress assessment, 167–168, 170; in shared decision-making scenario, 146–149

family of choice, 100, 154, 290; discussion question on, 131; Five-Dimension Assessment Model on, 109–110; of Krayger, 101, 103. *See also* same-sex marriage; same-sex partners

family of origin, 100, 154, 290; discussion question on, 131; emotional distress regarding, 242, 258; Five-Dimension Assessment Model on, 109–110; of Krayger, 101, 103; patient relationship with, 153; property ownership regarding, 201; same-sex partners regarding, 188; shared decision-making scenario involving, 140–142, 146–149

fatigue, 117, 290; of Brandt, 107–108; pain and symptom management regarding, *222–223*

fear, 290; of discrimination, 76; perceptual barriers to care, 88

Ferrell, B., 6–7, 249–250, *251*, 253, *254–255*

FICA Spiritual History Tool, 290; components of, 111–112; comprehensive history regarding, 106, 111–112; Five-Dimension Assessment Model using, 106

financial barriers to care, 87, 89, 91, *172*, 290

financial power of attorney, 192, 195

financial support, for Brandt, 34–35, 44–45, 49, 74, 81, 139, 244–245

fires, smoking regarding, 177–179, 180, 185–186

Five-Dimension Assessment Model, 130, 167, 290–291; Anticipatory Planning for Death dimension, 119–121; chapter activity on, 131–132; Decision Making dimension, 118–119; discussion question on, 131; FICA Spiritual History Tool used in, 106; Functional Activities and Symptoms dimension, 116–117, 211; Illness/Treatment summary dimension, 113–116; Knight and von Gunten's Whole-Patient Assessment incorporation into, 106; organ inventory, 108–109, 114–115; Patient as Person dimension 1A, 107, 109–111, 112–113, 252; Patient as Person dimension 1B, 122–123; plan of care based on, 160; psychosocial assessment in, 238; time commitment of, 166

FMLA. *See* Family and Medical Leave Act

focused history, 291

Functional Activities and Symptoms dimension, 116–117, 211

functional capacity, *172*

funeral: directive, 198–199; service, 120–121

Gardia, Gary, 167, 247
Gauvin, S. E. M., 58
Gawande, Atul, 184
gay, 65, 291
gay persons, nondiscrimination statement regarding, 267
gender, 154; agender, 60, 285; aliagender, 60, 285; childhood messages about, 47; cisgender, 56, 57, 287; cisgender patient, 92; discussion questions on, 71–72; diverse, 291; dysphoria, 57–60, 82, 291; euphoria, 58, 291; fluid, 60, 291; incongruence, 57, 58, 59–60, 292; key points for, 70–71; key terms for, 50; knowledge deficits regarding, 52; nonbinary, 60, 295; nonconforming,

gender (*continued*)
57–58, 59–60, 292; nonconforming persons, 127, *127*; presentation, 56, 57, 58–59, 64, 70–71; sex distinction from, 53–54, 62–64; SOGI data question collecting, 62, 63–64. *See also* nonbinary persons; pronouns; sexual orientation; transgender; transgender persons

gender affirmation surgery, 291; assigned sex regarding, 58–59, 71; regarding physical examination, 129–130

gender expression, 56, 57, 291; discussion question on, 71–72; gender identity regarding, 58–59, 64, 70–71; perceptual barriers to care regarding, 88

gender identity, 56, 57, 291; Civil Rights Act Title VII ruling on, 80; discussion question on, 72; disorder label, 82; gender expression and presentation regarding, 58–59, 64, 70–71; perceptual barriers to care regarding, 88; sexual orientation distinct from, 59, 71; transgender identity, 301. *See also* nonbinary persons; pronouns; transgender; transgender persons

genderqueer, 59, 292

genogram, 154–156, 292

Gibson, S., 6

goals of care, 179, 292; chapter activity on, 181; evolution of, 168, 190; expected outcomes regarding, 164–165, *165*; family identification of, 160; patient motivation for, 167, 181; questions for, 164; specificity for, 165. *See also* plan of care

GoFundMe. *See* Brandt, Kathy

Gollance, Richard, 99

grief, 292; anticipatory, 90, *126*, *173*, 201; effectiveness of, *125*–*126*; Patient and Family Outcomes-Focused Inquiry for Interdisciplinary Teams regarding, *173*–*174*; spiritual concerns regarding, *254*

guilt, *254*, 292

gynecologic oncologist, 34

hate crimes: discrimination, 83–86; Matthew Shepard and James Byrd, Jr., Hate Crimes Prevention Act regarding, 84; Pulse nightclub mass shooting, 84–86; against Shepard, 83–84

Hawkins, Jennifer, 22–23

health: discussion questions on, 71–72; key points for, 70–71; key terms for, 50; sexuality regarding, 68–70. *See also* sexual health

health care: ethics, 292; proxy, 293; system, xvii

health care decision-making: legal issues, 196, 198; same-sex partners regarding, 196, 198

health care power of attorney, 195, 206, 292–293; medical record regarding, 194; U.S. states governance of, 192–193

Health Insurance Portability and Accountability Act (HIPAA), 110, 203–204, 206

Helm, Kris, 151

HESTIA. *See* Home Evaluation System with a Triangulating Integrative Approach

heteroromantic, 66

heterosexual, 65, 293

Hilliard, Russell, 239–241

HIPAA. *See* Health Insurance Portability and Accountability Act

HIPAA Privacy Rule, 110

history: access to care regarding, 76, 77–78, 79–80; employment discrimination regarding, 79–80

HIV/AIDS: patients, 30, 166; treatment/prevention employee benefits, 271

HMDCB. *See* Hospice Medical Director Certification Board

Home Evaluation System with a Triangulating Integrative Approach (HESTIA), 176
Home Safety Self-Assessment Tool, 175
homophobia, 77, 230
homoromantic, 66
homosexual, 293
homosexuality, APA mental illness label of, 82
hope, 242–243, 247, 258, 293
hormone therapy, 89
hospice, 293. *See also specific topics*
Hospice and Palliative Credentialing Center (HPCC), 17
Hospice and Palliative Medicine (HPM), 16
Hospice and Palliative Nurses Association: on palliative sedation ethical defensibility, 142, 143; "Position Statement" by, 142
Hospice Medical Director Certification, 17
Hospice Medical Director Certification Board (HMDCB), 17
housing discrimination, 293
HPCC. *See* Hospice and Palliative Credentialing Center
HPM. *See* Hospice and Palliative Medicine
HUD. *See* U.S. Department of Housing and Urban Development
humor, 40, 293; communication regarding, 45, 48; context regarding, 46
Hunter, Lynn, 30
husband term, of patient, 37
hysterectomy, 67

IADLs. *See* instrumental activities of daily living
ICU Hospice Team, 137
Illness/Treatment summary dimension: drug or hormone question in, 114; Five-Dimension Assessment Model, 113–116; medical information sharing, 113; medication questions, 114; organ inventory, 114–115; sexuality questions in, 115–116
Improving the Quality of Spiritual Care as a Dimension of Palliative Care (Puchalski et. al.), 249–250, *251*, 253, *254-255*
"Inclusive Care at the End of Life," xix, xx
Indigenous communities, two-spirit terminology, 60
individual level change, 19
informed consent, 148–149, 293
insomnia, 117, *222*, 293
Institute of Medicine: *Dying in America* by, 6, 188; on living will, 193
institutional barriers to care, 87, 294; discrimination regarding, 90, 91; discussion question on, 92; inward-facing and outward-facing approach for, 90, 91, 92
institutional inclusiveness: advocacy regarding, 265, 269–270; chapter activity on, 277; discussion questions on, 276–277; employee benefits, orientation, and training regarding, 270–271; intake forms and processes regarding, 272–273; interdisciplinary/interprofessional team regarding, 263–265; key points for, 275–276; key terms for, 262; marketing and community engagement regarding, 273–274; nondiscrimination statement regarding, 266–270
institutional level change, 19
instrumental activities of daily living (IADLs), 116
intake forms and processes, 294; discussion question on, 276; institutional inclusiveness regarding, 272–273; questions incorporated into, 273
interdisciplinary/interprofessional team, 21, 238, 294; discussion questions on, 259; emotional distress assessments regarding, 241–242; family meeting

340 | Index

interdisciplinary/interprofessional team (*continued*)
coordinated and facilitated by, 100–101, 102, 156, 167–168; institutional inclusiveness regarding, 263–265; meetings, 168, 170, 174–175, 179; palliative sedation guidelines regarding, 149–150; psychosocial assessments regarding, 239; sexual health social assessment by, 70, 71; shared decision-making involvement of, 135, 136, 149–150; shared decision-making scenario involvement of, 142–144, 145, *145*, 146, 150–151
intersectionality, 9, 294
intersectionality of oppression, 77–78, 91
intersex, 53, 294; chromosomes regarding, 55; sex continuum regarding, 54–55
intersex persons: transgender persons experience regarding, 55; trauma-informed care for, 43
intersex status, 63
intrusive questions, 127, *127*, 131

Javier, Noelle Marie, 166
justice, 185, 205, 294

Kaiser Health News, xix, xx
Kallio, Jay, 77
Kemle, K., 11
key points: for access to care, 91; for advocacy, 232–233; for attitude, 91; for behavior, 70–71; for care coordination, 179–180; for communication, 46–47; for comprehensive history, 130; for education, 232–233; for ethical issues, 205–206; for family dynamics, 155–156; for gender, 70–71; for health, 70–71; for institutional inclusiveness, 275–276; for legal issues, 205–206; for physical examination, 130; for plan of care, 179–180; for psychosocial issues, 257–258; for self-awareness, 46–47; for sex, 70–71; for sexual orientation, 70–71; for shared decision-making, 155–156; for spiritual issues, 257–258
key terms: for access to care, 75; for advocacy, 210; for attitude, 75; for behavior, 50; for care coordination, 159; for communication, 25–26; for comprehensive history, 95–96; for education, 210; for ethical issues, 183; for family dynamics, 133; for gender, 50; for health, 50; for institutional inclusiveness, 262; for legal issues, 183; for physical examination, 95–96; for plan of care, 159; for psychosocial issues, 237; for self-awareness, 25–26; for sex, 50; for sexual orientation, 50; for shared decision-making, 133; for spiritual issues, 237
Knight and von Gunten's Module 3, 104
Knight and von Gunten's Whole-Patient Assessment, 105–106
knowledge deficits: regarding gender, 52; regarding sexual orientation, 51
Krayger, Nick: dad hospice experience of, 102–103; family of origin and family of choice of, 101, 103

Lambda Legal: checklist for funeral planning, 201–202; on nondiscrimination statements, 266
language, inclusive: for comprehensive history questions, 105; discussion question on, 276–277; for nondiscrimination statement, 266–268, 275; for spiritual and religious beliefs, 256; for spiritual/existential history, 252, *252*, 253; spiritual issues regarding, 252, *252*, 253
last will and testament, 195. *See also* living will
lavender family, 100
Lavender Scare, 79
Lawrence v. Kansas, 83
Led, Jen, 89

legal issues: advance care planning regarding, 187–188, 189–190, 191–195; confidentiality regarding, 202, 203–205; discussion questions on, 207; disposition of remains, 198–200; health care decision-making, 196, 198; key points for, 205–206; key terms for, 183; Patient and Family Outcomes-Focused Inquiry for Interdisciplinary Teams regarding, *172*; permanency planning, 202; property ownership, 200–201
legal power of attorney, 192, 195
lesbian, 65, 294
lesbian persons, 267
lgbtqia-inclusive.com, 22
LGBTQIA+ persons. *See* specific
license exams, 284
life completion and life closure, 21, 294, death regarding, *124*; developmental tasks, 245, *246*, 259
life insurance, of Brandt, 260–261
life-limiting illness, attitudes and beliefs about, 28
life review, 294
Limbo, R., 6
listening, 295
"little shiny gender breakthrough, A" (Beischel, Gauvin and van Anders), 58
"Living Their Values" (Aleccia), xix
living will, 295; chapter activity on, 207; forms for, 193; last will and testament regarding, 195; medical record regarding, 194; U.S. states supplementary instructions regarding, 193–194
Long Goodbye (Colby), 93
Lux-Sullivan, Holly, 128
Lynch, M., 142

Maine trip, Brandt on, 162–163
male-to-female (MtF), 87
marketing and community engagement, 295; institutional inclusiveness regarding, 273–274; marketing materials diversity for, 274, 276–277
mass shooting, Pulse nightclub, 84–86
masturbation, 67, 72
Matthew Shepard and James Byrd, Jr., Hate Crimes Prevention Act (2009), 84
meaning, 111, 258, 295; psychosocial issues, 242–243; spiritual questions of, 256
medical information sharing, 113
medical marijuana cost, 139–140
medical record: health care power of attorney regarding, 194; living will regarding, 194; medication management regarding, 224
medical students, 37–38
medication: questions, 114; reconciliation, 224, 295
medication management, 211, 295; discussion question on, 234; education regarding, 223–224, *225–227*
medicine discipline: competencies, 16; education, *282*
mental illness homosexuality label, 82
men who have sex with men (MSM), 295
Merriman, M. P., 245, 247–248
Missoula-VITAS Quality of Life Index (MVQOLI), 245, 247–248
mitigation plan, 250, 252, 258, 295; CAMPERS, 31, 32, 46; power imbalance minimized by, 31; self-awareness regarding, 31–32
Morgan, Vaiana, 272
MSM. *See* men who have sex with men
MtF. *See* male-to-female
MVQOLI. *See* Missoula-VITAS Quality of Life Index

National Academies of Sciences, Engineering, and Medicine, 62–63, 65
National Association of Social Workers Specialty Certification Program, 17
National Commission on Certification of Physician Assistants, 17

National Consensus Project, 8–9, 70. *See also Clinical Practice Guidelines for Quality Palliative Care*
National Hospice and Palliative Care Organization (NHPCO), 93–94, 123, *124–126*, 193
National Institutes of Health, 62
National Quality Forum, 96
nausea/vomiting, 117, 295; of Brandt, 13–14; pain and symptom management regarding, *222*
New York City Department of Health, 199
New Yorker, xx–xxi
next of kin, 198
NHPCO. *See* National Hospice and Palliative Care Organization
nonbinary, 60, 295
nonbinary persons: death certificates regarding, 200; discrimination against, 272
nonconsensual detransitioning, 200
nondiscrimination statement, 90, 271; accessibility of, 269; advocacy regarding, 269–270; inclusive language for, 266–268, 275; institutional inclusiveness regarding, 266–270; questions regarding, 268, 269; transgender persons regarding, 266–267
nonmaleficence, 185, 205, 295
nonverbal communication, 32, 47, 296
normalization, 296

observations, DAROP format, 240–241
Ohio State University James Cancer Hospital, 137
oncologist, 4
open posture, 296
opioids, 79, 136
organ inventory, 20, 296; Five-Dimension Assessment Model, 108–109, 114–115; transgender persons impacted by, 109
Orlando, Florida, 84

osteopathy education, *282*
Otis-Green, S., 7, 249–250, *251*, 253, *254–255*
outdated terms: male-to-female, 87; transsexual, 59
out-of-hospital/provider/physician/medical order for life-sustaining treatment (POLST/MOLST), 194, 296
Oxford Textbook of Palliative Nursing (Ferrell and Paice), 6–7
Oxford Textbook of Palliative Social Work (Altilio, Otis-Green, & Cagle), 7
oxygen use: in home, 177–179, 180, 185–186; plan of care regarding, 177–179, 180

Paice, J., 6–7
pain, *97*, 117, *223*; Brandt experiencing, 78–79, 181; management, 296; during physical examination, 129
pain and symptom management, 211, 233, 296; chapter activity on, 234; discussion question on, 234; education regarding, 220, *220–223*
"Palliative and End-of-Life Care" voluntary standards, 96, *97*
Palliative and Serious Illness Patient Management for Physician Assistants (Dimitrov and Kemle), 11
palliative care, 296–297. *See also specific topics*
palliative sedation, 134, 137, 297; ethical defensibility of, 142–143; ethics committee regarding, 150; euthanasia distinguished from, 138, 143, 148; informed consent form for, 148–149; interdisciplinary/interprofessional team guidelines regarding, 149–150; shared decision-making regarding, 149–150, 156; shared decision-making scenario regarding, 140, 141, 142–144, *144*, *145*, 148–149
"Palliative Sedation Position Statement" (American Academy of Hospice and Palliative Medicine), 142–143

"Palliative sedation therapy" (Schildmann, E., and Schildmann, J.), 149–150
panromantic, 66
pansexual, 65, 297
Parents, Families, and Friends of Lesbians and Gays (PFLAG), 242
PAs. *See* physician associates
pathology report, of Brandt, 23
patient: advance care planning regarding, 189–190; CAMPERS, 32–33, 37, 47; centered, 297; cisgender, 92; comprehensive history questions directed to, 102; family of origin relationship with, 153; Five-Dimension Assessment Model on, 106; goals of care motivation of, 167, 181; husband term of, 37; Knight and von Gunten's Whole-Patient Assessment regarding, 105–106; as person, 96; primary caregiver relationship with, 90; resuscitation preferences of, 119; self-awareness regarding, 32–33, 47; shared decision-making process driven by, 141–142; understanding, 32–33, 47; visits, 28–29; with HIV/AIDS, 30, 166. *See also* education
Patient and Family Outcomes-Focused Inquiry for Developing Goals for Care, 123, *124–126*, 297
Patient and Family Outcomes-Focused Inquiry for Interdisciplinary Teams, 123, 174, 180, 297; end-of-life caregiving regarding, *171*; grief regarding, *173–174*; legal issues regarding, *172*
Patient as Person dimension 1A: family of origin and family of choice in, 110; of Five-Dimension Assessment Model, 107, 109–111, 112–113, 252; household supports and stressors in, 113; social activities and hobbies in, 112; spiritual/existential/cultural history in, 111
Patient as Person dimension 1B, 122–123

patient-care skills, 233, 297; bathing, *212*; discussion question on, 234; dressing, *213*; education regarding, 211–212, *212–216*; incontinence regarding, *215*; meals and eating, *213*; movement regarding, *213–215*; nighttime bathroom needs regarding, *216*; questions assessing, 211–212, 234
Pediatric Palliative Care (Limbo and Davies), 6
Pennsylvania Gazette, xix–xx
perceptual barriers to care, 91, 297; discussion question on, 92; fears, 88; misperceptions, 87–88
permanency planning, 202
PFLAG. *See* Parents, Families, and Friends of Lesbians and Gays
physical examination, 128, 297; discussion questions on, 131; family presence regarding, 101, 102; key points for, 130; key terms for, 95–96; of transgender persons, 129–130
physician, hospice: ethics code and interpretive statement of, 265; primary care physician coordination with, 145; shared decision-making scenario involvement of, 142–144, 145, 147–148, 149. *See also* interdisciplinary/interprofessional team
physician associates (PAs), 10; education, 283; ethics code and interpretive statement of, 265; seminal texts of, 11. *See also* interdisciplinary/interprofessional team
plan, DAROP format, 241
plan of care, 297; collaboration for, 162; discussion questions on, 180–181; Five-Dimension Assessment Model regarding, 160; key points for, 179–180; key terms for, 159; oxygen use regarding, 177–179, 180; progress assessment regarding, 167–168, 170; quality of life regarding, 161. *See also* goals of care

POA. *See* power of attorney
(POLST/MOLST). *See* out-of-hospital/
provider/physician/medical order for
life-sustaining treatment
"Position Statement" (Dahlin and Lynch),
142
power imbalance, 31, 297
power of attorney (POA), 192. *See also*
durable power of attorney
presence, 297–298
primary caregiver, 90
primary care physician, 145
primary diagnosis, 230, 232
prognosis, 298
progress assessment, 167–168, 170
pronouns: application of, *65*;
confidentiality regarding, 204, 206;
multiplicity of, 64. *See also* gender;
gender identity; transgender;
transgender persons
property ownership, legal issues, 200–201
psychological distress, 241, 298. *See also*
emotional distress
psychosocial assessment, 298;
documentation of, 239–241; supportive
techniques and, 238–239, 259
psychosocial history, 106, 298
psychosocial issues: bereavement
care, 256–257; despair, 242–243;
discussion questions on, 259;
emotional distress, 241–242, 289;
hope, 242–243; key points for,
257–258; key terms for, 237; meaning,
242–243. *See also* life completion and
life closure
Puchalski, C., 249–250, *251*, 253, *254–255*
Pulse nightclub mass shooting, 84–86
purpose, 26–27, 46

quality of life, 298; Brandt prioritizing, 3–4;
MVQOLI regarding, 245, 247–248; plan
of care regarding, 161
queer, 298
questions: caregiver knowledge
assessed with, 211–212, *212–216*; for
comprehensive history, 102, 105;
education regarding, 234; for goals
of care, 164; regarding health care
decision-making, 196, 198; intake forms
and processes incorporation of, 273;
medication, 114; nondiscrimination
statement regarding, 268, 269; from
Patient and Family Outcomes-
Focused Inquiry for Developing Goals
for Care, 123, *124–126*; Patient and
Family Outcomes-Focused Inquiry
for Interdisciplinary Teams, 123,
171–174, 174, 180, 297; patient-care
skills assessed by, 211–212, 234; during
physical examination, 129; relevancy
and intrusiveness of, 127, *127*, 131;
sexual orientation identified with, 65,
71; for SOGI data collection, 62–64, 71;
spiritual/existential assessment, 248;
spirituality, 256. *See also* discussion
questions; Five-Dimension Assessment
Model
Quintana, Vicki, 37

rapport, 97, 98, 130, 298
reactions: CAMPERS, 36, 37–38; self-
awareness regarding, 36, 37–38
reflection, 38, 47, 298
registered nurse: education, *283*; ethics
code and interpretive statement of,
264–265; shared decision-making
scenario involvement of, 142, 143,
146–147. *See also* interdisciplinary/
interprofessional team
relevant questions, 127, *127*, 131
religion, 253, 255
religious beliefs, 1–2, 188; regarding Family
and Medical Leave Act, 22–23; inclusive
language questions for, 256; shared
decision-making scenario impacted by,
140–141, 148

resources, 22, *172*
Respect After Death Act, 199
results, DAROP format, 240
resuscitation preferences, 119
right to self-determination, 298
risk-benefit discussion tool, *144–145*, 148

same-gender-loving, 298
same-sex marriage: health care decision-making regarding, 196, 198; ICU Hospice Team recognition of, 137; U.S. state legalization, 128; U.S. Supreme Court federal legalization of, 203
same-sex partners: family of origin regarding, 188; health care decision-making regarding, 196, 198; health care power of attorney regarding, 153; hospice staff recognition of, 178–179; primary caregiver identification of, 90; shared decision-making scenario involving, 140–142, 146–149
Sandusky, Timothy, 136–137
Schildmann, E., 149–150
Schildmann, J., 149–150
scope of practice, 15, 298
self-awareness, 298; attitudes and beliefs regarding, 27–30; CAMPERS regarding, 26, 31, 38, 40, 46, 47, 48; discussion questions on, 47–48; emotion regarding, 36; key points for, 46–47; key terms for, 25–26; mitigation plan regarding, 31–32; patient understanding regarding, 32–33, 47; purpose regarding, 26–27, 46; reactions regarding, 36, 37–38; strategy regarding, 38
self-determination, 298–299; health care phrases regarding, 31; life closure regarding, *124*; in shared decision-making, 134
self-disclosure, 40, 299; communication regarding, 41, 42, 48; of sexual orientation, 41

Senate, U.S., 79
Serano, Julia, 53–54
sex, 299; complexity of, 55–56; continuum of, 54–55; difference of sex development, 63; discussion questions on, 71–72; gender distinction from, 53–54, 62–64; key points for, 70–71; key terms for, 50. *See also* assigned sex; intersex; intersex persons; intersex status
Sexual and Gender Identity Disorders Work Group, 82
sexual behavior, 299; discussion question on, 131; sexual orientation and, 65–67
sexual expression, 67, 299
sexual health, 68–69, 130, 299; in Five-Dimension Assessment Model, 107; interdisciplinary/interprofessional team social assessment regarding, 70, 71
sexuality, 299; health regarding, 68–70; humanity centrality of, 69; Illness/Treatment summary dimension questions on, 115–116
sexual orientation, 299; bisexual, 65, 68, 286; bisexual persons, 267; chapter activity hiding, 72; childhood messages regarding, 47; Civil Rights Act Title VII ruling on, 80; confidentiality regarding, 204–205; discussion questions on, 71–72, 92; gay, 65, 291; gay persons, 267; gender identity distinct from, 59, 71; heterosexual, 65, 293; homosexual, 293; homosexuality, 82; key points for, 70–71; key terms for, 50; knowledge deficits regarding, 51; lesbian, 65, 294; lesbian persons, 267; pansexual, 65, 297; perceptual barriers to care regarding, 88; queer, 298; questions identifying, 65, 71; same-gender-loving, 298; self-disclosure of, 41; sexual behavior and, 65–67. *See also* asexual; asexual persons; gender; same-sex marriage; same-sex partners; sex

shared decision-making, 20, 299–300; discussion questions on, 156; durable power of attorney in, 153–154; ethical principles of, 134; facilitation of, 134–136; family dynamics regarding, 152–154; interdisciplinary/interprofessional team involvement in, 135, 136, 149–150; key points for, 155–156; key terms for, 133; palliative sedation regarding, 149–150, 156; patient driving, 141–142

shared decision-making scenario: chaplain involvement in, 144, 147, 149; delirium regarding, 138, 140–142, 147–148; durable power of attorney in, 140, 141–142; emotional cutoff of, 152–153; facilitation of, 142–144, 145–149; family meeting in, 146–149; family of origin involvement in, 140–142, 146–149; final days goals discussed in, 147; hospice physician involvement in, 142–144, 145, 147–148, 149; interdisciplinary/interprofessional team involvement in, 142–144, 145, *145*, 146, 150–151; palliative sedation regarding, 140, 141, 142–144, *144*, *145*, 148–149; registered nurse involvement in, 142, 143, 146–147; religious beliefs impacting, 140–141, 148; risk-benefit discussion tool for, *144–145*, 148; same-sex partners involvement in, 140–142, 146–149

Shepard, Matthew, 83–84
Shick, Steve, 255
Sibley Memorial Hospital, 3, 4
signs and symptoms of imminent death, 211, 233, 300; discussion question on, 234; education regarding, 227, 230, *231–232*, 232; primary diagnosis regarding, 230, 232. *See also* end-stage disease progression
silence, 300
smoking: CDC on, 177; fires regarding, 177–179, 180, 185–186
social assessment, 70, 71

social work discipline competencies, 16
social worker: credentials and certifications of, 17; education, *283*; ethics code and interpretive statement of, 264; HIV/AIDS work of, 30; shared decision-making scenario involvement of, 142, 144, 147. *See also* interdisciplinary/interprofessional team
sodomy laws, 83, 300
SOGI data, 19, 300; National Academies of Sciences, Engineering, and Medicine report on, 62–63; questions collecting, 62–64, 71
special population, 5–6, 7, 9–10, 279–281
spiritual beliefs, 256
spiritual concerns, *254–255*
spiritual/existential assessment, 21, *251*, 252, 259, 300; chaplain regarding, 248, 250, 258; components of, 249; questions, 248; spiritual/existential/cultural history distinguished from, 248–249, 258
spiritual/existential/cultural history, 130, 300; in FICA Spiritual History Tool, 111–112; in Five-Dimension Assessment Model, 106, 111; spiritual/existential assessment distinguished from, 248–249, 258
spiritual/existential distress, 258, 300; discussion questions on, 259; spiritual concerns, *254–255*; support for, 256; transgender persons experiences of, 253
spiritual/existential history, 252, *252*, 253
spiritual history, 249–250, *251*
spiritual interventions, *251*
spiritual issues: bereavement care, 256–257; discussion questions on, 259; inclusive language regarding, 252, *252*, 253; key points for, 257–258; key terms for, 237; spiritual/existential history, 252, *252*, 253. *See also* spiritual/existential assessment; spiritual/existential distress
spiritual screening, 249

Index | 347

states, U.S.: hate crime laws in, 84; health care power of attorney governed by, 192–193; legal employment discrimination in, 80; legal eviction and housing discrimination in, 83; living will supplementary instructions regarding, 193–194; POA governed by, 192; same-sex marriage ban overturned in, 128; sodomy laws in, 83; transgender persons death certificates laws of, 199–200
suicidal ideation, 241, 257, 300
Sulmasy, Daniel, 256
support network, for Brandt, 81
Supreme Court, U.S., 80; *Dobbs v. Jackson Women's Health Organization* ruling of, 83; *Lawrence v. Kansas* ruling of, 83; state same-sex marriage federal legalization by, 203; state same-sex marriage U.S. state ban overturned by, 128
surgery: of Brandt, 3; Illness/Treatment summary dimension question on, 115. *See also* gender affirmation surgery
symptom: of Brandt, 13–14, 33–34, 44, 53; distress regarding, 172; end-stage disease progression regarding, 217–218; Functional Activities and Symptoms dimension regarding, 115–117, 211; management, 301; MVQOLI assessing, 247. *See also* signs and symptoms of imminent death
systemic level change, 19; strategies for, 278–279; textbooks regarding, 279–281

Taylor, Kathleen, 90
textbooks: discipline, 5–6, 7, 8, 9–10, 279–281; editor for, 280; invitation declined for, 280–281; marginalization impacted by, 280–281; special population standalone chapters in, 5–6, 7, 9–10, 279–281; systemic level change regarding, 279–281

thank you notes, 190–191
Tinder, 67
Title VII, Civil Rights Act, 80
touch, 40, 301; communication regarding, 42–43, 48; consent for, 42–43
Trans Bodies, Trans Selves (Erickson-Schroth), 52
transgender, 58; experience, 301; identity, 301
transgender persons, 87; APA gender identity disorder label of, 82; confidentiality regarding, 204; discrimination against, 89, 272; discussion question on, 92; eviction discrimination against, 82; financial barriers impacting, 89; funeral directive regarding, 198–199; healthcare employee benefits inclusive of, 271; hormone therapy, 89; intersex persons experience regarding, 55; intrusive questions impacting, 127, *127*; nondiscrimination statements regarding, 266–267; organ inventory impacting, 109; physical examination of, 129–130; SOGI data collection regarding, 63–64; spiritual/existential distress experienced by, 253; U.S. states death certificates laws regarding, 199–200
transition, 301
transphobia, 230
transsexual, 59, 301
trauma, of discrimination, 77
trauma-informed care, for intersex persons, 43
trauma survivors: physical examination impacting, 129; touch impacting, 42–43
two-spirit Indigenous communities terminology, 60

unconscious bias, 29–30, 301
University of Buffalo, 175
University of Virginia School of Nursing, 24

U.S. Department of Health and Human Services National Institute on Disability, Independent Living, and Rehabilitation Research, 176
U.S. Department of Housing and Urban Development (HUD), 82–83

van Anders, S. M., 58
Virani, R., 249–250, *251*, 253, *254–255*
volunteer handypersons, 176

weakness, 117, *222–223*, 301
weight loss, 117, 302; of Brandt, 39, 44, 48, 52–53; pain and symptom management regarding, *223*
WHO. *See* World Health Organization
will, 195, 302. *See also* living will
World Health Organization (WHO): sexual health defined by, 69; sexuality defined by, 68–69

Printed in the USA
CPSIA information can be obtained
at www.ICGtesting.com
JSHW021034280324
60129JS00002B/24